KIEL

LUBECK

ALTONA HAMBURG

Kiel Canal

Elbe

To Berlin

Meuse

HANOVER

T H

THERLANDS

ARN
no

ESSEN

G E R M A N Y

Eysden

COLOGNE

Rhine

IÈGE

GHQ
SPA

E N N S

COBLENZ

FRANKFURT

MAINZ

Main

LUX-
EMBOURG

Moselle

Longwy

ne
ontfaucon
Briey

Thionville

METZ

rdun
neulles

L O R R A I N E

Mihiel

Pont-à-Mousson

STUTTGART

Danube

gny-en-Barrois

STRASBOURG

A L S A C E

MUNICH

NOVEMBER
1918

NOVEMBER 1918

Gordon Brook-Shepherd

Little, Brown and Company / Boston, Toronto

Maps by Brian Elkins

Contents

Illustrations

Illustrations

Maps

Foreword

TO SAY THAT this particular narrative of how the Great War ended has never been written before may seem a bold claim to make, in view of the many thousands of books which have been published in all languages since that terrible conflict ended more than sixty years ago. I do so rather more readily since the idea was not mine at all.

Four years ago, my English and American publishers came forward with a joint concept to fill what they held to be a gap still existing in the histories of the First World War. This was to tell the story of the closing phase of that war on all four of its principal battlefields (i.e. Italy, the Balkans and Palestine, as well as the dominant Western Front); to show how those campaigns were inter-related in the approaching victory of one side and the approaching defeat of the other; and finally, to depict how the position on those battlefields affected the peace-making process fashioned by President Wilson, and when and where it contributed to the final collapse of the three empires (the Hohenzollern, the Habsburg and the Ottoman) which fell during those last months of 1918. In other words, what was required was a panorama of the whole closing scene, which would link, in one volume, all the main military aspects with the diplomatic and dynastic ones; would show how crowns were lost with battles; and how the cross-currents of war itself threatened, almost to the end, the incoming tide of peace. As often as practicable, the story was to be told in the language of the actors themselves, great and small, so that the reader would move from Supreme Headquarters to the front-line trenches, and from pavements to palaces.

I agreed to the idea in a somewhat dubious frame of mind. It was only after I started consulting the libraries and national archives of the six principal combatant nations – Britain, France,

9

America, Germany, Austria-Hungary and Italy – that I realized such a gap did indeed seem to exist. I knew from previous general reading that the memoirs or diaries of most of the famous figures involved – Foch, Haig, Pétain, Pershing, Ludendorff, Hindenburg among the commanders, for example, or Clemenceau, Lloyd George and Prince Max of Baden among the statesmen – were subjective to a dangerous degree. Even the broadest of such studies, like Winston Churchill's *The World Crisis*, had so much canvas to cover that parts of the war's climax were only sketched in.

But I then discovered that the enormous range of secondary works were usually even more selective, as well as being often very dated. Thus, probably the best single volume study of the diplomatic and political road to the peace, Rudin's *Armistice 1918*, was published thirty-seven years ago; moreover, it omits events on the battlefields altogether and, even on the political side, concentrates exclusively on Germany. It is much longer ago, more than sixty years, in fact, since the classic military account of the closing phase of the war, Major-General Sir Frederick Maurice's *The Last Four Months*, was published. The reverse of Rudin's study, this dealt only with the battle-fronts and, almost exclusively, with the West.

This same excessive concentration on the campaign in France and Flanders applies to the few relevant studies to appear in recent years. One of these, for example, which deals with the last year of the fighting, was written by a specialist on the battles of the Western Front, and is predictably sound on that subject. But the epic Allied offensive in the Balkans which, in September 1918, knocked Bulgaria out of the war, laying bare the southern flank of the Central Powers in the process, is dismissed in three paragraphs. General Allenby's equally brilliant campaign which, in that same fateful month, crushed the German-led Turkish army in Palestine and forced Turkey to sue for peace, gets precisely one paragraph. The offensive in northern Italy four weeks later, which shattered the armies of Austria-Hungary (Germany's principal partner) and forced Vienna to sue for a separate cease-fire, is not even mentioned, let alone described; nor is the baleful story of the Padua armistice itself, which cost the Habsburg armies more casualties from the conference table than they had lost in the battle.

Such an approach represents the philosophy of the 'Westerner' run amok. It is indisputable that the French front was, to the First World War, what the Russian front was to the Second: the primary theatre of action, the meat-grinder which slowly devoured the sinews of German military strength. Yet, apart from the strategic impact, the collapse of those three secondary fronts in the autumn of 1918 helped powerfully to destroy, in lightning blows, something equally important – the will of the German Supreme Command to go on fighting. To underestimate that psychological factor is to ignore the trauma of *'Einkreisung'* or 'Encirclement' which had shaped the fears of the German people, and the plans of German military planners, for decades past. It also, as we shall see, ignores the testimony of General Ludendorff himself, the virtual military dictator of the German empire in its death throes.

The capitulation of Germany's allies has a wider historical significance. When Germany, deserted by all her partners, finally surrendered herself, the map of Europe was barely changed by the territorial concessions she made. But the destruction of the Austro-Hungarian empire, a complex process which unfolded between the battlefield and the home front, meant that the map of central and south-eastern Europe was torn up for good. At first this was seemingly for the better; but then, as Stalin succeeded Hitler as the ultimate heir to the Habsburgs, it became clear that it had been for the worse. It is perspectives such as these which need to be kept in mind when chronicling the end of the Great War. Those last months are not simply the tale of how battles were fought and cease-fires negotiated. They are the story of how our continent was transformed, beyond recognition or redress.

The ending of the story declared itself – 11 November 1918. The only question was when and how to start. I finally chose the British victory east of Amiens on 8 August of that summer, not merely because this conveniently provided the last hundred days as a framework but because, as the famous 'Black Day of the German Army', this blow began the destruction of Ludendorff's faith in his own cause (the German Kaiser counted for little or nothing in all this) as well as the final rolling-up, on all four fronts, of his armies.

I was familiar, from earlier travels, with the general terrain of all four war-fronts and I have re-visited them again with the specific battles of 1918's last hundred days in mind. Nature's obstacles and amenities have not changed since then, and you have to see them to understand what the fighting meant. It is when you stand on the rocky Musmus Pass of present-day Israel and look down on the great bowl of the Armageddon plain below that you realize the significance of that marvellously foolhardy action by which, on 20 September 1918, a young English cavalry captain secured this crucial defile by night and then routed its would-be defenders with his Lancers at dawn. The savage mountain crests – range after range of them – which divide Greece from Macedonia have to be seen to appreciate the feat involved when Serbian and French troops did the impossible by storming them, and thus opened the road to Belgrade and Sofia for the so-called Allied Armies of the Orient. You have to stand on the banks of the Piave in flood to measure the achievement of another young British officer (then a brevet Lieutenant-Colonel, later to become a famous general of the Second World War) who forced that broad torrent against murderous gunfire and established the main bridgehead for the final Allied offensive in northern Italy.

Finally, in the paramount theatre of battle, only a tour of the dead flat country east of Amiens shows how the hundreds of tanks allotted to the British Fourth Army could cause the havoc they did on Germany's 'Black Day'; just as the deep canal cutting of Riqueval, the ravines which score the Argonne Forest, and the commanding heights of Mountfaucon demonstrate what the Allied soldiers faced in breaking the Hindenburg defence system along its entire length. These are battles that cannot be re-created simply from library books.

This was not intended as an anti-war book; but, almost unconsciously, I found it becoming one in its implications. This was inevitable when, in diaries or letters written the same day on both sides of the barbed wire on an identical sector of the same battle, I found directly opposing soldiers asking the same question: 'What's it all for?' in English; or the much shorter and more pregnant

'*Wozu?*' in German. That question we are still asking today, and there is still no answer.

The survivors themselves are getting very scarce. A mere bugler-boy who served only in the last weeks of the Great War would be seventy-nine today. Nearly everyone else still alive to tell their tales is well into their eighties or nineties. The vast majority of those millions of men and women who donned uniform for King, Kaiser or President between 1914 and 1918 are now dead, their memories, if they were ever recorded, existing only in letters, diaries, official reports or private memoirs.

But though their written testimony had to be the staple diet of research for a book like this, I had some lucky accidental finds of live reminiscence on the way. There was the octogenarian retired gunner colonel, for example, with whom I had spent dozens of unforgettable summer evenings trout-fishing on the Test, and who suddenly started talking about training the raw American artillerymen of General Pershing's army in a much less peaceful landscape many summers ago – thus converting himself temporarily from a fly-fishing friend to a military source. I am grateful to Tyrrel Hawker for putting all his recollections of the Western Front down on paper for my benefit – especially as the labour was completed despite a stroke which has banned him forever from his beloved river.

Elsewhere in Hampshire, I went to stay one weekend at a house where one of the other guests happened to be collating the papers of a famous British general of the Second World War. And it further turned out that, in the First World War, that general was the young lieutenant-colonel who had led the decisive Allied breach in the Austro-Hungarian lines in the last fighting on the Italian front. My thanks to old friends, Mr and Mrs James Hill, for putting Major James Nairne in my path; to Major Nairne for introducing me to General Sir Richard O'Connor; and my gratitude to the ninety-two-year-old general himself for allowing me to use his private diary of that action and for explaining much about the campaign which had been puzzling. By an odd coincidence, only a few months before, I had been given the private memoirs of an

Austrian acquaintance, Count Gerolf Coudenhove-Kalergi who, in October of 1918, had fought almost opposite O'Connor as an officer of the Habsburg monarchy. The fact that both the British general and the Austrian count died before this book reached the proof stage illustrates what a touch-and-go business it has become to find live contact with those days.

One such contact was, however, not accidental. I have been visiting her regularly at least once a year ever since 1966, for she is almost certainly the last person still alive today who knew both pre-1914 and wartime Europe from the very top table of the old order. I refer to the former Empress Zita of Austria-Hungary, now in her ninetieth year (though with a memory and vivacity which mock that age). For the last two years of the Great War, she sat with her husband Charles on the throne of their doomed empire and saw its political and military tragedy unfold not merely from the palaces of Vienna but at her husband's side at Supreme Military Headquarters; in travels around his war-torn empire; and in state visits to its allies. To be able, today, to ask someone what it was like to talk as an equal to the German Kaiser about the prospects for victory or peace, or to have his War Lords, Hindenburg and Ludendorff, at her lunch table, has been a precious and memorable experience.

Yet I have to admit that the search through the written material has never seemed an anti-climax by comparison. So much of it, from both sides of the various fronts, reads as vividly now as the day it was put to paper. The Imperial War Museum in London has a superb collection of these so-called 'P/E's' or 'Personal Experiences', and I must thank its Reading Room staff for their help in sifting the documents and Mr Willis of the Photographic Library for similar help in providing illustrations which, for the most part, avoid those familiar pictures which have been repro-duced time and again in so many books.

What is probably the finest British collection of First World War material outside the Imperial War Museum is that put to-gether over the years by the part-time labours of one man, Mr Peter Liddle, of the Sunderland Polytechnic. I have drawn on his remarkable archives for much additional material, both documentary and photographic, as the source notes will show. My special thanks are due to an old friend and neighbour in the country, Mrs Jessica Edgar, who first made me aware of Peter Liddle's existence.

On the continent, I have to thank, among others, the staff of the Bibliothèque Nationale in Paris for producing some of the more elusive French war diaries and memoirs; the Institut für Zeitungsforschung at Dortmund for photocopying German newspapers (which are surprisingly rare for the last days of the Empire); and the Heeresarchiv in Vienna (and in particular Dr Peter Broucek) for supplying me with much fascinating and hitherto unpublished material about the defeat and disintegration of the Austro-Hungarian army. Frau Annelise Schulz gave invaluable help in setting all this up.

As already indicated, I knew most of the battlefield areas well enough to organize my own tours, but I would like to express my appreciation to the Israeli authorities for arranging a visit, complete with an Israeli professor of military history as guide, to the terrain of Allenby's great victory in Palestine in September–October of 1918.

The source notes themselves I have arranged on a page and line reference basis, grouped together all at the end of the book. This method may be a little more tedious to consult (though not nearly so tedious as it was to collate!); but it has the great merit of leaving the text itself uncluttered by numerals which, in the case of some chapters, would have run into sixty or more sets of figures.

Finally, a warm word of thanks to Mrs Clare Guest who, from her house on the North Yorkshire Moors, converted my complicated manuscript chapter by chapter into an impeccable typescript.

GORDON BROOK-SHEPHERD
Hughs
Hambleden
Oxon.

June 1981

Bombon

A T 10.30 A.M. on the morning of 24 July 1918, four Allied generals – two of them French, the third British and the fourth an American, met with their advisers at a château about twenty miles north-east of Paris to ponder how their arch-enemy, imperial Germany, could finally be brought to her knees. The château was called Bombon, a flippant-sounding name for such an elegant eighteenth-century stone and red-brick building set in such a spacious park, more especially as it now served as the nerve centre of the entire Allied effort on the Western Front. General Ferdinand Foch had moved his own Headquarters there on 5 June and as, two months before that, he had been appointed 'General-in-Chief of the Allied Armies', Bombon was the nearest thing to a multi-national Supreme Command which the war in France had seen.

Foch who, as Generalissimo, had called the meeting, sat at the head of the table. He was then nearly seventy-seven years old and, at first sight, the high domed forehead, the aquiline nose and the pipe which he sucked incessantly, all gave the impression of an elderly professor; indeed, on his climb up the French military ladder he had served for five years as chief instructor at the *École de Guerre*.

Two things belied this passive, academic aspect. The first was the swaggering grey moustache, almost handlebar in its facial proportions, with sharply upturned tips he would tug at whenever (which was very often) he wanted to emphasize a point. The second was a pair of blue-grey eyes which, though calm, were extremely penetrating. 'The man seems to be charged with radium,' Georges Clemenceau, his Prime Minister, had once said of him, and old Clemenceau, nicknamed 'The Tiger', was no layabout himself. Perhaps it was Foch's native Pyrenean mountains which had imbued him for life with their own blend of granite and strong light. Perhaps that steady inner radiance came from the deep religious faith he owed to his family and the Jesuit colleges of his youth. At all events, it was his serene and unshakeable belief both in the just cause and in its final victory which, more than any other quality, had made him both appointed and accepted as *primus inter pares*. It was hard to resist a leader who, when things looked their blackest for the Allies during the great German offensive of that spring, had said to a colleague despairing of the outcome: 'Materially, I don't see myself how we can win. Morally, I am quite certain we can.'

'How we can win.' That was precisely what Foch wanted to examine with his colleagues on that midsummer Wednesday morning, when that German advance on Paris had been checked and even thrust some way back. Was this just a reflex action of the German giant, or was it something more?

Those other three generals were a strange contrast, both with him and with each other. On his right sat General Sir Douglas Haig, Commander-in-Chief of the British forces in France ever since December 1915, when he had ousted his discredited and exhausted predecessor, Sir John French, through some determined lobbying in high places. Haig was a thorough professional, like Foch, and he not only shared the Generalissimo's devoutness but had exalted it, in his own case, to a sense of holy mission. 'I feel,' he once said, 'that every step in my plan has been taken with divine help.' There, however, the similarities between the two men ended. There was precious little of the intellectual and even less of the Jesuit about Haig's aspect and make-up. His was the conventionally handsome, rather dashing face of the British cavalryman (he had, in fact, played polo for England as a young man). His riding boots were as highly polished as his manner and, quite unlike Foch, it was social graces and social connections which had smoothed his way to the top. A close friend of the late King Edward VII, in 1905 he had married, in the Private Chapel of Buckingham Palace, one of Queen Alexandra's Maids of Honour, the Honourable Dorothy Vivian. That was the era when the social register was also the tabernacle of power and, throughout his career, Douglas Haig had thus been able to help Providence help him. What neither had managed to accomplish so far, despite three and a half years of intense if remote-controlled direction by the British Commander-in-Chief, and the appalling losses, stoically endured, of his troops, was the defeat of Germany in the field.

The other Anglo-Saxon present was the American General John J. Pershing. His country had entered the war only fifteen months before, but his American Expeditionary Force in France, after a hesitant initial build-up, was growing by the time of that Bombon meeting at the staggering rate of a quarter of a million with every month that passed. It was still lacking, however, in everything from guns to coat buttons. An even graver deficiency, despite some recent blooding in front-line action, was battle experience. Pershing, as he had told Haig when the two men had dined quietly together at the Café Foyot in Paris the night before, was very anxious to increase that experience but also very insistent on gaining it with his own independently formed American armies.

In appearance and manner Pershing, though the tallest man there, was the least striking. He had neither the handsome elegance of Haig nor the luminous personality of Foch. His was a rather closed and puritanical face (typically, he had shown himself very keen on 'keeping our men clean', i.e. keeping them away from all French licensed houses of prostitution, and the repugnance was as much moral as military). But it was the face of a dedicated and doggedly stubborn man for all that, as his Generalissimo would learn before the summer was out. Like Haig, Pershing was a cavalryman. Like Foch, he was a former lecturer on military science. But unlike either of them he had not so much climbed the top rungs of the military ladder as been shot up them: his country's dearth of senior officers who had fought anybody anywhere meant that Pershing had jumped overnight from being a junior major-general to a full-blown Commander-in-Chief.

The fourth member of the quartet was General Pétain, the Commander-in-Chief of the French forces in the field. He was moustachioed, like Foch, but that was about the only resemblance between the two Frenchmen. The Generalissimo was a dynamic optimist; his compatriot a stolid sceptic. Foch, for all his formidable intellectual equipment, was a genial manipulator of men.

Indeed he saw himself, in his new role, rather as the American Supreme Commander General Eisenhower would see his part in another titanic struggle in France against the same enemy a generation later – the persuader, the co-ordinator, the reconciler who achieved fixed ends by flexible diplomacy. ('You have to march on ahead,' Foch told a friend later, 'have a plan and then apply it. That is the only way to bring the English along with you ... Instead of arguing with Haig, I never stop telling him how well everything is going before I tell him what we must do next; and then he follows me.').

Pétain would never have fitted that role. He seemed almost to mistrust humanity, so austere, even frigid, was his manner. Though a formidable military administrator and an ardent patriot, his peasant phlegmatism often led him to drift into such inertia that his own staff had dubbed him 'the great slug' (*'le gros ver blanc'*) – though they were careful to abbreviate the epithet to its initials, 'G.V.B.', in case they were ever overheard. This passivity had always made Pétain cautious as a commander and there were times – as, for example, earlier that year, his urging Clemenceau to abandon the capital – when it seemed to degenerate into defeatism before the awe-inspiring strength of the German military machine. Again, perhaps it was the shadow of things to come – in Pétain's case, his willingness to head the puppet regime which, from Vichy, administered that part of France Hitler had condescended to leave unoccupied. If Henri Pétain was something of a human enigma in the First World War, the Second transformed him as well into one of Europe's most prestigious figures of controversy. All this lay distant and undreamt of as he sat at that conference table in Bombon. But even his behaviour there was not without its portents.

Foch's purpose in calling the meeting was to get his colleagues' reaction to a paper drawn up by his Chief-of-Staff, Weygand, but reflecting his own views) which, after setting out the steadily growing Allied superiority in men, material and morale, culminated in the sentence: 'The moment has come to abandon the overall defensive attitude imposed on us up to now by our numerical inferiority and to pass over to the offensive.' That was stirring stuff in those days of hand-to-hand trench fighting, when every yard of soil lost or gained was gradually another yard of France drenched in blood. Yet the detailed proposals which followed were still framed in the barbed wire of static warfare. Foch was suggesting nothing more than the freeing of three key railway lines as the pre-condition for launching, perhaps in the autumn, 'a substantial attack, calculated to build up our advantage and deny any respite to the enemy'. Yet, according to Foch, after Weygand had finished reading out the memorandum, all three Commanders-in-Chief looked at him 'as though he were a madman'. And when he went round the table to get first reactions these (again according to his own colourful account) were the replies he was given:

> From General Haig: 'The British army was completely disrupted by the events of March and April and is still a long way from being restored.'

> From General Pershing: 'The American army asks for nothing better than to fight; but it has not yet been properly formed.'

> And, most depressing of all, from General Pétain: 'The French army has gone through the severest ordeals during four years of war. It is now worn out and bled white.'

Foch may well have been exaggerating Haig's reaction. Yet it remained true that his British armies, battered though they may have been, were still the only Allied forces with both the experience and the will for renewed early action. The Americans had too little of the former, the French too little of the latter.*

As things turned out, all three Commanders-in-Chief soon accepted the Foch–Weygand plan. In Pétain's case acceptance was as characteristic as the initial protest. Might it not be still better, he suggested, to strike in the Lys Valley and around St Mihiel? The first of these alternative targets of his lay in the British sector; the second was in the American.

* General Debeney, commanding the First French Army on Haig's immediate right flank, had made such a habit (according to the British) of attacking only after his neighbours had softened the resistance for him that the practice had produced a new word in the English language, the verb 'to deb'.

Yet the whole of this historic two-hour meeting at Bombon – including the degree of Foch's optimism as well as the depths of Pétain's pessimism – were typical of the mould of the war and the mood of that day. Those four men and their advisers formed the brains trust as well as the command platform of the Allied military machine and they were planning in terms of a major attack in the autumn with victory (as Foch had just written to Clemenceau) lying somewhere, and perhaps some long way, around the corner of the year. As things turned out, the German colossus, abandoned by all its partners, was not merely down on its knees before that autumn was over, but flat on its back, and the empire which it served destroyed for ever.

In July of 1914 the political leaders had stumbled backwards into war. In July of 1918, the military leaders were stumbling backwards out of it.

Anniversaries

A WEEK AFTER that Bombon meeting, the same mood of groping defiance was felt everywhere on the political fronts when the fifth year of fighting began. As the exact anniversary came round in turn to the warring capitals, the rulers of Europe drew up balance sheets and proclamations to urge their exhausted peoples forward. 'Four lagging winters and four lagging springs end in a word,' Shakespeare had written, as though of that moment. In the first week of August 1918 the word, it seemed, was deadlock.

On the key Western Front the last great German offensive of the war, the so-called 'Emperor's Battle', had been decisively repulsed. It had been launched four months before, when a hundred and ninety-two German divisions were thrown in against the hundred and sixty-nine of the combined Allied strengths.* The plan – whose aim was to smash the four armies of the British Expeditionary Force and drive them back into the sea as a preliminary to storming the River Marne and marching on Paris – cost the Germans nearly one million casualties. Even that staggering price had brought but fleeting rewards. By the last week of July Allied counter-attacks were slicing into the huge bulge the Germans had driven in their enemy's front. The 'Emperor's Battle' had carried German troops to within forty miles of the French capital, only to have them retreat again.

It was on 31 July that the soldiers of Crown Prince Rupprecht's Army Group, driven back from the Marne, were also ousted from the valley of the River Ourcq. Then, in the first days of August, they had scrambled back behind the next two natural defence lines to the north, the Rivers Vesle and Aisne. There, posted in strong positions, they stopped, incapable now of breaking their enemy, but also, to all appearances, still incapable of being broken them-

* 98 French; 57 British and British Empire; 6 Belgian; 6 American; 2 Portuguese.

23

selves. Indeed, it looked as though the fighting in France might now return to that all-too-familiar world of muddy trenches, festooned with barbed wire, sown with mines, blasted by barrages and ruled, as far as anything could dominate that inferno, by artillery and the machine-gun.

It was a dispiriting thought to take into the fifth year of the war. A German artillery man, writing home from Sailly in France as his comrades at the front started digging in once more, summed up the mood:

> 'Peace just will not come, and we must brace ourselves for static warfare again. So one year follows another and we still have to put body and soul into playing the soldier.'

Nor was there more promise from those secondary fronts where the so-called Western Entente (helped by its Italian, Greek and Serbian partners) confronted Germany's three allies – the shaky empires of Austria-Hungary and Turkey and the little Balkan kingdom of Bulgaria. Along the valley of the Piave in Italy; up on the mountain ridges of Macedonia; and across the deserts of the Near East there hung the same air of stalemate, with no hint of the explosions soon to come.

Yet, though neither antagonist could overthrow the other there was, by now, a difference in their grips. That last thrust of the 'Emperor's Battle' could only have been mounted in such desperate force because the Bolshevik revolution of 1917 had knocked Tsarist Russia out of the war, releasing more than fifty German divisions for transfer from the Eastern Front to France. Its failure was the failure of a giant whose sinews had already reached maximum strength. But in the global scales of power, the counterweight to the collapse of imperial Russia in the spring of 1917 had been America's entry into the war alongside Britain, France and Italy. More than a year passed before this new ally could begin to play any meaningful role on the ground. Then, in the summer of 1918, a handful of American divisions fought in their first offensive battles by helping to drive the German army backwards from the Marne. Among the flood of statistics, many of them doctored, that were released then, one of the truest, and certainly one of the most significant, was the announcement that General Pershing, the American Commander-in-Chief, now had one million of his countrymen in uniform and under his command in France. Compared with the static strength of the Germans, the hold which the Entente powers had on their enemy was now steadily increasing.

That underlying shift of pressure – sensed as yet rather than felt – was reflected even in the official postures struck by the two sides during the anniversary week. It fell to Germany, whose declaration of war on Tsarist Russia on 1 August 1914 had marked the beginning of hostilities, to lead the way.

The Emperor William, who had given his blessing and his name to the spring offensive, marked the day with two proclamations, one to the German people and the other to his armed forces. They were resonant, as befitted both the occasion and a sovereign much given to bombast and rhetoric. Yet the ringing tones had a hollow, uncertain echo. This was his message to the nation at large:

> 'The fifth year of the war, which dawns today, will not spare the German people from further sacrifices and trials. But whatever may lie ahead, we know that the worst lies behind us. What has already been achieved in the East by our feats of arms and secured by peace treaties, and what is being consummated in the West gives us the firm conviction that Germany will emerge, full of strength and energy, from this tempest which has uprooted so many powerful trees.'

After reproaching his enemies for rebuffing all Germany's peace overtures; for 'shamelessly besmirching the pure German name with repeated calumnies'; and for demanding Germany's total destruction, the Emperor ended:

> 'Therefore we must fight and labour on, until our enemies are ready to recognize our right to live, the right we have triumphantly defended and maintained against their overpowering onslaught. May God be with us!'

There was more defiance than confidence in those words. The

same blend appeared in the parallel message which the Supreme War Lord addressed on that first day of August 1918 to his army and navy. No more talk here, as in earlier years, of Germany's invincible strength, but rather of her unbreakable will; no more talk of conquest, but only of beating off the enemy's resolve to destroy. The strategic repulse just suffered in the West could hardly be left out altogether in a message to the Emperor's soldiers, so it was glossed over thus:

> 'You stand in the midst of the heaviest fighting. But, as before, the desperate exertions of the foe will be nullified by your bravery. Of that I remain convinced, and so does the entire Fatherland. We are not scared by American armies, for it is not numerical superiority but the spirit which is decisive. The history of Prussia and Germany teaches us that; and so does the course the campaign has taken up to now.'

Like the national proclamation, this one too ended with a call for God's help. Other appeals went out at the time to the shades of Germany's great heroes of the past, just in case the Almighty might not prove accommodating, or even equal to the task.

> 'German people, go into your church and pray that your Kaiser may be given strength to wake our Bismarck from the dead, and bring back this Hercules to purge Germany's Augean stables, slay the Hydra of dissension and save his people from faint-heartedness, treachery and ruin,'

ran one such invocation.

Indeed, the moment seemed right for the memory of any German feat of arms to be recalled, no matter in what context. The Director of the Berlin University Eye Clinic, for example, announced on that sombre fourth anniversary of war that he had just discovered the pear-shaped eye-glass Napoleon had worn on the battlefield of Waterloo – where, as every German knew, Prussian troops had helped the English to crush the mighty Corsican. Technical descriptions of the instrument followed, with the conclusion that when he was finally toppled, that greatest of military giants had been 'not too short-sighted'.

The Kaiser's Germany had, of course, its two living legends: the Army Chief-of-Staff, Field Marshal Paul von Hindenburg, and his nominal subordinate but effective controller, the First Quartermaster-General, General Erich Ludendorff. They were the men who, four years before, had muddled their way to a historic victory over the Russians in East Prussia. It mattered not that the triumph had been a flukey affair, a wound that the Russians had largely inflicted upon themselves with almost every military bungle of intelligence, command and organization in the text-book. Decisive for their legend was the name of the town deliberately chosen to foster it. Tannenberg had been the scene of the great defeat which the Teutonic Knights had suffered at Slav hands in 1410. The warriors who had wiped out that shame at last were, surely, predestined to lead their people to victory in this other massive conflict being waged five centuries later. It was unfortunate for the German nation that, in outward appearances at least, the two generals now gave every sign of sharing that conviction.

On the threshold of the new year of war, they gave a special press interview at Spa, the pleasant little Belgian watering place where, in the spring, the German High Command had placed its new headquarters. The failure of the four-month-old Marne offensive, and the German retreat across successive river lines to the north, inevitably dominated proceedings. Hindenburg's bland explanation culminated in the following:

> 'I have a duty to economize in losses and that is why I have transferred the battle to a terrain which favours us better.'

Ludendorff began with a show of frankness, but ended on the same note of deception:

> 'This time our strategic plan of attack did not succeed ... all we achieved was a tactical success. But we fight on French soil and, however painful it would have been to surrender even one village of our own homeland, we have enemy territory enough to spare. What we have given over to the enemy has been done according to plan.'

'According to plan'! The bland, familiar lie of a thousand communiqués, once pronounced again by those demi-gods, was taken
up and elaborated upon by almost every military commentator in
the capitals of the four Central Powers. Thus General Ardenne,
writing later that week in the *Düsseldorfer Nachrichten*, assured his
readers that 'the German ebb will soon be followed by the flood'.
His well-known colleague, Captain Salzmann, even went one
better than Ludendorff when he maintained, in the *Vossische
Zeitung*: 'During the past few weeks the German leadership has
shown complete strategic superiority.' A newspaper office on the
other side of the lines made a pungent comment on that refusal to
face the underlying facts, a refusal which would inflict deep
psychological damage on the German people. The Paris *Figaro*
commented:

> 'The Germans, who cover themselves with shame when
> they are winning, cover themselves with ridicule when they
> are losing. We do not ask for more!'

But however much the German High Command might lull the
nation with a sense of false security about happenings on the
battlefield, there were two other areas where, as the fifth year of
the war began, shortcomings could not be talked away, nor fears
stilled. The first was the elemental business of getting enough food
to eat: since the terrible winter of 1917–18 the years of Allied naval
blockade had produced not merely tightened belts and rumbling
stomachs among the German people but widespread malnutrition
and even semi-starvation. Ominously, all the defiance uttered over
the August anniversary period had coincided with furious rows
between Berlin and the provincial centres of the empire because
the Prussian capital had just alloted its citizens 250 grammes (8
oz.) of meat per week per head, instead of the national level of 200
grammes. Saxony joined Bavaria in the loudest howls of indignation, thus showing once again that, quite apart from the immediate
quarrel over food distribution, the long-standing hostility of these
southern Catholic kingdoms annexed by Bismarck had not melted,
even in the furnace of war. The agitation reached such proportions
that the Bavarian Minister of the Interior, Herr von Brettreich, felt

bound to call the local press to order for cheapening Germany's dignity abroad.

> 'This shouting about a wretched 50 grammes of meat a week has a repugnant and humiliating effect, giving the impression that the tribes of Germany are fighting like dogs over a bone for the scraps of food left in the country.'

He was not far wrong, especially as regards the 'tribes'.

The second menace, beginning to envelop the nation like a slow-rising fog, was Germany's steadily increasing isolation in the world. The only military voice to express this at the time was not Hindenburg's or Ludendorff's but that of a retired Prussian infantry general called Wilhelm von Blume. Drawing a balance between the growing numbers of the Entente camp and the unchanged block of the four Central Powers after four years of war, he wrote:

> 'We must face the fact that since the beginning of last year, the United States of North America and, following in their wake, China, Panama, Cuba, Liberia, Siam, Guatemala and Costa Rica had joined themselves to the coalition of our enemies; in addition, Brazil and eight other South American states . . . have declared their hostility towards us by breaking off diplomatic relations. This means that, out of 1,565 millions who currently inhabit this earth, more than 1,000 millions stand against us   compared with the 170 millions of our own four nation alliance.'

Nor did things look much brighter among the countries who had still not declared themselves. On the same day, 2 August 1918, that von Blume's sobering arithmetic appeared in the press Prince Max of Baden (who, as yet quite unbeknown to him, was soon to preside over the final act of the German drama) wrote, in a deeply pessimistic coded letter to a friend, of 'complete helplessness against the growing hostility towards us in the neutral countries'.

The same General von Blume probably brought little consolation to his readers when, echoing Ludendorff's line at Spa two days before, he totted up the foreign territory which the Germans and their allies still held ('almost the whole of Belgium; Serbia and

Montenegro; large areas around Venice and almost one-sixth of France which, like Belgium, has been in our possession for three and a half years without a break'). And Berlin's military propaganda office, the *Buro Wolff*, made itself somewhat ridiculous by announcing, in an attempt to cheer people up, the total of war material captured and the numbers of enemy persons held on the fourth anniversary ('over 3,800,000, of whom about 2,300,000 are in Germany alone'). To a people conditioned by years of earlier propaganda to dread the threat of '*Einkreisung*' or 'Encirclement', it was the feeling that Germany stood increasingly alone and friendless in the world – that world she had always tried so hard to dazzle and impress – which overshadowed all statistics. In short, the threshold of the fifth year of war was, for Germany, like the brink of an abyss, an abyss which its leaders forbade the nation to recognize, even to acknowledge, while preferring to look away from it themselves.

Yet (and here we come to an important irony which runs throughout much of the time ahead), Germany's enemies also failed to see her true plight. France had entered the war on 3 August 1914, a day earlier than England. Four years later, however, the two countries ran their anniversaries together, with formal messages exchanged between President Poincaré and King George V, and special Orders of the Day issued by their commanders in the field, General (about to become Marshal) Foch and Sir Douglas Haig. Both Heads of State repeated the ritual assurances of their determination to fight on to victory but, though the undertone was more confident than that of the Kaiser's proclamation, neither ventured any guesses as to how near that victory might be.

Characteristically, it was left to England's irrepressible Prime Minister, David Lloyd George, to sound the only note of optimism. His special message to the nation was 'Hold Fast'. That in itself was hardly an electrifying slogan; but he had chosen it, the Prime Minister explained, 'because our prospects of victory have never been so bright as they are today'. For the first time in the war 4 August fell on a Sunday, which presented problems with the distribution of the speech. These were got round, in the absence of radio and television, by delivering a copy of the message from 10 Downing Street by sealed envelope to the proprietor of every theatre, music-hall, concert-hall and cinema in the kingdom, and announcing the event in advance. Punctually at 9 a.m. on Monday morning, managers stepped up on stages the length and breadth of the country, doubtless with a rare sense of occasion at having more than an air raid alarm or a change of programme to announce, and read out the Prime Minister's words for him. As an exercise in mass media before the mass media age it was a spectacular success. It was reckoned that audiences totalling two and a half million Britons listened to their leader's exhortation in some five thousand places of public entertainment. At the Brixton Empire in London the speech itself was auctioned and raised fifteen guineas for the Soldiers' Comforts Fund. Many thousands heard the message away from home. It was the August holiday weekend and, war or no war, the customary rush from cities to seaside had taken place: queues for tickets half a mile long at London Bridge and Victoria Stations were seen in the metropolis on the Saturday.

The high clerics, of course, had had their say on the Sunday, and a strange say it was in some cases. In St Paul's Cathedral, for example, where the National Anthem preceded the hymns, a vast congregation heard the Bishop of London preach a disturbing sermon. He posed the question bluntly: 'If there is a God, why does he not stop the war? What is the good of another day of prayer when we have held so many already?' And his answer was even more disturbing, particularly to any very new of England's *nouveaux riches* who were sitting in his congregation. Perhaps, the bishop suggested, the Lord was turning a deaf ear because 'many people were not sincere in praying for the war to end'; and the reason for this lack of fervour on the delinquents' part might well be that 'never before in their lives had they made so much money'.

At the same hour a couple of miles away, his superior, the Archbishop of Canterbury, was preaching at a special service of intercession held at St Margaret's, Westminster. (It was indeed a very special service: the first time in history that the King and Queen of England, together with the members of both Houses of Parliament, had joined together officially in what was described as

31

'one solemn act of prayer, confession, thanksgiving, commemoration and resolve'.) Faced with such a congregation the Primate eschewed the challenging tone which his bishop was striking in the City of London. 'Four years have taught us much,' he began. 'They have not diminished, they have enhanced, the imperishable dignity of the deeds of heroic sacrifice.' Then he added, in a vein that had been entirely missing from the proceedings earlier that week in Berlin, that those four years had also taught 'the unspeakable hatefulness of war', leaving behind a resolve that 'a repetition of its ghastly horrors shall become impossible among men'. But even the Archbishop could not refrain from issuing a warning against the nation's high ideals being coarsened by 'prosaic selfishness and greed of gain'. Altogether, it was not a comfortable morning of devotions for England's war profiteers.

Those same gentlemen would, however, have regained their spirits had they read their *Sunday Pictorial* after the service. In it the newspaper's powerful proprietor, Lord Rothermere, was warning the nation against indulging in over-optimism, despite the recent Allied successes on the Marne: 'There is no prospect of the early collapse of Germany,' he told them, 'and there is much to justify those who believe that the war will last *at least three years more*.' (Italics in original.) This verdict, directly at odds with the bright note being sounded by the Prime Minister, was excessively gloomy. Yet it was true that not a single one of those experts whom Lord Rothermere was invoking had the faintest inkling that the war had not three years, but only three months to run.

That was especially true of the mood in the Allied capital of Paris over the anniversary weekend. The Germans had indeed just been halted and finally pushed back in their advance on the capital, as they had been in that first dreadful summer of the fighting four years before. But the formidable foe, if no longer at the gates of Paris, was still entrenched in the courtyard. As if to rub home the fact the German long-range guns opened up again on the capital in the early hours of 5 August after a silence which had lasted since 17 July. After all the heady successes of the past few weeks, 'Big Bertha's' voice seemed to be announcing a return to the sober hardships of a city under siege. And the preparations for a seemingly endless struggle only reinforced the message. The French Chamber was debating whether to accelerate the military call-up of the 1920 class by eighteen months in order to meet the acute manpower shortage in the field. The measure was duly passed, though not without criticism. One Socialist deputy, M. Renaudel, while accepting that some other countries had been forced to take the same step, still questioned whether France could be expected to follow suit, 'in view of the grand total of French sacrifices already'. And it was those battle casualties, some three and a half million to date, which loomed largest in France's anniversary balance sheet.

On the other side of the Atlantic the first days of August had, of course, no special significance in the nation's war diary; but the Americans had nonetheless commemorated fervently with the British and French on the fourth. One leading New York paper declared in its editorial that day:

'The Tricoleur, the Union Jack and the Stars and Stripes are now bound on the same errand, and please God they shall never part.'

Its sister paper paid this glowing, if slightly bizarre, tribute to America's one-time colonial masters:

'August is indeed England's day, and there is no day in the ten centuries [*sic*] of English history that shines more brilliantly.'

As for President Woodrow Wilson, he gave the world another taste of that severe and almost messianic Founding Fathers spirit which he was soon to cast over the entire imbroglio of peace-making. On the occasion of England's 'Sunday of Intercession', he formally proclaimed a date for the American people to indulge in 'public humiliation, prayer and fasting'. He went on to exhort his 'fellow citizens of all faiths and creeds to assemble on that day in their several places of worship and there, as well as in their homes, to pray to Almighty God that he may ... purify our hearts ... in these days of dark struggle and perplexity'.

The occasion produced many an oddity which reflected

America's all-too-keen awareness that, as yet, she had not begun to match the terrible blood-letting which her allies had been suffering on the battlefields for four years past. Any gesture which might show willingness to atone for the gap was seized upon. Thus, on 4 August, the 'Society of Cincinnati' (which had originally been formed by General Washington and the Marquis de Lafayette from the officers of the 'Continental Army') sent a telegram from New York to Mr Lloyd George announcing that, just as 4 July was their Independence Day so, from now on, 4 August 'will ever be held sacred as "Dependence Day", in honour of the great Motherland who drew her sword without hesitation for the cause ... of world freedom'. The signatories, who had met in New York's 'France Tavern', were headed by Theodore Roosevelt. Despite being launched with such fervour by such illustrious sponsors, it is doubtful whether 'Dependence Day' was ever celebrated, or even heard of, again.

In a search for some more popular crumb of anniversary comfort, New York managed to unearth a counterpart to that item about Napoleon's eye-glass which had been produced earlier in the week in Berlin. America's little morale-booster was not quite so prestigious; it concerned the German Crown Prince's teeth. Dr Davis, a New York dentist who had earlier practised in Berlin, revealed that when 'Little Willy' had visited him for treatment there he had proved so craven in the chair that it had been almost impossible to work on his teeth at all. The Kaiser's eldest son had apparently confessed to Dr Davis: 'The future ruler of Germany ought to be brave at all times, but I just hate going to the dentist.' In normal circumstances most people would have had nothing but fellow-feeling for the Hohenzollern prince. This, however, was a war anniversary; and the anecdote carried the appropriate message that, even at the very top, the German bullies were really cowards at heart.

But the two messages from the United States which really counted that week concerned the vital topics of money and men. The first was a calculation, made on 1 August, that America's war bill, including loans to her Allies, totalled some £3,000 million in English money and was now running at £12 million a day, compared

34

with the £7 million a day Britain was still finding for herself after four years of costly hostilities. America was right to draw attention to this, for she had saved her allies with her dollars long before she could begin to save them with her doughboys.

The second statistic, appropriately enough, was published in Washington on the exact Allied anniversary date of 4 August. It concerned a new draft bill to enlist all eligible American men between the ages of eighteen and forty-five. This, it was stated, would result in a US army in France of between three and four million men before the year 1919 was over. In all, it was pointed out, America could draw on a manpower reservoir of no fewer than twenty-two million men of military age. Figures like those were calculated to inspire even the most pessimistic experts in London and Paris; and, just as certainly, to cause many a shiver of apprehension in Berlin.

As for the junior partners of the two alliances, the most important of them, Italy and Austria-Hungary, behaved like the odd men out they really were. In Rome, as in Washington, the August date had no special meaning; and the Italians, unlike the Americans, had little reason anyway to celebrate their true anniversary. It was on 23 May 1915 that they had entered the conflict on the Entente side by declaring war on Austria-Hungary, thus breaking the pledge with Vienna to which they were bound. The lever that had broken this treaty was one of the greatest bribes of modern times: the promise by England and France to give Italy, after the common victory, all the Hapsburg realms south of the Brenner plus large tracts of islands and coast in the Adriatic and Dalmatia. Even allowing for the fact that ever since Italy's struggle for unification had begun the century before, Austria-Hungary had been her traditional enemy, such a political somersault was nothing to be proud of. Nor was Italy's military record in the war much more illustrious, despite much evidence of her soldiers' bravery and even some of good generalship. The national shame was Caporetto, the name of the town up in the Julian Alps north of Trieste from where, in the autumn of 1917, a surprise Austro-German attack had chased the Italian armies down into the plain and then driven them in headlong retreat across the Tagliamento and Piave Rivers.

With so little to boast about it was not surprising that the Italians concentrated on their hopes. It was perhaps symbolic that on the exact date of the Anglo-French anniversary a statue to '*Regina Pacis*', the Queen of Peace was unveiled in Rome; but even Italy still regarded her as a very distant princess. Messages were exchanged on that day between President Orlando and the Heads of the Allied States, and the Italians seemed grateful for even the most ritual of tributes to their loyalty and valour. There was a distinct air of condescension about the reply from the French Prime Minister, Georges Clemenceau. This expressed pride in the victory just won by the French armies on French soil through French endurance; and the 'generous and effective' support of France's other allies, including Italy, was acknowledged. The moment was hailed when, some time in the future, peace and liberty would reign in the world. 'At this glorious hour,' the 'Tiger's' telegram to Rome concluded, 'Italy will receive the reward which admiration and gratitude owe to her.' No plainer nor more embarrassing reference could have been devised in a public message to that massive bribe which tied Italy to the Entente's coat-tails.

As for Vienna, as the fifth year of fighting opened there, the yearning and the clamour for peace – for peace through any means and almost at any price – came out above all else, louder and clearer than in any of the other warring capitals. There was one prime reason for that: the character and convictions of the young Emperor Charles who, in the middle of the war, had succeeded his great-uncle Francis Joseph when that most venerable of all Europe's monarchs had died at last, on 30 November 1916, after his enormous span of sixty-eight years on the throne. It was not for nothing that the new ruler, destined to be the last in the six and a half centuries of the Habsburg line, would go down in history as the '*Friedenskaiser*' or 'Peace Emperor'. From the first day of his brief reign he had striven to put an immediate end to the conflict he had inherited with his crown.

Approach had followed approach to the Western Allies – through the Vatican, through Switzerland, Holland, Spain or any of the other neutrals willing to act; by the hand of diplomats, soldiers, ministers, professors, industrialists. No channel and no intermediary offering the faintest prospect of progress had been scorned. In March of 1917 – encouraged by Zita, the vivacious and highly intelligent Bourbon princess he had married three years before war had broken out – Charles even embarked on the desperately dangerous move of bidding in secret for a separate peace with France. This venture, dubbed the 'Sixtus Affair' after his French wife's brother who had served as chief go-between, was probably the last venture of dynastic diplomacy in the old Europe. It was certainly the most disastrous. The negotiations led to nothing and the approach blew up in Charles's face when Clemenceau was goaded into exposing the secret a year later.

Despite these humiliations and set-backs the ill-fated young monarch had pressed on. He did so not merely because he loathed war with every fibre of his gentle being – unlike his fellow-Emperor in Berlin, who played out all the fantasies of his life in the charade of military uniforms. Charles's motives were down to earth as well as up in the heavens. He knew that the faded and ragged quilt of his eleven-nation empire would come apart altogether if the strains of war tore at it much longer.

Even his great-uncle may have felt this in his ancient bones four years before. At any rate, largely for military reasons, Austria-Hungary had acquired anniversary dates very different from those of her principal ally. It was not until 6 August that the Dual Monarchy had declared war on Russia; and, despite the urgings of Berlin, parallel action against France and England did not come until a week after that – marking, incidentally, the first occasion in their long histories that the British and Hapsburg realms had been directly, as distinct from indirectly, opposed on the battlefield.*

There had been a much more significant delay on Vienna's part when the United States entered the conflict. Germany responded immediately to the American declaration of war. Austria-Hungary did not follow suit until four months later, as though cherishing the fond hope that this life-line of peace to the Western democracies could be kept open. That hope had inevitably failed then; and, in

* In the Seven Year War, 1756–63, Austria's ally had been at war with England who was in turn supporting Austria's enemy, Prussia, with money.

37

Vienna's eyes, the unfathomable President Wilson had been failing them, less avoidably, ever since.

Indeed, for the Austrian propagandists of August 1918, Woodrow Wilson had become the arch-villain of the people. A drawing widely circulated in Vienna with the caption 'On the threshold of the fifth war year' showed a slender angel of peace, wings held tautly back, walking nervously down a woodland glade. Waiting in hiding to waylay her with a bludgeon and a pistol are Wilson, Lloyd George and Clemenceau. It is the American President who stands closest to the path, a look of keen anticipation on his lean features. Vienna's leading newspaper spelt the message out in words which a later generation would call Gaullist:

> 'The greatest obstacle to peace at the beginning of the fifth year of war is Wilson who ... has taken up the idea of destroying our Monarchy. It is 'Tsar' Wilson who feeds, clothes and arms France and England. It is he who decides on war and peace and so brings Europe under alien rule.'

On the other hand, Austria's main Socialist organ, with its natural pacifist leanings, was allowed to use the occasion to attack both the war and the Austro-German alliance and to support one of the President's pet schemes for the post-war world, as enunciated among his famous Fourteen Points for peace six months before. 'Instead of peace,' the journal thundered, 'more people are starving to death than ever ... We are now even further from a decision. This is the terrible reality that must be brought home to Germany. The war will not be ended by any battle victory won by the Central Empires. It will end only if they consent to a new world order with a League of Nations, disarmament and arbitration.'

Nobody who knew the Emperor Charles or Count Burian, his Foreign Minister, need have been surprised that this remarkable outburst got past the censors. Whatever their differences with the Socialists over domestic policy, both the monarch and his minister were at one with them over that. By then peace was not just an imperial priority in Vienna; it was an imperial obsession.

So much for the political capitals in the anniversary week, and the voices of Emperors, Prime Ministers, Presidents and newspaper editors. It is time to return to the front-line soldiers who knew they would have to contest the new year of conflict. Their mood varied of course with the man, the moment, the regiment and, to some extent, the battlefield. But, to judge from the many personal diaries which have survived in various languages, and also from general censorship surveys analysing thousands of unidentified letters, it was a feeling of helpless and hopeless exhaustion which prevailed, particularly in the Austro-German camp. And on both sides of the line, that heady, almost light-hearted enthusiasm with which they had marched off to fight four summers before had totally evaporated.

This contrast is vividly illustrated by a private journal which a remarkable Austrian aristocrat, Count Gerolf Coudenhove-Kalergi, compiled for his family. For his Austrian friends, who had left with their regiments for the Russian front in August 1914, it had not been even a case of 'Back home for Christmas'. Hunters almost to a man, they all confidently expected to have the war finished long before then, and be back on their estates for that great event of the sporting season, the stag-shooting of the autumn. And the mood in which they had gathered for battle was summed up for Coudenhove in one message sent back to him from the front by a friend. The field postcard had only three words on it: '*Riesenhetz, Masse Bekannte*' ('Tremendous fun, lots of familiar faces.'). It might have been a holiday greeting written in deepest peace-time from Karlsbad or Nice.

Four years later Count Coudenhove, now an artillery lieutenant* on the Italian front, described the very different atmosphere:

> 'For us, the war had now become a permanent state of affairs which we had simply come to accept without questioning ... but a certain war-weariness was widespread and also a contempt for everything behind the battlefield.

Elsewhere on that same front a brother-officer of humbler origins,

* A man of his family would normally have been commissioned into one of the Monarchy's crack regiments; but his father, in a romance that had rocked Viennese society of the day, had married a Japanese lady and this counted heavily against the son.

who had risen to much greater military rank and position (he was, in fact, Chief-of-Staff of the élite Austrian Edelweiss division), was writing the following entry in a diary he kept in his own special stenograph:

'1 August: Another new month, and the first to come round for a fifth time. It seems to begin everywhere with us in a mood of depression. Today, one can hardly imagine anymore how the war is going to be won ...'

The ordinary soldiers on that front who, by then, were suffering severe privations, inclined more to bitterness than philosophy. In the same month of August 1918 the Austrian authorities intercepted a whole batch of troop mail which had been sent home by the civilian post in an attempt to evade censorship. Here is one typical outburst:

'There's nothing more for us to eat, and no fresh clothing ... The only things we have enough of are lice. They are half the size of your thumb and everyone is eaten bare by them, like a leaf with caterpillars ... I can't describe to you how ravenous we are, for one cannot even believe oneself that men could endure such hunger ... Nothing but turnips and rotten cabbage ... I do as I am ordered, but just about as willingly as cattle or a machine ... There's no joy in living for me anymore, I'd rather by lying under the grass at home. Truly, it is a lucky man who manages to get home, even if he is ill or a cripple ... There will be no peace until we do what so many of us have already done – desert.'

Perhaps the most interesting thing about this pile of correspondence which never reached its various destinations was the comment of the officer to whom they were sent for possible disciplinary action:

'I decided against punishing any of those who wrote these letters because what they say is, for the most part, the truth.'

On the Western Front that type of outburst was, as yet, much rarer

– not only because German discipline was tighter but because the German High Command was still managing to feed and clothe its soldiers adequately. But any intelligent German who, as the new war year opened, sat back to think instead of living simply by conditioned military reflexes, could hardly escape the same rising feeling of despair.

One such man, a divisional liaison officer, had written this in his diary (*'West of Rheims'*), while the retreat from the Marne was going on:

> 'Confusion and muddle on the increase . . . today the situation seems to have stabilized, but I can no longer believe that we will get freedom of movement. The American army is here – a million men. That's too much.'

And on 4 August, when the Germans were dug in behind their new river lines, and he had time for more spacious thought, the same officer wrote:

> 'People are tired of the war. You hear it said – and not just by the worst elements but by brave front-line soldiers – "Let's give them this cursed Alsace-Lorraine!" . . . There is a feeling that this year of which so much was promised . . . has passed uselessly by . . . You tell yourself that you are not here simply to be consumed any more in this crazy, never-ending business . . . The most idiotic sort of static warfare is starting up again . . . it might in the end lead to something you could call peace. But I'm not properly convinced of it; therefore I cannot properly carry on any more.'

As for the Allied armies which were now pressing the Germans hard across the rivers north of the Marne, they were at least carried forward by a hope their enemy could no longer feel – the hope that the worst was over and that, conceivably, the corner might now have been turned. A British company commander with the 42nd Infantry Division in France reflected this mood exactly in a letter written to his father as the fifth year of battle was starting:

> 'I am writing this on the anniversary of our declaration of

war ... I am sure we can keep this day this year in a far happier frame of mind than we could last year. At any rate, we know the Boche has done his worst and from now onwards his resistance must gradually slacken.'

Yet, hope or no hope, there was no recapturing, for them either, that *bravura* of the early days. One of the most moving expressions of this on the French side was surely a letter that a young French private had written from the front line to his parents on 18 March 1915, his twentieth birthday:

'To be twenty years old, and to be a soldier. At this moment that's a whole fortune ... Dear Papa and dearest Mama, do not distress yourself if, in a week or two, I am struck down doing my duty. I shall still have the courage to cry again with all my heart: "My soul to God, and my twenty years to France!"'

The writer of that letter was, in fact, killed in action soon after. Yet even had he survived into the fifth year of fighting, it is unlikely that such ecstasy would have survived the numbing months of horror with him.

A French infantryman who did survive to take part in the great counter-attack wrote this, for example, on 2 August 1918, after crossing the Meunière Wood on the Marne front, from which the Germans had just been driven:

'I seem still to see those two Boches lying across a road. One without his head; a foot cut off and stretching across his belly; his hand torn away and fallen several yards from the body. The other bent backwards, has spatters of bloody mud over his forehead and chest; his right eye, partly hanging out of its socket, seems to be looking at you strangely, while the flies already begin to crawl out of his open mouth ...

'Not far away an even odder sight awaits us: all round a large round dining-table, properly laid in the middle of the wood, are spread the corpses of a dozen officers, all killed by the same shell. It must have been a meal or a staff conference which one of our projectiles rudely interrupted . . .'

There is precious little exhilaration of victory in those lines; rather a feeling of comradeship for the enemy' my friend, who had drawn steadily closer during the four years of battle. That feeling comes out more strongly, with even a sympathetic echo from the foe, in the French diarist's final entry for that day:

'But our most unexpected discovery is certainly that of a placard which the enemy had propped up in full view against a tree and on which we read these words in French:

"Long live the Kaiser and all honour to the 18th French Infantry Battalion".

And later that day, one of our officers found this message addressed to him, also in French:

"Two months ago you were not so proud of yourselves; but we will meet again on the Seine!" '

It seems that the advancing French troops who came across those greetings felt no surprise at their confident and chivalrous tone. The forces which had opposed them on that sector were known as familiar antagonists from several previous engagements, and were mainly drawn from élite troops of the Prussian Guards.

Whether the French infantrymen knew it or not, by August 1918 that apparently undiluted spirit of defiance was becoming ever rarer among even the best of the enemy's troops. The German High Command went on planning as though it still had at its disposal that magnificent military machine of 1914 – acknowledged by none other than Foch to be the most formidable army the world had ever seen. But by August 1918 the machine had begun to splutter and even to seize up in places. The cause, apart from general metal fatigue, was the poor quality of the spare parts sent from home. These twin weaknesses of morale and manpower were about to be exposed in spectacular fashion at the heart of the Western battle-front.

43

3

One Man's Black Day

THE BLOW DELIVERED on the plains of Picardy on 8 August 1918, which was to create such havoc on a key sector of the German army's front and even greater havoc in its High Command, was not mounted by the Allies with any such ambitions. In the darkest days of the 'Emperor's Battle' both Foch and Haig had still found the time and the confidence to discuss possible counter-offensives against the centre of the enemy's line. With the Germans pulling back, in good order but in poor spirit, from the Marne now was the obvious moment to launch such a move, before the juggernaut had time to steady itself on its backward lurch.

There was no thought, however, of turning the juggernaut right over. What the French Generalissimo had worked out with Haig in the last days of July was, as we have seen, a series of local stabs to keep the initiative, improve Allied communications and so win more elbow-room for a really savage swing at the enemy later on. In other words Foch intended to begin with the rapier, rather than the bludgeon, as befitted the man who had once talked of his strategy more like an excitable fencing master than a sober War Lord:

> 'I attack them. Good. I say "Into Battle. Everyone into battle." Good. I give them no rest, the Boches ... They don't know what to do, but I do. I have no plan. I await events. Good. The event arrives and I exploit it ... I carry on ... I press them. We strike everywhere ...'

All this and more, delivered in a monologue while striding quickly up and down his office, the staccato sentences punctuated with lots of play-acting as the Generalissimo imitated a bayonet thrust or a revolver duel.

That was one aspect of the man. Yet there was a reflective as

44

well as an impulsive side to his nature, typical of the soldier who had first made his name as a military theorist. This other Foch was more the methodical plodder than the intuitive improviser; and he had once likened this approach of his to that of a parrot climbing carefully to reach its food: 'See how it starts from the bottom of the ladder ... it grips the first rung and only lets go when it is sure of reaching the next. Finally it reaches the top rung and seizes its grain. I am this parrot.'

It was the cautious old bird, still very much confined to his cage, who, on 24 July, had proposed those three separate but connected operations to free the railway lines linking Paris with northern France.

As it happened, the most pressing of those operations, to free the line which linked Amiens to the capital, was not Foch's idea in origin but rather the brainchild of Field Marshal Haig. This dour but dapper Scot – always impeccably turned out and seemingly never flustered – looked such a perfect copybook general that it was hardly surprising if performance did not live up to appearance. An American soldier with the 107th US Regiment describes the impression Haig made when, earlier that summer, he had come to inspect the unit:

> 'The general walked down our lines and looked us over. He seemed a small man physically to have the whole weight of the Empire on his shoulders, but those shoulders were square and soldierly and the face, worn and pale, was businesslike ... With little personal magnetism, he impressed one as a man who would stick to the job until it was finished.'

What Haig might well have been wondering while he was doing that inspection was whether, in fact, he would be allowed to stick to his job. He had carried the burden of the Supreme British Command for three and a half gruelling years and he knew that Lloyd George, Prime Minister since the previous winter, was yearning to replace him as an exhausted, unadventurous figure. But Haig knew too that now, if ever, the moment had come to beat off this pressure from a politician whom he in turn despised as a

45

dangerously impulsive bounder. Moreover, the prime enemy target was on his front – the vulnerable German Second Army commanded by General von der Marwitz, who had been one of the star performers in the 'Emperor's Battle' in March.

As early as 13 July Haig had accordingly instructed the GOC of his Fourth Army, Sir Henry Rawlinson, to draw up plans for an attack on the Amiens salient. On the 17th, as soon as the outline proposals were ready, Haig had submitted the project formally to his Generalissimo. At Bombon, therefore, Haig had been handed back his own idea.

By the end of the month the operational plan was complete. The main blow was to be delivered by the Fourth Army, striking due east at the Amiens bulge, and driving north and south of the marshy River Luce which divided it. For this purpose Rawlinson (described by Sir Winston Churchill, who had known him since the battle of Omdurman, as a 'tough, cheery gentleman and sportsman') had a formidable array of Commonwealth forces. He now commanded four British divisions with one American division attached to get its baptism of fire; the British Cavalry Corps; five Australian and four Canadian divisions; two thousand pieces of artillery and an entire Royal Air Force Brigade (as it was then still styled).

Most important of all, he disposed of the greatest concentration of fighting tanks ever employed – three hundred and forty-two heavy Mark Vs and seventy-two mediums, the so-called 'Whippets'. The armoured *Blitzkrieg* of later wars was not dreamt of in the martial philosophy of those machines. Their performance ruled it out, for a start. The heavy model, going flat out on a hard surface, could only manage a brisk walking pace; even the Whippet rather belied its name, with the maximum speed equivalent to that of a trotting horse. Nor was that the only curb: unreliable engines and caterpillar tracks produced frequent breakdowns which quickly overwhelmed the relatively primitive maintenance resources of the day.

None of that mattered unduly at the time, for their purpose was not to roll up the enemy's flanks and strike terror and confusion hundreds of miles behind his lines, but simply to punch holes in his

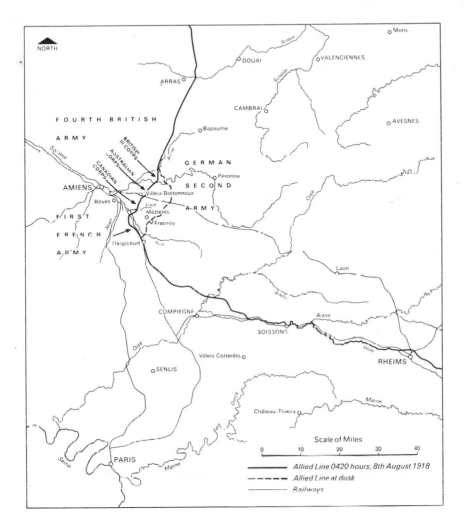

NORTH

o Mons

SCARPE

o DOUAI

o VALENCIENNES

ARRAS o

CAMBRAI o

o AVESNES

FOURTH BRITISH

ARMY

o Bapaume

BRITISH III CORPS

AUSTRALIAN CORPS

GERMAN

CANADIAN CORPS

o Péronne

SECOND

AMIENS

o Villers Brétonneux

ARMY

Bovès o

Luce

Mézierès

FIRST

Fresnoy

FRENCH

ARMY

Harbonnières

Oise

Laon

COMPIÈGNE o

SOISSONS

Aisne

Villers Cotterêts o

RHEIMS

o SENLIS

Ourcq

Château-Thierry o

Marne

Scale of Miles

| 0 | 10 | 20 | 30 | 40 |

Seine

PARIS

Marne

——————— Allied Line 0420 hours, 8th August 1918

– – – – – Allied Line at dusk

——————— Railways

8 August 1918, showing Allied Advance

front through which the accompanying assault infantry and cavalry could pass. The omens for that sort of manoeuvre seemed hopeful. To begin with, the terrain east of Amiens, as can be seen today, is ideal for armoured operations, being either dead flat or gently rolling; in that summer of 1918 its chalky soil was also as hard as a billiard table after a hot, dry spell. Moreover, Marwitz's men seemed to have been leaning on their spades, for no new defence systems of note had been added to the old trench-works of 1915 and 1916. Everything pointed to a leap-frogging advance once the tanks had made the first ground. But how far?

The general staff had calculated that, along the whole of the ten-mile front, 10,500 yards might be hoped for as the average advance from the starting line on the first day. On the second day the French First Army under General Debeney, with fewer forces and with far fewer tanks, was to put in a supplementary attack against the southern side of the bulge. Though the entire operation was placed under the personal command of Haig, the man who had inspired it, General Foch, who was about to be raised to the rank of Marshal of France,* was not going to be left out of things entirely.

If the plan were to succeed (and, by the standards of French warfare, an army front advance of 10,000 yards in one day's fighting was a wild success) it would have to be sprung as a surprise. That was a tall order, for the reinforcements which were poured into the Fourth Army's sector during the first week of August alone needed some two hundred and thirty extra trains for men and guns and more than sixty extra trains to bring up their ammunition. Night movements helped; so also did the fact that none of the men and relatively few of the officers who got on and off those trains knew exactly what was afoot. Until the last possible moment knowledge of the operation was kept to a handful of commanders and their staffs, who constantly changed their meeting places to avoid drawing attention to the conferences. Tank movements were blotted out as far as possible by aircraft noise. The massive assembly of artillery was ordered to calibrate its guns for the barrage by indi-

---

* On 6 August Clemenceau had arrived at the Chateau de Bombon to announce that he was making the recommendation to President Poincaré.

vidual batteries firing a fixed number of rounds at fixed intervals, so that a preparation which had, in fact, been worked out to the last round would sound like routine, even desultory, shelling on the other side of the line.

Every trick of deception (in this war, as in the war to come, a British speciality) was brought into play to strengthen such routine camouflage. The aim, which was at least partly achieved, was to keep the eyes of the German High Command fixed further north on Flanders while the real blow was being mounted in Picardy. Thus, while the Canadian Corps, a fresh and powerful source of strength, was being moved southwards from Arras for the attack, rumours were put about that it was really destined for a new push on the Ypres front, where new hospital units and air bases were ostentatiously established. Bogus radio signals elaborated on the charade which, even if it only confused the enemy, completely took in the Belgian army fighting with the Allies; its commander, the valiant King Albert, indignantly demanded why he had been kept in the dark about this important new move to be launched on his own soil.

As for individual security, every officer, NCO and man in the strengthened Fourth Army was issued with a special pamphlet, entitled brusquely 'Keep Your Mouth Shut', which told him what not to say or ask before the battle and what not to tell the enemy should he be taken prisoner during the battle.

That enemy knew, of course, that an attack was to be feared, here as anywhere else along the new battle line. And, so far as the Second German Army was concerned, its commander also knew that he was in no great shape to meet it. So many statistics were to be produced weeks, months and even years afterwards on the German side to explain or excuse what went wrong in that famous Amiens battle that it is refreshing to find one set of significant facts and figures which were drawn up five days before the engagement started. On 3 August 1918, General von der Marwitz, a cavalry officer well-known for his dash (and by no means, therefore, given over to pessimism), reported back to his Army Group commander, Crown Prince Rupprecht of Bavaria, on the condition of the thirteen formations under him. Only two, the 27th Württemberg and the 117th, could he rate as 'completely fit for battle'. Five others were classified as 'fit for operations in static warfare only'; three more only for 'defensive roles on a quiet sector'; and the last three as 'in need of replacement'.*

What reaction, if any, General von der Marwitz got from Army Group we do not know. But the next day, 4 August, he received, together with all German field commanders, an order signed by Ludendorff in which the Quartermaster-General sought to revive the sagging spirits of his troops and to give advice as to how any future Allied blows should be parried. There was nothing, in Ludendorff's view, to justify the 'certain degree of apprehension' which prevailed in many quarters of his army. Then came this extraordinary passage, commenting on the French counterstroke of 18 July which had started the German retreat:

> 'It is to the tanks that the enemy owed this initial success. These however would not have been formidable if the infantry had not allowed itself to be surprised and if the artillery had been properly positioned in depth. We now occupy everywhere positions which have been strongly fortified and we have, I am convinced, carried out a judicious organization in depth of infantry and artillery ... We should wish for nothing better than to see the enemy launch an offensive, which can but hasten the disintegration of his forces.'

Ludendorff's inability to grasp the growing importance of armour in modern warfare was by now ingrained; but, addressed as it was at this juncture to the Second Army, his warning to the infantry and artillery not to let themselves be surprised by a tank attack had a particular irony. We know from that army's regimental records that, despite all the Allied precautions, the German forward troops

---

* General Rawlinson's Intelligence Officers had come to similar conclusions in respect of several of these divisions, though basing their judgements mainly on the freshness of the Second Army's formations. They knew for example that the 27th would be a tough nut to crack because it had only just been brought down from reserve in the Lille area. They also knew that the 109th, one of those marked down as 'in need of replacement', would be a much softer target because it had been in the front line for three and a half months without a break.

had picked up the noise of what they took to be large numbers of tanks forming up at Villers-Bretonneux and at various other parts of their front in the days before the attack. Though most of their reports were dismissed as nervous fancies, the 41st East Prussian Division, which was holding the Villers-Bretonneux sector, went so far as to report the possibility of an imminent enemy tank attack on its front. The warning was echoed by army command. Nothing was done about it.

Then, on 6 August, a German photographic reconnaissance plane (one of only seven allowed by Allied fighters to complete its mission over the critical area in the week before the attack) returned to base with the startling information that a column of no fewer than one hundred enemy tanks had been seen moving up on the road to Morcuil. Again, no special precautions were ordered from Army, Army Group or Supreme Headquarters. In the philosophy nurtured by Ludendorff, a tank was merely a moving target for a gun.*

The Allies had one final bit of luck. That same day the 27th Württemberg Division had shown its mettle by carrying out a short sharp attack on the northern sector held by British troops; and they had brought back as prisoners five officers and two hundred and thirty-one men of the 18th and 58th Infantry Divisions. If any of the captives knew what General Rawlinson was about to do, not one of them breathed a word under interrogation. Security had held until the last minute of the eleventh hour

So 8 August dawned on an unsuspecting German Second Army. Back at his comfortable headquarters in the Chateau de Beaurepaire near Montreuil Haig, who knew better than anyone what was at stake east of Amiens both for the army and for him personally, got up at first light and noted laconically in his diary: 'Glass steady. Fine night and morning – a slight mist in the valley. An autumn feel in the air.' He soon had more exciting things to record.

But it is another diary, kept not by a general but by a modest

---

* Thanks to this scepticism, the German army, in the summer of 1918, possessed fewer than a score of tanks, and some of those were captured Allied models.

Royal Artillery subaltern, which best conveys the atmosphere on the Allied side of the battlefield that day – and above all the sense of sheer disbelief that this German juggernaut could, perhaps, be rolled over on its back after all. The young English officer wrote of that 8 August:

'Up at the guns Zero Hour was at twenty minutes past four; down at the wagon lines I was wakened by the bombardment. I got up and looked out of my tent. It was quite dark in the wood and there was a thick mist ... I tried to distinguish the sound of enemy shells bursting from the cannonade of our own guns but Boves Wood was a long way back and at a distance it was all one noise, a sullen, ceaseless reverberation. The drum of death.

'For once I was not directly concerned. I was in safety at the wagon lines, I could go back to sleep for another hour ...

'When I woke again the noise had almost stopped, and this was surprising. Battles lasted for more than an hour or two, whether we won or lost. The silence was rather disconcerting. I could interpret noises but silence, even this comparative silence, was a new feature in a battle ...

'From Boves I could see the enemy observation balloons against the sky, looking no further away than usual. If the attack had been successful they would have been forced further back. We hated these sausage balloons. They could watch everything we were doing.

'No cancellation order to move up to the front line at 9 a.m. was received and we got away at the right time. It was much emptier now. The Canadians had gone up the night before. They were attacking on the right, the Australians in the centre, and British troops on the left, across the Somme. The roads were blocked; at first we moved very slowly, but there was no enemy shellfire. That was a good sign. Then we saw prisoners coming back, a lot of them. Another good sign. But still there were those damned balloons watching us. They must be able to see all the wagons and lorries on the road. Why weren't we being shelled? What was the matter with his guns?

'Then an extraordinary idea occurred to me. Could they be *our* balloons, not his? Could the attack have been so successful that our balloons were already up there where his had been only yesterday?'

The subaltern had been riding at the rear of his column when this thought struck him. He became so excited that he galloped ahead to the front to put his 'extraordinary idea' to his fellow officers at Battery Headquarters. He goes on:

'They nodded their heads in agreement. "If everything goes according to plan," the Major said, "we shan't know what to do ..." I galloped away. It was unbelievable. Nothing like this had ever happened before.

'I saw Hughes and Durham standing by the guns and I shouted to them, "What's happened? Who's winning?" "We are," said Durham. "Forty-love." "Jerry's on his way back to Berlin," Hughes said.'

'Forty-love' was not a bad description, in tennis terms, of the contest, for though Jerry was not yet heading for Berlin, when night fell on 8 August 1918 his Second Army had been driven back by between six and eight miles along a twelve-mile front. Even the six miles exceeded (by sixty yards!) the average target planned; but what went far beyond the wildest Allied estimates was the overall ease of the advance and the damage inflicted. The Amiens salient had already been as good as wiped out, and with it, on that day alone, had been eliminated more than twenty-seven thousand German troops, of whom nearly sixteen thousand from eleven different divisions had been taken prisoner. More than four hundred guns had been captured together with masses of other enemy war material; and all this at the cost of some of the lightest ratio of casualties ever sustained in such a major attack. How and why had this happened? The element of complete surprise; the devastating impact of the massed tanks; the bonus of a dawn mist, and the advantage of complete air mastery when it lifted; change-

53

over problems at the critical period in the enemy's lines – all these helped to explain the victory. But even rolled all together, they were not the full explanation.

The surprise had been completed by the fact that Rawlinson's two thousand guns had opened up their deafening bombardment only at the precise moment, 4.20 a.m., the first British tanks had moved forward. (Normally, a big artillery barrage preceded a ground attack and thus gave warning of it.) Then the tanks: they had no fixed plan of manoeuvre as at that British armoured attack at Cambrai the year before. This time, though they were of course allotted objectives, it was left to them how to get there. Their job was to take on any opportunity target, crushing resistance from trench, machine-gun nest or gun-battery wherever it occurred, and leaving it to their infantry which followed (closely but not right on their tracks)* to make good the ground flattened. As their Regimental journal put it: 'Owing to lack of effective communication in battle, company and section control . . . were out of the question. Each tank fought individually; co-operation between them was a matter of chance.'

This tactic meant that when the two hundred-odd first-wave tanks lumbered into sight of the German trenches ('like saurian ghosts from a pre-historic era' as one graphic description put it) the mist that covered the dawn battlefield hampered them far less than the enemy. That grey blanket, which only began to lift six hours later at around 10 a.m., was a combination of Allied smoke shells and natural causes. It constantly swirled and eddied, and that afterwards led to varying estimates of how thick it had really been. Most of the attackers put the visibility at about ten yards. However, two German officers of the 13th Infantry Division, fighting in neighbouring regiments south of the Somme, put it at only four and five yards respectively. And on the next sector, held by the 41st German Infantry Division, a front-line company commander noted that at 5.30 a.m., when he released a carrier pigeon to warn his Regimental Headquarters that a major attack was developing,

---

* Experience at Cambrai had taught, among many other lessons, that if the infantry stuck too close to the tanks, which were the obvious targets for enemy machine-guns, they were in danger of bullets ricocheting off the armour-plate.

the bird had immediately turned back in disgust in the murk and re-joined him in the trench.

Whatever the pigeons and the German messenger-dogs (who also tended to lose their way) thought about it all, and however differently their masters assessed the mist, the fact that it was there at all during the first crucial hours of the offensive could only help that type of attack. The business of the tanks was to sow dread and confusion, and it mattered little to them if they wandered off their advance line, or even got hopelessly lost – as some did – in the process.

But General Rawlinson would have been unhappy to have faced bad visibility all day; and, as it happened, the clearing of the mist towards mid-morning gave his airforce all the time it needed to re-assert its superiority and add its own contribution to the victory. Some planes laid phosphorus smoke bombs at precise tactical points of the advance. Others took on any chance target they found, like the 11·5-inch railway gun which had been used in the long-range bombardment of Amiens and was now showing its enormous barrel to infantry of the 5th Australian Division little more than half a mile away. The big gun was bombed to such effect by two Sopwith Camels that when the Australians reached it shortly afterwards they found the entire crew either dead or wounded.

Then, after midday, when pilots reported that German troops were streaming back to the Somme, absolute priority was given to an attempt to destroy the bridges across that river. In all, two hundred and five individual bombing attacks were made that afternoon on the bridges, leading to a battle with German fighters officially described as 'dramatic as any in the war in the air'. The German High Command was well aware of the peril its Second Army now faced if the river crossings could not be secured. At Péronne, the Somme takes an abrupt turn southward. It was towards that elbow that thousands of German soldiers and hundreds of vehicles poured. If crammed up against the pocket of land on the left bank and unable to get across, they would be wiped out or captured where they stood.

A red alert had accordingly also been sounded on the German

side. Fighter squadrons were called in not only from the neighbouring armies but also from Flanders to help save the bridges. And so there arrived over the Somme that day the most famous fighter unit of the First World War, the Richthofen Squadron; and, with it, a man who was to become one of the most infamous figures of the Second, Hermann Goering. Goering had taken over command of the squadron two months before, after the death in action of the 'Red Baron' and the subsequent death of his successor, Captain Reinhard, in a flying accident. The 'Flying Circus' itself was torn to shreds in that 8 August battle against heavy odds. To try and even things up Goering kept his pilots at it for combat after combat, allowing them only the minimum time on the ground for re-fuelling and re-arming, and no time at all for rest. Many of them, including the commander, were in the air that day for ten hours; most did not return. In the first engagement alone the squadron was reduced from fifty machines to eleven. When Goering collected together what was left of his unit and led them up against the Allied bombers again, the eleven became only seven, and the shattered unit was withdrawn.*

But they had helped powerfully to achieve the German High Command's objective. By intercepting the British planes *en route* to the river, or attacking them only a thousand feet up, just as they were diving to bomb their targets, the German fighters prevented any of the five key bridges from being blown up, though at least one was severely damaged. As for Captain Goering, even the enemy acknowledged the 'reckless courage' with which he and his comrades tackled their task. It might be said that, unlike Shakespeare's Thane of Cawdor, what was to become him most about his life was its beginning.

When we look at the German Second Army's troops who were milling around in confusion and consternation on the ground below the picture is much more mixed and the élan which their comrades were showing in the air appears only in patches. But some of the fine detail of that picture repays a closer look, since the historic importance of 8 August is not how far the German Second

* Allied air losses were also considerable – nearly one hundred planes shot down or damaged beyond repair.

Army was driven back, but why. The generals on both sides debated this question on the day and the military historians have been analysing it ever since. Again, some of the best, and certainly the most vivid clues are to be found in the German unit battle reports and, even more, in the personal diaries written at the time. The latter, in particular, take no account of the controversy touched off in their own Supreme Command by the débâcle, let alone of the political repercussions in Berlin, events of which the writers, mostly front-line infantry and artillery officers or their NCOs, would have been totally unaware.

First, an impression of what it felt like to receive the first shock of that dawn battle, as recorded in his diary by a lieutenant of the 265th Infantry Regiment north of the Somme, where the British III Corps were doing the attacking. The regiment formed part of one of the weakest divisions under General von der Marwitz's command, the 43rd Reserve, one of the three tersely classified by him on the eve of battle as 'in need of replacement'. The lieutenant wrote:

'A murderous artillery fire started up, the lighter guns trained on our forward lines, the heavies striking further back. It lasted only about a quarter of an hour but in that time we all made our wills. We all fell flat on top of one another in the trench or else crept into the primitive holes just in front, the fog, which was getting steadily thicker, meant we could see nothing. Suddenly, as the barrage moved forward we heard shouts, the crash of hand grenades and the uncanny sound of tank engines. A forward patrol reported no sign of the enemy in front of our company yet Tommy already seemed to have swept everything with him on our left flank ...

'Everyone who still had his head and legs on after the barrage now collected together and we started firing off into the fog ... Three machine-guns, about forty rifles and all our hand grenades – all blazed off blind into the landscape! We knew we had scored some hits from the cries we heard ahead ...

'What now? A patrol sent out to the right reported that the enemy had long since broken through the neighbouring division on his flank too. That meant we were a sort of island in a sea of flames. Should we evacuate? Then we would have had to answer for abandoning our position in the face of the enemy ... Suddenly, uttering frightful yells and sounding quite drunk, English troops came at us from behind, hurling hand grenades ... Our own were, alas, all used up. We couldn't get to the last machine-gun in all the tumult. Every man fired and defended himself as best he could ... and then another wave of English soldiers appeared ... Surrounded as we now were, bombarded and shot at from all sides, there was no point in thinking of further resistance. So we laid down our arms – the twenty men who were all that was left of my company.'

That was a straightforward infantry scrap, with British tanks heard somewhere ahead in the fog, but not seen. South of the Somme where, in better going, the tanks played a far bigger role, the Australian and Canadian infantry following behind them took everything by storm, and had seized nearly all of their first objectives within two hours. In view of the distinctions made later by Ludendorff between the performance of crack troops and poor quality reservists on this day, the record of the 117th German Infantry Division, fighting south of the Amiens-Chaulnes railway line, is worth noting. They were officially rated as 'one of the freshest and most effective divisions of the German army'. Admittedly some of the front-line battalions had only reached their lines a few hours before the attack began, so that they had never even seen the position by daylight. But as one trench on the Western Front was much like another, and as precious little could be seen anyway, the disadvantage was not too serious. The fact remains that that élite formation, commanded by a first-rate officer, Major General Hoefer, did little better in that critical sector on the day than the rest of them.

A German artillery lieutenant, cut off from his captured battery in the early fighting, had tacked himself on to some infantry of the 117th whom the Canadians were pushing relentlessly back towards Caix. He left this graphic account of the British Fourth Army simultaneously deploying every arm of land warfare as it swept forward:

'I stayed with the infantry. Perhaps I can be of some use. We dig ourselves properly in, using old rifle trenches. And now a shattering sight, and yet a glorious picture – squadron after squadron of English cavalry galloping towards Wiencourt! More and more of them, I can count almost 1,500 horsemen, and, following at high speed behind them, rows of light tanks that seem never-ending ... I send messengers back to try and find any staff HQ and warn them of the steadily worsening position; perhaps they can give us artillery support soon. But no one returns. Little point in sending any more people back ...

'The enemy is bombarding our rear with heavy guns and we haven't long to wait before thick swarms of his planes come over us, in masses the like of which we have never seen before. We shoot down two of them, but it doesn't do us much good. The pilots give us a hell of a working over. Flying so close over us that we could almost touch them, they toss bundles of hand grenades into our position and their machine-guns cause heavy casualties. Then enemy tanks loom up, coming at us across the field-path. We open up with rifle and machine-gun fire against the monsters.

'We are surrounded from all sides and our ammunition is running out ... the few of us now left must abandon the position ... we cross the Luce stream and try to reach Caix ... No German units of any size to be seen anywhere, only the enemy. At last we come up with one of our anti-tank guns, cut off from its unit, firing all alone. It finds a worthwhile target and knocks out a tank. We take the crew prisoner with us ... wounded and bleeding heavily ... The air activity is still enormous. Only in the evening do the first

German planes arrive and the enemy aircraft now leave us in peace. But what does it look like at the front, if one can speak of a front any more . . . the 117th and our division are shrunk to nothing, hardly any infantry left. And the best part of them are captured. Only the artillery checks the enemy, almost on its own . . .'

That same evening, another young artillery officer, the one who had been awakened in Boves Wood by the dawn bombardment of his own guns, took his horses to water in the sunshine in that same little stream the German lieutenant had crossed a few hours before. The Englishman wrote:

'It was a glorious summer evening, and the little River Luce was beautiful. It was like a little river in England and the flowers growing at the water's edge, where my horses were drinking, were English flowers. The water was so clear, the field in front of me looked utterly peaceful but, only fifty yards away, there was that trench, full of dead Germans. We should see them again on our way back, the grey faces, the poor twisted bodies. They had been bayoneted by the Canadians in the morning. You can't take prisoners in a front-line trench in an attack. Wives, mothers, sweethearts wouldn't know yet. They would still be writing letters, but the letters would never be read. It might have been us.'

It might have been; but it wasn't. The next day, 9 August, the attack of the French First Army went in from the south side of the fast-vanishing 'Amiens bulge'. On the eve of the attack Haig had found the commander, General Debeney, 'much distressed and almost in tears' when he called on his headquarters at Conty. The cause of this Gallic anguish was three battalions of French Colonial Infantry who, in a preliminary skirmish with the enemy, had turned tail and bolted under the fire of a single German machine-gun. However, everything went smoothly for the distressed general on the day; in fact, the First Army's initial attack, against an enemy disorganized and demoralized by the blow already delivered on his right flank, turned into a military promenade. By nightfall on the 9th Foch could register with satisfaction a six-mile advance by his troops and the capture of more than thirteen thousand enemy prisoners and three hundred guns. (Thereafter, Debeney got bogged down in the face of stiffening resistance and failed to get within striking distance of the key communication centre of Roye, where seven roads converged: this despite frantic messages from Marshal Foch that he should get to the town 'without losing a minute, beating down all hesitation and delay. It is here that the decisive result will be obtained.')

Meanwhile, the Fourth Army was continuing its eastward advance and by 10 August had regained the whole of the outer defence lines which had originally been established by the Allies to protect Amiens. In some sectors they had been pushing at open doors, as the Germans either evacuated their second-line trench systems in time or else surrendered without a fight. The German dug-outs which our young British artillery diarist inspected on the 9th, for example, were all empty, undamaged, and cosy. He had time to reflect on the national characteristics they displayed:

> 'Their home was very like one of ours, maps and pictures stuck on the walls, shelves cut out of the earth, a sheaf of orders on a hook, newspapers on the table, a half-written letter, a pair of spectacles. I looked at their books, but I could not tell whether they were like ours, whether they were novels or not. Their pictures were certainly different. There was one of a German U-boat arriving at Constantinople, I could tell it was Constantinople because of the domes and minarets, and sailors from the other ships in the harbour, waving at the submarine, were all wearing red fezzes. Fancy wanting to pin up a patriotic propaganda picture! We only had girls on the walls of our dug-outs, girls in underwear or in nothing at all. Jack had *La Vie Parisienne* sent to him and he allowed us to cut out what we liked.'

But elsewhere on the British front there were clear signs that the best of the offensive was already behind them. On 10 August the whole of the Canadian Corps, for example, struck far stiffer resistance and far tougher terrain. Some of its units, to quote the official history, found they were now fighting 'an enforced and very unwelcome reversion to trench warfare, involving slower progress and more numerous casualties'. They also faced determined counter-attacks by the 119th German Division, one of several which had now arrived to reinforce the Second Army; one of its determined assaults was stopped only fifteen yards in front of the Canadian lines. The British III Corps and the Australians were also being slowed down by an enemy who seemed to have regained much of his old zest for battle. Australian infantry who took Crépy Wood that day only cleared it after the bitterest fighting. The Germans then counter-attacked; got a foothold in the wood again; were in turn surrounded; but then refused to surrender and fought it out to the last man.

As for the picturesque Cavalry Corps, their bravura had never quite yielded the required results, even on the first day, and they now found themselves virtually immobilized in a terrain gashed by old trench-systems and spiked with belts of barbed wire hidden from sight by the long grass. The German machine-gunners were often able to rake the floundering horsemen almost at will and at nightfall on 10 August the whole Cavalry Corps, having fought one of its last major engagements of the war, was withdrawn into reserve.

Yet by the time Haig suspended the offensive the following day (despite urgent pleas from Foch, who had now totally deserted his cautious parrot-in-a-cage approach), both the British Supreme Commander and his Fourth Army had every reason for jubilation. Almost everywhere they were back on the lines between the Somme and Oise rivers, lines which they had last held in the summer of 1916; and of the twenty-four enemy divisions engaged, six or seven had been mauled beyond recognition.

It was a very different story on the German side as, surprised and relieved that the enemy could not or would not press his advantage, they now looked at their own sorry balance sheet. Why had this humiliating defeat been suffered; and what were the lessons to be drawn? Let us move upwards in taking the German verdicts, from Army to Army Group and, finally, from Army Group to Supreme Command.

An interesting order issued after the battle by the Second Army's defeated commander paid the familiar tribute to the role of the enemy's armour, though General von der Marwitz expressed it in an indirect way: 'Tanks are no bogey for front-line troops who have artillery in close support,' he told his men. He then gave reassuring examples where the armoured monsters had been destroyed by individual acts of bravery – one put out of action by a single hand grenade; another by a corporal who had clambered up on to the turret and fired through the slits with his revolver; plus many more knocked out by German guns. The English cavalry, he suggested, had been 'shot to pieces', while the enemy's infantry was still inferior when taken on its own. The order ended with the extraordinary tergiversation: 'Our troops in the Front Line have never before considered themselves so victorious as they do now.' Propaganda, clearly, was not the general's strong point.

Back at Army Group, Crown Prince Rupprecht,* commenting on the Amiens battle day by day in his personal diary, could afford to be more level-headed. The initial attack, he noted on 8 August, had caught some sectors of the Second Army on the hop through no fault of their own: two of its divisions, the 108th and 217th, were just in the process of being relieved by the 43rd and the 209th respectively. His long entry of 9 August begins with the familiar refrain . . . 'It was above all the fog which favoured the attackers by concealing the many advancing tanks from our guns.' And tanks feature in his final summing-up three days later, though with

---

* A war which had divided the inter-married dynasties of the old Europe produced many tragic ironies, with cousin fighting cousin and even brother fighting brother. But the most extraordinary confrontation lay in the fact that it should have been Crown Prince Rupprecht who commanded the German Army Group against which the British had struck this heavy blow, for the soldiers of the Fourth Army were attacking the man whom some of their compatriots revered as the rightful King of England. English Legitimists traced the Stuart succession down a clear line which ran through the Houses of Orleans, Savoy, Sardinia and Habsburg-Este to Rupprecht's mother, Queen Marie-Thérèse of Bavaria. Each year, on the anniversary of that January day in 1649 when Charles I was executed, the Jacobites would send white roses to her in Munich as 'the lawful Queen of England'.

comments which show that the Bavarian Crown Prince, at any rate, now realized that the whole approach which the German Supreme Command had hitherto adopted towards armoured warfare was wrong. He writes, on 12 August:

> 'That the Second Army's opponents have scored a *significant initial victory*, thanks above all to their massive employment of tanks, cannot be disputed; nor can the fact that we will not be able to sustain repetitions of such attacks. As the Second Army correctly points out, our field artillery must be made more mobile if it is to fulfil its anti-tank role. It cannot go on, as up to now, being tied down to precisely determined positions but must move about more freely in open country.'

The Crown Prince concluded with a cool assessment of the options now open to the enemy and to his Army Group; on balance, he was against mounting a costly counter-offensive south of the Somme, though the strong river-line itself should be held.

The calm commonsense of all this contrasts with the near-hysteria which seemed to prevail back at Supreme Headquarters at Spa – or rather in the mind of the most powerful figure at that headquarters, the First Quartermaster-General. For it was above all Ludendorff who transformed the battle of Amiens from being just a serious military set-back into a decisive political event. And he did this with one phrase and one sentence. He declared 8 August 1918 to be the 'Black Day' of the German army, and from it he concluded: 'The war must be ended.'

It is only when Ludendorff's verdict is placed at the end of the affair (instead of, as almost invariably, at the beginning) that it can be properly tested. For it is clear that, driven by some sudden emotional impulse which rarely touched the brain of this military computer, he had grossly over-reacted. The Crown Prince had been closer to the truth as he was closer to the front. A major set-piece battle had been lost, setting grave lessons to be learned. But the campaign in France was not yet lost, let alone the whole war. And in any case, 8 August had been fought in a combination of special circumstances which would not easily come together a second time. The Allies still had their tanks; but they could not count again on springing such a surprise, let alone on conjuring up such mists to help them on the day.

Ludendorff himself soon seemed tacitly to accept all this. Within a few days, as the front steadied so did his resolve, and he moved on into a mood of qualified gloom which was in fact to give his emperor, army and people the very worst of both worlds. But what mattered was not that he regained his nerve, but that on 8 August he totally lost it. Why?

His own memoirs are, of course, a key document in trying to follow both the course he set himself and the course which the war took in general during the final months. But they should not be taken as German gospel. Though he started putting pen to paper immediately after the armistice* he wrote, as he admitted, chiefly from memory. Moreover, like the other prominent military memoir writers of the day (Foch and Pershing were similar cases) he sought to carve out for himself the niche that he desired to fill in the history of his country. There were several occasions when the truth came under his chisel if it got in the way. 8 August was one such time.

In his account of the Amiens battle tanks are mentioned only once, when he records that 'strong squadrons' of them took part in the initial Anglo–French attack, an attack in which the enemy 'was otherwise in no great superiority'. Hardly a glimmer of recognition of what it had meant to his front-line troops to see them looming up out of the mist in such unheard-of numbers. No recognition at all of the fact that it was thanks to his own obstinacy and short-sightedness that the German army in 1918 had neither been trained to fight tanks properly, much less to use them. No recognition either of the important part that surprise had played in the Allied success; and not even a mention of the warnings – few but significant – the Second Army had passed back that the enemy was massing armour

---

* Ludendorff began his memoirs at Hessleholmsgård in Sweden in November 1918, where he remained until the following February. The work was completed in Berlin in June of 1919.

against its front. Even before battle was joined, German Intelligence had failed.*

'The report of the staff officer I had sent to the battlefield as to the condition of those divisions which had met the first shock of the attack perturbed me deeply. I summoned divisional commanders and front-line officers to Avesnes to discuss events with them in detail. I was told of deeds of glorious valour but also of behaviour which, I openly confess, I should not have thought possible in the German army; whole bodies of our men had surrendered to single troopers, or isolated squadrons. Retiring troops, meeting a fresh division going bravely into action, had shouted at them expressions such as "Black-leg" and "You're prolonging the war" ... In many instances, the officers lost control and allowed themselves to be swept along with the rest ...'

Now it was clear to everyone that an army which suffered nearly two-thirds of its losses through men taken prisoner must have experienced a collapse in morale in addition to a defeat by more effective weapons and superior strategy. But, in his memoirs, Ludendorff produced the wrong explanations (or rather, inadequate ones) even for this one failure of one army on one day. He put everything down to the low quality of the German reserves, which were steadily diluting the old fighting strength of the forces, introducing a spirit of defeatism, insubordination and even Bolshevik agitation, all imported from the Russian campaign via the German home front. (Somewhat illogically, however, his other reason for suddenly wanting to throw in his hand was that he could not get enough of these reserves.)

* In an Order of the Day circulated to all troops on 11 August Ludendorff was rather more frank about the débâcle than in his memoirs. But even here, he seeks basically to exonerate the High Command. The Second Army on 8 August had 'lost its head'; it had not made proper use of its artillery nor built enough obstacles. The Order lays down, among the precautions to be taken in the future, increased emphasis on gathering information of the enemy's intentions, including more 'aerial reconnaissance'. It was an ironic instruction, in view of the way the German pilots' report that a hundred tanks were gathering on the Moreuil sector on the eve of the battle had been ignored.

This, of course, is a convenient version to leave behind for posterity in a personal apologia. But it also matches the man as he really was. From the beginning he gives the impression of a dry and humourless fanatic, and his natural reserve was doubtless accentuated by the personal chip he carried on his shoulder. Erich Ludendorff had earned his place among the top military élite of Germany. But he did not also belong – as was almost *de rigueur* – to its social élite. Far from being a landed Prussian Junker like his nominal superior, Paul von Beneckendorf und Hindenburg, a man whose stolid square face might have almost been designed for a spiked helmet, Ludendorff was the son of an estate agent.

Without the army he was little or nothing. He therefore demanded even more from it. Moreover, he demanded it as though from an automated machine for, after four years regarding soldiers as rectangles or triangles on his huge headquarters map, he was less and less able to sense that what the pins of these formation flags were stuck into were only masses of ordinary humanity in uniform. And by the high summer of 1918 those German masses, like their families at home, were approaching total exhaustion, an exhaustion that was even more of the spirit than of the body.

The enemy too were exhausted, and particularly the French, as their Commander-in-Chief, General Pétain, had gloomily admitted at the outset of the Allied counter-offensive. Ludendorff seized on the comparison to defend himself against any suggestion that he had been asking too much of the Second Army's battle weary formations. The divisions which had attacked them on 8 August, he claimed, 'had been fighting just as long in the forward areas as our own'. This ignored the cardinal distinction that the French were liberating their own soil whereas the Germans were being driven out of a hostile land where so much had been endured and so much promised – all of it, seemingly, now for nothing. With American manpower thrown in behind them the Allied armies had the first faint sniff of victory in their nostrils; the Germans, both the good soldiers and the poorer ones, had only the ever-stronger sour smell of defeat. '*Wozu?*' 'What's it all for?' was what most of them were saying to themselves; and many were saying it out loud.

If Ludendorff had ever had the time or the opportunity to read through the hundreds of Second Army unit reports and personal diaries about the Amiens battle which were collected afterwards he might have better realized, though perhaps still not have admitted, what he was really up against. Lieutenant Herbst, a front-line company commander fighting on the critical sector just south of the Somme, left this fairly typical account of how he and his sergeant were captured by Australian infantry soon after dawn:

'The engine noises worried us. We were convinced they came from tanks rolling up the Hamel-Cerisy road and that planes were flying overhead to try and drown the sound. As the enemy artillery fire jumped further to our rear I rushed to the crossroads with my signaller and Sergeant Kade, to get our reserve group to bring explosives up on to the road ... When we got to the crossroads, we were for a moment speechless. Smoke was pouring up from the craters where our reserve group had been lying. My own people, and the artillery observation unit which had also fetched up here, were all finished. Then my batman appeared out of the smoke and reported that Australians, coming up from the right, had thrown phosphorus bombs; apart from him everybody had been taken prisoner ... At this moment I heard shouts from several groups of Australians who were coming up in a close firing line also from the right: "Hands up!"

'I pulled my pistol from its holster. But then Sergeant Kade caught my arm and said: "Lieutenant, sir, there's no point in that; we would be finished off straightaway, and I have a wife and children."

'And, heaven knows quite why, with that he persuaded me not to offer any resistance. They moved us off westwards...'

The lieutenant was not indulging in false heroics, and his sergeant had certainly not spoken like a Bolshevik agitator. Their story, repeated many times during that battle, answered the question Ludendorff was angrily posing in more orders of the day: what had happened to the old German army maxim that surrounded units which had not received orders to retreat always stood their ground and fought it out to the last man and the last bullet? The answer was that other question which Sergeant Kade had put in his own way: '*Wozu?*'

Ludendorff's initial reaction to the Amiens débâcle had in fact been the same, though he obviously would not admit as much to the troops. He was not the only commander who had begun to think like Sergeant Kade. Seated at the very top of the military pyramid, in theory if not in fact, the Emperor William, Germany's Supreme War Lord, now came to a similar conclusion. His military aide describes the scene the day after the Second Army's rout, when the Kaiser had hurried to Forward Headquarters at Avesnes, to get a first-hand impression from the Supreme Command. As Ludendorff finished his report Field Marshal Hindenburg read out a telegram he had just received from General Cramon, the German liaison officer at the Austrian General Headquarters at Baden, near Vienna. The message described the depressing effect that the news of the Amiens defeat had had on Germany's principal ally and added a depressing comment of its own: 'The physical and moral strength of the Dual Monarchy is nearly exhausted.' The aide continues his account:

> 'The Kaiser kept his outward calm. But anyone looking into his face could see in the strained features and blazing eyes the inner turmoil he was keeping down.
>
> ' "I can see," he said, "that we must draw up the balance. We have reached the limits of our strength. The war must be brought to an end." '

After that, the aide wrote, a silence reigned in the close atmosphere of the conference room. The Kaiser broke it with the laconic command: 'Very well. I shall await you gentlemen in the next day or so at Spa.'

With the military situation apparently stabilizing again, as the reinforced Second Army dug in on shorter lines before Roye and Chaulnes, and the panic ebbing away, it was in that agreeable Belgian watering-place far removed from the fighting, rather than on the battlefield, that the echoes of 8 August rumbled on.

4

Post-Mortems

FOUR SUMMERS BEFORE, almost up to the day when Europe started tearing itself to pieces, the season at Spa had taken its usual placid course. The eight thousand population of the little Ardennes town was swollen by the annual complement of twenty thousand visitors, mostly English and Americans, who had come to take the waters and enjoy the many non-medical distractions. By August the flat racing was over and the steeple-chase meetings were still to come; in the meantime, however, there was pigeon-shooting, lawn tennis, golf, concerts and the theatre to be enjoyed, as well as excursions into the wooded valleys of the Spa and Picherotte rivers. Yet everything – out of medical necessity or merely convenience – revolved around the cure. Spa prided itself indeed on being the oldest European watering-place of note, so old that Pliny had once mentioned it in ancient times; so old that, for centuries, it had given its generic name to all such resorts throughout the Western world.

Its own waters were described in the travel literature of Edwardian Europe as 'sparkling, easily digested and cheering'. Apart from treating disorders of the bile and liver, they were, so it was claimed, especially efficacious for hysteria. These properties would have come in very handy in this midsummer of 1918.

The German Supreme Command had set up its headquarters in Spa five months before as the control centre for the great 'Emperor's Battle' that was to bring victory in the West at last. Now, with that gamble finally lost, the Emperor and his ministers from Berlin converged there to discuss with the generals what had gone wrong and what should be done next. If, as Ludendorff had suggested (and his words were still ringing in everyone's ears), the battle of Amiens had been the military turning point of the war, that conference at Spa should have been its political turning point.

The truth, though very confused, was very different.

The headquarters building was the Grand Hotel Britannique in the Rue de la Sauvenière. With its spacious gardens, private mineral baths and 165 bedrooms, it had headed the peacetime list of the resort's large first-class hotels, charging the tidy sum of fifteen Belgian francs, or twelve English shillings a day, for full board. Now coal-scuttle helmets had taken over entirely from panama hats, and sentries with fixed bayonets had replaced the commissionaires at the entrance. At 8 a.m. on 13 August they gave their smartest salute to two very familiar figures, Field Marshal von Hindenburg and General Ludendorff, who were the first to arrive for those three days of critical talks. Their purpose, as set out in the official conference papers, echoed the Kaiser's words on the evening of 8 August: 'To draw up an unadorned balance sheet of the war.' The problem set for posterity was that, afterwards, each of the main participants did in fact adorn or disguise his own part in the proceedings, in order to avoid being put in the Rogue's Gallery of German history. As a protocol was only kept on one day (and that only for the formal sessions) the charges and counter charges that appeared later in the various memoirs and official enquiries can only be weighed against each other without striking any precise balance. But implicit in all accounts is that, at this Spa post-mortem, Germany wasted even such last weak cards as she still had.

At 10 a.m. on the 13th, the day before the Emperor was due to arrive to hold a formal Crown Council, the principal military and political leaders of his empire met in Hindenburg's rooms for a preliminary inquest of their own. Apart from the Field Marshal himself, the quartet consisted of the inescapable Ludendorff; the ageing and ineffective Chancellor of the day, Count Hertling; and Paul von Hintze, lately the German ambassador to neutral Norway, who had only arrived back in Berlin a month before to assume control over German diplomacy as State Secretary for Foreign Affairs. In experience as well as in prestige, therefore, the field-grey uniforms around the table far outweighed the black frock-coats. There was nothing new for Germany in that, but it was a particularly dangerous time for the scales to be so lop-sided.

As it had been Ludendorff, from the battlefield five days

before, who sounded as though he had blown the whistle on the entire war, everyone hung on his words. Hintze, who knew and admired the Quartermaster-General, described how Ludendorff took him aside before the morning meeting began and confided: 'In the middle of July, I told you I was certain that our own offensive would break the enemy's will and oblige him to seek peace; I no longer have that certainty.' And when the diplomat asked how, in that case, Germany was to conduct the war from now on, Ludendorff had replied: 'We should gradually paralyse the enemy's will to fight on, through a strategically defensive campaign.'

When the four sat down together, Ludendorff (who makes no mention in his account of this exchange with Hintze) more or less repeated that line adding, that as a defensive campaign could scarcely force the enemy to sue for peace, 'the termination of the war would have to be brought about by diplomacy'. And that seems to have been that. All versions agree that, for most of the remainder of the morning session and throughout an afternoon one which began at 5 p.m., the two military Titans spent nearly all their time weighing into the civilian pigmies for spoiling their war for them.

At any top-level meeting held in such grave circumstances in England or France, Lloyd George and Clemenceau, the Prime Ministers of those countries, would have been pummelling the generals for an explanation of the battlefield débâcle, and even calling for changes in command and future strategy. But at German Supreme Headquarters the voice of the military was as unquestionable by outsiders as the words of high priests in a temple. So the pounding went all the other way. Count Hertling was obliged to defend himself as best he could against accusation after accusation thrown at him across the table. Why was his government not doing more to stem the decline of morale at home, a rot that was spreading from there to the front line? Why was enemy propaganda getting so successful, and what was being done to curb its baleful effects on soldiers as well as civilians? Why were the manpower reserves for the army so inadequate? Why were there breakdowns in food supplies for the front?

Hours were spent debating these charges, so that Count Hertling must have ended up by feeling – as was doubtless the intention – that it was he in his Berlin chancellery and not this formidable duo at Spa who had lost the battle of Amiens. Hintze (who throughout was to show far more resolution than his Chancellor) finally brought the discussion back again to political problems by raising the future of Poland and Belgium, both still under German occupation. But when he went on to give his own sober assessment of the present state of Germany's three allies (Austria-Hungary morally and physically exhausted; Bulgaria ineffective and ready to fall away; Turkey set on its own course ever since the spring), Ludendorff reproached him for being too pessimistic. Any Turkish disloyalty he dismissed as 'not dangerous'; as for the Bulgarian army, it would fight stoutly again against the Entente in the Balkans as soon as Germany sent it 'supplies of food and new uniforms'.

It was Ludendorff in other words who, abandoning his alarmist role, acted as the soother of troubled nerves and the exorcizer of ghosts – at least in front of civilians. Ironically, it was that seemingly calm and confident tone which did the most pernicious damage. The link between diplomacy and the battlefield in ending the war, the admission that the war could indeed no longer be won without peace moves, all that was still present. But the anguish behind Ludendorff's *cri de coeur* of 8 August seemed to have died away completely. The Chancellor got up from the table feeling that, though all was obviously not well, there was no desperate urgency about the matter. The generals would let him know when their 'strategic defensive' had sufficiently sapped the enemy's resolve, and that would be the time for Berlin to act. As for the German public, they were merely informed that 'a thorough and fruitful conference' had taken place.

The following day, 14 August, the Hotel Britannique welcomed an even more august set of visitors: the Kaiser; that dissipated string-bean, Crown Prince Willy (who was in nominal command of an Army Group on the Western Front); and the chiefs of the Military and Civil Cabinets with an attendant swarm of lesser dignitaries. The position was now to be reviewed by the supreme forum of Germany, the Imperial Crown Council.

Before the meeting convened at 10 a.m. in the general staff conference rooms, von Hintze took his Chancellor, the aged Count Hertling, aside. The State Secretary's fears about the true military crisis had not been allayed by Ludendorff's smooth performance the day before and, having slept on the matter, the minister had woken up more alarmed than ever. He now informed his Chancellor that unless full support were given him to launch peace moves, he would offer his resignation. But the only weary reaction he got was: 'Well then, at least let an old man like me go first.' It scarcely needed a Ludendorff to quell such a feeble civilian spirit as this. Any Major with the broad red band of the German general staff running down his trousers could have done the same.

As for the Crown Council meeting which followed, neither the débâcle of Amiens nor Ludendorff's traumatic reaction to it might have happened at all, so vague and temporizing were the exchanges made across the table. The Chancellor expounded on how tired the German people had become of the war and how short both food and clothing were (neither of them exactly novel revelations). Ludendorff responded with another of his calls for stiffer discipline on the home front and stronger civilian support for the military. Von Hintze was the only one of the Emperor's advisers to get away from such excuses and recriminations and attempt an objective *tour d'horizon*. He repeated his warnings that Germany's three war allies were each, for different reasons, fast becoming broken reeds. He reiterated the formula set out by Ludendorff the day before that, though the war could not be won by military action alone, the High Command nonetheless intended 'gradually to paralyse the enemy's resolve to fight by fighting a strategic defensive campaign'. And he added the highly significant gloss: 'The political leadership bows before this judgement made by the greatest generals which this war has produced.' Both the terrible strength and the mortal weakness of Wilhelmine Germany lay in that one sentence.

Everything now depended on the monarch with the withered left arm concealed under a blaze of gold braid and decorations who sat at the head of the table. As Germany's Supreme War Lord he, by law and hallowed tradition, was the unquestioned master of them all, with few of the constitutional restraints which limited the

74

power of Presidents, Prime Ministers and sovereigns in the
Entente camp. Yet the four years of fighting had already amply
demonstrated that this brilliant but unbalanced fantasy-king who,
in peace-time, had alarmed the world with his various threats to
wrest control of the seas from England, dislodge France from her
North African empire, thrust the German sword right down to the
Persian Gulf, and even quell the 'yellow peril' of China's distant
millions, was only capable, in fact, of acting out a military charade.
When the charade became reality and war began in earnest he had
accepted, without protest, the role of the sanctified ceremonial
puppet. His less intelligent but far shrewder English uncle, King
Edward VII, had got his nephew absolutely right when, ten years
before the war broke out, he had predicted to a close friend:

'He is even more cowardly than vain, and, because of this,
he will tremble before all those sycophants when, urged
on by the General Staff, they draw the sword in earnest . . .
It is not by his will that he will unleash a war, but by his
weakness.'

The Kaiser failed again now to rise to his responsibilities. At that
crucial meeting, which he himself had convened to face unpalatable
truths and set a completely new course for his country's salvation,
he behaved instead like the chairman of a company in temporary
financial difficulties, appealing to its directors to stop bickering and
at the same time reassuring them by pointing to the problems
which rival companies also faced. The enemy, the Emperor declared, was also suffering. England, for example, was facing a bad
harvest. Her shipping tonnage available to bring food in from
overseas was steadily being reduced by Germany's U-boats 'and so
England might gradually be induced to the path of peace through
these shortages'. As for Germany's own peace strategy, the Kaiser
was vagueness itself: 'We must have regard to the appropriate
moment at which to seek an agreement with the enemy.' In the
meantime, as the High Command had insisted, there must be
tighter discipline at home; a new propaganda effort 'to raise the
confidence of the German people'; while the civilian power, and in

particular the War Ministry, 'must support the commanding generals and not leave them in the lurch'. In that rambling and half-complacent survey there was not a mite of clear direction to his ministers about diplomatic moves to end the war, and not a word from the Supreme War Lord about the war situation itself.

As a result both Chancellor and Foreign Minister got up from the meeting feeling that there was no great urgency about peace moves; (indeed, Hertling had been unchallenged when he suggested that the right time for such moves would be 'after the next German success in the West'). Moreover, when it came to drawing up the official protocol from the military side, Ludendorff decided to strike a distinctly more optimistic note than Hindenburg, who was usually the less gloomy of the two. The Field Marshal had written that he 'hoped that we would after all succeed in standing on French soil and finally forcing our will upon the enemy'. His Quartermaster-General took up the pen, altered the 'hoped' to 'stated' and deleted the words 'after all'. It was as though Ludendorff, awakened rudely but only momentarily by the shock of 8 August, had now gone back to sleep-walking. There was no one in the room prepared to shake him by the shoulders.

That same afternoon the most illustrious of those wavering allies whom von Hintze had been warning against arrived in Spa in person – the Austrian Emperor Charles, accompanied by his Foreign Minister, Count Burian; his Commander-in-Chief, General von Arz; and General von Cramon who, since January of 1915, had served as principal German liaison officer at the Austrian Headquarters. In his own memoirs Cramon, who strove to be a faithful servant to both of the allied empires, describes how the news of the Amiens defeat had been received in Vienna and how the journey to Spa came about:

> 'The reversal of the situation which had taken place on the Western Front had a cataclysmic impact in Austria. The belief that German might could work miracles was so deep-rooted in the mass of the Austrian people that the disillusionment struck them like a hammer-blow. The Emperor himself was profoundly affected; he summoned me and told me that even the Austrian set-back on the Piave had

not left such a strong mark on his peoples as the changed position on the West.'

He added that he wished to have a personal meeting with the German Emperor as soon as possible:

> 'They would have liked it in Vienna if the Emperor William could have used this opportunity to return the last visit which the Emperor Charles had paid to him. But our supreme chief could not leave the Western Front. He conveyed as much to the Austrian Emperor who thereupon declared his readiness to go to Spa.'

Sixty years after these events the Empress Zita, widow of the last Habsburg ruler, who was also at the Baden Headquarters when the 'Black Day' was being discussed, gave a rather different version of her husband's reactions. According to the Empress, however shocked the Austrian people may have been by the sudden bad news from the West, this turn of events did not astonish the young monarch. She recalled of this period between 9 August and 13 August:

> 'The Emperor Charles had been sceptical all along of the victory boasts which the German Supreme Command had been making throughout the spring and summer about its offensive in the West. To begin with, he had received very different reports from his own Liaison Officers on that front, and he had anyway always predicted to me that when the German collapse came, it would come suddenly. And for him such a collapse was inevitable from the moment America entered the war. So, when the news of the 8 August defeat reached us at Baden, his first words to me were simply, "Well, so now here we are."
>
> One big problem in such a situation was that the Emperor's natural link for advice and support was that with the Emperor William and, as the latter had once declared quite frankly to me: "I've never had so little to do in my life as now in the war!"'

But astonished or not, Charles had every reason to be stirred into immediate action. It was vital for him and his principal advisers to get a first-hand impression of how deeply this crisis had struck at his allies, and where it might lead them. And what the Emperor Charles hoped and intended it should lead on to was yet another of his cherished peace initiatives, launched either jointly with Berlin, or independently from Vienna, if possible with German blessing. That, and not just another review of military strategy, was what he had in mind when he and his party boarded their special train in Baden on 13 August and headed north for the long journey to occupied Belgium.

The meeting at Spa on 14–15 August was destined to be the last time the two emperors would ever see or talk to each other. It is a good moment to underline the glaring contrasts, not only between the two sovereigns themselves but also between the empires they ruled. The Austro-German alliance was generally regarded by the Western powers as the unshakeable corner-stone of the enemy camp. Certainly, it seemed the most obvious of European pacts, this bond between two German-speaking realms with a common boundary and a common culture, as well as a common language; and it was indisputably the oldest of all alliances between major European powers, having been founded almost forty years before, in the confident hey-day of Bismarckian diplomacy.

Yet just as the gentle young 'Peace Emperor' who had mounted the Habsburg throne two years before through such a long chain of family mishaps and disasters was as different as could be from the German Kaiser – (William never felt happy out of uniform, for example, Charles never happy in it; William sought all his life after effects, Charles only after solutions; William was drugged by power, Charles humbled by responsibility) – so also did their empires pull in opposite directions, behind their façade of unity. Charles had been bequeathed, through the six centuries of his dynasty's haphazard growth, a jumble of different peoples to reign over, and his only hope of holding the patchwork together was the supra-national symbol of the Habsburg crown. The nationalistic and racist creeds of the nineteenth century could only rend that patchwork into shreds. William ruled the *parvenu* among the

European empires, an arbitrary creation of Bismarck's will and the Prussian sword which, even by 1918, was still less than half a century old. And the only thing that could hold this brash new realm together and assure the continued supremacy of the Hohenzollern crown over the lesser German princelings it had so recently subdued was strident nationalism, a nationalism coupled with that fateful creed of the dominance of the German race.

Thus, what was cement for the one emperor was dynamite for his ally. No division among Entente powers – neither that between monarchical England and republican France nor that between these two European democracies and their transatlantic partner – went half as deep as this fundamental contradiction between Vienna and Berlin. Yet, with few exceptions, of whom Lloyd George was perhaps the most distinguished, the Allied leaders could only see the rock face of this Central Powers bloc which faced them, never noticing the cracks in its granite.

It was not surprising that this last 'summit' between the two emperors and their advisers, if not quite a dialogue of the deaf, was a conversation between the very hard of hearing. On the military side, General Arz asked Ludendorff for the same clear-cut verdict which the German ministers had sought the day before. He received only the same delphic answers, coupled with similar demands from the Quartermaster-General for stronger support. The only thing resembling a strategic decision to emerge from those military talks was a consensus that the threatened Western Front should now be given priority by both powers. Arz accordingly agreed to drop the plans he had been toying with for a new offensive against the Italians and promised to dispatch more Austrian troops to help his allies in the West. As both sides knew, this promise amounted to little. Arz himself put a bracket round it by telling his German opposite numbers with brutal frankness that the end of the year marked the absolute limit for Austria's military support; the armies of the Dual Monarchy could not, and would not, fight on into 1919. And even if Hindenburg and Ludendorff could not quite bring themselves to take that dire warning at its face value, they knew that Austria-Hungary under its 'Peace Emperor' would never commit substantial forces on the main battlefield against

79

France, England and America. Such a move could only prejudice his overtures to those same powers to bring an end to the war on all fronts. That, as expected, was the theme he immediately launched into at the conference.

He and Burian had come to Spa to get approval for what the Germans contemptuous'y dubbed amongst themselves 'Austria's cry to the world' – a public appeal from Vienna to all the belligerents to attend a peace conference at an unspecified date in an unspecified neutral country and with no terms or commitments laid down in advance. On the afternoon and evening of 14 August everyone in the Austrian party from the Emperor downwards hammered away at that plan with his German opposite number, but without making a dent. The Germans stuck to their own leisurely approach, evolved the day before, of awaiting a 'favourable opportunity' on the Western Front to start more precise peace moves through their favoured neutral intermediary, Holland.

In the end yet another temporizing compromise was reached. Nothing was to be done by either side for the moment. Burian, under the strongest pressure, agreed not to 'go it alone' with his project and not to launch a separate Austrian peace initiative of any sort without his ally's previous consent. There was also some inconclusive and, given the dark military outlook, somewhat academic discussions as to which princeling should be nominated for the intended post-war kingdom of Poland;* and that was that. At midday on 15 August Charles re-boarded his train for Vienna, and the last opportunity to decide an Austro-German strategy for peace or war by top-level face-to-face talks steamed off into the distance with him. Ludendorff's paralysing philosophy of fearing the worst but hoping for the best (and doing nothing in the meantime until a miracle or another disaster pointed the way ahead) had prevailed.

Analysing that dreadful example of Micawberism displayed at Spa, Britain's war leader wrote later:

---

* The final choice fell on Prince Frederick Charles of Hesse, though his crown was never to materialize.

'There was no man strong enough to admit that it was no longer possible for Germany to dominate the peace negotiations through the strength of her armies and the extent of her conquest. Two courses were at this moment open to such a man had he been at the top. Either he would have insisted on immediate negotiations being opened while his armies were still capable of a dangerous resistance and the area they occupied was considerable; or ... he could have thrown all his energies into the development of formidable defence works along the German frontier ... abandoning Belgium before he was driven out, and massing his forces on a very greatly shortened line which he could hold against any attack with the troops he still possessed until peace terms had been agreed ... The German leaders took neither course. They fell between the two stools.'

That summing-up of Spa was, however, written with the benefit of much hindsight and many post-war revelations. At the time, in mid-August of 1918, it was not only David Lloyd George who was in the dark. No leader, political or military in either camp, had any clear or confident picture of the difficulties which confronted its enemies. Europe was groping its way out of the Great War almost as blindly as it had blundered into it four years before.

On the purely military side, for example, the German Supreme War Lord and his High Command had gone into the Spa meeting quite baffled as to why Foch and Haig had suddenly broken off their offensive after that mighty blow east of Amiens. Ludendorff had been steeling himself for further major retreats which proved to be unnecessary when, as he put it, the enemy failed to drive home that advantage 'with sufficient vigour'. The Germans could only ascribe that sudden and, to them, unaccountable slackening of pressure to some broader Allied master plan. Little did they know that Foch had been imploring his obdurate British colleague to press on at all cost with the advance (motoring to Haig's Headquarters to make his plea in person on the evening of 11 August) and had only given up when persuaded that, even if the German Second Army was in tatters, the British Fourth Army was, for the moment, quite out of breath. (Rawlinson, at a conference with his corps commanders at Villers-Bretonneux earlier that day, had concluded that exhaustion among his men, wear and tear on his tanks,* and the shaky supply situation to his rear, all made it imperative to call a temporary halt.)

The Germans would have been mightily cheered had they known that when the British Chief of Imperial General Staff, Sir Henry Wilson, had lunched at Marshal Foch's Headquarters, also on 11 August, he had been told that the Generalissimo's plans for the rest of the year consisted only of 'disengaging the lateral railways of Amiens and Hazebrouck, Compiègne and St Mihiel'. Only in 1919 was it hoped to clear the main Lille–Metz line and so prepare the way for a really decisive attack. And if the German High Command had had a spy at the meeting of the British War Cabinet held in London three days later to discuss the overall situation, he would have heard the South African Prime Minister, General Smuts, affirming that he still 'did not believe in a decisive victory against the Boches in the West'. The truth was that whereas Ludendorff had failed to appreciate the importance of the tank weapon altogether, even his more progressive opponents were unable either to grasp or to exploit its full potential. Neither side realized, in August of 1918, that what had just been enacted in Picardy was a prelude to the *Blitzkrieg* of the future. The pall of four years of trench fighting and static warfare still hung too heavily over the military mind.

For their part, the Allies were equally ignorant of the parlous condition and state of mind of the Central Powers. Not until the war was over did they hear of 8 August as Germany's 'Black Day' or imagine that, at Amiens, they had broken Ludendorff's nerve as well as his Second Army. As for the Spa meeting itself, they assumed this to be a natural stock-taking in the enemy camp, and they probably guessed that the Germans would be pressing their reluctant allies to send more divisions to France. On the political

---

* By 9 August, two hundred and seventy of the tanks which had spearheaded the Fourth Army's attack the previous day were out of action; by 10 August the number of serviceable tanks had shrunk to eighty-five; by 12 August it was down to six only.

side, all that leaked out from Spa were reports of the fruitless discussions over which Germanic prince might wear the Polish crown. In London and Paris they had not the faintest notion that the Austrian and German Emperors had spent twenty-four hours debating who should move first, and in what direction, to seek peace; even less did they imagine that the Austrians had just told their allies that Vienna could only hold out for another four and a half months at the most. That deadline of December 1918 announced by General Arz for dropping out of the war altogether was the same modest target date initially set by Marshal Foch for clearing a handful of railways in northern France. Whereas Foch was to exceed his target beyond his wildest dreams, the gloomy General Arz was to be proved not pessimistic enough.

The Emperor Charles, as his widow recalls it, got back to Vienna slightly reassured by the Spa Conference:

'But this was not because he believed the military situation to be anything but dark and growing darker, but because he thought the chances for peace now looked somewhat brighter, despite the clear difference with the Germans over how to go about it. At Spa, as at almost every time the two rulers had met during the war, he had again emphasized to the German Kaiser the seriousness of the threat to their crowns, repeating his old warning that if the two dynasties did not make peace, their peoples would do it for them over their heads. But the German Emperor, who cut a pitiful figure at the talks, seemed incapable of taking the warning in.'

During the month that followed, as the German position in the West crumbled further – though still without collapsing – the political conflict between Vienna and Berlin moved remorselessly towards its climax.

Eight days after the Spa meeting the text of Austria's proposed peace appeal to the world was officially presented to the German Foreign Office; and a week later, on 30 August, the sorely-tried Austrian ambassador in Berlin, Prince Hohenlohe-Schillingfürst, had to go to the German Chancellor with the message that his government could wait no longer and was resolved to try and end the war immediately off its own bat. Hertling, at his wits' end to gain time, decided to send von Hintze to Vienna to try and box up the impatient Austrian peace-doves in their dove-cotes. It was, of course, the German High Command which continued to pull the strings of the Berlin Chancellery. Ludendorff was still moving back on the Western Front – partly of his own accord but mainly because he was being driven – and there was no sign of his famous 'strategic defensive' which was supposed to induce the right mood of conciliation in the enemy. That meant there was no 'all-clear' as yet for Hertling to indulge in serious peace moves of any sort. The battlefield situation thus exercised a fatal braking action on diplomacy during the last summer weeks.

It was able to do this because, though the military set-backs continued to cause concern, nothing for a while happened in France which was drastic enough to raise another panic. True, the new Anglo-French offensive launched on 20 August had succeeded, by the end of the month, in capturing the towns of Péronne and Bapaume, turning the German defence line along this sector of the Somme and costing the Germans far more casualties than they had bargained for in what was supposed to be a measured withdrawal. A more significant blow came on 2 September. That day six British and Canadian divisions, with the help of forty tanks, carried by assault a northern spur (known as the Drocourt-Quéant switch) of the Hindenburg defence line itself, routing, in less than seven hours, nine German divisions from positions which had been fortified for over eighteen months.

Moreover, to those on the battlefield, there were abundant signs that though the German army was still functioning magnificently for such a battered fighting machine moving in reverse gear, the rust of despair and disillusionment was eating into its metal deeper and deeper with every day that passed. Even a senior staff officer at the headquarters of the Tenth German Army allowed such fears to surface openly in a strictly confidential letter to his wife written at that period:

'It is less the military situation which depresses me . . . than the complete hopelessness of our global position, the lack of

reserves and new material and all the rest which will force
us to give way and rescue as much out of the business as we
can ... But quite a few storms will set in for us at home
before everything settles down smoothly again. All this is
only for you, my dearest. On no account should you talk
about it to anyone else ...'

The German rank and file were less punctilious about keeping up
appearances, especially when captured. On 28 August a British war
correspondent, visiting a compound for German prisoners just
taken by the Canadians on the Arras front, wrote in his diary ...

'When those who had been first taken saw batches of their
comrades coming down, they cheered and jeered and
laughed, with shouts of "Bravo", as though they had
gained the best of luck. They became excited when some of
their officers were brought in, a Battalion Commander
among them, with his Adjutant and the survivors of two
battalion staffs, and they lounged up to the barbed wire of
the enclosure which separated them with cigarettes hanging from their lips and no sign of discipline or deference.
One of the officers was angry and commanded the men to
stand to attention when he spoke to them but they shook
their heads and grinned as much as to say, "All that is
finished ... We are equal in captivity."'

Two days later the same diarist put his finger on one of the main
causes of this sullen defeatist mood. The Germans were retreating
across ground they had held since they had rolled back in triumph
over the Somme battlefields in the spring of 1918; their opponents
were taking sweet revenge with every yard recaptured. On 31
August he wrote, in the blackened streets of Bapaume:

'I picked some roses today at Bapaume, red rambler roses
which would make a garland for the steel helmet of one of
the New Zealand boys, to whom honour is most due for the
capture of the town. Bapaume is not a fragrant place for
rose-lovers and when I went into it early this morning,
when the new battle was in progress outside, German shells

were smashing among the houses and there was a smell of
corruption and high explosives in its ruined streets; but I
noticed how, against a broken wall, these roses were in
bloom and marigolds and sweet williams among the red-
brick dust of the ruins, and I picked a bunch out of sheer
maudlin sentiment. For there is a sentiment about the
recapture of Bapaume for all our soldiers and for me. It is
the second time that we have entered it with triumph after
stern fighting up a long, long trail ...'

Yet the writer also felt compelled to pay tribute to the German
army, so formidable even in its retreat. It was not just the tough
resistance of some rear-guard units, and especially of the artillery
men and machine-gunners, which symbolized the enemy's continued strength. It was the renowned organization of the German
army, still unbroken and still in evidence on ground it had just
abandoned:

'They are great sign-writers, these Germans, and
everywhere for miles and miles at every turn in the road, at
every broken wall leading to a village smashed to dust and
ashes, there are notices on big boards warning German
soldiers not to loiter there because of English aircraft,
pointing the way to dug-outs and fire-trenches, signifying
wells, dressing-stations, isolation camps for mangy horses,
work-shops and field kitchens, and the inevitable
"*Kommandantur*".'

A robot like this seemed to have a momentum all of its own.

It was that belief in the invincibility of the German army –
diminished, yet far from destroyed – which paralysed the civilian
ministers in Berlin, and through them, held back the desperate
peace-makers in Vienna. Even such a relatively clear-headed figure
as von Hintze had found fit, on 21 August, to assure the leaders of
Germany's political parties: 'There is no reason to doubt our
victory. Only when we doubt that we shall win are we defeated. In
the opinion of the Supreme Command we are justified in hoping
that we can establish a military position which will enable us to

achieve an acceptable peace.' And to the layman, even if the Somme defences had been turned and a spur of the Hindenburg line itself snapped off, the main body of that line which guarded the approaches to the fatherland was quite intact. By the second week of September the German army was moving into the outposts of those fortifications in what the Berlin war communiqués described as good order and good spirits. It still looked entirely possible to the public that the victors of Tannenberg and many another battle could impose their will yet again upon the fortunes of war.

That, at any rate, was the message which the Germans tried to impress during those same weeks on Vienna, though the Austrians proved a difficult and, eventually, an impossible audience to persuade. Von Hintze began the task, arriving in the Austrian capital on 3 September on what was officially described as his courtesy call as new head of the German Foreign Office. The real purpose, of course, had nothing to do with protocol, and little to do with courtesy. Two days later he and Burian, flanked by their advisers, tried to thrash out the problem of a peace strategy in a mammoth session held in the Ballhausplatz. The Austrian Minister put his case. Mediation by a neutral power, as the Germans favoured, would be 'ineffective, devoid of authority, a mere jab in the air'. In order to proceed this way the Central Powers would be obliged to declare their own peace aims in one form or another at the start; and that, in itself, would mean they would get no further. The only feasible method at this late and critical stage ('and every day in the future will be worse than today') was a direct appeal from one belligerent camp to the other, without entering into preconditions.

Von Hintze elaborated, just as obdurately, on his brief from his Chancellor and the Supreme Command. A public approach as proposed by Austria would only make the German people feel that their ally was betraying them, while persuading the Entente that their enemy had admitted defeat. A neutral country like Holland might not have much political weight; but it did possess moral weight – 'something which the great powers lacked'. And what, he asked, would be the impact of a separate Austrian initiative inside the Dual Monarchy itself? It would only strengthen the yearning for peace among the ordinary people, while the effect on the army would be 'immeasurable'.

That stung Count Burian into a reply which was to go the rounds in Berlin and eventually enter the history books. It was no good, he said, falling into phraseology; they had to act. 'Austria-Hungary cannot continue the war any longer. We are at the very end.' Von Hintze returned home the next day knowing that he had gained nothing for his masters but a little time.

After he had gone the delaying task was taken up by General Cramon. The German army liaison officer at Austrian General Headquarters, acting under direct orders from Hindenburg and Ludendorff, thus temporarily supplanted the German ambassador in Vienna, Count Wedel, in what was, by its very essence, a diplomatic issue. The mere notion that anything of the sort could have taken place in the Entente camp – a British general at Marshal Foch's headquarters, for example, taking personal orders from Haig as to when and how their respective governments might enter into peace talks – reveals again the gulf that yawned between the Western democracies and the Central Powers.

In the week that followed Cramon had three audiences with the Emperor Charles, each time begging him, in the name of Field Marshal Hindenburg, to hold back. And each time the argument was that same siren song which the German Supreme Command had used on their own sovereign and their own Chancellor at Spa: though the German army in the West was taking up its proposed positions the military situation there was not yet favourable for launching a peace initiative, since the enemy's will to fight had not yet been broken. But Charles was too desperate to be lulled. The most that General Cramon could achieve at his last audience was, in his own words, that the Emperor 'allowed the promise to be extracted from him to telegraph the Emperor William immediately before making the peace offer, in order to obtain his consent'. In the event all that the German ruler got was notification of a *fait accompli*. Charles sent the promised warning telegram on the morning of 14 September. Austria's 'cry to the world' was published that same evening.

The cry itself turned out to be a very protracted affair. It was also much too elaborate in its phrasing to convey the genuine sense of emergency behind it; more of an operatic aria in the listener's ear than the shout of a dying gladiator. There was a long philosophical introduction stressing the 'strengthening of the will towards peace and understanding' among the masses and growing realization among the governments of all the warring powers that, if the struggle went on much longer, it would leave Europe 'in ruins and in a state of exhaustion that will cripple its development for decades to come'. Yet, the note continued, some of these governments seemed prepared to risk their standing with their own public opinion by openly offering concessions. A round-table discussion without pre-conditions was the only way out of the *impasse*:

> 'The Imperial and Royal government would like, therefore, to propose to the governments of all the belligerent states that they should send delegates to a confidential and non-binding discussion on the basic principles for the conclusion of peace at a place in a neutral country and at an early date to be agreed.'

Once gathered together, these delegates 'would request and give frank and candid explanations on all those points in need of precise definition'. It was, in true Viennese style, just an Invitation to the Ball, though without even a *carnet de bal*.

Whether anyone would have accepted the invitation even without the disturbing noises that had just come out of Berlin is doubtful; what is clear is that this German distraction destroyed any faint chances that the Austrian peace note possessed. Two days before it was issued the German Vice-Chancellor, Herr von Payer, stood up in Stuttgart and delivered a speech on war aims which, though it appeared much too pacifist for his pan-German colleagues, struck the enemy camp as being far too arrogant in tone and quite unacceptable in most of the precise conditions it advanced.

In eastern Europe, according to Payer, Germany would retain every inch of territory given her under the settlement of Brest-Litovsk with Communist Russia. In western Europe, Germany might consider 'restoring Belgium' (provided certain economic guarantees were given and the Flemish issue satisfactorily resolved); but there was no question of surrendering Alsace-Lorraine. As for the rest of the world, all Germany's colonies must be restored to her and so must all territories belonging to her allies (meaning anything that Austria stood to lose in Italy and everything that Turkey had already lost in Arabia and the Near East.

It was a classic demonstration of the Austrian thesis that any pronouncement on peace which laid down rigid terms in advance was doomed to failure. The Entente powers could not fail to reject Payer's ambitious ideas of a Pax Germanica. The return of Alsace-Lorraine was a pivotal demand for France; Austria's territories south of the Brenner Pass had been secretly promised to the Italians three years before; chunks of the crumbling Turkish empire in both the Balkans and the Near East had more recently been ear-marked for the Serbs and the Arabs; and nobody in Paris, London or Washington proposed leaving Germany a post-war African empire.

That unfortunate speech threw a pall over both the secret moves being made by Germany to open up a mediation channel with Holland and the public move made by her ally for a broader round-table conference. Those two approaches were, in fact, rivals to one another, the end product of four weeks of bickering at all levels from emperors down to ambassadors. Yet the irony was that the Western powers, quite unaware of the great rift which had opened up in the enemy camp, assumed that Berlin and Vienna were working hand-in-hand throughout and that all the warlike speeches and all the peace initiatives formed part of an agreed Machiavellian strategy to win time and to divide and befuddle the Entente. That illusion runs throughout the speech which the British Foreign Secretary, Mr Balfour, made at the Savoy Hotel on 16 September, in which he rejected the Austrian proposal:

> 'I cannot bring myself to believe that this is an honest desire on the part of our enemies to arrive at an understanding with us on terms which it would be possible for us to accept ... This is not an attempt to make peace by understanding, but to weaken those forces which are proving too strong for them in the field.'

Mr Asquith, the leader of the Opposition, echoed the rejection a few days later, adding an intellectual's rebuke ('I do not want to find myself bogged and befogged in a jungle') for the baroque style of the Austrian note. The French reaction was summed up in two comments by leading Parisian newspapers. *Le Figaro* warned (again misreading the true situation): 'We must not forget that behind the Austrian puppet there is the German tragedian pulling the strings.' And *Le Gaulois* asked simply: 'Do the Kaisers in Berlin and Vienna take us for idiots?'

From Washington President Wilson – by now convinced that Austria was merely the docile puppet of Germany – sent an even more dismissive reply. The United States, he told Vienna, 'could entertain no proposal for a conference on a matter concerning which it has made its position and its purpose so plain'. That struck even the British Prime Minister as slamming the door on the Dual Monarchy with unnecessary violence; he himself, he told friends, favoured 'a more reasoned answer'.

As for the Emperor Charles, it was the speed and severity of President Wilson's reaction – almost like that of a venomous snake striking back at him – which was the biggest blow. Only four weeks before, the direct threat which he had long been dreading to his dynasty had begun to take shape when England formally recognized the exiled Czech movement as an Allied belligerent power. France soon followed suit and so, at the beginning of September, did America, with a statement by her Secretary of State, Robert Lansing, recognizing the 'Czechoslovak National Council as a *de facto* belligerent, clothed with proper authority to direct the affairs of the Czecho-Slovaks'. That formula seemed to range the White House alongside those in Europe who sought to dismember the Dual Monarchy.

That new political toughness had its counterpart on the battle-fields, where the growing strength of the United States as a military power had just been demonstrated for all to see. On 12 September, two days before the Emperor Charles ran out of patience and issued his 'cry to the world', the American army on the Western Front finally came of age.

5

'We Have Come to Die
For You'

IT WAS THEIR ZEST FOR LIFE, even on that journey laden with
death, which amazed their allies and dismayed their enemy the
most; that and their burning sense of mission, a flame long since
turned low or snuffed out in the ranks of all the veteran armies.
When fresh drafts of English soldiers landed in France in the
summer of 1918 they could be forgiven, after the four years of
slaughter their comrades had gone through before them, for plodding off the troop-ships like cattle heading for the abattoir. But the
Americans poured eagerly down the gang-planks, a mixture of the
crusader and the tourist, as though holding a shield in one hand and
a Baedeker in the other rather than rifle and pack. The tourist, if
anything, was uppermost for, as well as the excitement of war, this
was also the 'European trip' which the hometown American boy
would otherwise have spent his whole life just reading about in the
social gossip columns. The mood comes through vividly in the first
impressions they recorded.

A captain of the 107th US Infantry Regiment wrote this in his
diary, for example, while in the train taking him and his men from
their disembarkation port of Brest up towards the Somme:

> 'It was a beautiful ride through Normandy in apple blossom
> time. Little groups of women, children and old men stood
> at the stations or along the tracks and waved to us. Every-
> thing seemed so peaceful and content and we were all in
> such high spirits. There was big adventure in the air and,
> surely, the whole trip was going to be such a lark! And
> where do you think we were sleeping on that night? Right

---

* The American General Bliss to Foch.

on the edge of the forest of Crécy! Shades of the Black Prince!'

Another American officer, setting off on foot with his company from the same port, felt a similar sentimental curiosity:

'Can anyone who took part in those route marches in France from the sea ever forget them? It seems to me that we were always marching along those splendid shaded French roads with a gridiron of sunshine falling through the tree trunks that stretched their endless double row along the white ribbon that disappeared for ever and ever over the edge of the next hill ... It was like a river flowing through a tunnel, a river of men ...

The whole population turned out to see us. Women held up their babies to *les braves Américains* as we went down streets between the shuttered houses ...'

A twenty-eight-year-old infantry corporal, also on the inland march from Brest, was struck most of all by the way these tiny French children behaved as soon as they could walk by themselves:

'The little French tots followed us a long ways. When we made our first halt, they all asked "Gimme cigarettes," little kids about seven years old ... They would puff away at them like veteran smokers ...'

But nearly always, those diaries or letters are suffused with the sheer romance of it all. A young artillerist with an obvious feel for history wrote home to his father after exploring his first Norman town:

'I got lost in the dark and wandered for an hour. I remember particularly one crooked cobbled street which led up a steep hill. There is one pale street light at the foot and one half-way up. The latter was hung from a wrought iron bracket and lit up a beautifully carved door, above which was a coat of arms. It needed only that the door should open and close with a crash and there, sword gleaming in his hand, should stand D'Artagnan crying "*Qui demande un Mousquetaire du Roi?*" So, from the middle of the seventeenth century, I send you my very best, Daddy dear.'

And an American woman who was living in Paris summed it up as she watched the boulevards, swarming with American boys in their khaki clothes and new tan gaiters, 'all behaving as though they were here for a sort of glorification'.

> 'In a sense it is a big adventure for them, and for some it will be *the* big adventure – to come over the sea, all dressed up in new uniforms, to walk about the streets of Paris, before going "out there". No one blames them for enjoying it . . . In fact everyone likes them just as they are, and the French are quite daft about them . . .'

Troops like those may have been green but they were bursting with sap as well, and the battlefields of France had seen nothing like them since that first heady summer of 1914. The only trouble was that, for the British and the French, they were painfully slow in coming, and there were indeed moments when both Allies despaired that the rescue could come in time.

Unflattering though it may be to cast God-fearing men like Foch and Haig in the role of Dracula, there is something of the famished vampire in the way both commanders, throughout 1918, jostled with each other to fall on this supply of fresh American blood and draw it off in order to revive their own exhausted armies. Like the Transylvanian count they could never get enough, despite the fact that unlike him they were able to go at it at all hours of the day and night.

Though the AEF's build-up that year ended by being spectacular, the Americans themselves shared the despair of their allies at the beginning. On 1 January the American Expeditionary Force in Europe numbered a mere 9,804 officers and 165,080 men. Moreover, despite the fact that by then America had been in the war for nine months, she still did not have a single formation capable of taking over a stretch of the front line; and there was more to such a depressing balance sheet than a shortage of men. After the

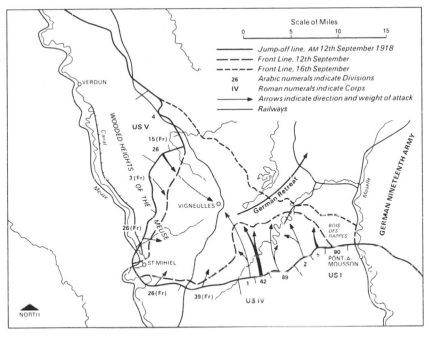

St Mihiel: Allied offensive, September 1918

advance guards of the 1st US Division had arrived at St Nazaire it soon became known that 'many recruits had received their rifles just before boarding ship in New York, that newly-organized units like the howitzer companies, mortar sections and 37 mm cannon crews not only had no howitzers, mortar or cannon but had never even heard of the weapons'. And the most their officers knew about trench warfare on the Western Front was what they had managed to mug up from a single military manual on the subject borrowed from a British officer on the voyage. The million strong AEF originally envisaged for May 1918 seemed a mirage even as the winter ended; and the Americans, who had tackled mobilizations and supply as though it were just another big business problem which their renowned expertise would crack, were suitably embarrassed. On top of that they were temporarily dependent on their allies for almost everything needed to make their precious manpower effective – British ships to bring the troops over, French and Italian horses for their supply trains, British tanks for their

95

embryo armoured units, British and French artillery to back up their infantry.

If they were to survive that long spell on the leading rein with dignity and grow into a cohesive, independent force, they needed a man of exceptional pride and obstinacy to lead and speak up for them. They were lucky that President Wilson had picked the right one: John J. Pershing. The First World War had no truly great commanders, otherwise it might have been over a little sooner. But within a few months Pershing emerged as one of its strongest military personalities; and no one, not even the French Generalissimo himself, served his own country's interests more faithfully.

His own appointment symbolized the dire straits of the force he was to command.* There were only six major-generals on the army list when America entered the war and Pershing, a fifty-four-year-old cavalry officer from Missouri, was the most junior of them all. But he had one qualification which, in American eyes, helped him to jump the ladder. Four weeks after the outbreak of war, when he was stationed at Fort Sam Houston in Texas, he received what he describes as this 'somewhat puzzling' telegram from his father-in-law, a senator in Washington: 'Wire me today whether and how much you speak, read and write French.' He was able to report that, nine years before, when he had been studying the language in France, he had acquired the basis for a 'satisfactory working knowledge'. He had barely sent off his reply before another telegram arrived – this time a top secret service message in code -- announcing that he was to command America's proposed expeditionary force to France.

Though linguistic ability was at a premium in Washington, Pershing's other qualifications were paramount. They added up to the nearest thing the United States had to an all-round combat General. Pershing had commanded troops in the Cuban campaign, where he had won the Silver Star for gallantry, and in the Philippines. Nearer at home he had served in South Dakota in the wake of

---

* When sent into war the US army held in its arsenals only four hundred light field guns and a hundred and fifty heavy pieces. Its 'Air Service Section' had sixty-five officers, of whom only thirty-five could fly, and none of those had any experience of aerial combat or bombing.

the 1890–91 Indian War with a company of Sioux Scouts, and from April 1914 to March 1916 he had actually led an American expeditionary army of sorts, the primitive strike force, fifteen thousand strong, which drove down into Mexico in pursuit of the famous bandit leader, Pancho Villa. Compared with the battle experience which all the European generals had acquired by the time Pershing appeared in their midst, those skirmishes of his with Red Indians and Mexican marauders must have seemed slightly comic. Probably none of them paused to think that Pershing's experience of military action was more varied and, above all, more recent than anything that a single one of them could have boasted when they set sail for France three years before him. But, quite apart from that, President Wilson had picked a man whom he felt could be relied on to carry out his instructions to the letter, and without developing any political ambitions of his own. Pershing was to justify his confidence on both scores.

The key passage of those instructions, as set out in a letter from his War Department, read as follows:

> 'In military operations against the Imperial German Government, you are directed to co-operate with the forces of the other countries employed against that enemy; but in doing so the underlying idea must be kept in view that the forces of the United States are a separate and distinct component of the combined forces, the identity of which must be preserved.'

He had had to fight for that principle even before his men got across the Atlantic. Only the British could supply the ships he needed. They duly offered to provide sea transport for an extra 150,000 men, provided that these troops were split up into one hundred and fifty battalions which were then to serve with British divisions for several months at a stretch. This was a recipe for annihilating the AEF's identity from the start, not preserving it. Pershing successfully dug his toes in. What the British were finally promised was the use of six American divisions, on recall whenever he decided.

The tug-of-war continued as the AEF built up, with first one ally, then another (and sometimes both) at the other end of the

97

rope. The French, for example, tried to talk Pershing into a scheme for allotting whole regiments of raw American troops to their divisions, to be used not merely on quiet sectors, but in the front line if needed. It was another blatant daylight raid on the American blood-bank and again Pershing fought it off, despite the awkward fact that he was still dependent on the raiders in order to carry on business at all.

That dependence extended even to the trivia of a great war machine, as the episode of the British button was to show. Because American factories had failed to meet the demand for heavy winter clothing there was nothing for it at first but to buy supplies from British depots. No soldier can be expected to show much enthusiasm for wearing the uniform of another army; but reluctance turned to near-mutiny when one American unit, whose soldiers were largely of Irish descent, was called upon to wear British tunics with the original buttons still attached. They indicated in no uncertain manner that they would rather freeze to death than walk about displaying the royal coat of arms all over their chests. A consignment of American army buttons was hastily dispatched by car.

When the long-awaited German offensive was finally launched and Paris itself was threatened, the pressure on Pershing to fling his troops into the battle, no matter what protocols might say, or the cost might be, became intense. It was indeed a question of numbers as well as of strategy and morale, for when the 'Emperor's Battle' began, the Germans, thanks to their divisions transferred from the now-silent Russian front, had a clear front-line superiority.* Pershing responded to the crisis by offering the French the entire fledgling divisions he now possessed, on the understanding that the loan would last only as long as the emergency and that the American formations would eventually be re-assembled under their own command.

The height of the military crisis, which came in the early

---

* British Intelligence estimates put the strength of the German army in the West at this time at 1,569,000 rifles compared with the 1,245,000 of the Allies. A French estimate of total 'combatant effectives' in the summer of 1918 put the overall balance the other way – 4,002,104 for the Allies compared with 3,567,000 for the Germans.

summer of 1918, also saw the climax of this perpetual debate over command. At a two-day sitting of the Supreme War Council at Abbeville on 1–2 May, Pershing held out against the combined onslaught of Lloyd George, Clemenceau, the British and French Commanders-in-Chief and the designated Generalissimo Foch – all of whom wanted to draw on the filling reservoir of American manpower, trained or untrained, for their own forces and thus postpone the creation of an independent American army. During a heated exchange Pershing told Foch that, if need be, he was prepared to see the French army being drawn right back to the Loire to secure the American aim of independence at the earliest feasible date. He added, in the tone of a man whose increasing confidence was now underpinning his determination:

'The time may come when the American army will have to stand the brunt of this war, and it is not wise to fritter away our resources . . . The morale of the British, French and Italian armies is low while, as you know, that of the American army is high. It would be a grave mistake to give up the idea of building up an American army in all its details as soon as possible.'

Haig wrote in his diary that night: 'I thought Pershing was very obstinate and stupid. He did not seem to realize the urgency of the situation.'

The obstinate Pershing was not to be budged on his cardinal principle then, nor at a similar debate which was held in the same forum and with most of the same actors a month later. He agreed to a crash programme of shipping over half a million American troops during June and July, even if some were insufficiently trained, but only as 'a temporary and exceptional' measure to meet the emergency on the Allied front. The vast figures that were being bandied about in those telegrams to Washington showed where Pershing's air of authority was coming from. If projected into the spring of 1919 (and no one in the Supreme War Council was in any doubt that the fighting would continue into the coming year) the manpower demands being made for Pershing would have given him by then a total of some four million American combatant

99

troops under his command – as much if not more than all the Allied armies in the West put together. As it was, the flood of American reinforcements pouring across the Atlantic had, by midsummer, transformed the Allies' front-line inferiority of the spring to a clear superiority over the Germans of some two hundred thousand men. The tall cavalryman from Missouri could afford to ride high.

Such was the debate going on that summer between the politicians and the generals. How did those same problems of command, amalgamation and joint training strike the troops on the ground?

Before the induction of the AEF into battle could be done on a unit scale (first, American battalions attached to Allied brigades and, later, whole regiments serving, under their own commanders, as brigades in Allied divisions) the British and French got their first sight of their new comrades in small batches. Their initial attitude was one of understandable condescension. These, after all, were 'rookies' being shown a few tricks of their terrible trade by the old hands. Yet, from the beginning, there was also respect for the newcomers' courageous spirit, and for their eagerness to learn.

One British artillery officer serving with the 51st Highland Division recalls:

> 'The adjutant sent us two young American officers on what we called a Cook's tour, to see how we managed to annoy the Germans without casualties on our side ... We gave them the best lunch we could and I took them up to see our observation posts in our infantry front line ... As we strolled up the track, the Germans started a straffe on our farmhouse cross-roads, possibly in retaliation for a few salvoes I had fired at a cross-roads in their back area ... From long experience, one gets to know by the sound of the shells screaming overhead whether they will fall close, or, as more often, far away. These newcomers, who had never heard shells going by overhead, just vanished into abandoned, muddy bits of old trenches, from which I helped them out with sympathetic explanations that everyone did the same until they got used to the noise.

Actually, at this short range, if a shell was coming directly at you, it reached its target before the sound, so it was not worth taking cover ... This explanation did not seem to cheer them up ...'

A company commander in the British Guards Division who has a batch of American officers, NCOs and men attached to him 'for forty-eight hours' instruction in trench duties' gives another typical reaction in his front-line diary entry for 8 August:

'More Yankees came in last night, and the old lot departed. They make one laugh, they are so green, but they are so devilish cautious not to be caught napping they are positively dangerous to anyone going round the line – every sentry you visit receives you with a bayonet in your face. Some of them went out on patrol last night and, as usual with novices, thought they saw an army of Huns in every row of stakes. I ordered them to fire on everything they thought suspicious and the result was a ripple of shots all night. I wonder what the Huns think has happened. Broncho came round this morning with the American major, a southerner called Gordon. He was a long hard-looking fellow, and very thirsty. Without saying a word he took hold of a bottle of diluted peroxide I use to clean my teeth and had a long drink. "Gee," he said, "that's the strongest water I have had for some time!" I hope it won't hurt him.'

And the next day:

'One unfortunate American killed by one of our own shells. There is a small percentage that drop short and an occasional one of these hits ... These Americans are not bad. They are very keen, willing and good-tempered. Everything goes wrong with them in the process of learning ... but they keep up their spirits well ...'

As for the Americans on attachment to the Guards, they were able to witness a prime example of that stolid 'gallows humour' in which the British at war always seem to specialize. Describing 'a burst of hurricane shelling' which descended on the unit, the diary continues:

> 'Toby and his orderly were hit – I fear both badly. They were very cheerful and kept on asking each other how they were. Mags, the orderly, with a bit of his nose off, his hand smashed, and his knee-cap torn off, observed that he was "well cam-u-fladged".'

From the other side of the Allied camp a French war correspondent, attached to the so-called 'Terrible Brigade' of Michigan and Wisconsin troops who were fighting in the same offensive, paid this glowing tribute:

> 'After six months in France, they have behind them some magnificent baptisms of fire, and neither the French, alongside whom they have fought, nor the enemy, whom they have vigorously thrown back, would dispute their nickname of "Terrible".'

That was, at best, only a semi-professional military verdict. But the same writer, with a journalist's eye for the human detail, spotted some of the reasons why the 'doughboys' were so popular as comrades as well as so welcome as reinforcements. The brigade delighted the French soldiers by composing 'a pleasant marching song out of fragments of student songs ... and a few notes of the Marseillaise'. The refrain made up in sentiment what it lacked in rhyme:

> 'The Kaiser has no chance
> We will shoot him in the pants.'

And the soldiers and civilians alike were touched when one of the regiments of the American Brigade decided to adopt as their 'mascot' the twelve-year-old son of one of their French comrades who was found abandoned after his father had been killed in battle. These new allies had some odd habits. The French, for example, found it odd that the Americans spent so much time brushing their teeth, or complained about the lack of drinking water when there was so much wine around. And General Pétain must have suffered a considerable shock when an American unit he visited during that summer's offensive greeted him with an impromptu jazz concert followed by a 'Buck and Wing dance in the old plantation style' – all provided by a Negro band. On the other side of the cultural divide, an American officer attached to a battalion of the British Royal West Kents could scarcely believe his eyes and ears when an orderly appeared in the trenches one afternoon to announce, with the colonel's compliments, that 'tea was ready'. But they were all fitting in. As one American, an officer from the Pacific coast, told a friend of his French comrades:

> 'It's odd. These people do not look a bit like us. They don't speak our language. I speak very little of theirs. But somehow they are like us. I felt at home with them at once and every day I feel more at home. I don't know why it is – just can't explain it.'

In some ways, the Americans appeared as close to this ally whose language they did not understand as to the other ally whose tongue and culture they shared. The fact that Britain, unlike France, was a monarchy may have had something to do with it, at least in the eyes of the ordinary soldiers. One American private, recording in his diary how, on 12 August 1914, he caught his first sight of a real live king, might have been writing of a visitor from Mars:

> 'At eleven on this sunny morning the heralds came up the hill and soon the royal car shone in the sunlight as it moved between the two rows of poplars that for a quarter mile border the road to the chateau at the top of the hill.
>
> 'An American soldier near me rushed back and called to his comrade: "Hurry, here comes the king." "What king?" "George King." We crowded the sideways, silent in expectancy. The long limousine, black and sleek drew near and one American called out loudly – "So that's the big stiff!"
>
> 'King George V of England led the procession on the

green back of the chateau. General Pershing walked on his left; then came General Bliss, General Henry Rawlinson and General Bell, and after them a host, including myself. About twenty officers and men of the 131st and 132nd Infantries stood at attention. The movie cameras clicked, the king pinned an English medal on each, the band played "God Save the King", and then the "Star Spangled Banner"; the procession returned to the chateau, the band played "Illinois", and the little white-bellied donkey that wanders around our headquarters every day, stood nearby half asleep thru it all, ready to kick King George in the rear side as readily as a soldier of the ranks.

'It has been a great day for the Thirty-third Division. I saw a king for the first time. I saw together the only two full generals of the United States Army, of whom there have been less than ten in our military annals; I saw a king give for the first time a decoration to an American soldier.

'This evening at the theatrical performance, we sang "God Save the King"; and I saw no conquering warrior, no awe-inspiring leader, no merry mighty monarch. He was a little man, perhaps five feet four inches tall; the dark rings around his eyes marked his every movement with tiredness. A dozen times he scratched his beard furiously with his fingers. Aides rushed to his side and spoke this or that each time he was about to perform some act. And they placed him like a child in the automobile, as it carried him away and we stood at attention – George V, by the grace of God, king of Great Britain and Ireland and the dominions beyond the sea, Emperor of India, the monarch of a greater portion of the earth than any other human has ever ruled.'

But whatever psychological problems the Americans may have had with their one-time colonial masters, and however tenaciously Haig and his generals fought for the British lion's share of American blood,* the nearest thing to a flaming row Pershing had

---

* Haig had been particularly pained when, on 12 August, Pershing told him that the five

with anyone was his confrontation with Foch over the AEF's first solo battle.

A French marshal had called it 'the hernia of St Mihiel'. It was a pungent and not inappropriate description of the German bulge, some fifteen miles deep, which still protruded into the Allied lines between the Meuse and Moselle Rivers. Vulnerable though it had become after four years of secure occupation, the German High Command was reluctant to abandon the salient which protected both the fortification of Metz and the key industrial region of Briey to the rear. For his part, Pershing had been equally determined to reduce it ever since the AEF started landing in France. As early as 24 February 1918 he wrote to his Secretary of War, Mr Newton Baker:

> 'In accordance with a tentative agreement made by General Pétain and myself, we shall in time have a sector of our own as soon as our divisions are able to act independently. It will probably begin where the 1st Division is now finishing its training, between St Mihiel and Pont-à-Mousson, from which base we shall likely extend [sic] both to the west and east.'

In the following months, American logistics were based on the assumption that St Mihiel would, indeed, be the AEF's first independent operation. Their main training area was set up opposite the sector and field hospitals and supply depots were all established with reference to that one target. Throughout the spring and early summer Pershing had been badgering Foch to make the understanding a formal one, and to write it officially into the Allied war plan. This finally happened on 24 July, at that same conference of the Commanders-in-Chief which had decided on the 'freeing of the Paris-Amiens railway line', as the great blow against the German Second Army had been modestly christened. The next of Foch's 'railway attacks' was laid down as 'The clearing of the

American divisions then in training with the British army (and partly equipped by Britain) were to be withdrawn and would not be available for the 'big push' Haig was planning against Kemmel at the end of September. 'What will History say regarding this action of the Americans?' he asked his diary. The answer was nothing at all.

Paris-Auricourt line in the region around Commercy, by reducing the St Mihiel salient. This operation should be prepared without delay and executed by the American army as soon as it has the necessary means.'

During the month that followed, Pershing wasted neither time nor effort on those preparations. By the end of August, forty thousand tons of ammunition had been placed in dumps; a telephone switchboard with thirty-eight circuits had been set up at Ligny-en-Barrois (operated partly by expert women operators plucked from the city exchanges of New York, Boston and Philadelphia); nineteen railheads had been established for the movement of supplies; a hundred and twenty water-points had been formed, capable, between them, of furnishing 1,200,000 gallons a day; more than twenty thousand hospital beds and sixty-five evacuation trains had been prepared for the wounded and enough American railway material had been piled up to build forty-five miles of standard gauge line. Admittedly, at the sharp end of the build-up, Allied equipment still predominated. Not one of the 3,010 guns assembled for the barrage was of American manufacture, and some forty per cent of the crews manning them were French. It was the same story with the two hundred and sixty-seven light tanks gathered for the attack; and even the airforce of nearly fourteen hundred planes assembled for the operation was composed mainly of British bombing squadrons and one entire French air division. But whether begged, borrowed or home-produced, that massive arsenal of weapons and supplies collected together to reduce one weakly-held enemy salient was an impressive forerunner of the lavish style in which the Americans were to fight all their subsequent wars in the twentieth century, whether in Europe or in Asia.*

And then, at the end of August, when Pershing had already started to move his units up quietly into their battle positions to

---

* The only thing they seem to have been economical in, at least in 1918, was staff work. When Pershing took over the St Mihiel sector, the French general handed him two thick volumes, each of a hundred and fifty pages, containing plans drawn up respectively for the attack and defence of the salient. The Americans handed over their corresponding plans, which were of eight and six pages only.

seize their prize, Marshal Foch tried to take that prize away from them. In the circumstances this was not just a blow at the American First Army but at the United States itself.

It was Field Marshal Haig who first seemed to have put the idea in the Generalissimo's mind. In his diary entry for 27 August, the British C-in-C wrote:

'Sir J. Du Cane, who stayed last night, left for Foch's HQ. I took the opportunity of sending Foch a letter. I urged him to put the Americans into battle *at once* in order to enable an important advance to be made without delay, concentrically, *viz.* against Cambrai, against St Quentin and against Mezières from the south ...'

And two days later, after a long discussion with Foch, Haig comments:

'As regards our future plans, he is in full agreement with me. I noted however that *since he received my letter* he had decided to put in the American attack down the left bank of the Meuse towards Mezières instead of against the St Mihiel salient which was his original plan. Pershing is still preparing for the latter operation. F. will tell him as soon as possible of the change.'

'As soon as possible' came, in fact, only twenty-four hours later. On 30 August, the very day when Pershing assumed formal command of his sector, he was visited in his sumptuous residence (a chateau at Ligny-en-Barrois) by the Generalissimo, who promptly 'presented an entirely new plan for the employment of the American army'. According to this, the attack on the salient was to be downgraded to a limited thrust against its southern face only – little more than a harassing operation. The moment this little diversion was out of the way (and Foch's manner implied that he would not object if only one afternoon were wasted on it) the American First Army would then be split up again for the really serious business ahead – two major thrusts against the enemy along the line of the River Meuse and beyond the Argonne Forest. Moreover, for these attacks, which would both be launched with French troops, some of the American divisions would pass again under French command.

It would be hard to say which of these two announcements shook Pershing the more – the news that his coveted St Mihiel offensive was being brushed aside, or the threat of losing the First Army's independent role before it had enjoyed even one proper chance to assert it. In all probability it was the latter, for his first reaction, though objecting to both proposals, ended with the words: 'This virtually destroys the American army that we have been trying so long to form.' A long and very tough exchange followed between the two men, with Foch insisting again and again that the real and urgent battle for the Allies now lay beyond St Mihiel, and Pershing insisting that though he would fight on any sector assigned to him, his troops would have to be under American command, 'and no other way'.

The climax came in the following confrontation:

'Pershing: "Marshal Foch, you have no authority as Allied Commander-in-Chief to call upon me to yield up my command of the American army and have it scattered among the Allied forces where it will not be an American army at all."

Foch: "I must insist upon the arrangement."

Pershing: "Marshall Foch, you may insist all you please but I decline absolutely to agree to your plan. While our army will fight wherever you decide, it will not fight except as an independent American army."'

At this, the Generalissimo, looking, according to Pershing, 'very pale and exhausted', gathered up his maps and left, after handing the American a memorandum of his proposals 'for careful study'.

The outcome of this 'careful study', and of forty-eight hours of equally careful sparring between the French and American general staffs, was another top-level meeting, held this time at Foch's chateau headquarters, Bombon. That was more of a conference than a confrontation, for the Generalissimo already realized that he might have to meet Pershing part way over the St Mihiel operation, and all the way over the question of command. The compromise finally reached was that the attack on the salient should go ahead; it would be launched by only eight to ten American divisions who would make an all-out assault from both north and south, though limiting their advance to a line rather shorter than Pershing's original target. The moment that line was reached, however, Pershing was to re-group his First Army, move it sixty miles to a new sector between the Moselle River and the Argonne Forest, and then be ready to take part in a grand French-American offensive west of the Meuse between 20 and 25 September. It would be a tough assignment to take on even for an experienced army with full logistical support of its own. For Pershing's raw staff officers, still learning by their mistakes and still dependent for transport and equipment on their Allies, the task must have looked somewhere between herculean and impossible.

Pershing, however, seemed quite happy to take on the challenge. One reason, perhaps, was that it was primarily a challenge to American efficiency, and he would have soon despaired of that as of American valour. But the prime reason was that, on balance, he had won. His First Army was to get its battle of the bulge, and, after that, a ninety-mile sector of the front line in a major Allied attack. Moreover, both operations were to be under his own unfettered command. That, he knew, was how it would be from now on until the day of victory, with his authority swelling steadily as the weight of new American divisions built up behind them. One might say indeed that on 30 August 1918, at the château of Ligny-en-Barrois, America's second declaration of independence from Europe was proclaimed.* As with the first nearly a century and a half before, it now had to be tested in battle. A fiasco at St Mihiel would do more than damage Pershing's pride: it would completely destroy his arguments. Fortunately for him the conditions under which

---

* Foch's own account of this whole episode is notable for its blandness and its omissions. No mention appears of the role Haig played before the confrontation with Pershing and not a word of the heated exchange which took place at that confrontation. Either the Generalissimo was trying to present for history a picture of totally unruffled Allied relationships; or he was reluctant to admit he could not always impose his will. In either case, his memoirs are misleading.

America's first solo operation on the Western Front was finally launched made an American fiasco well-nigh impossible.

'Pray for fog!' Pershing replied to Mr Baker when the American Secretary for War, who could not resist turning up in person to watch the First Army's début, had asked his general, on the eve of the attack, what he, as a civilian, could do to help. At 5 a.m. the next morning, Thursday 12 September, Mr Baker could see from his observation post close to the battlefield that his prayers had been answered. When the first waves of American infantry went in against the southern face of the salient, mist and drizzling rain enveloped the landscape. This helped to nullify one of the only two advantages the enemy possessed – his ability to watch every move of an attacker from the wooded heights of the River Meuse above and around St Mihiel itself. (In 1915 the French had tried again and again to dislodge the Germans from those commanding heights, but had always been repelled with heavy losses.)

The only other advantage the defenders possessed was the formidable nature of their defences. The ground had been held by them ever since September 1914 when, in the course of their first offensive, they had tried to break through to the south of the great French-held strongpoint at Verdun. In the four years that had followed (three of them quite unmolested) they had had ample time to convert the salient into a classical fortress of trench warfare. Four or five defensive positions ran from the outposts west of St Mihiel to the base of the bulge twenty miles behind it – the line at which the Americans, with their reduced objective, were now aiming.

A very experienced British observer, looking over those rear defences soon after they had been overrun, wrote this description in his diary:

'A long glacis, several forward trenches, much wire; and a concreted main position withdrawn some 150 yards behind the crest of the ridge ... Good dug-outs and bomb-proofs, and a daedelus of trenches ... The wire of several kinds, the oldest very thick and all over strong barbs; the latest un-barbed and thin but in great coils, hard to get through. The strong points were surrounded by interior *zaribas* of the wire. I do not think that the Germans of six months ago could have been turned out of such a position at the gallop...'

But that, precisely, was the weakness of the defenders, a weakness that far outweighed all the advantages of terrain. They were neither the same force in quality or in relative quantity as the troops who had won ground, and held it, as recently as the Kaiser's great spring offensive. When the American attack opened the salient was held by a mixed force of nine German and Austrian divisions under the command of General von Fuchs. No fewer than six of those were rated as second-class formations. Even second-class troops might have held out longer in the formidable defence-works had not the entire force been in the process of withdrawal. After the battle of Amiens and the follow-up attack of the French along the Oise valley and the British and Belgians on the allied left flank, the St Mihiel bulge looked every bit as vulnerable to Ludendorff as it was inviting to Pershing. Moreover, despite all the Americans' efforts at camouflage and concealment, their increased activity in front of St Mihiel had been noted at the end of August by German Intelligence, who predicted an imminent attack. On 8 September, four days before that attack came, the Germans began to evacuate the salient, on order from General Headquarters at Spa. It seems to have been a fairly leisurely operation, in keeping with Ludendorff's serene directive 'to keep the enemy at arm's length'. But it meant that only their covering forces were left in the forward trenches by 12 September and, more seriously, that some of the heavy guns had already been moved out while others were no longer at their emplacements. It was thus a weakened defence, caught off balance, that the Americans struck at. All that was needed to knock it right over was a blow of overwhelming force.

That the First Army duly delivered. The preliminary night-time barrage by Pershing's three thousand guns was hailed in itself as the 'most intensely concentrated of the war', hurling nearly one million shells within the space of four hours into the salient. Then, at dawn, the infantry went in: seven American divisions delivered the main punch against the southern face of the bulge while two more American divisions and four French made supporting attacks all round the nose of the salient and along its north-west flank. Pershing had every right to point out with pride afterwards that, of his nine formations in the front line, four had 'never before been engaged in offensive combat'. But in that context it was the sheer weight of numbers which mattered – that and the zest with which the entire First Army hurled itself at the enemy.

In the 60th Regiment of the 5th Division (one of those attacking for the first time) was the youngest American soldier ever to reach the front line, a thirteen-year-old infantry runner who had managed to enlist by using a false name and giving his age as eighteen. He later gave a vivid description of the St Mihiel operation in which, once again, the Americans' sense of adventure comes through far stronger than any sense of horror or danger. His account begins at 1 a.m. on 12 September when his regiment sent the delightful code message 'Roosters waddling' back to Divisional Headquarters to indicate that all its units were ready in their battle-stations. At that moment too, the barrage started; and, as he waited in the pouring rain listening to the stream of shells overhead, the schoolboy warrior, doubtless remembering maternal instructions for more pleasant outings, found time to change into clean socks and underwear. There was another homely touch as H-hour arrived and, in the 'unbelievable silence' which followed the thunder of the guns, they went forward against the southern face of the salient:

> 'As our first lines passed over the ridge, a lone rabbit scampered out of the brush. A doughboy of the second wave knocked it over, rifle in one hand, the rabbit in the other. He wasn't bothered by his buddies' remarks, saying only, "We gotta eat sometime, ain't we?"'

Then this description of the ease of the American advance:

> 'The heavy tanks assigned to smashing the wire entanglements never made it: they were behind us, bogged in a sea of mud. The first wave had to advance through the wire;

fortunately the guns had made this possible.

'Waves of mud-coated men, helmeted, with full packs, swept across the open fields like an avalanche, descending on the few scattered Boches in their lonely outposts ... Everywhere complete destruction. Reinforced concrete pill boxes were a mass of twisted rubble. As expected, resistance had been negligible – Jerry had been caught napping. The enemy's plans for pulling back had not been executed soon enough and as we moved forward we noticed dead Boche [*sic*] and wrecked equipment scattered over the entire area ...'

Finally, the passion for collecting mementos, which seized schoolboy and veteran soldiers alike:

'A short distance ahead I spotted a dead Hun, and it appeared he had been pinned to the ground with a bayonet ... In one of his stiffened hands he held a post-card; he must have given it one last look as he "went west". I took the card and stuck it in my blouse. I'll keep it as a souvenir, I decided.'

The sweeping advance of the 60th Regiment was fairly typical. By midday, only seven hours after H-hour, the entire I Corps of General Liggett, with its four divisions which carried out the attack on the right flank, had already reached the objectives assigned to them for the second day of the operation. One brigade commander on that front had strolled ahead, quite unescorted, to find out where the retreating enemy had got to. Not a shot was fired at him and the story goes that he sent back a message to his divisional commander: 'Let me go ahead and I'll be in Metz and you'll be a field-marshal.' But neither suggestion (and particularly the second) was in Foch's plan. On the morning of the 13th the main American force driving up from the south linked up at Vigneulles with the secondary American–French forces advancing into the bulge from the north-west, and the limited target of cutting off the base of the salient had been achieved. It was time to pause, count the cost and measure the prize.

The First Army's casualties in the St Mihiel operation numbered some seven thousand which, by Flanders and Picardy standards, was a dirt-cheap price to pay for an advance of twenty miles. General Fuchs had lost four hundred and forty-three guns and some sixteen thousand men in prisoners alone; if the northwest pincer had moved in more aggressively (American heads rolled over that afterwards) the tally would have been even higher. But it was good enough for a start. The last salient on the Western Front had been reduced and, more important than any territorial gain, the Americans had demonstrated that they were capable of independent action, even if it was only a straightforward nutcracker operation against a very brittle nut. One visitor to an American Divisional Headquarters during the battle used a different metaphor. It was, he said, 'like listening to election returns when things are going one's way'.

Some American ground commanders, perhaps understandably, were persuaded by the exhilarating success of their first independent battle into believing that, if given their heads by the Generalissimo, they could have almost marched into Germany and won the war there and then. General Dickman, for example, who had commanded IV Corps in its rapid advance into the southern face, later declared: 'The failure to push north from St Mihiel with our overwhelming superiority of numbers will always be regarded by me as a strategical blunder for which Marshal Foch and his staff are responsible.' Pershing himself felt he might at least have taken the key German strong-hold of Metz had he been allowed to press on immediately from the salient.

Others, including General Liggett, Dickman's neighbouring corps commander, gave a more sober verdict, pointing out that all these projections of further victories seemed to be based on a totally false assumption – namely that the First Army was already a trained and well-oiled fighting unit. Quite apart from the supply problems which a further advance would have thrown up, the military balance itself was swinging back more in favour of the Germans, now that the Allied armies had come up against the forward positions of the great Hindenburg defence line. As General Pershing and his ebullient troops were to discover, a frontal attack against an enemy on well-fortified ground of his own choosing was to prove a very different matter from squeezing out a hideously vulnerable bulge which the enemy was already in the process of abandoning.

The debate is one of those numberless military 'might-have-beens' which the Great War left behind. But, in that particular case it is irrelevant, for St Mihiel was attacked by the AEF less for its military value than for its psychological and political significance. The operation was part of the back-drop, on the field of battle, to that dominance which President Wilson was about to exert in the field of Allied diplomacy. A contemporary cartoon by the Dutch artist Louis Raemakers about the first tentative German peace moves expressed the connection perfectly. Wilson, a swaggering cowboy, is shown fingering his gun holster in front of a glowering Kaiser with a lowered sabre. Cries the presidential gunman: 'You want to sheathe the sword. I have only just begun to draw it!'

6

The 'Gardeners'' Harvest

IT WAS CLEMENCEAU who dubbed them 'the gardeners of Salonika' when he heard that the expeditionary force in Greek Macedonia spent so much of its spare time – of which it usually had more than enough – just digging itself in. The French Prime Minister's sarcasm matched perfectly the disdainful neglect of Paris and, for that matter, of London for the Balkan theatre. Indeed, the grandiloquently named 'Allied Armies in the Orient' are best thought of as a swarm of beached crusaders whose mission, for three years, was ridiculed in their home countries and often doubted by the men themselves. The fact that this Cinderella among expeditions finally got to the ball in spectacular style just before midnight barely compensated for all the bitterness and frustration that had gone before.

Their presence on the coastline of the Aegean Sea stemmed, of course, from the alliance with Serbia, whom Austria-Hungary immediately attacked at the outbreak of war as the presumed instigator of the Sarajevo murders. Geographically, Serbia was a most awkward ally to have. She was surrounded on all sides by enemy or neutral states and the only feasible access, from the south, was hampered by some of the fiercest mountains and poorest communications to be found anywhere on the continent of Europe. For the first fourteen months of the war France and England, absorbed and obsessed by the gigantic struggle on the Western Front, left the Serbs to cope as best they could with the invaders. That best proved good enough until, in the autumn of 1915, the odds against isolated Serbia began to multiply. Bulgaria entered the war against them, determined to get back the whole of the disputed Macedonian province which she had conquered, briefly occupied, and then lost in the Balkan Wars which erupted just before the Great War itself. Then the Germans, who had long been irritated by the poor military showing displayed by their Austrian allies, mounted a new invasion of Serbia alongside these new Bulgarian partners. It was a desperate outlook for the Serbs. Against their 194 remaining battalions – all of them by now exhausted and depleted – was raised a fresh army of 341 battalions, of which 111 were German and 177 Bulgarian.

The Entente powers had to respond if the entire Balkan peninsula were not to be lost to them. Fortunately they had some troops available only two hundred miles away, though in the most dismal of military settings. The Gallipoli campaign against the Turks had by now almost run its disastrous course, and for the invaders the evacuation of the Anglo-French invasion force was only a matter of time. The end of one tragedy was thus fused into the launching of another desperate venture. On 5 October 1915 two troop transports dropped anchor off Salonika with elements of the 10th British and 156th French divisions on board. Veterans both of the Dardanelles fighting, they seemed to bring something of the doom-laden confusion of that campaign with them as they stepped on this sullenly neutral Greek soil:* the British advance guard, for example, was clad in a mixture of thick winter great-coats and tropical drill shorts. It was not an auspicious beginning; and neither was their first sortie up the Vardar Valley into the mountains to help their beleaguered Serbian allies. Before Christmas all of Serbia was in enemy hands and the Orient Army, some two hundred thousand strong, was driven back to Salonika to start its digging. By the New Year a seventy-five mile arc of defence works had been thrown up around the port. With them had come the trenches and barbed wire of Flanders.

Salonika itself was one of the strangest of all the temporary military capitals which the Great War threw up. The city, named after a sister of Alexander the Great, was no stranger to foreign occupation. Indeed it had known little else since its foundation in 315 BC. Once capital of the Roman province of Macedonia it had first been seized and plundered in turn by Avars, Bulgars and Normans; then held by Byzantium for close on two hundred years; next taken by the Turks after a terrible massacre in 1430 and

* Greece only entered the war on the Allied side in June 1917.

absorbed into the Ottoman empire until being finally annexed with southern Macedonia to the Kingdom of Greece only three years before the Great War began. Garish, strident, treacherous, opportunist and overcrowded, the city bore traces of all those cultures though, curiously enough, the biggest single element in its population – sixty thousand Spanish Jews who still spoke a bastard Spanish dialect – belonged to none of them.

Once their ranks were complete the new military garrison of Salonika fully lived up to those polyglot surroundings. Six armies were represented: British, French, Serb, Italian, plus a few Tsarist Russians and the Greek soldiers of the reluctant host country. The Italian who was made liaison officer to them all commented:

> 'Never in any other city did one see such a collection of different uniforms as at Salonika ... British khaki, Highland kilts, French *bleu horizon*, Italian *grigioverde*, the Serbs in grey, the Greeks in uniforms combining features of all the others, Russians who invented their own and colonials of various kinds – coal-black Sudanese, swarthy Algerians, yellow Tonkinese and Annamites, dignified Indians in imposing turbans.'

Occupiers and occupied thus somehow matched each other, different sides of the same multi-national coin. Salonika cannot have been very impressed by the Army of the Orient, at least not in its formative stages, when the soldiers arrived short of everything from nose-bags for their mules to tent-pegs for themselves. And the first sight of the city cannot have been inspiring to the disembarking troops. As one modern historian of the campaign aptly put it: 'To the Frenchmen ... it had all the appearance of a Balkan Marseilles. To the men of British regiments, it was a second-rate Port Said with Alexandrine undertones, neither in Europe nor in Asia, but of both.'

The first of the three French Commanders-in-Chief appointed to lead the Salonika army might have been hand-picked for this sleazy city. The white-haired General Sarrail was to prove, despite his affable manner and good military bearing, a positive disaster at his job. He rarely went to the front, and then to pin on medals

The Balkans: September to November 1918

rather than conduct operations; and his life in Salonika seemed devoted in equal measure to indulging in political intrigue, promoting French commercial interests, and pursuing a string of love affairs. One of his mistresses, a Russian noblewoman who was herself suspected of espionage, summed the man up, after his departure, with the acid comment: 'It has been stated that when General Sarrail was here, it was I who commanded the *Armée d'Orient*. Unfortunately, this was untrue; if I had commanded it, far fewer *bêtises* would have been committed.'* This early setting was more music-hall than martial – rather like a non-stop performance of *The Chocolate Soldier*, the comic opera whose scene is set in the Serbo-Bulgarian war of 1885 and which was, in fact, staged more than once for the Salonika garrison.

As for living conditions, these became fairly tolerable in time, despite the extremes of the temperature, the notorious 'Vardar wind' which blew for days on end, and the high disease rate. A British nurse was thus pitching it rather high when she wrote home from the Salonika hospital:

> 'The men out here have the mud of Flanders, the cold of France, the heat of the tropics and nothing to look forward to. Rest out of the line does not mean a comfy billet in a village; it means only a few bell-tents (if they are lucky) still being potted at and ever in sight of the Bulgars who command the high ground. No concert parties ever come our way from Blighty; the only concerts are those the men get up. And so they camp out on those hills, with malaria swamps all round, sand-fly fever, and ever the dread of dysentery . . .'

The strong British contingent met the challenge to morale in characteristic style by developing amateur entertainments and regimental sports on a scale unheard of on any active front. It was puzzling that the enemy rarely interfered with their football

---

* The irrepressible Sarrail finally settled down into marriage with a French Red Cross nurse, but even caused a scandal with his entry into domesticity. It was a rule that no Allied officer of any rank could have his wife with him in Macedonia. The C-in-C ignored the rule and installed his new bride in his villa.

matches and horse-jumping shows even when these were held in forward areas. British officers gratefully put this down to the fair play instincts of 'Johnny Bulgar'. They ought, in fact, to have attributed it to the astuteness of enemy intelligence. Bulgarian army papers captured after the war revealed orders that no major sporting event on the other side of the lines was to be interfered with as they yielded such valuable information. For days in advance the organizers would sit on the telephone happily chatting to units throughout the Salonika enclave who would be taking part, and whenever these conversations could be tapped an excellent picture of the British order of battle emerged.

But what no amount of troop concert parties and football tournaments could dispel (or, as in the case of the French officers at their Cercle Militaire club, excellent food and wine) was the sense of boredom and isolation. The worst of all the evils listed in that British nurse's letter was the feeling that there was 'nothing to look forward to'. The gloom was well-founded. In the long battle between the 'Easterners' and the 'Westerners' of the Entente – those who advocated striking at the weaker members of the enemy camp by substituting a war of movement for the horrendous rigidity of Flanders, and those who championed the undiluted priority of the French front – the 'Westerners' always held the strong upper hand, especially after the Gallipoli débâcle against the Turks. Lloyd George, the most influential as well as the most impassioned of the 'Easterners', could appreciate why Clemenceau, his opposite number in Paris and nearly all the French Generals, opposed him on this. For them Germany was not only the enemy *par excellence*; she was also the enemy at their gates. But the impatient and imaginative Celt could not understand why so many of his own ministers and military commanders – with all the imperial traditions of global warfare behind them – should echo the French view. Surely, their argument that victory, however costly, could only come in the West because Germany would fight on whatever happened to her satellites, weighed lighter in the scales of war than the blunt fact that defensive weapons reigned supreme on the French front, thus apparently ruling out any prospect of a decisive breakthrough there? Apart from most of his own

Commonwealth Prime Ministers, Lloyd George could convert few of his colleagues with his eloquence.

But then, through one of the many ironies of this war, it was a crisis on the Western Front which gave the 'Easterners' their decisive impetus by unexpectedly furnishing the Orient Army with the finest leader it or any other force could have wished for to tackle its ordained task. On the evening of 17 June 1918 Louis Félix Marie François Franchet d'Espèrey landed at Salonika to take over command. Then aged fifty-eight, he was heading for an astonishing climax to an already unusual career; and the Orient Army was to go all the way with him.

Few top appointments can have been made in a more haphazard way. As summer came, the second round of the 'Emperor's Battle' was reaching its climax on the Western Front and the outlook for the Entente powers was grim, with the French armies broken and reeling back on their capital. Clemenceau, running through his army list for commanders to meet the crisis, soon stopped at the name of General Guillaumat who, six months before, had been sent out to Salonika to replace the woefully unsatisfactory Sarrail.* Guillaumat had been far from idle during his short spell with the Orient Army; but, in the eyes of his Prime Minister, he was just too good an officer to be left languishing in a Macedonian side-show when his own homeland was in danger. On 6 June Clemenceau recalled him to France, initially to defend the capital but later perhaps, if things went from the desperate to the disastrous, to take over the Supreme Command. This was Clemenceau's immediate problem: what should be done about Foch and Pétain, who were ultimately responsible for the French collapse? Deciding that to remove either of them at that juncture would do more harm than good to the nation's morale (and needing anyway a new man in Salonika) the 'Tiger' took even less time to find his man. On the afternoon of that same 6 June General Franchet d'Espèrey, whose Northern Army Group had been

---

* As early as June of 1917 Lloyd George had been pressing for Sarrail's removal and had taken the extreme step of writing to the then French Prime Minister, M. Ribot, about the number of reports 'which reflect very gravely on the fitness of General Sarrail for the command'.

driven back in the overall German advance, was told to hand over his command on the Western Front and take over the Orient Army in Guillamaut's place.

When Clemenceau received d'Espèrey in Paris the following morning he made it clear to the general not only that he was being treated as a political scapegoat but also that he was being handed a military demotion. D'Espèrey's biographer, who describes Clemenceau's attitude at the meeting as 'sarcastic but friendly', says that the general was even told outright that his being sent to Salonika amounted to being 'sent to Limoges'.* When d'Espèrey protested that, after all, he had just been appointed a Commander-in-Chief, Clemenceau dropped his sarcasm and confided:

> 'Yes, yes, you must understand the situation. I know as well as you do who is responsible. But I have had too much trouble in securing a unified command to destroy it without serious reasons. Your Army Group has suffered a severe set-back; I have to calm Parliament down ... Leave as soon as you can and come back and see me before you go ... All will be well.'

A few days later d'Espèrey set out. He had been given no chance to meet Foch who, as Chief of the French general staff, had the overall supervision of the Macedonian operation. Neither had he been presented to the Supreme Allied War Council at Versailles nor told of any of its strategic thinking or political agreements over the Balkans, though these vitally affected his front. He might have been leaving Paris to take over a training division somewhere in southern France rather than to assume command of an inter-national army in the most explosive area of Europe. Yet none of this would have disturbed him unduly, for he had his own ideas about the Balkan theatre, ideas that were cherished and long-standing. That is the unique romance of the appointment. For Clemenceau it was a cynical, almost dismissive exercise in political juggling. For d'Espèrey it was the realization of a dream.

The germs of his dream lay in his travels before the war.

---

* A minor military command for retired or failed officers.

D'Espèrey, in a long and varied career, had had his fair share of postings overseas: Algeria, Tunisia, Indo-China, Morocco and even an assignment with the international force dispatched to Peking in the summer of 1900 to quell the Boxer Rising. But he had also taken every opportunity, private or official, to study at first-hand the Danube Basin, which held a professional as well as a historical fascination for him: there, after all, was the vulnerable southern flank of Germany's vulnerable Habsburg ally in the conflict for which every French officer was being prepared.

For the first two months of the war d'Espèrey had no time to think of anything excepting parrying that first murderous sweep which the German army made through Belgium and northern France towards Paris. As commander of the 1st Corps and then of the Fifth Army* he had proved a tower of confident strength amid all the despair and confusion of the fight to save the capital. When, at the beginning of October, the front seemed to have stabilized, President Poincaré left Paris to thank and encourage his field commanders, and his tour took him inevitably to the headquarters of the 5th Army in Champagne. It was when the President, discussing the overall situation, mentioned the likelihood that Turkey might soon join in the war on the German side that d'Espèrey saw again the mountains and valleys of Macedonia, valleys which led, however awkwardly, up to the Central European plain and the twin capitals of Austria-Hungary. He aired his views, a classical statement of the 'Easterner's' philosophy, and Poincaré was sufficiently interested to ask for a memorandum on the subject.

As a result, on 1 December 1914, a detailed project was handed in at the Elysée Palace for a French expeditionary force some 185,000 men strong to be landed at Salonika, march up the Vardar Valley and join hands with the Serbs (who were, in fact, just in the process of abandoning their capital, Belgrade, to the Austrian army as Poincaré was reading the memorandum). The military crisis in the West made d'Espèrey's paper study of victory in the East look somewhat optimistic, for it lacked nothing in grandeur. The French were to concentrate ('in conformity with our tempera-

* With characteristic aplomb his only comment to Marshal Joffre when offered the promotion in the heat of the battle was: 'The higher one goes, the easier it is.'

ment') on mobile operations during the advance to the Danube, while the Serbs would hold their left flank by clearing the mountains of Bosnia. Once the two armies were united in triumph on the Danube Basin, two possibilities were open to them – either to cross and strike north for Szegedin and Budapest or to keep south of the river and head westwards for Vienna. It was a vision of Napoleonic proportions which must have looked extravagantly remote when viewed from a beleaguered Paris in the first autumn of the war. Yet, before the last autumn of that war was over, the visionary was to enact the greater part of his dream in real life himself.

The man who now landed at the Salonika of his 1914 memorandum can best be described as the aristocratic fireball among Allied Commanders-in-Chief. Like quite a few of the minor nobility of the French provinces d'Espèrey, with his squat frame, close-cropped hair, short neck and bullet head looked, at first sight, less like the lord of the manor than one of the peasants from the fields outside. But the Roman nose and the voice that cut through the worst din of battle left no doubt that here was a man born to give orders, not to receive them. If doggedness was the characteristic of Haig and serenity the mark of Foch, what stamped d'Espèrey above all was his confident bustle. 'A stranger to depression', Poincaré had called him. A British liaison officer who had seen him at work in France wrote:

> 'He moved quickly, almost fiercely, bent arms keeping time like those of a runner with the movement of his legs. His dark eyes were piercing, his voice sharp, his diction precise ... He kept all in place by his manner. Never did he solicit or permit advice or suggestions, which indeed no-one would have dared to offer. He was a genuine commander ...'

Another liaison officer – the Italian who now had to deal with him constantly in Macedonia – gave a more subtle portrait:

> 'When he was in a good humour he was gay, *bon camarade*, and one could tell or ask him anything, whereas when something had gone amiss, he was irritable and difficult to

deal with ... But as a strategist he showed qualities of the highest rank ...'

Those were the qualities d'Espèrey started to display from the moment he stepped ashore.

Locked in the safes of his new headquarters were all manner of plans for attack and withdrawal which the Orient Army had worked out, and in some cases tried to implement, over the past three years. The withdrawal plans could now be burnt as far as d'Espèrey was concerned. As for the offensive projects, he dismissed the most ambitious on the files because it was also the most obvious – a strike up the Vardar Valley which the enemy would always be half-expecting, since this was the main north-south road and rail artery of the entire front. But his immediate predecessor Guillaumat – who had shown more initiative in his six months of command than Sarrail had mustered in more than two years – had been mulling over a more exciting idea: to concentrate a great mass of men in a mountainous sector so savage that even the chamois trod there with caution, and then use this as the seemingly impossible launching-pad for the main attack.

The idea owed much to the Chief-of-Staff of his Serbian allies, Jivoïne Misić, whose battle headquarters were at Yelak, a wooded basin high up in the Moglena Massif, eighty-five miles from Salonika on the north-western arc of its forward defences. The Serbs had stormed those heights in the autumn of 1916 and had sat there defiantly ever since. It was as close as they could get to that beloved homeland from which the combined armies of Germany, Austria and Bulgaria had driven them. Guillaumat had already launched, just before his recall, a highly successful local offensive in similar mountain country, attacking along a seven and a half mile sector of the Skra di Legen front, where more than a mile of ground had been won and two thousand prisoners taken. But could not other peaks of the area now be used to leap forward a hundred miles, not just one; to liberate Serbia; and knock Bulgaria out of the war altogether? The three leaders who, on 29 June, met at Yelak – d'Espèrey, Misić, and his commander, the exiled Serbian Prince-Regent Alexander – were all fired by the same thought, the two Serbs because it was the shortest way home, the Frenchman because it was the most difficult. From an observation post hollowed out of the rock 7,500 feet up, they looked across at the enemy's mountain line which, if it could only be smashed, would open the way to the Upper Vardar Valley and so both turn his defences and imperil his retreat.

We are fortunate that, among his French troops, d'Espèrey numbered an infantry sergeant who was a university professor in private life and who, as his Commander-in-Chief once said, 'really had eyes to see with'. Looking at the terrain ahead the sergeant saw 'a series of forbidding crests, strange towers of stone and saw-toothed shapes ranged one behind the other right up to the far horizon'. And of its dark, forbidding atmosphere he wrote: '*C'est un pays pour faire bigorner le monde, et jouer cache-cache avec les noirs.*'

More specifically, the military chiefs crouched in their stone eyrie on the afternoon of 29 June took stock of the four giant granite pillars of the Bulgarian defence system ahead, each of which would have to be turned or toppled if the Allied attack were to succeed: in the foreground the Sokol and Vetrenik peaks with the jagged ridge of the Dobropolje running between them; and, a few miles behind, the summit of Kuchkov Kamen which crowned the enemy's second line of resistance. Their heights ranged from 5,000 to 6,000 feet, and their flanks were laced with little more than goat-tracks. It looked, at first sight, a stronger natural barrier than anything man made out of barbed wire and pill-boxes along the Western Front d'Espèrey knew so well. Moreover, this was unfamiliar territory, despite all his pre-war travels around the Balkans, while the men at his side were unknown partners. A key to the problem, as he had instantly appreciated, was whether enough heavy artillery could be dragged up and massed in the Moglena jumping-off area so that the assault could be preceded by the obligatory barrage. Special roads would have to be built and vast exertions of mule- and man-power expended on the task. He slept on it down at Trelak and in the morning told the delighted Serbs that the attack was on.

D'Espèrey had told the staff officers who had greeted him at the quayside of Salonika that he would expect them to show 'ferocious energy', and he now led the way himself. By 6 July, a week after his visit to the mountains and less than three weeks after taking over command, his outline plan was ready. A new task force, the so-called 'Central Franco-Serbian Group', was to be formed for the main blow-up at Moglena, consisting of all four Serbian divisions with two French divisions placed under Serbian command. They were to make the decisive breakthrough, and, once past the high granite barrier, the six formations, with Italians on their left and more French on their right, would all fan out, heading for Prilep to the north and Gradsko and Veles on the Vardar River to the north-east. Beyond those targets d'Espèrey certainly dreamed, but did not as yet dare to think.

The main supporting effort was to be made by the British force under General Milne* which held the sector around Lake Doiran east of the Vardar Valley. That was where the enemy expected the attack and where he had posted some of his best troops. Milne's job was to encourage him in that belief and so prevent those troops being switched as reinforcements across the Vardar. It was an honourable but thankless task, promising much bloodshed and few laurels, for the mountains ahead of Lake Doiran had already taken a heavy toll of British lives.

Having settled matters with his subordinates in Salonika, d'Espèrey now had to clear the lines with his political and military masters in Paris and London. This proved almost as arduous as scrambling up the Moglena, for the summer of 1918 saw one of the last bitter rounds in the four-year-old struggle between the 'Easterners' and 'Westerners' of Allied strategy. D'Espèrey could see why the Salonika army had to take a back seat while any crisis was raging on the Western Front, and even be bled of troops – as it was during June – to feed that battlefield. He could therefore understand, even if he did not welcome, the instructions which Clemenceau had sent him on 23 June, calling for a continuation of limited thrusts until, at some unspecified date in the future, the Orient Army was to be allowed to lash out in earnest. But his patience got

---

* Under the somewhat complicated arrangements by which the Army of the Orient worked, Milne had supreme authority in his own command but was under the control of the French C-in-C for any joint operations.

shorter as July passed by, with American reinforcements flooding into France all the time and the outlook then looking distinctly rosier, yet still no agreement loomed in sight for his own offensive.

Not until after the tide had turned in the West, with Foch's counter-offensive from the Marne, was d'Espèrey given approval in principle from Paris on 3 August to launch a major attack; and even then the British withheld their blessing for another month, starving Milne of the extra ammunition and supplies he was pleading for as they did so. Finally, on 4 September, Lloyd George, who had been temporarily straying from his old 'Easterner' philosophy, got into his stride and carried his reluctant general staff with him. (Guillaumat had done the Salonika army one last supreme service by coming over to the Downing Street debate in person to plead their cause.) At last, on 10 September, after more than two months of long-range tussling, d'Espèrey received direct clearance from Clemenceau to commence operations 'when judged appropriate'. He left his masters little time to change their minds. The moment he fixed as 'appropriate' was only five days later.

D'Espèrey could look forward to his 'J-Jour' or D-Day' with well-founded confidence. The 29 divisions of his Orient Army gave a total of 574,000 men, providing him with a front-line rifle strength of 157,000. Though the Germans, Bulgarians and Austrians who faced him were somewhat larger on both counts, on that critical central sector where he was to deal the surprise blow on which all depended he led in numbers by two or three to one.* Moreover, his two hundred aeroplanes, which were soon to play such an unexpected star role, came to more than twice the size of the enemy's airforce; and he was ahead too in both machine-guns and artillery. What was even more important, that artillery was now where he wanted it. Batteries of heavy 155 and 105 mm guns had been brought forward on approach roads built by a conscript labour force of all nationalities (including prisoners of war) and the great weapons with their ammunition had then been heaved up by tractor to heights approaching 8,000 feet, from where they domi-

---

* 45,000 French; 40,000 Greeks (thrown into the Allied scales after Greece abandoned its neutrality); 32,000 British; 30,000 Serbs and 10,000 Italians were the national components.

nated even the loftiest emplacements ahead. The men who were to go in right behind the shells knew what this could mean for them. Just before the attack, when the air was ringing with shouts of 'Navred' or 'Forward!', the French sergeant-diarist wrote:

> 'Some old Serbian soldiers came to look at the guns, which they gazed at respectfully and at length. One of them fervently kissed the barrel of a 120 mm ... Another called out "God bless you, and *au revoir* in Serbia!"'

Such was the mood in d'Espèrey's camp, now that *le grand farniente de Salonika* was coming to an end at last. What of his opponent, the German General von Scholtz, a veteran of Tannenberg, who now commanded the Army Group which bore his name, based sixty miles to the north on Skopje? Numbers, as we have seen, need not have troubled him. So far as quality went the forces under his command included a stiffening of German units mixed in with the Bulgarian mass, and one army, the Eleventh, whose commander, General von Steuben, and both corps staffs, were also German. In addition there were some ten Austro-Hungarian battalions on the extreme right of Scholtz's a hundred and thirty mile front. His main concern was the morale of the Bulgarian First Army under General Nerezov which held the Vardar Valley itself, facing the British across Lake Doiran. Would its three divisions, commanded and staffed entirely by Bulgarian officers, stand firm when the test came?* Above all, what would happen back in their capital, Sofia, where the ruler, King Ferdinand, had been rumoured for months past to be ogling at the Entente behind his allies' backs?

'Foxy Ferdinand', as he had been dubbed by Edwardian Europe, was, without doubt, one of the most preposterous of all those Coburgs† who, during the nineteenth century, had married or lobbyed their way on to the steps of foreign thrones. A slippery,

---

* It was hardly an inspiration to the Bulgarian army that their Commander-in-Chief, General Jekov, had chosen this moment to repair to the safety of an ear-clinic in Vienna for a prolonged cure; he had been replaced by General Todorov.
† So many indeed that Bismarck could refer sarcastically to the tiny German state as 'the stud-farm of Europe'.

vainglorious homosexual, he was as far removed as could be imagined on all accounts from his kinsman Albert of Saxe-Coburg-Gotha, whose memory was still respected in England as Queen Victoria's painstaking Consort. It was from London that, during that September crisis of 1918, the most blistering personal attack on Ferdinand came. An Englishman, who had known the Bulgarian ruler before the war, wrote:

> 'He combines the brains and vices of the worst type of Italian *condottiere* of the Middle Ages without the one redeeming virtue of personal courage which they usually possessed.'

That was pitching it a bit high. It is true that he wore a protective vest whenever moving among these wild subjects he had been imported to rule over in 1887; but Balkan thrones being as vulnerable as they notoriously were to the assassin's bomb or bullet, the precaution could be put down as much to prudence as to cowardice. There were two ways to survive as a German princeling in Sofia. One was to be a warrior-king like his predecessor, Alexander of Battenberg (the handsome 'Sandro' so beloved of Queen Victoria). But Ferdinand, a notable botanist, was more at home with the butterfly net than the sword. The other – and the only course for which this dandified, devious but highly intelligent man was suited – was to juggle for survival on the diplomatic field rather than fight for it in battle. In that capacity the shiftiness in his nature matched the needs of the day, for throughout the summer of 1918, Bulgaria had once again been forced to weigh loyalty against self-interest.

On the surface both the king and his ministers continued to be all smiles and fraternal embraces towards Germany. A telegram from Sofia to Berlin on the occasion of the fourth anniversary of the war, for example, had conveyed the 'warmest wishes and blessings of a loyal ally' and had drawn 'sublime confidence from three years of true brotherhood of arms'. Shortly after that message was sent the Bulgarian ruler had gone to Germany to assure the Kaiser in person of his unswerving fidelity. If William II was taken in by these protestations it would have been against the better knowledge and judgement of his own Intelligence staff. Peace-feelers from Bulgarian Opposition spokesmen had been extended westwards for months past and, as the United States had not declared war on either Bulgaria or Turkey, it was American diplomatic missions in Europe – especially those in Berne and Copenhagen – which offered the best channels. Mr Murphy, the American Chargé d'Affaires in Sofia, was also busy spreading both blandishments and bribes inside Bulgaria; and his efforts were intensified after June 1918, when Ferdinand installed a new and allegedly pro-Western government in power, headed by the Democratic Party leader, Alexander Malinov. In London, where a Bulgarophil sentiment was nourished by long memories of Turkish oppression, the Foreign Minister, Mr Balfour, was also full of ideas for weaning Bulgaria away from the enemy camp. At one point he even floated the extravagant suggestion of giving her Constantinople in exchange for those Macedonian lands she had seized by force in 1915 and would ultimately have to disgorge again to Serbia and Greece.

Yet Bulgaria's unreliability as an ally stemmed, paradoxically, from the fact that – with that misplaced serenity which is at the core of so much fanaticism – she was convinced she would never have to give Macedonia up. The last of President Wilson's famous Fourteen Points (which had been widely distributed by Mr Murphy) had, after all, pledged that all 'well-defined national elements shall be given the utmost satisfaction', provided this did not introduce new elements of antagonism, or perpetuate old ones. To the average Bulgarian that meant Macedonia was his for keeps, and as that was absolutely all he had entered the war for, why fight on any longer?

On top of that came the ever-growing friction with the German army, which treated Bulgaria rather like a colony, and plain weariness with fighting as such: Bulgaria's casualties in her various wars from 1912 onwards had killed four per cent of her population and crippled another ten per cent, a staggering cost even for such a fatalistic peasant people. But whatever his peasants thought 'Foxy Ferdinand' was still the key who alone could spring open or close the lock of Bulgaria's loyalty. His allies staked much on the dynastic appeal of fellow sovereigns of the same blood. That was why, in the mid-summer of 1918, King Ludwig III of Bavaria (first cousin of the compulsive castle-builder, 'Mad Ludwig') and King Frederick Augustus of Saxony paid three visits between them to their Coburg colleague. The Saxon ruler was still in Sofia when, on 14 September, d'Espèrey's heavy guns boomed out in the mountains above Moglena to sound the Allied advance.

The bombardment would have been a fairly routine headache for a single defending division to endure in France. But the five hundred French guns which opened up at 8 a.m. that morning against the six-mile sector of the Dobropolje, and boomed on until nightfall with only one half-hour pause for the barrels to cool, were a concentrated barrage the like of which the mountains of Macedonia had never felt. At dawn on the 15th, with the guns now quiet behind them, the French and Serbian infantry went in. The enemy positions on the Dobropolje pyramid itself were cleared by the French 122nd Division after only two hours of fighting, with a moderate loss to the attackers of seven hundred men. But it had taken flame-throwers to roast the last Bulgarian machine-gunner out of his rocky nest, and this initially tough resistance was a good example of what was to come during the next forty-eight hours. Of those other key peaks which the Orient Army had to storm, the Vetrenik was not taken by the Serbs until the afternoon, and the Sokol held out until nightfall. The Serbs may have been fighting like heroes to re-cross the old border of their country; but the Bulgars seemed no less determined to cling on to 'their' Macedonia, and both were at home in those mountains. It was the same story the next day when Misic, having moved his men stealthily forward throughout the night, attacked the Kozyak ridge six miles further north. It looked to begin with as though all von Scholtz's misgivings were unfounded.

Then, suddenly, as though the backbone had been ripped clean out of a fighting salmon, the Bulgarian line sagged and gave way. First, they gave up to Kozyak, despite the arrival of a good quality German Saxon Jaeger battalion to stiffen them. Then, with that second-line citadel fallen, the commander of the Bulgarian 2nd Division seemingly panicked and withdrew precipitately to the third line of defence, imperilling all formations on his flanks. More ominously still, mutinies broke out in some units of the 3rd Bulgarian Division. Von Scholtz was forced to order a general withdrawal, and just as he was wondering, on the morning of the 18th, whether he had not been fooled after all and whether this mad surge across the central mountains was not, in fact, a calculated thrust to the Vardar, the British on his left flank played their appointed role by fooling him a little longer.

General Milne's code message to his divisions to start their attack from Lake Doiran – '508 bottles of beer will be sent to you' – was quite in keeping with that zany concert-party mood which the British had managed to preserve amid all the tedium and mosquito bites of Salonika. But it was to be the only cheerful thing about the disastrous operation which now began. The targets of Milne's Anglo–Greek force – three hills known as P (or 'Pip') Ridge, the Grand Couronne and the Petit Couronne, which reared above the western shore of the lake – were already familiar names, each full of bitter memories for the Salonika army. The French had tried in vain to storm them in 1916; British troops had followed up with two more assaults a year later, and those had also collapsed, at a cost of five thousand casualties. Fourteen out of the twenty-two battalions which had failed in 1917 were going forward again now, and the hundreds of old hands in their ranks had no illusions as to what faced them. Those three hills were known to be among the strongest defensive positions along the entire front and were held by the toughest and most ably-led soldiers of the Bulgarian army.

Any evil forebodings that the attackers felt as, in obedience to that droll signal, they went in at eight minutes past five on the pre-dawn gloom of 18 September, proved more than justified. After two days of murderous fighting General Milne's men were left with only the limited ground they overran in the first hours of the attack, the Petit Couronne and the ghost town of Doiran itself which it overlooked. The Bulgarians remained masters of the other two hills, and their machine-guns had meanwhile taken a dreadful toll of the attackers. The 7th South Wales Borderers, for example, who, on the first day, had fought their way up to sparse scrub just below the summit of the Grand Couronne, finally pulled back with only one wounded officer and fifty-five men left alive out of the whole battalion.* The Scottish Brigade, which took over the assault from the Welsh the following day, got no further and suffered almost as much, one of its battalions losing seventy-five per cent of its strength in casualties, and the other two each being cut down by half.

When the attacks were abandoned and the dismal tally made, it was found that the British alone had lost 3,871 men, killed, wounded and missing in the two days' fighting. Like the artillery barrage which had opened d'Espèrey's offensive, that was modest compared with the daily slaughter that took place on the Western Front. But it was savage by Balkan standards, and came to more than twice the total losses suffered by the French and Serbs in their assault. What made the higher price so hard to accept was that, unlike their allies on the central sector, General Milne's men had failed to take their most important objectives. Endless explanations and excuses were produced: his battalions were far below strength; many were weakened by influenza and malaria; the supply position was inadequate; there had been muddles with Greek units during the advance; there were too few artillery shells for a proper barrage; some of the gas shells which were fired had hampered or knocked out the attackers themselves, and so on. All factors may have played a part, and some certainly did. But one cannot help feeling also that, for all the great valour which the British troops displayed, they just did not possess that extra cutting edge of savage fanaticism for the task which had driven their Serbian comrades to the top of the Vetrenik, the Sokol and the Kozyak. After all, none of those Macedonian mountain ridges spelt a return home to the English, Welsh or Scots.

Very fortunately for their morale the British were only given forty-eight hours to lick their wounds and count their losses. On

---

* Its CO, Lieutenant-Colonel Dan Burges, was badly wounded three times in the attack and was carried into a Bulgarian dug-out behind the hill where he was attended to by the enemy. He was recovered during the Allied advance, and awarded the Victoria Cross to add to his DSO. He was more fortunate than other fellow-officers of his rank. Two battalion commanders of the British 66th Brigade, for example, were killed at the head of their troops.

the morning of 21 September Major F. A. Bates, commanding 47 Squadron of the RAF, sent up two of his De Havilland planes to reconnoitre the valleys behind the Doiran front. They reported back that a defile west of the town of Rabrovo was jammed with military transports, with hundreds of lorries and horse-drawn carts queueing to join the stream already on the road. Rabrovo was two miles to the rear of Dedeli, where the Bulgarian First Army had always had its headquarters. This could only mean that the whole army was now withdrawing, and other pilots confirmed a similar picture on every other route leading north. When British and Greek patrols picked their way gingerly that night up to the summits of 'Pip Ridge' and the Grand Couronne they found only deserted defence-works and the unburied bodies of the hundreds of men who had fallen there on both sides earlier in the week. It was a chastening way to reach their targets.

What had happened was that, two days before, at a top-level conference convened by the 11th Army commander, General von Steuben, at his headquarters in Prilep, the Germans and their allies had held a lively debate as to what they should do next. Todorov, the newly-appointed Bulgarian Commander-in-Chief, was so buoyed up by the defeat his men had just inflicted on the British above Lake Doiran that he even proposed an all-out offensive, to sweep the Allied Army of the Orient right back into the sea. Von Steuben was horrified at such over-sanguine folly and, like his Army Group commander, was increasingly worried by that sharp, strong wedge which the French and Serbs were still driving into the central sector. Realizing too late that this might well be the main threat, von Steuben persuaded his Bulgarian colleague to join in a general withdrawal, arguing that d'Espèrey would waste himself in the mountains of Serbia just as Napoleon had spent himself in the steppes of Russia. Not surprisingly, the German had won the argument.

Von Steuben may have been thinking soundly according to his Prussian text-books. But in that reality of war which supersedes all theory, he had failed at Prilep to allow for three things. The first was the Sixteenth Wing of the British Air Force with its advanced base at Janesh aerodrome. The second was d'Espèrey's French

Colonial Brigade of Moroccan cavalry waiting patiently back at Florina for its hour to come. The third was the phenomenal endurance of the Serbian foot-slogger now to be displayed along the entire battlefield.

The British planes not only signalled the start of the enemy withdrawal. They then helped to convert what was intended to be an orderly retreat into a chaotic rout. As a still unborn Israeli airforce was to discover in a great desert battle half a century later, a handful of bombs which block a key mountain pass can do more damage than hundreds dropped on the fleeing enemy in open country. When, as in this case, the retreating force consisted largely of peasant-soldiers still unaccustomed to air attack, and encumbered with mule-, horse- and even ox-drawn transports, the impact was lethal.

'Fighter planes, like monstrous birds of prey, plunged down on the enemy at full throttle, as though drawn towards the earth by the streak of their machine-guns,' wrote our literary French NCO of a similar action. In more prosaic language, the British official air historian of the campaign describes the scene at the narrow Kosturino Pass, where the cruising reconnaissance plane, a De Havilland 9 fitted with a powerful wireless, had reported long columns of vehicles, guns and men struggling northwards. In one sortie alone, twenty-five RAF machines dropped five thousand pounds of bombs and sprayed twelve thousand rounds of machine-gun bullets on the target, an enormous concentration for a secondary front of 1918. 'The defile was choked with helpless troops. From the air the road looked a continuous line of dots, like an enormous trek of ants.' Other accounts describe how the Bulgarians at first tried to clear the pass by lifting the smashed wagons off the road and hurling them down the ravine; but then, as the British planes returned again and again, many of the enemy simply fled the death-trap, leaving guns, stores and dead comrades behind, and took to the relative safety of the mountain tracks.

It was 47 Squadron which had done the damage, and its intelligence officer, inspecting the scene a few days later, reported finding three hundred smashed transport wagons in a single section of the pass, horses and oxen dead beside them as well as 'a vast number of pack animals' lying at the foot of the ravine. In the nearest hospital, at Rabrovo, 'more than seven hundred human bodies had been collected for burial'. There were similar scenes of havoc at the Kryesna Pass, through which the Struma River flows down from Sofia. There six pilots of the squadron dropped forty-four bombs on a Bulgarian convoy in one attack, half of which exploded in the middle of the column, blowing some vehicles clean off the road. Machine-gunning from heights as low as twenty feet completed the carnage. And, all this time, there was no retort at all from the eighty planes of the enemy's airforce, which had been worn away into immobility by earlier engagements. It was all a far cry from February 1917 when Baron Richthofen himself had brought his famous 'Flying Circus' down from France to the Salonika front, and German planes had dominated the Macedonian skies for weeks on end.

If those RAF raids, which had pulverized the Bulgarian First Army, were the first such application of air power ever seen in the Balkans, the blow now unleashed across the other side of the Vardar against the German Eleventh Army represented the last great cavalry operation of the entire war.* Once it was clear that the Bulgarians were scrambling for home d'Espèrey issued a general Order of the Day to all his forces calling for 'a ceaseless and resolute pursuit'. The hour of the cavalry, he declared, had come, to drive through the ragged enemy lines and open up the way for the advancing infantry. The main task force for this, held in readiness back at the Allied start-line, was the 'Jouinot-Gambetta Brigade' of Spahis and Chasseurs d'Afrique, commanded by a nephew of the great Leon Gambetta, hero of the Paris Siege of 1870. The brigade moved off to take up the chase on 22 September. Riding day and night (the men dismounting to lead their horses up the mountain tracks), with hardly any sleep and even less food, the advance guard were in Prilep, twenty-five miles inside Serbia, by the following afternoon. Two days after that, together with the Franco–Serb force which was advancing on their right directly up the Vardar Valley, they stormed the town of Gradsko after tough resistance by a German and Bulgarian rear-

* By a few days only; see Chapter 7.

guard. Its capture meant that the key to Macedonia's primitive road and rail communications was now in Allied hands. Moreover von Scholtz's forces were now split in two, his German Eleventh Army, which was still resisting, being separated from whatever was left of the Bulgarian First Army that was either willing or able to fight on.

The infantry, and especially the Serbs, had performed even greater feats of endurance, for they had done everything on their feet. Their supply system for the advance was grimly simple: they carried no food with them at all, just ammunition, relying on whatever the impoverished peasantry of their homeland could provide. As a result many who had set out as bronzed fighting men ended up as walking wraiths, mahogany turning into wax. But they went on walking, out-distancing not only the French horsemen but even the British ration-lorries. Such fanaticism was the answer to the puzzled comment Hindenburg made later: 'Without rest, it seemed impossible for the enemy to bring up strong forces forward to Skopje and the frontiers of Old Bulgaria. How would he overcome the problems of supply, for we had completely destroyed the railways and roads?' What the Germans could not destroy was the Serbian spirit.

On 26 September 1918 the road to Skopje, the second largest town of Serbia, and even to the capital, Belgrade, two hundred and fifty miles further north, seemed feasible in military terms. That same morning it became wide open as politics momentarily took over. 'Foxy Ferdinand' decided he had had enough; or rather, his ministers and his people had decided for him.

The pressure, from Bulgarian generals and politicians alike, to end the war had been growing ever since the Allied offensive began. As early as 16 September, when the attackers had only made a dent in one sector of the line, General Lukov, commander of the Second Army, asked Sofia for permission to put out peace feelers. (Lukov, a former Bulgarian military attaché in Paris, was credited with pro-Entente sympathies.) The King's reply to that somewhat premature request was to tell the general to go out and die defending his present positions – instructions which were duly ignored. On 21 September, when the main Bulgarian force was in full retreat, Ferdinand, accompanied by his son, Crown Prince Boris, and General von Scholtz, travelled to the battle area together to try and talk the Bulgarian First Army into putting up a fight. That was a pretty hopeless task from the start, and the fact that the royal train was bombarded by Allied planes as it arrived did nothing to help.

By then war-weariness or outright mutiny among the troops in Serbia was reflected and heightened by a growing upheaval at home. On 23 and 24 September those harbingers of red revolutions, local Soviets, sprang into life in three Bulgarian provincial towns; the next day the unrest struck at one of the nerve centres of the war. A large band of deserters from the Dobropolje front arrived at Kustendil, seat of the Bulgarian army's Supreme Headquarters, and pillaged the town. As the marauders commandeered trains to take them home, scandalized and petrified staff officers fled to what they hoped was the greater security of the capital.

Yet Sofia was also coming apart at the seams. By then, Ludendorff at his own Spa headquarters on the other side of Europe realized that a major political and strategic crisis was looming up in Bulgaria, with an ally on the brink of collapse and the entire south-eastern flank of the Austrian and German Empires threatened with exposure. He did what he could to stem the tide. Nine German and Austrian divisions were rushed from all over Europe to the Balkan Peninsula including, from the Western Front itself, the crack Alpine Corps with its mountain equipment. 'We are coming to help and save you with every man available,' Ludendorff signalled the Bulgarian Commander-in-Chief. To stiffen Ferdinand and secure the capital, General von Steuben, who had great influence with the Bulgarian military, was dispatched to Sofia (where the refugees from Kustendil had set up their new headquarters); and there was even serious talk among the Germans of setting up an outright military dictatorship, headed by General von Scholtz.

But the position could no longer be held. On the morning of 26 September, the day before Steuben arrived in Sofia to greet the first reinforcements of the 217th German Infantry Division from the Crimea, a British regiment deep down in Serbia, the Derbyshire Yeomanry, had some surprising visitors as it was watering its horses in the Struma for the day's advance. A German staff car with a large white flag flapping alongside its bonnet, loomed up in a plume of dust from the direction of Strumica and pulled up in front of the British troops. Out stepped two Bulgarian officers, the senior of whom bore a letter signed by his Commander-in-Chief, General Todorov. This stated that the Government in Sofia, with the consent of the King, had authorized him to seek British mediation with General Franchet d'Espèrey to secure 'a suspension of hostilities for forty-eight hours to allow for the arrival of two delegates authorized by the Bulgarian Government . . . who are coming . . . to arrange conditions for an armistice, and eventually for a peace'.

Whether, in fact, Ferdinand was a willing party to this step has been disputed by three weighty French and German histories which all insist that the Bulgarian Cabinet, thrown into a panic by the sacking of Kustendil, had acted against his wishes. The probability is that, in this as in all other matters, the King was playing both sides against the middle – assuring the German generals in Sofia and his imperial allies in Spa and Baden of his undying loyalty, while at the same time putting out preliminary armistice feelers to the Entente.

In the event it hardly mattered, for 'Foxy Ferdinand' was soon swept on, and then washed away, by the tide of events. D'Espèrey sent the two Bulgarians back saying that, though a temporary cease-fire was out of the question, he was willing to receive properly accredited delegates 'with all suitable courtesy'. When that accommodating reply reached Sofia all German attempts to halt the slide to a separate peace were doomed, as a series of armistice missions set off southward for the Vardar Valley and Salonika. The next vehicle which reached the British lines the following day was flying two flags – one white and the other the Stars and Stripes. Here, we have a British eye-witness account:

'Stopped first by an advance point . . . an enclosed motor car came slowly to the CO and drew up a few yards away . . . Out stepped a gentleman attired in morning dress. Inside the car, sternly and sadly staring ahead, sat a Bulgar general with a leather case . . . So surprised were we to hear the English greeting given by the civilian (American, someone said) that only one camera snapped the scene . . .'

The 'gentleman attired in morning dress' was indeed a civilian, a Mr Walker of the American Legation in Sofia, which had played such a big role in gradually seducing Bulgaria away from the Central Powers alliance. But, much to the chagrin of the Chargé d'Affaires, Mr Walker and his Stars and Stripes, though let through the lines, were to be allowed no part in the armistice negotiations. This was Franchet d'Espèrey's hour as a conqueror, the one he had first dreamed of out loud almost exactly four years before, and he did not propose to share it with a civilian who, in that part of the world, was also a neutral. The diplomat was received politely by d'Espèrey at Salonika, told that there was no need for America's help as mediator, and sent back to Sofia.

By now d'Espèrey had received approval from Clemenceau for all the proposed armistice conditions he had telegraphed to Paris on the 26th. The two illustrious figures who were to be allowed to share the triumph with him – Prince Alexander of Serbia and the Greek Prime Minister Venizelos, who had brought his country into the Entente's camp fifteen months before – had also arrived on the scene. Everything was therefore ready for the agreed enemy plenipotentiaries, General Lukov, the Bulgarian Second Army Commander, and the Finance Minister, M. Liachev; and these duly turned up at Salonika on the afternoon of the 28th, driving in 'a huge German staff car, adorned with the Royal arms of Bulgaria'.

D'Espèrey received them in his headquarters building, which ironically had formerly housed the Consulate-General of Bulgaria. He took advantage of their fatigue and chastened frame of mind (they had been blindfolded by the British with white handkerchiefs for a short stretch of their long journey) to produce immediately a copy of his conditions, which he handed over with the following crisp lecture:

'You marched against us without any cause; you must now pay for that delict. I will not tamper with your government as I do not want a revolution. But as I want to end this war

swiftly and thoroughly, you will furnish me with everything I need for that end.'

It is unlikely that the two plenipotentiaries intended to put up
much of a fight in the first place; certainly, any such thoughts would
have been dispelled as, after receiving that magisterial dressing-
down, they were led away to their food and quarters for the night.

When the two sides met at d'Espèrey's villa with its view
of Salonika Bay and Mount Olympus (the venue emphasizing the
personal nature of triumph) at 9 a.m. the next morning, the
Bulgarians duly accepted every single clause in the conditions
imposed upon them. These were brief and tough. Bulgarian forces
were to be withdrawn immediately from any Greek or Serbian
territory they still held, but were forbidden to take with them
'cattle, wheat or foodstuffs of any kind'. The Bulgarian army was to
be entirely demobilized except for a small force assigned to guard
their eastern frontier and their railways. All arms, ammunition and
vehicles belonging to the demobilized units were to be put in store
under Allied control, and all horses to be handed over. Bulgarian
prisoners were to be employed by the Orient Army until peace was
signed, but without reciprocity for the prisoners they held. Finally,
as regards the mighty allies Bulgaria had just deserted, Germany
and Austria-Hungary were each given four weeks to withdraw their
troops, their diplomatic missions and all their nationals from Bulgarian soil. When the agreement was signed at half past ten that
night (to come into force at noon on the 30th) Bulgaria had been
transformed from an opponent in the field into a mere corridor of
convenience for the Allied advance. The Bulgarian delegates set off
again to Sofia the following day after a shopping excursion in
Salonika during which, the shops reported, they purchased 'large
quantities of female underwear'. So, with a final touch of *The
Chocolate Soldier* the first armistice of the Great War had been
imposed – by the forgotten army of that war.*

What was its impact? As far as the ordinary soldiers of
d'Espèrey's force were concerned, many were too dazed by a
fortnight's non-stop marching and fighting to realize it was all over.

* For text of armistice terms *see* Appendix B.

A sergeant of the French 17th Colonial Division describes in his diary how the news reached his unit as the men were taking a morning rest at a ruined village north of Skopje, all flopped out in ditches, their rifles not even stacked. Suddenly, the divisional commander, General Pruneau, appeared on horseback with his staff officers:

'The general calls out, "Now then, my friends, something to celebrate! It's all finished with the Bulgarians! The armistice was signed yesterday. There'll be no more fighting from noon today!"

'Silence. Those not asleep who have heard don't move. Weariness and hunger glue the men to the ground, crushing their spirits. Under steel helmets slid down over noses, one or two dazed faces turn towards the horsemen.

'The general gets impatient. "Where's your colonel? Go and get me Colonel Pichon." The colonel emerges from his roofless house. "Ah, there you are, Pichon. Well, tell your men. For God's sake, they don't seem to understand. It's all over with the Bulgarians, as from noon. They signed the armistice yesterday, accepted all our conditions ..."

'At that, one of us leans up on his elbow. Another rises on his knees, as though arousing himself from some terrible torpor. Then the helmets begin to fly in the air. "Long live France! Long live the general! Long live the colonel!" But the very next words were: "When is the food arriving?"'

As for the Germans, General von Scholtz's headquarters had received the first news of Bulgaria's intentions as early as 25 September, through their liaison officer with the Second Bulgarian Army, Captain von Bardeleben. For the next four days, during which time the officers tried to keep the news from the men, they did their best, helped by the newly-arrived German troops, to gather together scattered units of any description they could find and so make an orderly withdrawal to Bulgaria, fighting all the way. (Indeed, in the hills east of Skopje, a German rear-guard continued to resist throughout 30 September, despite the fact that the cease-fire was in operation from that same midday, and the town itself was in Allied hands.)

But it was in Sofia itself where the German reinforcements played their most decisive role. As the news of the impending armistice spread, the revolutionary tumult grew. On 27 September, after a republic had been formally proclaimed in the provinces, a force of insurgents, six to eight thousand strong, marched on the capital and reached its south-western outskirts on the evening of the 29th. The Governor of Sofia, General Protogerov, whose loyalist garrison had by now shrunk to one reserve battalion, three companies of the cadet school, and the squadrons of the King's own bodyguard, appealed to the Germans for help. The freshly-arrived troops were willingly thrown in and the republican 'army' wiped out. This first action of the German army against Bulgarians was also its last on Bulgarian soil; von Scholtz now ordered his forces back to defend Sofia from an Entente attack which never came.

For 'Foxy Ferdinand' it was also the end. His death sentence had in fact been pronounced during the armistice discussions in Salonika when d'Espèrey had remarked to M. Liachev: 'We would find it easier to deal with Crown Prince Boris.' Ferdinand, who was given this verdict in softened form when his plenipotentiaries returned, shut himself in his palace for a few days to mull over it, and to consider the general situation. The German troops would soon be withdrawing from his country and they, as had just been demonstrated, were the only guarantee of his personal safety. The game was up, especially as he had always lived in terror of a violent end. His two castles in Austria and six estates in Hungary* suddenly seemed more desirable residences. On 3 October he summoned Malinov and handed the Prime Minister an instrument of abdication, already signed, in favour of his elder son. The next evening he left by rail for Budapest and Vienna, travelling in appropriate oriental style. The royal train had two saloon coaches apart from his own special 'court coach'; two more waggons, filled with personal baggage and treasures; and, finally, some freight cars carrying his automobiles and state carriages. It was a fitting close to a reign given over to display and self-indulgence.

In the world outside the collapse of Bulgaria was widely seen

* An inheritance from his Hungarian great-grandfather, Prince Koháry.

for what it was: the beginning of the final phase of the war. Winston Churchill, in Paris at the time, 'recognized at once that the end had come'. For Maurice Hankey, the influential secretary of the British Cabinet, 'the first of the props had fallen'. Over in America President Wilson was told about the Bulgarian armistice bid as he was preparing to make a War Loan appeal speech at the Metropolitan Opera building in New York. According to one of his intimates, 'He immediately realized that, for the Central Powers, the beginning of the end was here.'

But of all the reactions recorded in the West the most incisive came, not from any statesman, but from an ordinary British cavalry officer in France who heard the news while fighting with his unit east of Rheims. He described the 'dramatic effect' it had on the troops and then wrote:

'Towns and prisoners and guns and ships had been captured by both sides for four years past without any apparent effect on the war ... But when whole nations began to fall and capitulate without conditions, then indeed there seemed ground for hope. If one fell away, others would surely follow ...'

What, finally, of those others? The Central Power most immediately affected by the Bulgarian collapse with the Austrian empire, for it was her own back door which had suddenly caved in. It was at seven-thirty on the evening of 25 September that a personal telegram from King Ferdinand to the Emperor Charles, announcing the armistice negotiations, arrived at the Austrian Supreme Headquarters at Baden and was taken over to the 'Emperor's Villa' nearby. The Empress, who was with him when the message arrived, recalled the scene many years later:

'The Emperor was not really surprised. We knew that Ferdinand had been fishing in all waters for months past, especially towards the Americans. Indeed, earlier that same summer, after our own official visit to Bulgaria in May (when King Ferdinand was, of course, all smiles and fidelity) my husband had warned the German Emperor about him. "But Ferdinand is completely loyal to us; why, he even warned me against *you*!" was the indignant reaction. To which my husband replied: "Yes, and he is always trying to put *me* against you; that's typical."

'The military danger to the monarchy was obvious. After all, we had never forgotten that it was from this direction, the south-east, that the Turks had come to Vienna more than two hundred years before. But for the Emperor Charles, the military side was already somewhat academic.* It was the political aspect which he was mainly concerned with and, for him, the collapse of Bulgaria only made it even more urgent to start peace talks up with the Western Powers while there was still something to talk about.'

There was another priority which appeared just as pressing in light of the news from Sofia: the reconstruction of the Austrian empire itself along more liberal lines. Charles had been personally committed to this long before he came to the throne and, during the two years of his reign, had been struggling away with that old Habsburg conundrum: how could centuries-old quarrels and ambitions of his eleven so-different subject-peoples be resolved within one democratic framework? It was, for him, the domestic parallel to all his peace efforts abroad. The paradox was that though Charles needed peace to tackle this problem, that peace would not be entertained by the Western Powers until the problem had been disposed of first. Later generations were to dub this a 'Catch 22' situation.

But, however daunting the task was of launching major constitutional reforms within an empire fighting for military survival, it had to be approached again now for, as the Austrian Foreign Minister Count Burian graphically put it to his master: 'In jumping clear from us, Bulgaria has knocked the bottom out of the barrel.' That verdict was pronounced at an emergency meeting of the

---

* The Bulgarians had appealed to the German High Command for reinforcements the moment the Allied offensive began. Feeling at first that this was a matter his Austrian allies could deal with, Hindenburg had passed the request on to Baden. Ironically, it arrived the very day that Charles launched his peace move to the West.

Austrian Crown Council convened by Charles in Vienna on 27 September, the day the Bulgarian plenipotentiaries were setting out for Salonika. Its protocol shows a desperately worried sovereign and his advisers surveying the fulfilment of their worst predictions. The defection of the Bulgarians, a Slav people just outside the empire, could only foment the movements for Slav independence within the empire, Burian warned, and went on:

> 'The South Slav danger in its broadest form now stares us right in the face and positively demands a solution ... We must act, act as quickly as possible to avoid the impression of our hand being forced. There is not a day to lose ... Once a South Slav state has been created of its own accord, then the Bulgarian question will arise to square the circle.'

Charles summed up by calling for 'energetic pressure on Germany in the peace question' and by ordering 'the speediest start on the internal reconstruction of Austria'. That start was to be made in less than three weeks' time, and was to prove how dangerous it was to change the framework of a multi-national empire while it was also a multi-national army at war. As for the 'energetic pressure' on Germany, for once, that was not needed. As well as knocking the bottom out of Austria's barrel the Bulgarian capitulation finally knocked sense into Germany's head.

The Kaiser was passed the bad news while he was at Kiel, but as he had been out at sea all day happily watching his submarines at torpedo practice it was not until he returned to his train late in the evening of 26 September that the teleprinter message from Hindenburg could be read to him. His first reaction was one of fury. Had not Ferdinand renewed all his pledges of loyalty when they had met only a few weeks before? How could he break faith with the alliance so peremptorily and so soon afterwards? Anger soon gave way to concern. The political consequences, the Kaiser mused aloud to his entourage, could be grave in both Central Empires, and especially in the increasingly unstable Habsburg monarchy. Perhaps these ill-effects could still be warded off. As always in such a crisis William turned, not to his capital and his ministers, but to his Supreme Command and his generals. The royal train was ordered straight to Spa.

At the Supreme Headquarters in occupied Belgium, Hindenburg and Ludendorff were already drawing up another of their military balance sheets, and wherever they looked, the prospects looked darker than before. On the Western Front, so far from their being any signs of that 'strategic defensive success' which they had talked of in mid-August as the best basis for peace moves, the enemy had now begun to attack the main fortifications which guarded Germany's own borders. On the Italian front a new Allied offensive against Austria-Hungary was expected at any time; and the Habsburg monarchy, with strife and discontent mounting amongst its Slav peoples, seemed in worse shape than ever before to parry the blow. On the German home front the Bulgarian capitulation had driven a shaft of black panic into the nation's mood of slowly-gathering despair. The behaviour of the Berlin Stock Exchange was the best barometer of the change. It had remained steady, even firm, throughout the series of military setbacks (duly reduced in scale, of course, by the German propaganda machine) which had been registered over the previous six weeks. But this public defection of an ally could neither be concealed nor explained away; and when the news of the armistice reached the German capital shares plummeted in waves of selling. Clearly, less resolution than ever could be expected out of Berlin from now on.

But it was in the south-east, from where the disaster had come, that things looked grimmest.

'It was obvious' [Ludendorff wrote soon afterwards of his gloomy stock-taking] 'that the Entente would attempt to liberate Serbia, and from there to make an attack on Hungary, thus delivering the *coup de grâce* to the Dual Monarchy. Our Balkan front was unstable and it was quite uncertain whether we would be able to reconstruct it in Serbia and Bulgaria, or even along the Danube ... The overall military position could only get distinctly worse. Whether things would move slowly or with terrifying speed

could not be foreseen but it was probable that it would all
be over in a relatively short time . . .'

Ludendorff was, in fact, living through his second 'Black Day' and,
unlike its forerunner of 8 August, this vision of total catastrophe
had come to stay. This time no second thoughts held him back as he
rushed headlong towards that peace table he had tip-toed around
for six long, lost weeks. There was indeed little time to lose if the
Central Powers were to survive as a negotiating force. The fall of
Bulgaria had reduced the solid-looking Quadruple Alliance to a
nervous band of three. By the time Ludendorff was doing his
fateful calculations at Spa, it seemed inevitable that they would
soon be down to two. Turkey, all land links with her allies already
severed by the Bulgarian collapse, was about to fall herself.

'Jerusalem by Christmas'

NOBODY WOULD HAVE DESCRIBED the British empire forces
fighting the Turks in Palestine as 'gardeners'. Though they too had
at times been busy enough with the spade, digging out trench
systems, the very thought of a garden was foreign to that arid
desert. The terrain was as different as could be imagined from the
battlefields of Macedonia and Picardy. Rocky defiles rising above
the scrub and sand-dunes were the nearest approaches to the great
chains of Balkan mountains. Better even than topography, water
symbolized the contrast with France. A cup of that slimy mud in
which men drowned on the Western Front would have saved many
a life here.

Yet the three landscapes were linked in their past history as
they were bound together in the present conflict. It was from his
Macedonian homeland that Alexander the Great had marched
down those same wastes to conquer nearly all of the world then
known to European man. And, fifteen centuries after him, the
knights of France and England had journeyed here to liberate the
cradle of Christendom, Crusaders fighting an earlier Moslem
enemy in a very different cause.

In the year of our Lord 1918 there was another link far less
romantic – at least for the soldiers of the Salonika and Palestine
forces. Both were sideshow actors, fighters in armies which were
neglected even when they were not forgotten; both with their
supplies and manpower always up for sacrifice on the high altar of
France. And now, in the same week of the closing months of the
war, both were to enjoy triumphs on a scale so spectacular that,
between them, they temporarily eclipsed everything else in the
Allied calendar.

It had been a strange affair from the start, that war against the
Turkey of Enver Bey, leader of those 'Young Turks' who in 1908

had overthrown the last of the Sultans, 'Abdul the Damned', and had tried to build a thrusting republic on the rubble of the Ottoman Empire. That new Turkey could have been an ally of the Western Powers, not their foe, had Great Britain accepted the proposal for a permanent treaty which Enver had put up to London three years before the Great War broke out. Only seventy-two hours before Germany formally opened that war the friendless Turks, whom nobody in Europe seemed to want or trust, made the same suggestion to Berlin. It was snapped up, for the Black Sea, its outlet to the Mediterranean controlled by Turkey, was the vital waterway between Russia and the Western democracies, whose alliance in arms the Kaiser knew he would soon be facing. Even then, it took further high-handed action by Britain to prod Turkey into actually signing the Berlin treaty on 3 August, the eve of general hostilities. Even higher-handed action* was then needed by the Germans before, on 4 November, after twelve weeks of ducking and weaving, this slippery new partner of theirs was finally dragged into the war. It was not until the beginning of 1916, when the last British troop transports steamed away from the Gallipoli Peninsula with their defeated invasion army on board, that Turkish enthusiasm for the war was kindled. Not only was their capital, Constantinople, now safe from the threat of enemy occupation which had hung over it for eight months. They had, in the process, defeated a great European power, the possessor of the greatest empire and the strongest navy in the world; and the same power, moreover, which had spurned their overtures of 1911 as coming from a political and military lightweight. With that revenge and that achievement behind them, was there any reason why the new Turkey should not emulate the conquests of the old?

The mood of exhilaration was not to thrive for long but, while it did last, the Germans, who controlled the Turkish army, found it easy to exploit and direct to their own strategic purposes. In that same spring of 1916 Turkish troops were sent marching south-

---

* The German battleships *Goeben* and *Breslau* which, on 10 August, had slipped their British pursuers in the Mediterranean and were allowed to enter the Dardanelles, steamed north on 28 October, flying the Turkish flag, and bombarded Russia's Black Sea ports.

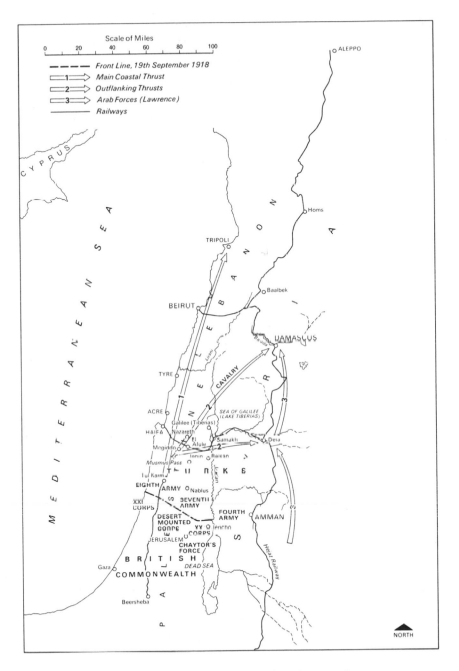

Scale of Miles
0   20   40   60   80   100

- – – – – Front Line, 19th September 1918
- ⇨1⇨   Main Coastal Thrust
- ⇨2⇨   Outflanking Thrusts
- ⇨3⇨   Arab Forces (Lawrence)
- ———— Railways

ALEPPO

CYPRUS

MEDITERRANEAN SEA

Homs

LEBANON

TRIPOLI

Baalbek

BEIRUT

DAMASCUS

TYRE

CAVALRY

ACRE

SEA OF GALILEE
(LAKE TIBERIAS)

Galilee (Tiberias)

HAIFA   Nazareth

El   Samakh   Deraa
Megiddo   Afule

Jenin   Beisan

Musmus Pass

THURKIS H

Tul Karm

EIGHTH ARMY   Nablus

XXI
CORPS   SEVENTH
ARMY

DESERT   FOURTH
MOUNTED   ARMY   AMMAN
CORPS

XX   Jericho
CORPS

JERUSALEM

CHAYTOR'S
FORCE

BRITISH

Gaza   DEAD SEA

COMMONWEALTH

Hejaz Railway

Beersheba

P

NORTH

Palestine: September to October 1918

wards towards the Sinai Desert, aiming once more for the Suez Canal, whose banks they had first tried to storm the year before. Like the 1915 raid, this more ambitious Turco-German operation failed in its ultimate objective of blocking Britain's man-made sea-artery to India. Yet, this time, the mere threat had drawn large forces from the British garrison in Egypt far out into the Sinai, to establish advance defence positions in the desert; and so the two-year campaign in Palestine began.

It had started in depressing style for the British. In March 1917 their so-called Egyptian Expeditionary Force decided to make a lunge for Gaza, the Turkish fortress and sea-port some twenty miles inside the Palestinian border. Its defenders were commanded by the same dashing German officer, Colonel Freiherr Kress von Kressenstein, who had managed to drag a fleet of pontoons across the Sinai all the way up to the eastern bank of the Suez Canal two years before. But it was less that formidable opponent than the flabbiness of the attack itself which was responsible for the Gaza fiasco. By dusk on 6 March the cavalry of the assault force had penetrated the town and Kress was actually preparing to withdraw when the attackers, whose command had suddenly lost its nerve, beat them to it. Deceit only compounded the damage when the British Commander-in-Chief back in Cairo, General Sir Archibald Murray, sent a totally misleading telegram back to London suggesting that, out in Sinai, a victory had just been won. That produced a message of congratulations from Buckingham Palace and from the War Office an instruction to press on with the offensive. The outcome of that instruction was a defeat which not even Murray attempted to disguise. In four days the British, trying to force the Gaza–Beersheba road, were repulsed with a loss of over five hundred men killed and nearly six thousand wounded or missing – exceptionally heavy casualties for this type and scale of warfare. The new British Prime Minister, Lloyd George, who, true to his 'Easterner's' passion, had pressed for this Palestine campaign from the moment of taking office, was livid with disappointment and frustration; and the anger was still smouldering when he came to recall the episode in his memoirs:

'The attack . . . on Gaza had been the most perfect sample exhibited on either side in any theatre of this Great War of that combination of muddleheadedness, misunderstanding and sheer funk which converts an assured victory into a humiliating defeat.'

Yet, ironically, salvation was to rise straight out of this débâcle in the form of a new British Commander-in-Chief. On 27 June 1917 General Sir Edmund Allenby arrived in Cairo to take over from the discredited Murray, and with that burly, short-tempered cavalryman the Palestine army received the equivalent of its own Franchet d'Espèrey. Like d'Espèrey Allenby had yearned all the war for the independence of his own supreme command. Like the Frenchman he had fretted under the static warfare of the Western Front which devoured so many lives and soured so many souls, and had longed for a campaign which would give him air and space to work in. Like the Frenchman, too, he knew his own mind and brooked no shortcomings among his officers. Above all, he had the same restless energy and supreme self-confidence, both of which were needed to lift up a dispirited army. There was at least one difference, however. The British troops in Palestine had no need to compose any elaborate nick-name for their new commander as their comrades at Salonika had done. Allenby was already universally known as 'The Bull', and he promptly set about justifying the label.

Lloyd George's orders to his new commander had been crisply romantic: 'Jerusalem by Christmas'. Allenby beat the schedule by a fortnight. First, Beersheba was taken, its precious water-wells luckily left intact by the retreating Turks. With his base secure, Allenby drove his rejuvenated (and reinforced) army northwards up the coast road and then swung eastwards into the Judaean hills. On 9 December, after a long and tough battle which cost eighteen thousand casualties, he entered Jerusalem. As the official British historian of the campaign commented: 'Lloyd George's somewhat amateurish demand for the Holy City as a Christmas present had been fulfilled, but not cheaply . . .' Cheap or dear, Allenby pressed on. In February 1918, the walls of Jericho fell and, by the time spring came round, he was thrusting forward to Transjordania.

Then two things brought his Egyptian Expeditionary Force to a halt. The first was the searing summer weather, its temperatures of up to 120 degrees Fahrenheit accompanied by the added torments of high humidity and swarms of malarial mosquitoes. The second was the emergency produced by the great German offensive on the Western Front. Again like d'Espèrey at Salonika, Allenby was forced to yield some of his best troops to strengthen Allied ranks depleted by the 'Emperor's Battle' for France. Two complete infantry divisions were transferred, plus another twenty-three battalions with artillery batteries and machine-gun companies plucked out of the divisions which remained. Though, in due course, his original numbers were made up, principally by Indian troops, the army as a whole needed time to assimilate those new men and re-arrange its battle order.

So the last war summer dragged by in Palestine. Two Australian and New Zealand mounted divisions sweltered it out under canvas in the deadly Jordan Valley, partly to hold the area, but mainly as part of a long-range deception plan to persuade the enemy that the main blow against them would be mounted from that river line in a direct lunge eastwards at Amman. For those unfortunate Anzac troops it was a case of 'They also serve who sweat and wait.' Serve they did, but the physical cost was great. They became 'as poor as crows', and, at the end, 'were but gaunt ghosts of the splendid bodies which had moved across the Jordan in the spring'. And while that cruel camouflage was going on between Galilee and the Dead Sea Allenby, encamped seventy-five miles to the west in the orchards and olive groves of his General Headquarters at Ramleh, was preparing a very different attack.

The first plans for that had been laid the previous winter in a manner which displayed at its best the Anglo–Saxon aptitude for combining business with pleasure. On 14 February 1918 (after the usual wrangle between 'Easterners' and 'Westerners' in the Allied Supreme Council had been grudgingly and conditionally settled in favour of the former), the South African leader, General Smuts, had arrived at Ramleh to work out with Allenby a strategy for a Palestine offensive which would not drain any strength away from the Western Front. Though Ramleh at that time of the year was looking its best, with cyclamen, columbine, and the crimson Rose of Sharon all in full bloom on the plains and hillsides, the two great men decided that it was not restful enough for deliberating the future; so off the planners went, with their delighted batch of advisers, to Luxor in Upper Egypt. There, as one of the party put it: 'In the intervals of sight-seeing there was much serious discussion of plans.' It is difficult to imagine any Prussian general putting the tombs of the Pharaohs before the defeat of the enemy.

Beyond agreeing on the obvious point that Palestine, unlike France, offered open country which invited a strategic cavalry swoop, the touristic excursion seems to have produced little of lasting value. At all events when, on 1 August, Allenby revealed his own campaign plans to his corps commanders, they bore little resemblance to the ideas which Smuts and his experts had been airing six months previously among the temples of Upper Egypt. Any thought of breaking through to Damascus – the strategic and political goal of the operation – by battering down the main gate of the enemy's defences through an all-out attack up the Jordan Valley had been abandoned. Instead Allenby, for once not so much the bull as the fox, decided on the exact opposite: he would swing the gate on its hinges by breaking the lock which rested on the sea.

So, to begin with, the centre was left to one divisional group with Arab irregulars roaming the desert beyond it, while no fewer than five infantry divisions with all the heavy artillery were secretly massed on a narrow front only eight miles wide against the coast. Once this lock had been forced by a sudden surprise blow and the gate was opening, the mounted troops were to pour through the gap and cut road and rail communications in the Turkish rear. Three weeks later, while retaining the essence of the plan, Allenby substituted something far more daring for this limited enveloping concept. In the final version the cavalry were not merely to probe and harry but to crush and conquer. Once through the coastal lines they were now to ride straight for El Afule, thirty-five miles away to the north-east, and then wheel down into the Jordan Valley at Beisan, thus drawing a fast-running noose behind the entire enemy force.

That was boldness indeed, for it meant that the cavalry would be riding far ahead of their own supply lines and forced therefore to fight on what they could carry with them or forage from a seemingly barren landscape. The second gamble that Allenby took was that his long-standing deception scheme would go on until the end deluding the enemy into thinking that the main attack against them was still coming in the central sector. This scheme was ingeniously elaborated upon as, early in September, the count-down for the offensive began. Thus Fast's Hotel in Jerusalem, once a German-owned tourist establishment and used since Christmas as quarters for British officers, suddenly found itself emptied of its lodgers, plastered with flags and signs, surrounded by barbed wire and sandbags, and guarded by sentries. The bazaars were soon buzzing with the planted rumour that the building had been earmarked for Allenby's new Forward Headquarters; and that could only mean an offensive was planned along the Jordan. From the bazaars the rumours rapidly reached the enemy who was very inclined to believe them, not only because they made military sense but also in view of what he saw – or thought he saw – happening in the Jordan Valley itself.

During the first fortnight of September, as two whole mounted divisions and an infantry formation slipped away westwards to line up for the coastal attack – marching across Judaea by moonlight and hiding as best they could by day – the Allied strength in the valley was reduced in fact to the so-called 'Chaytor's Force', which consisted of General Chaytor's single Anzac Mounted Division plus a very mixed bag of native Indian State soldiers, two battalions of British West Indians and two more of Jewish volunteers collected everywhere from Birmingham to Beersheba. But, between them, they made enough display for an entire army. New tented towns arose behind the front to suggest the arrival of reinforcements. Fifteen thousand dummy animals, made of canvas draped loosely around wooden frames, were assembled in the horse lines for enemy reconnaissance planes to observe. (Fortunately the pilots failed to notice that not a head tossed and not a tail swished as they flew over these strangely docile ranks.) By night hundreds of unattended camp fires were lit along the valley. By day the horsemen jogged about, raising all the dust they could, while the West Indians and the Jews marched busily up and down in columns. That youthful legend, T. E. Lawrence, whose meteoric two-year career as a leader of Arab guerillas was approaching its climax (and anti-climax), played his own hand in the game. His agents surfaced as far away as Amman, their pockets heavy with golden sovereigns, the army's 'horsemen of St George', with which they began buying up all the animal feed they could find. The inference, plain enough, was spelt out, just to make sure: they were supposedly laying in forward supplies of fodder for a major British cavalry thrust up the Jordan.

The first, if unintended, accolade for the success of this deception plan was a captured German Intelligence map which had been drawn up of Allenby's presumed order of battle only forty-eight hours before his attack went in. It showed units still positioned in Jericho which, by then, Allenby had safely transferred to the orange groves of Jaffa by the sea. And so far from realizing that the Jordan Valley had been almost stripped of cavalry, that same German appreciation spoke of a recent *addition* of some twenty-three enemy squadrons. The fifteen thousand dummy horses had won the first round of Allenby's battle for him without moving one wooden leg.

By coincidence, on the day that map was drawn, an Indian sergeant deserted to the German lines with information which totally and startlingly contradicted it. The British attack, the deserter assured his interrogators, would come on the coastal plain of Sharon and not inland along the Jordan. But the new German Commander-in-Chief, General Liman von Sanders, would have none of it. How much, after all, did the Indian sergeant know? Was he a British plant? If genuine, did he mean a strong subsidiary attack or the main offensive itself? Ever since the summer of 1917, when Allenby had deliberately consigned Anzac forces to roast in the Jordan Valley, the Germans had had their eyes glued on that central sector. One Indian NCO was not going to divert their gaze now, especially in view of the latest picture being painted by German Intelligence.

Liman von Sanders, who had taken over from the famous

General Falkenhayn* in March of 1918, knew his Turkish allies perhaps better than any other German officer. A cavalryman like Allenby, he had been head of his country's military mission in Istanbul before the war, and so had helped to build the Turks into something resembling a modern army. It had been an uphill task all the way. Some of the first peasant recruits were so raw and poorly trained that they had gone into action holding the rifle butt square between their eyes in order, with luck, to get a better aim; the result, of course, was chins and noses smashed by a recoil that only their shoulders could properly cushion. After Gallipoli there had been that surge of Turkish martial ardour which, at one point, had led the Minister of War, Enver Pasha, to dream of leading an army of fourteen Turkish divisions, stiffened by six thousand Germans, to sweep across Mesopotamia and re-take Baghdad. That had been in Falkenhayn's day, and even in the winter of 1917–18, he had dismissed the operation – codenamed 'Yilderim' or 'Lightning' – as utterly impracticable, not least on logistical grounds. To his successor, surveying the balance of forces ranged against each other in Palestine the following summer, the mere thought of Operation 'Yilderim' would have seemed a sickly joke.

On paper Liman von Sanders had under his overall command in September 1918 a force of ten Turkish infantry divisions, with one Turkish cavalry division and a Caucasian cavalry brigade stationed in and around the Jordan Valley. But the infantry, grouped into three armies (the Eighth, the Seventh and the Fourth, numbering from the coast to inland east of the Jordan), were in a sorry state. Eight of the ten divisions had been in the front line without a day's relief ever since the spring. Many battalions were down to half-strength. Sickness was one cause for the shrinkage. Desertion was another. In the one month between mid–August and mid–September of 1918, eleven hundred Turkish soldiers crossed to the enemy lines and surrendered. The reason they invariably gave – that they were hungry, without boots or underwear and down to one set of ragged uniform – needed no questioning; they walked in looking like scarecrows in winter. Liman von Sanders

---

* Erich von Falkenhayn was a former Chief of the General Staff, and commander of the forces which had knocked Rumania out of the war.

would have despaired of his task altogether had it not been for the handpicked group of German staff officers which he had under him (the most notable being Colonel von Oppen, who commanded a corps in the Eighth Army on the coast); and the six battalions of German troops plus some Austrian artillery and ground units which he had in his Army Group. These he would use as nails to shore up the soggy mass of Turkish timber. But, in the event, there were too few nails, and far too many creaking timbers.

Even Allenby's own estimates of the relative strengths of the two sides demonstrated his clear numerical superiority: 57,000 rifles against 26,000; 540 guns against 370; and finally (a count made almost for the last time in modern warfare) 12,000 sabres against 3,000. But there was more to this dominance than figures. The British rail network behind Allenby's lines had been gradually extended and improved, with nearly all of the track relaid in the broader standard gauge. Road convoys were assured by fleets of motor lorries, backed up by more than 25,000 transport camels and some 8,000 donkeys. The Egyptian Labour Corps who supplied the two-legged element of the operation had swollen by September to nearly 135,000 docile and cheerful men. Moreover, the supplies themselves were of a high order. Thanks to the army's firm base in Egypt and the Royal Navy's hold on the Mediterranean, Allenby's army enjoyed good and varied rations — American and Argentinian canned meat, Canadian flour, fresh vegetables and sugar from the Nile Valley, fish from Port Said and, of course, limitless oranges from the groves of captured Jaffa.

Compared with this plenty, von Sanders stood at the end of a very parched limb. His motor transport was limited; his trains of bullock carts primitive and slow. Above all, his rail-borne supplies had to reach the front down the single narrow gauge line from Rayak, the overburdened Hejaz railway, whose bridges and culverts constantly received the loving attention of Lawrence's specially designed 'tulip' demolition charges. It was fortunate that his Turkish peasant-soldiers could live as frugally as they did; but, even for them, the daily rations were shrinking to a point where both body and spirit had begun to shrivel in proportion. Canned delicacies, including consignments of bottled asparagus, were shipped down for the German and Austrian officers' messes, but even they were often reduced to frugal fare.

That imbalance on the ground was repeated, with emphasis, in the skies. Each corps of Allenby's army had its fully operational RAF squadron attached, with four more squadrons of Bristols, SE5s, de Havillands and Nieuport fighters in army reserve. The pride of the so-called Palestine Brigade RAF was one Handley-Page bomber which had been specially flown out from England in secret stages via Paris, Rome, Otranto, Crete and Cairo between 28 July and 8 August. This giant of 1918 aviation, with its Rolls-Royce engines driving two four-bladed propellers, its eight-hour flight endurance and its unheard-of wing span of a hundred feet, had a prestige value almost as great as the destructive value of the sixteen 112-lb bombs it carried. Lawrence describes the impact it had on his Arabs when it landed among them one day to bring urgently needed supplies of petrol, food and medicines:

'Twenty miles short of Ul em Surab we perceived a single Bedawi, running southward all in a flutter, his grey hair and grey beard fluttering in the wind, and his shirt (tucked up in his belly-cord) puffing out behind him. He altered course to pass near us and, raising his long arms, yelled, "The biggest aeroplane in the world," before he flapped on to the south, to spread his great news among the tents.

'At Ul em Surab the Handley stood majestic on the grass with Bristols and Havillands like fledglings beneath its spread of wings. Round it admired the Arabs saying "Indeed and at last they have sent us *the* aeroplane, of which these things were foals."'

The Air Corps alloted to von Sanders's Army Group had, on the other hand, been ground down into almost total immobility before the main fighting even began. Throughout the summer the pilots of the Palestine Brigade had been picking off its machines (inferior in any case to those of the RAF) in ones and twos so that, by the time Allenby attacked, his adversary allegedly disposed of only five machines fit for combat.* Von Sanders relates how, at the beginning of September, Colonel von Oppen, the one German corps commander in his force, had pleaded with him to call off air reconnaissance altogether, 'as the sight of the now invariably luckless air fights was calculated to reduce further the low morale of his troops'.

Given that crushing superiority at the front line, behind the front, out at sea to the west of the battlefield, and in the skies above it, there was no reason to suppose that Allenby would lose this final round in the struggle for Palestine. What still remains remarkable, however, was the manner in which he won it. One who took part in what was, for him personally, to become a bitter victory wrote: 'The Syrian campaign of September 1918 was perhaps the most scientifically perfect in English history, one in which force did least and brain did most.' And the historian of the campaign was to describe it later as 'one of the most brilliant cavalry operations in the history of warfare'. That text-book battle is normally known by the name of Megiddo, after an ancient town on the Musmus Pass where the decisive breakthrough into the Plain of Esdraelon was made. It was a classic setting. The Pharaohs Thothmes III and Necho were among the many other commanders who, long before Sir Edmund Allenby, had won glory at that same pass.

Allenby began precisely as d'Espèrey had done in that other backwater triumph of the month: a pre-dawn bombardment, from a concentrated mass of artillery unheard of on such a dispersed, secondary front. In this case it was 384 British guns which opened up on the Sharon Plain at 4.30 a.m. on 19 September; all were ranged along an eight-mile coastal sector which had hitherto known only desultory fire from a quarter as many pieces. The destroyers *Druid* and *Forester* added to the enemy's discomfiture by pouring more shells into his lines from the seaward flank. When, after fifteen minutes, the initial barrage lifted and the four infantry assault divisions under General Bulfin went forward against the

---

* That figure, supplied to General von Sanders by his Chief of Air Staff, was certainly too modest. Colonel Lawrence who, on 16 September, was making a major demolition attack on the Hejaz railway found his party on this one foray being bombed by 'three two-seaters, four scout planes and an old yellow-bellied Albatross' (*Seven Pillars*, p. 615).

Turkish Eighth Army, they found that surprise had been complete. At some points inland, especially where the so-called Asia Corps of Colonel von Oppen was involved, the defenders regained their balance and put up a stubborn fight before yielding their ground. But the Turks virtually made a present of it to the attackers where this mattered most, on the extreme left of the line against the sea. General von Sanders later claimed that one whole Turkish division in this sector, the 7th, plus two regiments of the adjoining 20th Division, 'completely disappeared on 19 September before the hostile infantry offensive had been launched'.

How many of his Turks melted away before or after they felt the enemy's bayonets is immaterial; one way or the other, it was the 60th British Division attacking here which made the swiftest progress. Within a few hours they were in possession of their first objective, a bridgehead across a little stream eleven miles from their starting-point, and by the afternoon of that blazingly hot day they had taken their second, the little town of Tul Karm, the point where the coastal railway bent sharply inland towards Nablus. The Londoners and Punjabis of the division who carried this assault were moving across famous battlefields: it was on those same sand-dunes of Asruf eight centuries before that Richard Coeur de Lion had defeated Saladin. (Unlike Allenby, however, the English Crusader-King had scored against heavy odds.)

With the Turkish defences against the coast either pierced or abandoned, the Allied cavalry, here composed of the 4th and 5th Indian Divisions and the Australian Mounted Division, could move into what was to become its greatest action. By 7 a.m. the horsemen were picking their way across the first shattered line of Turkish trenches. Half an hour later – and only three hours after the offensive had started – they were already moving through the ranks of their pathfinders, the 60th Infantry, and were streaming northwards up the plain, ignoring any Turkish stragglers unless these came straight under the points of their lances. Their aim was not to kill or capture but to keep the gate swinging open, and by mid-morning the whole Turkish line was cracking under their pressure. Von Oppen's Asia Corps, fighting on the next sector inland from the coast, were the first to feel the strain. The relatively stubborn resistance they offered was, in those circumstances, reduced to tactical value only. By nightfall von Oppen had been forced to bend his line right back in an attempt to escape envelopment. It was a similar tale with the whole of the Turkish Seventh Army, fighting next to him in the foothills of Samaria. Helped by terrain which favoured the defenders, they had given the British XX Corps of General Chetwode plenty to think about; but in the end they too pulled back – partly forced by the pressure against their front and partly persuaded by the threat to their right flank.

Liman von Sanders wrote of the parlous position which confronted him that evening:

'In the rear of the front-line divisions of the Seventh and Eighth Armies ... there was on 19 September an area more than 125 miles deep which was entirely denuded of combatant troops. In all this space were to be found only the remnants of two Arab depot regiments; a few German, and many more, though much inferior Turkish troops from the lines of communications; labour units; air force stations with their personnel; motor transport groups, supply and engineering depots; the numerous overcrowded hospitals and convalescent homes; and the Arab battalions of the coast guard.'

That was a fragile egg-shell indeed to be caught between seven British infantry divisions bearing down in front and twelve thousand Indian and Australian cavalry already swooping round behind. But the most alarming feature of the German commander's appreciation was that he was only able to reconstruct it bit by bit by information given to him after the battle itself had been lost and won. Before Allenby struck at his adversary's body on 19 September, he first went for his eyes. For much of that day, thanks to the Palestine Air Brigade, von Sanders had been fighting blind.

The communications in his Army Group had been kept, as far as possible, in the hands of German and Austrian personnel. (It was one way of ensuring control over his Turkish troops; another was to keep the supply lines also in the hands of his own men.) But though there was therefore no lack of expertise in his signals corps, the system itself was antiquated by Western Front standards. The central telephone office at El Afule (some ten miles south of Nazareth, where von Sanders had his headquarters) was a vulnerable civilian exchange which Allenby had made one of his prime objectives. The mighty Handley-Page delivered the first blow. It had taken off from its base aerodrome at 1.15 a.m. on the morning of the 19th, and loomed up over its target at daybreak to unload all its sixteen bombs over the signals complex and the adjoining railway junction. Two bombing runs by smaller aircraft followed and similar attacks were made on the buildings which housed the headquarters of the Seventh and Eighth Turkish Armies and on the tented camps of their corps commanders. Other relays of planes took it in turns to sit on top of von Sanders's own air base at Jenin, twelve miles south of El Afule, to pin to the runway what was left of his own airforce like so many butterflies sealed in a case. Not a single German machine took off that day.

Though the Australian pilots reported plenty of hits it was not until their comrades on the ground moved into the target areas that the extent of the havoc became clear. The cavalry that rode into El Afule later that same day, for example, found almost every bomb crater festooned with the broken ends of Turkish telephone wires. Out in the desert Lawrence and his Arabs had already given similar dedicated attention to the enemy's land lines.

> 'It was pleasant' [he wrote] 'to imagine Liman von Sanders' fresh curse, in Nazareth, as each severed wire tanged back from the clippers. We did them slowly, with ceremony, to draw out the indignation.'

Whether the Army Group commander swore at the time or not, the tribute he paid later to all this co-ordinated sabotage was brief and to the point:

> 'Telephonic and telegraphic communications between Tul Karm and Nazareth ceased at about 7 a.m. The wireless station of Eighth Army Headquarters also failed to respond when called . . . Not a single direct report was received from

that headquarters and it was learned later that it had been without wire communications with its divisions on the coastal sector since morning, as all links had been cut or destroyed by projectiles.'

For the first vital hours of the Allied offensive von Sanders was thus fighting like a man in a fog. When, in the afternoon, the fog lifted a little with the partial re-establishment of signals links, he could only catch glimpses of a battle that was already lost. Indeed, he soon had to run to save his own skin.

The single engagement which was to give its name to the entire campaign was not dramatic in numbers; but it was decisive nonetheless. Elements of the forward brigade of the 4th Cavalry Division had reached the ancient ruins of Megiddo, near the southern end of the Musmus Pass, in the early hours of 20 September. Just before darkness fell they had ridden down a Turkish officer who supplied the valuable if not very surprising information that a Turkish infantry force with machine-guns was under orders to march down from the bomb-battered town of El Afule to block the pass at its northern exit. The divisional commander, Major-General Barrow, had been told by Allenby to clear the defile at all costs. His worry, in the hour left before dawn, was whether he dared to press forward with the few squadrons he had up with him for, among other delays, one of his brigades had lost its way altogether in the darkness and was several miles off course behind him. Too weak a force might get mown down; on the other hand every minute was precious if the enemy were to be denied their counter-attack. He rightly decided to press on and so, at 5.30 a.m. on the 20th, his vanguard, the three squadrons of the 2nd Lancers, trotted out on to the Plain of Esdraelon, having cleared the pass by night without incident.

There, on the open ground right in front of them, was the Turkish force they had been expecting. It turned out to be a Depot regiment from Nazareth which von Sanders had dispatched at lunch-time the previous day with orders to march into the Musmus Pass and block it. Second-rate infantry though they were, they would have presented severe problems had they carried out their

167

instructions, instead of taking all afternoon and evening over an easy march of some fifteen miles and then sitting down on the plain. Even there, their machine-guns were a deadly threat to charging horses. But the young British captain who had the good fortune to be leading the 2nd Lancers that day (both his commanding officer and second-in-command were sick) was made of the same stuff as General Barrow. With all his light armoured-cars massed in the centre and firing at the enemy's front, the two squadrons of horsemen charged from either flank. It was lances against machine-guns, yet the spectacle of fearlessly galloping horsemen bearing down, each with his lowered spear tip glinting in the sun, seemed to put the Turkish soldiers off their aim. They managed to kill only twelve horses and one single man before their lines were crashed into and rolled up. Forty-six of their number were lanced to death and the remainder, four hundred and seventy in all, taken prisoner. The whole affair had lasted only a few minutes but it had opened the way for Allenby's grand concept. Before Megiddo, the Turkish gate had been swinging open; now, it was smashed.*

How far events had moved beyond von Sanders's best intelligence and worst imaginings can be gauged by what happened to him next. An hour after daybreak on the 20th, almost at the same time as the cavalry charge which, unbeknown to him, was clearing the Plain of Esdraelon, he was aroused from his sleep by the sound of rifle and machine-gun fire coming from the southern sector of Nazareth. A party of Gloucester Hussars and Indian Lancers belonging to the 13th Brigade of the 5th Cavalry Division (the formation advancing on General Barrow's right) were in the streets of the German Commander-in-Chief's headquarters – with orders to take him prisoner in his bed. The brigade had turned inland after galloping across the Sharon Plain the day before and had then been led by Arab guides along the bridle-paths of the hills of Galilee to this town which General Allenby coveted as a military prize almost as much as he revered it as a Christian shrine. He came within an ace of scooping it up completely at the first bid.

As von Sanders had no idea how grave his position was and had

---

* When Allenby was raised to the peerage he took Megiddo as his title, a permanent tribute to the significance of this one crucial engagement.

received no messages of any importance during the night, only normal outposts – made up mainly of German clerks, chauffeurs, and signalmen from the Nazareth depot regiment – had been posted at the southern and western outskirts. Those were soon dealt with by the cavalry, who went on to shatter a German motor-lorry convoy they encountered crawling up a steep trail. The vehicles were ridden off the road and sent crashing down into a gorge. Minutes later the invaders were at the town centre and inside the Hotel Germania – appropriately named, since it housed a number of German officers and administrative staff who were taken prisoner before they had time to dress. The same fate almost befell the Commander-in-Chief who fled his nearby headquarters building, the Casa Nuova, in his pyjamas. He soon returned however, presumably in uniform, to direct a counter-attack. A wild street battle ensued with German and Turkish staff officers seizing carbines and joining their infantrymen in firing from windows and balconies at the cavalry. However confused that fighting was, von Sanders remained clear in his mind on one point. The western heights of the town had to be held at all costs, for they commanded his one free escape route, along the valley to Tiberias.* After three determined assaults by remnants of the German depot regiment (directed by von Sanders from an Emergency Headquarters set up in a French orphanage) the British were successfully driven off. Half an hour later the attackers were withdrawn from the town entirely. Both their men and their horses were exhausted, and the brigade was further burdened with a load of some two thousand prisoners.

The German Commander-in-Chief records in his factual style:

'After the departure of the British, I rode down to Casa Nuova and found the HQ offices almost completely empty. Some of our men were still firing out of windows towards the south, though no enemy remained in sight. Such of the records as had not been burned were loaded into cars and

---

* The inexplicable failure to close that road, an operation which a handful of men with machine-guns could have carried out, was eventually to cost the British Cavalry Brigadier his command.

lorries and sent to Tiberias, as was the last of the personnel.'

Nazareth, a ghost town, was occupied in strength by the British the next morning. From his new headquarters, twelve miles to the north-east, von Sanders surveyed the wreck of his command. Twenty-five thousand men had already been taken prisoner; in one engagement alone twenty-eight hundred had surrendered to twenty-three Australians. Apart from Colonel von Oppen's corps (which managed to pull back losing only thirty per cent of its strength) the Turkish Eighth Army had almost ceased to exist, and the Seventh was reeling alongside it. The only hope of survival that the remnants of both forces had was to get back across the Jordan and join up with their comrades of the Fourth Army which, at that point, was still intact. But they first had to negotiate the roads and wadis which led, often through narrow ravines, to the river valley, and it was against those that Allenby's Air Brigade struck its second telling blow.

At 6 a.m. on the morning of 21 September a dawn reconnaissance patrol of two Bristol fighters spotted the long columns of Turkish guns and transport writhing forward like a giant caterpillar east of Nablus and Beisan. Relay after relay of planes was called up throughout the day – the aim being to have a pair of bombers over the target area every three minutes, with an additional formation of six every half hour. By nightfall, 90 tons of bombs and some 56,000 machine-gun bullets had been dropped and fired into the retreating Turks. It was an identical operation to that which other Allied airmen had carried out a few days before against the demoralized Bulgarians in Macedonia, but here the carnage was, if anything, greater. Even the official account of the campaign, normally so factual, seeks prose to match it:

'Drivers were seen to jump from their lorries, which crashed out of control into the transport in front, and often carried a piled-up mass into the ravines below. Horses were seen to stampede and men to rush anywhere in panic, many of them waving signals of surrender to the pilots, some of them prostrating themselves, as it were in supplication from these new mechanical furies from out of the heavens.'

When Allenby's troops reached that particular defile they found it blocked solid with a tangled mass of about a hundred guns, fifty-five motor-lorries, four motor-cars, 837 four-wheeled wagons, seventy-five two-wheeled wagons and twenty water-carts and field-kitchens. Strewn among that impedimenta were the torn bodies of hundreds of men, horses and bullocks. It took days to restore either order or sanitation.

It was not only the victims who had never known anything like this before in the war. For the pilots, too, it was a novel experience, and most of them were sobered by this first application of a technique that was later to be perfected by German Stukas in Poland in 1939 and Israeli fighters at the Sinai passes in 1966.

One Australian who bombed a Turkish convoy on a precipitous road near Beisan wrote, for example:

'It was a slaughterhouse! It was horrible! I don't even like to think about it, but I had to take part in it. We had so many aeroplanes working the road that we got in each other's way. When we finished we left eight solid miles of carnage ... Wagons, trucks, carts, kitchens were piled up, torn up, blown up ... vultures fed on the bodies of countless Turks and horses. It was ghastly!'

A British pilot in action that day (one of his less distressing tasks had been to drop a lunch-basket to a hungry general cut off from his mess) also noted the carnage, adding, in a letter to his father, 'We are commonly alluded to as the butchers now.' But this particular young man seemed to have few pangs of conscience about it; indeed, his letter ended ruefully, 'We shall never have such a good war as this again!' Appropriately, his family nickname was 'Biffy'. He later became commandant of the RAF's training school at Cranwell where his path crossed again with Colonel T. E. Lawrence, though, by then, the great man was calling himself Aircraftsman Ross.

By that time Liman von Sanders had pulled his own headquarters right back to Damascus (for Tiberias, being in the battle zone, could only serve as a transit camp). He had thus escaped either suffering or seeing all this havoc. But he realized, as fragmentary reports came in from survivors, or sometimes by indirect wireless messages, what it signified. The retreat of his Seventh and Eighth Armies had now been converted into a disorderly rout. The lost war material was itself irreplaceable, as were the lost men. Even more serious was the shattered morale of the Turkish units which remained intact. The destruction of the entire Army Group stared him in the face. In the midst of this extremity, a personal telegram reached him from the German Military Mission back in the Turkish capital, his base to which he had been signalling every phase in the fast-developing crisis since Allenby had first unleashed his offensive. The message contained neither advice nor information nor even sympathy. It merely wished to enquire whether the general would be willing to offer a prize for a sack race to be run at a soldiers' competition in Constantinople on 8 October.

To get his own legs out of the sack that Allenby had wrapped around them von Sanders needed, above all, a breather to regain his strength. On paper, large elements of his command remained unbroken and battleworthy, if only they could be re-united. There was the Fourth Turkish Army under Jemal Pasha, for example, which faced Chaytor's Force in the Jordan Valley. It had held up well during the first three days of the offensive; and though it began to evacuate the valley and fall back on Amman once the Turkish disaster on the coast became known, it was still withdrawing as a coherent fighting force. To it, again on paper, could be added most of the Asia Corps of the redoubtable Colonel von Oppen (which, after a precarious retreat, had managed to get across the Jordan on 23 September); and the bulk of the 146th German Infantry Regiment. Von Sanders's first hope was to establish a rearguard line at Tiberias and the Yarmuk Valley, behind which he might regroup. But the key to this line – the road and rail centre of Samakh just east of the point where the Jordan flows out of the Sea of Galilee – fell on 25 September. That was, for once, an evenly matched and fiercely contested struggle between an Australian Light Horse Brigade and a determined German–Turkish garrison under Captain von Keyserlingk. As at the Musmus Pass, it began with the cavalrymen charging machine-guns; but then the village had to be cleared house by house until almost the entire defending force had been wiped out or captured. Even one last detachment of Germans who tried to get away across the lake on a motor-boat tied up at the pier perished when a well-aimed artillery shell smashed up their craft in the water. The Australians lost nearly half their animals and had fourteen men killed and twenty-nine wounded; but they found ninety-eight corpses in the ruins of the village and took four times as many prisoners.

As so often, both here and in the Macedonian fighting, it was the thin strip of German steel which had stiffened the resistance. Indeed, it was the courage and steadfastness of these German detachments fighting in Palestine which produced from a famous pen one of the most vibrant and heartfelt tributes ever paid to the enemy on this or any Great War front:

> 'Here, for the first time, I grew proud of the enemy who had killed my brothers. They were two thousand miles from home, without hope and without guides, in conditions mad enough to break the bravest nerves. Yet their sections held together, in firm rank, steering through the wreck of Turk and Arab like armoured ships, high-faced and silent ... There was no haste, no crying, no hesitation. They were glorious.'

The fall of Samakh coincided with the capture, also on 25 September and also largely by Australian cavalry, of the key city of Amman a hundred miles away to the south-east. Here the horsemen had to dismount and charge the stone breast-works with the bayonet before the enemy surrendered; but the defence had been tenacious enough to allow many of the garrison to escape northwards by train. They still had to face bombardment from the air, and an Austrian lieutenant serving in von Sanders's supply lines has left in his diary a vivid picture of the terror which Allied bombers were wreaking in this sector. The lieutenant had decided to cheer up his little army of construction workers (mostly Armenians and Caucasions with their wives and children) by declaring a premature pay-day. Despite the distant noises of aircraft, the wooden chests laden with coins were dragged into the open and the workers crowded around their paymaster, who was using two corn-sacks for a table and an iron bucket for a chair. The next minute, two British planes swooped in over the surrounding hills, unloaded their bombs in the middle of the assembly, and, within seconds, dozens of his labourers were killed by the very money they had been queueing to collect:

> 'Afterwards [he wrote] we found gold and silver coins scattered far away. We found them driven by the explosion deep into the wooden frames of the huts, and the doctors had to cut them out of the bodies of the wounded. All around the tragic scene lay bundles of paper money, tattered and scorched, most of them reduced to dust and red with the blood of our comrades.'

Blessed by that luck which often goes with rashness the lieutenant himself, protected by his corn-sacks, escaped with nothing worse than a bump on the head.

Though an essential prize, the capture of Amman still left the main body of Chaytor's Jordan Valley force more than a hundred miles behind the cavalry on the left flank of the advance. It was Lawrence and his Arabs who, on 27 September, straightened out the line by seizing the key rail junction of Dera, which Allenby had allotted to him as the main Arab objective while the whole operation was still being planned in the groves of Ramleh. For Lawrence, that was the last major action in a saga that had begun with the raising of the Emir Feisal's standard of revolt against the Turks deep in the Arabian desert more than eighteen months before. It was also a last reversion to the primitive savagery of those early days. The British officer who had latterly been skimming delightedly across the desert at nearly seventy miles an hour in a Rolls-Royce tender ('Great was Rolls, great was Royce!') now mounted his camel for an orgy of killing in the pursuit of Turkish columns fleeing north from Dera. 'By my order, we took no prisoners, for the only time in our war.'

Lawrence had arrived in Dera just too late to catch Colonel von Oppen, who had got there the day before him; hurriedly repaired the Arab demolitions along the line; and had entrained northwards in the nick of time with every man of his Asia Corps that he could cram into the waggons. But now that Lawrence's irregulars had made contact with the 4th Cavalry Division under General Barrow it was the turn of the Turkish Fourth Army to be put through the meat-grinder, together with the remnants of its fellows. Lawrence's last swoop may not have been decisive in winning Palestine and Syria (indeed Allenby's victory was as good as assured after the first forty-eight hours); but it certainly contributed towards shortening the campaign. With the last of his three Turkish armies shattered and his precious German units being whittled down further with each desperate rearguard action, von Sanders was now forced to pull his line right back to Damascus, while he himself moved further north to Baalbek.

Counting the garrison of Damascus and all the columns of Turkish and German troops retreating towards it during these last days of September, there might in theory have been anything up to forty-five thousand Turks and Germans available to hold it. But, as the campaign's official historian wrote:

> 'In no case could there be a serious defence of Damascus. There never has been in its history. It is in no sense a fortress, and if its possessors were defeated outside it was always captured and generally sacked.'

That was to be its fate again now. The 'possessors', in the shape of von Sanders' Army Group, suffered further heavy losses as their pursuers snapped at their heels on the approaches to the city — General Barrow's division and Lawrence's irregulars moving up from due south, with the 5th Cavalry Division and other Light Horse units closing in from the south-west on their left. It was those light horsemen who caused the greatest carnage when, from the crests of the Barada River gorge, they spotted below them long convoys of Turkish and German units trying to escape to the Baalbek Plain by the road and railway which twisted along the narrow defile. It might have been another helpless bombing quarry for the Air Brigade as, from the heights, the Australians opened up with their six machine-guns, Hotchkiss guns and rifles:

'All along the gorge the unequal issue was joined. The result was sheer slaughter. The light horsemen, firing with fearful accuracy, shot the column to a standstill and then to silence. For miles, the bed of the gorge was a shambles of Turks and Germans, camels, horses and mules. Never in the campaign had the machine-gunners found such a target.'*

All the while the attackers' task was being eased by the mounting chaos within the city walls, where four centuries of corrupt and self-indulgent Turkish rule were crumbling, almost overnight, into dust. The Christian Syrians, who accounted for about one-fifth of the three hundred thousand Damascenes, were already dreaming of their own independent state. The Arab majority, though split into working factions, were all convinced that, on the contrary, the advancing British would give them such a kingdom – and one, moreover, which would stretch all the way from Arabia to the Taurus mountains. Christians and Arabs were united only in their hatred of the Turkish presence, a hatred fired more and more by insolent contempt with every hour that passed. Few empires have been so utterly friendless in the hour of their collapse. Even the commander of the Turkish garrison, General Ali Riza Pasha, a Baghdad Arab who had served his whole life in the Ottoman army, finally decided that the Crescent had nothing more to offer.

On 30 September, he had seen his Turkish comrade-in-arms, Jemal Pasha, commander of the retreating Fourth Army, flee for Beirut in despair as the first green flags of the Hejaz unfurled in the city, proclaiming Damascus to be part of the new Arabian kingdom. So, that night, as Jemal Pasha headed north just before his escape route was cut, General Ali Riza galloped off with a bodyguard in the opposite direction – straight into the arms of the 4th Australian Cavalry Division, to which he promptly surrendered. At 2 a.m. in the morning of 1 October, over breakfast with General Barrow, he revealed such defence secrets as the Damascus garrison possessed. The most intriguing of them was that he

* The German troop trains evacuating Damascus managed to get through the Barada Valley despite the fact that, for several miles, the road and railway ran very close together.

himself had incapacitated his heavy artillery batteries by positioning them in sites so inaccessible that no regular water supplies could reach the gun crews. As the genial deserter recounted his tale he flung himself back with a roar of laughter, kicking the table over as he did so and scattering the mugs of cocoa and plates of scrambled eggs in the darkness. It was a cheap price to pay for such information.

The fall of Damascus was now a military formality. Soon after dawn the advance guard of Barrow's cavalry, having picked its way between the shattered vehicles, dead soldiers, horses and cattle which still blocked the Barada Gorge, galloped with drawn swords into the city, scattered the last remnants of the Turkish garrison, and accepted the token surrender of the city by constables.

'The old city' [one description went] 'was now delirious with excitement. Christians and Arabs, in all the colours of their varied dress, crowded about the light horse column. Rugs and silks, flowers and perfumes, with fruits and other delicacies were thrown from the windows and the mob fought for the privilege of holding and touching the stirrups of the victors. Only with great difficulty was the stern march to action stopped from degenerating into a tumultuous and indefinite triumphal procession about the streets and bazaars.'

The 'stern march to action' which this Australian vanguard was concerned with, was not the capture of Damascus but the pursuit of the retreating enemy to the north. Accordingly, having extricated themselves from the delirious Damascenes, they clattered off again and disappeared along the road to Homs. That left confusion worse confounded, as the main body of the Australians had not yet reached the city. Lawrence and his Arab irregulars (who may or may not have entered Damascus before the first Australian cavalrymen; the issue is disputed) now stepped into the breach. He deposed the acting governor and installed his own Arab nominee Shukri Pasha in his place, to administer the city in Feisal's name. He then organized police to combat, as best they could, with flailing sticks, the orgy of pillage led by the Bedu who had streamed in from the desert bent on plundering the fabled city. He got the power-house working so that street-lighting, the symbol of security, could go on again that night; organized a fire brigade in order, as he rotundly put it, 'to circumscribe the flames'; cleared corpses from the sewers; turned the filthy charnel-house of a Turkish hospital into something approaching a medical centre; and set about restoring the shattered railway (for him, a complete reversal of roles). Then, sitting alone in his room and looking back on the turbulent day, he heard, through the window, the last call to prayer coming from a nearby mosque. At the end of the age-old invocation to Allah the Muezzin dropped his voice and added: 'And He is very good to us this day, O people of Damascus.' Lawrence found that he could not share in this moment of reverent joy. 'Only for me, of all the hearers, was the event sorrowful and the phrase meaningless.'

The reasons were not hard to find. To begin with he was certainly suffering from what the astronauts of a later age were to call 're-entry problems': after two years as a romantic swashbuckler fighting a private desert war with a handful of other British officers he was back again on the unromantic army treadmill, in ordinary uniform like all the rest, and soon to be entered on ration strengths and movement orders. But more painful to bear than the end of his adventure was the end of his dream. When General Allenby arrived in Damascus himself by motor-car on 3 October, one of his first acts was to summon Prince Feisal, who had reached the city by train soon after, and inform him that any new Arab administration would have to be confined to territory east of the Jordan River. Though Feisal knew that Syria and the Lebanon had both been allotted to France as zones of influence,* he had attempted to forestall the French by getting secret Arab committees to hoist his own Hejaz flag in Beirut and Tripoli. Now 'The Bull' had forcefully put paid to this vision of a Greater Arabia whose western boundaries would run along the shores of the Mediterranean. In a bid to restore that vision at the Allied negotiating table Lawrence left abruptly for London the following day. It was an uncharacteristic and somehow undignified exit. That enigmatic man, always so

* Under the so-called Sykes-Picot agreement of May 1916.

indifferent to rank and so contemptuous of discomfort, now demanded and obtained immediate promotion to full colonel in order to enjoy the luxury of a sleeping-car berth and a more rapid journey home on the route through Taranto, Paris and Cherbourg to London. The world at large took no notice of his movements. T. E. Lawrence had yet to fashion with his pen the monument which had eluded him with the sword.

All eyes were on Allenby's army as it surged north through Tripoli, Homs and Aleppo towards Constantinople. Turkey's formal surrender did not come about until the last days of the war. But it was a foregone conclusion by the time Allenby left Damascus. When the final count was made, his army had captured seventy-five thousand prisoners (including some three thousand seven hundred Germans and Austrians) and three hundred and sixty guns as against British losses in killed, wounded and missing of five thousand six hundred and sixty-six. For a fraction of the casualties which could be suffered in one single day of heavy fighting in France Allenby had advanced the Allied front by some five hundred miles, had destroyed or disbanded the enemy divisions in the process, and had knocked the Kaiser's second most powerful ally out of the war. There was the deepest impact of his victory. His blow had been aimed at the Turks and had duly felled them; but, as with d'Espèrcy's elimination of the Bulgars, the recoil struck hardest at Germany herself.

A Beleaguered Fortress

HOW HARD THE RECOIL of all these defeats would strike the enemy and how Berlin and Vienna would respond to the challenge were questions which now began to preoccupy the Entente powers. But at first they seemed intrigued, rather than obsessed, at finding the right answers. There was still, at the end of September 1918, no suspicion that both the German giant and its reluctant Austrian paladin would soon be sinking to their knees as their Eastern partners had just done. One distinguished Western observer, trying to see the problem through the eyes of the German Supreme Council, put it in these words:

> 'The alternatives before the Council will be to throw over the East or throw over the invaded provinces of Belgium and France west of the Meuse . . . One is inclined to think that the Council will prefer the second alternative . . .
>
> 'At the same time, there will probably be some species of sham political reform in Germany to please the people at home and also impress America – if America is in a state to be impressed – which is more than doubtful.'

The political part of that analysis proved strikingly accurate on each and every count. The military assessment was almost completely wrong. Though doing what they could to shore up the East the Germans never hesitated to hold on in the West, where they felt themselves on relatively firm ground, rather than move all their last flimsy reserves to the Danube basin, there to be swallowed up by the Balkan quagmire. Yet, also on the Western Front, the High Command found that it could no longer dictate even the pace of the battle, let alone its terms. It was not a case of 'throwing over' the occupied territories west of the Meuse. The German army was being thrown out of them, and the eviction process went far beyond one bank of one French river. Germany's main defensive system, which stretched some two hundred miles south-eastwards from Lille to Metz and which, at its centre, was more than ten miles deep in the front sector alone, now started to crack and crumble. The so-called Hindenburg Line (the name given to it by the Entente armies) behind which the fatherland was supposed always to sleep secure – a breakwater shielding the civilian population from whatever storms raged out on the battlefields of France and Belgium beyond – was falling, as had remote Skopje, Sofia, Nazareth and Damascus, to the invader.

German soldiers and civilians alike could be forgiven for having put so much trust in it. Some of the construction work went as far back as September 1916 and the main fortifications had been mostly completed by 1917, the year when Ludendorff had deliberately shortened the central arc of his lines in France, resting and re-modelling his army for the 'Emperor's Battle' of the following spring. Everything inside the great bulge of French soil he chose to evacuate had been systematically laid waste before his troops moved out: the towns and villages looted and their able-bodied inhabitants borne away eastwards; all buildings solid enough for military use levelled to the ground; every bridge blown; every railway line torn up; every water well blocked or poisoned; and every orchard felled. It was a grimly classical exposition of what was later to become known in warfare as the 'scorched earth policy'.

The Hindenburg Line was drawn along the rear of this devastated bulge of French territory, the unbreakable chord of the abandoned arc. One of the best of many descriptions of it comes from an American military historian:

> 'It was neither a line nor a single system of fortifications; it was a defensive zone varying in width from three to twelve miles, making use of every hilly ravine, river, and natural obstacle but in the main deriving its strength from the successive fields of wire entanglements backed by trenches, block-houses, concrete emplacements. Each point of cover was a machine-gun nest, and every art of modern engineer-

Allied offensive: 8 August to 11 November 1918

Scale of Miles

0   20   40   60   80

—————— Allied Line, 8th August, 1918
— — — — Allied Line, 11th November, 1918
- - - - - German Defence Lines
———— Railways

ANTWERP

BRUSSELS

L/GIUM

LIEGE

GHQ
SPA

NAMUR   Meuse

A R D E N N E S

Sambre

L U X E M B O U R G

Mézières

Moselle

F R E Y A

BRUNHILDE

Longwy

Grandpré   Thionville

IMS   KNIEMHILDE

Montfaucon   M I C H E L

Verdun   METZ

G E R M A N Y

2E SEPT   2E SEPT   12 SEPT   L O R R A I N E

ARGONNE
FOREST

C   St Mihiel   Pont-à-Mousson

E   A M E R I C A N S   12 SEPT

Meuse

ing ... was employed to increase the obstacle.

'The theory ... was not that the enemy would be broken before it but that the force of such an attack would be lost ... and that the enemy, checked in the tangle, would be slaughtered by the concentrated fire from all sides ... or thrown back by a well-timed counter-attack.'

To this end, everything which might obstruct a clear line of fire in front of the fortifications had been removed, down to the last tree and bush. To complicate the enemy's counter-battery fire, the Germans had sited most of their own guns on the reverse slopes of ridges, where their fire would be difficult to pinpoint. Everything that the best military machine of the age could create had been put into place.

It was intended, through those gigantic exertions, to create a psychological as well as a strategic bulwark; and so, to fortify it further, the Germans had called on their legends as well as on their engineers. Wotan, chief of all the ancient gods and himself the creator of Valhalla, lent his name to the extreme right-hand sector south of Lille – an appropriate flanking post, considering he only had one eye. South of that, the key section covering Cambrai and St Quentin was called after Siegfried, again an apt choice for such a vital task, since the Siegfried of mythology, slayer of the fearsome dragon, had forged the sword that could never be broken and worn on his head the magic 'Tarnhelm' which gave him the added powers of invisibility. True, there was not much that was invisible about the elaborate defences which now faced the Third and Fourth British Armies under his name; but the unbreakable sword was a splendid symbol and so, give or take a couple of hundred miles on modern maps, was the fact that Siegfried had also been known in legend as 'Lord of the Netherlands'.

Other evocative names from the sagas lent their aura to the rest of the system: Alberich, the sinister dwarf who was Lord Treasurer of the Nibelungs, guarded the central sector south of St Quentin and west of Laon where the First, Third and Tenth French Armies took over from the British. Behind him was a reserve line called after Hundung, who slayed Wotan's son Siegmund and had to be killed by Wotan himself. Brünnhilde, Wotan's favourite daughter, gave her patronage to the next sector of the line east of Rheims, while the Meuse-Argonne sector which confronted the First and Second American Armies towards the southern end of the system was named after Kriemhilde – no docile lady this, for she had killed Alberich's half-dwarf son Hagen with her own hands.

None of those names carried the mystical reassurance of Siegfried himself. As the war crept a little closer to Germany's own frontiers, cartoon after cartoon and allegory after allegory appeared in contemporary German periodicals, looking above all to him for strength and comfort. One typical example was a whole-page drawing in a youth paper showing Siegfried, complete with breastplate, horn, magic helmet and invincible sword, towering like a contemptuous giant over a swarm of enemy tanks which are crawling like puny ants towards his toes. '*Bis hierher und nicht weiter!*' ('So far but no further') runs the caption. In the event it was the armoured ants who were to prevail, reducing the giant into a pygmy as they advanced.

The overrunning of the Siegfried position was, in fact, the military as well as the psychological key to the breaking of the whole defence line – against which, in the last days of September, Foch launched a co-ordinated attack all the way from Flanders to the forests of Champagne. The Siegfried position was not merely the solid centre of the system. It fell in the only area along the entire front where, when the Allied offensive began on 26 September, the German defenders actually outnumbered the attackers. For that central battle the Germans had concentrated fifty seven divisions, eighteen of them assault formations, against the forty British divisions supplemented by an American corps which was at Haig's disposal. By comparison, for the northern battle in Flanders, the Allies had sixteen infantry divisions (eight of them Belgian) plus six cavalry divisions against twelve German; while on the southern sectors nineteen German and one Austrian division faced thirty-one French and thirteen American divisions – the latter with double the rifle strength of anything else on the Western Front. Haig's British army had already lost 7,700 officers and 166,000 men in the summer counter-attacks which had prepared the way for this last great offensive; and there was no hope of filling the gaps in time. But the French, who had lost 100,000 more over the same period, were in far worse shape and had been obliged to reduce all their infantry companies to a mere 175 men. It was the familiar story of those last hundred days on the Western Front. Pétain's troops were seasoned but drained; Pershing's were lusty but green. They all fought and gave of their best; but only the British combined experience with sufficient reserves of strength, and even a touch of dash added on.

They had shown this in important clearing operations (notably the capture of Havrincourt and Epéhy) earlier in September; they were to display it even more in the so-called 'Battle of the Canals' which was now joined. Even the seasoned British, however, approached this new fight against such a powerfully massed enemy sheltering behind such formidable defence works with some apprehension. On the eve of the attack a young English subaltern of the 27th Infantry Brigade wrote to his mother at their Hertfordshire home:

> 'I am going into a particularly offensive offensive [*sic*] tomorrow, so just thought I would tell you what a perfect mother you are, in case anything happens. If you get this letter and haven't previously had a telegram from the WO saying that I've been "biffed", all is well and you needn't worry ...'

On 27 September, after a fearsome preliminary bombardment (in all, about one million shells were poured from the British front line into the German defences) the British First and Third Armies jumped off at dawn in the general direction of Cambrai with the Canal du Nord, which blocked part of their advance, to be negotiated first. The waterway itself, the marshes which oozed around it, and the high ground which the Germans commanded on its eastern bank, all combined to make it a formidable bonus for the enemy's engineers. Nevertheless, it was crossed on the first day (thanks largely to a brilliant out-flanking manoeuvre by General Currie's battle-hardened Canadian Corps); and by nightfall the two British armies were fighting four miles inside the German defence network, with a bag of some eight thousand prisoners captured between them. At the end of the second day, they were across the River Scheldt and stood at the gates of Cambrai itself. Despite German resistance, which was always methodical and often fierce (no repetition of the 8 August panic), the whole of that sector of the Hindenburg Line had thus been stormed within forty-eight hours. Siegfried here was flat on his back. That British subaltern was now able to scribble another, and more reassuring note to his mother: 'It's all right so far and things are going swimmingly. Splendid victory, everything OK. Too busy going after Fritz to write.'

On this same day, 28 September, the Flanders Group of Belgian, French and British forces under the overall command of King Albert of the Belgians* launched its pre-arranged assault against the Fourth Army of General Sixt von Arnim which was holding the extreme north of the German line resting against the sea at Nieuport, near Ostend. There was no Hindenburg line up here, and Arnim forces were both weaker and wearier than the attackers (the Belgian forces in particular had enjoyed a relatively restful war). The big gamble was with the early autumn weather. This was the blackened wasteland of Ypres and Passchendaele, a naturally flat and marshy area, pock-marked everywhere by four years of shelling and trench warfare. Too much rain would invoke a demon more formidable than anything in the Nibelung: Flanders mud. But the Allies' luck held out. By 30 September, when a spell of bad weather set in in earnest to bog down the advance, the first and second German defence lines had been overrun; ten thousand prisoners and two hundred guns had been captured; and a score of strongpoints all too poignantly familiar to many British veterans from the summer fighting of 1917 were again in Allied hands. Those included the whole of the Passchendaele Ridge itself, the land of invisible crosses, where the martyrdom of so many terrible months was now resolved, if not avenged, in two days.

---

* The King had been prudent enough to request a French officer as Chief-of-Staff when the operation was being planned and Foch had been delighted to supply one – General Degoutte, whose services Pershing had refused earlier in the campaign.

By now, another of Foch's co-ordinated blows had gone in. General Rawlinson's Fourth British Army, the heroes of the August breakthrough, were engaged on the extreme south of the British line in a waterway battle of their own. It was to prove a far tougher business than that breathless leap forward at Amiens. On this southern sector of the Siegfried Line, the St Quentin Canal, which had been built in to the German defences, posed by far the biggest problem, as it was, on average, some thirty-five feet wide, up to eight feet deep and cut through banks which rose at steep angles above it. No modern armour would relish negotiating this, let alone the primitive machines of 1918. There was, it seemed, only one stretch where the Fourth Army could hope to stage another Amiens triumph, and that ran between the village of Vendhuile and the bridge of Riqueval, south of Bellicourt, between which points, more than a century before, Napoleon had constructed a massive tunnel to carry the canal for six thousand yards underground. The tunnel itself was almost impregnable to any form of shelling or assault, for it lay an average of fifty feet beneath the surface and had been converted by the Hindenburg Line engineers into an electrically-lit underground fortress complete with stores, stables, offices and hospitals, with a long string of barges for accommodation. But the ground above was, in effect, a four-mile bridge over the troublesome waterway, and that nominated itself to both attackers and defenders as the arena for the main tussle. The Australian Corps of General Monash, the toughest but also the tiredest troops which the Fourth Army possessed (they had been in almost continuous front-line action since the spring), were again given the breakthrough task, but replacements simply had to be found for their two most depleted and most exhausted divisions. And so the American 27th and 30th Divisions, formations which had never fought in battle before and were anyway woefully short of officers, were brought up to join in the main assault over the tunnel. There was a glow of Anglo-Saxon missionary fervour when all four divisional commanders met to discuss their joint operation ('America, a great English-speaking democracy on one shore of the Pacific, was to co-operate with Australia, its younger sister-democracy on the opposite shore ...' etc. etc.). As things turned out, that mixture of weary veterans and enthusiastic greenhorns was to prove a very unhappy one.

A young British artillery officer, looking round the front line with his battery commander just before the attack went in, describes their own misgivings:

'"Christ! What a place!" the major said when we saw it for the first time. Old trenches, barbed wire, shell holes. There was nothing else to see in any direction ...

'We walked for about half a mile, finding a way through the barbed wire, until we came to a trench full of Americans.

'"Hello," said the major to them.

'"Hello you!" they replied.

'It was a surprise to learn that an American division, not an Australian one, was holding the line in front of us and that they had never been in action before.

'"No wonder they had the jumps," the major said as we were walking back. "I should have had them myself had I known," and he added that he could not see a new division with no battle experience cutting the Hindenburg Line into little bits.'

The major was right, for it was those American troops of the 27th Division who were cut into little bits when, at 5.30 a.m. the next morning, in damp and foggy weather, they jumped off to try and clean up the German outposts as a preliminary to the main attack. The leading American regiment was required to knock down less than a mile of the enemy's forward screen, and for this, apart from the usual creeping barrage, it was given the support of a dozen British tanks. But after a day of conflicting reports it became evident, not merely that the attack had failed but that, even worse, there had been neither advance nor retreat, so that whatever remained of the regiment was stranded somewhere in No-Man's-Land, thus inhibiting Allied artillery from opening up again. It transpired later that seventeen of the regiment's pathetic complement of eighteen officers had soon become battle casualties, leaving their utterly inexperienced troops leaderless and floundering in the mist. But though those raw American soldiers, most of them straight off the streets of New York, were as disorientated as headless chickens, they resisted like fighting cocks. Of the two thousand men of this 106th Regiment which made the assault, some fifteen hundred fell killed or wounded during that disastrous day.

There were similar tales of confusion when the main attack went in on the 29th. Australian and American infantry got tangled up with each other in shrouds of mist in the same fateful sector, enabling the Germans to inflict further casualties. Moreover the British tanks failed to repeat their success at Amiens: more than half of the 141 Mark Vs and Whippets which rumbled forward were knocked out, blown up or ditched. Most of them fell victims to carefully co-ordinated artillery fire, some within a few minutes of going into action. On this day's balance sheet, Ludendorff's contemptuous dismissal of enemy armour as being merely a target for German guns seemed justified.

Gradually, however, the Fourth Army managed to press its enemy back along the twelve-mile front, as the combined weight of five army corps, sixteen hundred guns and three hundred planes was brought to bear. No small part in the victory was played by British troops achieving what had seemed almost impossible to attackers and defenders alike, the storming of the canal itself by frontal assault. The section chosen was the stretch running towards Belleglise from the tunnel's southern exit. Even today, one only has to stand on Riqueval Bridge, which marks that exit, to appreciate what General Braithwaite's IX Corps had, voluntarily and systematically, taken on. The high-arched stone bridge is much as it was then, though a new parapet, now weathered to the same dull grey, replaces the superstructure shattered in the fighting. The banks are now wooded and green, in contrast to the blackened pock-marked ramparts of September 1918. But the dimensions of those ramparts remain just as they were – cuttings rising sixty feet high at a sheer angle of more than forty-five degrees, and flowing between them, the band of deep dirty-green water.

The Territorial Division, the 46th, which was selected to make the crossing, was no élite formation; indeed it has been described as 'not a distinguished division'. Yet the men of its Midlands Regiment certainly covered themselves with glory on this day. Using the fog as an ally, not as an encumbrance, they first overran with the bayonet the German outposts which guarded the eastern bank, then slid down the sheer slope to the water's edge and ferried, swam or splashed their way across to take the far bank as well by storm. The German defenders blazed away at them with surprisingly little effect. It was not merely the dawn mist which upset their aim. It was the sheer improbability of such targets as they could discern – soldiers paddling across on collapsible boats or wooden rafts buoyed up by petrol cans; others half-walking, half-wading on canvas mats carrying scaling ladders as though they were besieging some medieval fortress; and, most unlikely sight of all, hundreds festooned with life-belts which had been collected from cross-channel ships and sent up from Boulogne. This was a triumph of the unexpected and the improvised over the orthodox mind of the defenders, and the dividends were commensurate. In less than three hours, the assault brigade, the 137th, had taken the far bank and captured two thousand of its astonished defenders for the loss of six hundred of their own men. The other two brigades of the division then passed through to take objectives beyond the canal and by 5.30 p.m., General Braithwaite's other division, the 32nd, had leapfrogged its way through the lines to take up the pursuit. Close to the Riqueval Bridge is a small memorial to the soldiers from Tennessee killed in this same canal battle, and another vast one towers above the village of Bellicourt to the north, where the American 30th Division broke through with heavy losses. The feat of the British is enshrined only in their regimental and divisional histories. Most of these are full of under-statement.

But whether through muddled and bloody slogging or through daring and economical use of force, by the 30th, the Fourth Army was through the first line of the Hindenburg defence; by 3 October it had taken the next line, which ran through Beaurevoir; and two days after that the canal and the entire fortified network which surrounded it were in General Rawlinson's hands. Our young artillery officer records what must have been the emotions of many of his fellows during these days. When the attack began, he was looking longingly through his field-glasses at Beaurevoir, Joncourt and Villers-Outreaux, villages on a crest behind the far bank of the canal:

> 'I could see unspoiled country ... undulating hills, little woods, villages fit to live in, trees that bore leaves, a hillside without shell-holes. It was like a Promised Land ... I longed to walk on those green hills, hills on which no British soldier had ever set foot, to ride through those unspoiled villages, to hear the rain falling on leaves on living trees ... then the mist came down and all the green unspoiled country was obliterated; only the white scars of the trenches remained and the lines of wire.'

Three mornings later, 'like a man in a dream', he was in his promised land.

> 'Bellicourt, where the canal came out of the tunnel, was still being shelled, not heavily but with a sulky persistence, and a cloud of dirty-coloured smoke hung over the shattered villages ... I could see the major up in front leading us. Now he was turning left, away from the canal, towards the enemy again, into the unspoiled country I had seen from the OP where ... the trees bore leaves ...
>
> 'We came to Etricourt, a hamlet only ... the servants were pitching a tent under a bank ... A tent in the line! It was absurd ... Two German sausage balloons had been watching us, they had seen us coming in ... and there was a German trench at no great distance ... But the major said we had finished with trenches.
>
> '"It's all over bar the shouting," he said. "It's come sooner than anyone could have expected. We may have heard our last shell, we shall soon forget the sound they used to make."
>
> 'And then the battery commander added: "I'm beginning to feel sorry for Fritz. He's put up a damned good show. I mean to say, he's had most of the world

against him, and it's taken us all this time, but he's down for the count now." '

Britain's war leader later paid his own tribute to the tenacity of the German defenders during those October battles:

> 'Starved, decimated, despairing, the German soldiers fought on, making us pay a heavy price for every mile we wrestled from them ... There was nothing finer in their record than the pluck with which they continued to withstand us in the hour of their defeat. They could not but know that they were beaten ... Yet in the month of October, the last whole month of the war, the British forces in France suffered 120,000 battle casualties, as evidence of the resistance they encountered.'

Both the artillery major's verdict and the British Prime Minister's summing up are reflected in two directives which Crown Prince Rupprecht, Commander-in-Chief of the German Army Group now recoiling back along the whole northern sector, received during these critical days. On 29 September, the day the British Fourth Army's attack went in, he received a telegram from Hindenburg warning him that, 'due to the lack of battle-worthy reserves and the overloaded situation of the railways no dispatch of further reinforcements can be expected'. Everything, Hindenburg added, had to be fought for; but it was now left to the discretion of divisional commanders whether they should simply try to seal off any breaches, or actually counter-attack. This abandonment of the usual style of categorical directions drew from the Crown Prince the weary marginal comment: 'At Last!'

The second message from Spa arrived the following day. Repeating, in even more emphatic form, the warning about reinforcements, Hindenburg continued:

> 'Nonetheless, an enemy breakthrough must be prevented at all costs ... What is needed is to win time, to inflict heavy losses on the foe, to bring back our own war material while systematically destroying railway and communications

installations ... A firm resolve is called for to beat off the enemy's onslaught and no ground must be yielded too soon ...'

Nowhere was this firm resolve displayed to greater effect against the Allies than in the fourth and most southerly thrust of their autumn offensive – the advance, by the American army, through the forests of the Argonne and across the line of the River Meuse. After the discordant overture of the St Mihiel operation, General Pershing had rightly demanded his grand solo act. Now he was given it, to play out in the most uninviting theatre and in the worst possible conditions.

As at the St Quentin canal cuttings, the problem of terrain emerges as clearly today as it did in the autumn of 1918, especially when viewed at the same time of year. After the open land around Chalons and St Menehould (mostly one dead flat beet or maize field after another) the Argonne Forest looms up like a vast rock in a calm sea. It is not only immensely thick and seemingly impenetrable, especially when most of the summer leaf is still on, but is also scored at all angles with deep ravines. To cap everything, at the time of the attack, there were only three main roads available. One, running up the Meuse Valley on the far right of the eighteen-mile front, was exposed to German guns sited on the heights above the eastern bank of the river; a second, skirting the woods on the far left of the line, was also under fire from enemy batteries in the forest; and the third, a lateral one running at right angles to the advance through the key objectives of Montfaucon, was a poorly-metalled minor road which soon collapsed under the pounding of these new hordes of men and vehicles. No experienced staff in normal circumstances would have dreamt of launching a major offensive against such a target until at least the approach roads had been improved and extended. But though General Pershing's planners* were learning fast, they still approached their tasks with the breezy optimism of American big business sorting out administrative

---

* They included the then Colonel George Marshall, later to rise to fame in the Second World War. One of Pershing's officers on the ground was to rise to even greater heights – Harry S. Truman, then captain of 'D' Battery of the 129th Field Artillery Regiment.

snags in the factory. Moreover, the circumstances were far from normal, especially for the American Commander-in-Chief in person. After harrying Foch for so many months to strike a major blow on his own account, Pershing could scarcely lag behind now. His next chance might not come until the spring, and by then, the war could be over, with his immense Expeditionary Force having to go home with little more than one long promenade across France to its credit. He really had no choice; but in taking the only political option open to him, Pershing had to gamble on the vitality, ingenuity and sheer numbers of his force to turn the military odds. There was a heavy price to pay before the gamble paid off.

Pershing's problems began long before the attack went in. As we have seen, he had only been allowed to conduct his modified operation against the St Mihiel bulge earlier that month after undertaking to have some of those same divisions, together with many fresh formations, ready for this far greater offensive on a different front less than a fortnight later. It was a very tall order indeed. The astounding thing, looking back, was not that his administrative machinery creaked and faltered under the stain, but that it managed to function at all.

To begin with, the whole of the French Second Army, which had been holding the Argonne sector, had to be moved out, except for one corps left behind to support Pershing. That meant evacuating some two hundred and twenty thousand French soldiers with all their staffs and impedimenta. Then six hundred thousand Americans had to be moved in (fifteen divisions with their Army and Corps Headquarters and supporting troops). Two-thirds of these men came at top speed from the St Mihiel battlefield, nearly fifty miles to the south-east, and some of the artillery from St Mihiel had to be shifted before the fighting there had even ended. Truck transport was somehow found for four hundred and twenty-eight thousand; the rest walked. Ninety thousand horses lugged up most of the three thousand guns which were moved into the attack area; the forty thousand tons of ammunition needed for the initial bombardment came up by rail, as did the three thousand tons of shells needed every day from then on.

For three hours before daylight on 26 September, those guns

opened up against the German defences with a noise like 'the head-on crash of a million express trains'. Then, at dawn, the American First Army moved forward, nine divisions abreast along the whole front, supported on the ground by 189 light tanks and overhead by 821 planes, mostly piloted by American aviators. America's first – and last – great battle of the war had begun. The grand objective was to roll up this Kriemhilde section of the Hindenburg Line (aided by the Fourth French Army marching on the American left), cross to Meuse and then cut the vital Lille-Metz railway near Sedan. An important subsidiary aim was to draw some of the fifty-odd German divisions away from the St Quentin front, and thus lighten the formidable opposition which faced the British there. But this proved illusory for, days after Haig had broken through his canals, Pershing remained stuck in his forests.

The Americans, despite the haste of their build-up, started with two advantages. The first was a good degree of surprise, thanks to a successful deception plan suggesting that their heaviest blow was being mounted further east. The second was sheer weight of numbers. Only five German divisions, four of them low-grade, defended this sector, as against the nine American divisions, with three more in close support, which attacked. Given the larger size of American formations, this worked out as a rifle superiority of some eight to one. Pershing's main drawbacks were the rawness of many of his assault troops, some of whom had only handled a rifle for the first time a few weeks before. On top of this came the nature and depth of the obstacles ahead. Whereas Haig had started on the very outposts of the Hindenburg Line, Pershing had to slog his way through a broad band of difficult country dotted with strong-points, before he even confronted the Kriemhilde defences. Five miles in front of the Kriemhilde Line, for example, lay the for-midable strong-point of Montfaucon, which rises a thousand feet up in the centre of the sector and where, even today, the ruins can be seen of some of those seventeen German blockhouses whose machine-guns in 1918 dominated the ground below.

Though both the flanking corps made good progress on the first day (even the forest on the far left proving less fearsome than had been thought) it was the check in the centre which drained the momentum from the attack. Pershing had fondly hoped that his army would not only reach the Kriemhilde Line on the first day, an advance of eight miles, but actually break through that line as well. In fact, the terrible 'Mountain of the Falcon', which was three miles short of the Hindenburg Line, did not fall until the second day, and, acting on Pershing's directive, the divisions on each flank waited – in vain – for the centre to catch up with them. By the time it did, three fresh German divisions had arrived to strengthen the defending forces, which then counter-attacked and regained ground at several points. Two more general offensives were launched by the Americans on 4 October and 14 October but 'achieved little at large cost'. Pershing's dream of breaking the Hindenburg Line before the British (who were in fact clear of it and in open country by 5 October) lay in ruins. Eleven more days of battle after the first thrust gained barely two more miles of ground. In all, there were to be forty-seven days of hard and costly fighting before the tenacious enemy on this sector was finally overcome. The beautifully sited cemetery of Romagne, where most of the American dead from the Meuse-Argonne battle lie buried under endless rows of white crosses, bears tranquil witness to the cost: with its 14,246 graves, it was the largest United States military cemetery in Europe. St Mihiel, by comparison, had less than one-third of that number.

The comparison with St Mihiel, when fighting the Germans had seemed so easy, was very much in the minds of the puzzled, frustrated attackers. One soldier who took part in both first-wave assaults wrote in his diary:

'We remembered the victorious dash at St Mihiel and went forward ... expecting to take everything in front of us. But what the hell is wrong? Heinie is getting tough, sticking until the last, and fighting like hell to hold every inch of ground. Within a very few minutes, we were hit by another devastating barrage. All hell broke out ... it was like a band of steel across our front. As our thinning ranks topped the crest of the hill, we were met by a withering blast from Jerry's machine guns ... men fell on all sides. Heavy shelling made the soggy, muddy fields one huge sea of death ...

Though there were some remarkable exploits – for example by the 1st Division of regular troops fighting on the left, or by the 79th, which managed to storm Montfaucon on the second day – there were some sad failures, which find no mention in Pershing's own bland account of the battle. The 15th Division (of Missouri and Kansas National Guardsmen) made what one of the American Corps Commanders called 'a costly mess' of its advance up the Aire Valley, while the 92nd Negro Division virtually took to its heels twice in the battle and had to be removed altogether on the insistence of the French.

An American surgeon whose diary of the campaign is full of shrewd comments, wrote this when the battle was five days old:

> 'We have unquestionably been severely handled. The 35th Division ... lost three of its four colonels, all of the lieutenant-colonels and majors and probably most of its captains and subalterns. The 79th came out much be-draggled ... and will probably be broken up or have its number changed ... the National Army has not made such a good showing as was expected ...'

But the American showing which caused the biggest Allied rumpus was not so much at the front line as behind it. On Sunday 29 September, the third day of the offensive, Clemenceau visited Pershing's headquarters. He was delighted with the capture, the previous day, of Mountfaucon, and asked to be taken up there. Pershing agreed, with some reluctance in view of the danger. But what defeated the 'Tiger's' motor-car was not German shells but the unholy tangle of American trucks he ran into. Pershing's severely misleading account of that abortive car trip reads:

> 'We failed to reach Montfaucon and he left rather disap-pointed, thinking, no doubt, that our transportation was hopelessly swamped, as we soon began to hear criticism to that effect, not only by the French but even by some Germans.'

In fact, the French Prime Minister was both furious and totally disenchanted with the chaos he had seen (somewhat unjustly, for a divisional relief had been in progress the day he tried to reach Montfaucon). Whatever the rights and wrongs, there were more than 'criticisms' when Pershing's front line seemed to get every bit as bogged down as his lines of communication.

To understand the episode which followed, we need to look again at the 'Tiger's' massive but highly volcanic structure. Apart from his life-long worship of women, Clemenceau only had one other imperishable idol – the glory of France. That aside, he was something of an iconoclast at heart and always a brutal non-respecter of persons. When, in November of 1917, President Poincaré – all solemnity and protocol – had greeted him for the first time as Prime Minister, in a ceremony which included the usual ritual embraces, Clemenceau had horrified both the prim Head of State and the assembled company by bellowing out: 'So, Raymond, shall we now make love, you and I?' And when he had formed his Cabinet, Clemenceau blandly introduced its members as 'the geese who have saved the Capitol'.

A man who could talk like that to his ministers and to the President of France was not going to equivocate in dealing with an American general – more particularly as it was Clemenceau himself who had coined the *bon mot* that 'war was too serious a matter to be left to the soldiers'. Moreover, he regarded even Foch as a subordinate general and, in his constitutional capacity as head of the French army Clemenceau wrote to Foch one of the most extraordinary letters ever dispatched in the war by a political leader to his Generalissimo. Complaining sarcastically that 'our worthy American allies, who thirst to get into action and who are unanimously acknowledged to be great soldiers, have been marking time ever since their forward jump on the first day', he tried to prod Foch into taking over direct command of Pershing's troops, in order to surmount 'the crisis existing in the American army'. Clemenceau expressed willingness to take the matter up with President Wilson if need be, and tell him 'the truth and the whole truth about the situation of the American troops'. But perhaps that would not be necessary. 'If General Pershing finally resigns himself to obedience, if he accepts the advice of capable generals, whose presence at his side he has only permitted up to now so that he might reject their counsels, I shall be wholly delighted.'

Foch, having, in his words, 'a more comprehensive knowledge of the difficulties encountered by the American army' and realizing what a minefield his Prime Minister was sowing, calmed Clemenceau down with a reply that was both factual and evasive. Eventually, as he knew, success along the whole front would carry any lagging sector with it, and erase all recrimination. But, as can be seen, the Allied advance on the Hindenburg Line was producing set-backs as well as victories and causing complications for the Allies which were both political and military. What, meanwhile, was going on behind the lines in the enemy camp? It is time to return once more to German Supreme Headquarters in occupied Belgium.

The first critical moment at Spa came as early as 26 September. That, it will be remembered, was the day after Bulgaria had capitulated to General Franchet d'Espèrey's Army of the Orient, thus opening a way for an Allied advance through Serbia right up to the line of the Danube. It was also the day when, in the Palestine fighting, the Germans and Turks had been driven from the key city of Amman, thus exposing Damascus to the all-conquering British empire forces of General Allenby. On the Western Front, the French–American attack in the Argonne had begun at dawn that same morning; but, as we have just seen, it had been halted short of Montfaucon, which was itself some miles in front of the main Kriemhilde defence lines. Whatever other Allied offensives in France were thought to be in the offing none had, as yet, been launched, and the whole of the Hindenburg Line was still intact.

Yet it was on this day, 26 September 1918, that Ludendorff summoned State Secretary von Hintze to Spa to end the war as soon as possible by diplomacy because it could no longer be resolved by force of arms. There is good reason to believe that the decision to send for von Hintze had in fact been taken the day before by a young group of so-called military 'realists' on Supreme Headquarters staff led by Colonel Mertz von Quirnhem and Colonel Heye, who had just been transferred to Spa from his former post as Chief-of-Staff to Crown Prince Rupprecht's Army Group. Ludendorff, who, according to von Quirnheim, 'still had the desperation to fight but not the courage to make an end of it', immediately confirmed the invitation when Heye raised the matter with him at midday on the 26th, and seemed relieved at the initiative taken by his subordinates. As the Supreme Headquarters archives for the Great War were destroyed in Potsdam in 1945, there is no complete official record against which all these personal accounts can be placed.

In his memoirs, which make no mention of any such preliminaries, the First Quartermaster-General does, however, make it abundantly clear that it was the grave news from the Eastern Fronts and not any fresh disasters in the West (which, indeed, had not yet emerged) which made him decide, for the second time in seven weeks, to throw in the military sponge. Everything that he records in the four pages of gloomy analysis explaining that appeal to von Hintze concerns the collapse in the East. The West is only mentioned once, as the 'hard-pressed' front which had now lost six or seven badly-needed divisions rushed to the Balkan theatre because the even harder-pressed German commanders there needed them still more.

'It was obvious' [runs his catalogue of woe] 'that the Entente would attempt to liberate Serbia, and make an attack from there on Hungary, thus giving the *coup de grâce* to the Dual Monarchy. Our Balkan front was unstable and it was quite uncertain whether we would be able to reconstruct it in Serbia and Bulgaria; or even on the Danube ...

'Turkey too was now in great difficulties. Her Palestine front was broken beyond repair ... the English were gaining ground rapidly northwards along the coast and the railway towards Damascus ... Constantinople was bound to fall and whether it fell in November or December made little difference ... Once the city fell, it was to be expected that Entente fleets would establish communication with Rumania through the Black Sea and send troops through Bulgaria to the Danube. We could not hope to keep Rumania neutral ...

'In Italy, an attack was sure to come, and it was very dubious how the Austro-Hungarian troops there would fight ...

'In these circumstances I felt compelled to take on myself the heavy responsibility of hastening the end of the war, and for this purpose to move the government to decisive action ...'

Even writing of this fateful decision in a lengthy memorandum composed a month later, when the Allies had almost completely broken through in the West, Ludendorff does not alter the broad balance of the arguments which drove him to act as he did on 26 September:

'The treachery of Bulgaria came as a surprise ... she could not longer be counted on ... I was convinced that Serbia could not be held. That meant the enemy would stand on the frontiers of Hungary and that, inevitably, would shake the crumbling Hapsburg state ...

'I was reckoning with an attack on Constantinople in November which would fall without resistance, for the Turkish Army was pinned down elsewhere ... I state in conclusion that the events in Bulgaria were bound inescapably to lead to the collapse of our allies. The war was now lost and there was nothing more we could do about it.'

And Ludendorff added that, when at 4 p.m. the following day, 27 September, he had communicated this scenario of military despair to Hindenburg, he found that the Field Marshal had already reached the same conclusions independently and was about to voice them himself.

This conference at Spa during the last days of September was a crucial turning-point in the story of the last hundred days, and on that account alone, it is worth establishing its genesis. But there is another reason for being quite clear about the true sequence of events, and that is to get the famous argument between 'Easterners' and 'Westerners' into some sort of perspective. During the war itself that debate grew so acrimonious that the rival partisans in

London and Paris often ended up by shouting and sniping at each other from behind their respective barricades, with little thought for the common ground which lay between them. The battle has continued to rage academically for more than sixty years after the war's end, sometimes with equally little respect for common ground or common sense.

Certainly, the French front was always the primary theatre in the First World War; just as, from June 1941, the Russian front was paramount in the Second. Each was the great meat-grinder which, alone, could relentlessly consume German strength. But, in both conflicts, the other fronts, though secondary, were far from trivial. And what the 'Westerners' failed to grasp during the Great War (and their apologists ever since) was that the Italian, Balkan and Near Eastern battlegrounds possessed a deep psychological as well as strategic significance for the enemy. For decades before 1914, the Germans had been forced to contemplate, constantly paraded before them, the dual spectres of '*Zweifrontenkrieg*' and '*Einkreisung*' ('War on two fronts' and 'Encirclement'). Nor were these just propaganda phantoms. They were also the real-life bogeys of the German general staff, who had spent these same decades planning how to overcome them. For both the German military and the civilians, the Kaiser's English uncle, Edward VII, who had done so much to strengthen his country's links with Republican France and Tsarist Russia, was the bland arch-villain of the piece. After the collapse of imperial Russia in 1917 it seemed that this baleful circle of enemies which ringed Germany was broken at last and that the eastern approaches to Berlin and Vienna were firmly secured.

But, less than eighteen months later, it was as though the garden gates had suddenly been thrown down, and it could only be a matter of weeks, perhaps days, before the back door itself would be splintering. The panic which seized both capitals of the Dual Alliance on 26 September can only be fully explained by the mental conditioning both peoples had undergone ever since the 1880s. So, in a more sober and professional context, can the pang of despair which gripped Ludendorff on that same day; and it cannot be said too often that one of the decisive battles of 1918 was the losing battle which Ludendorff waged with his own nerves.*

It was not only Germany's War Lords in Spa who were being driven to far-reaching decisions. The nation's political leaders back in Berlin were also preparing to cross the Rubicon, or rather several Rubicons at once. By the time von Hintze set out for Spa he and his circle of friends and advisers were clear about two things. The first was that the new German peace move which now lay, almost tangibly, in the air, would have to go to President Wilson and not to his European allies. In this, Hintze was to find no opposition either from the military or the crown. America was a relatively new opponent on the battlefields, and one with whom in peacetime Germany would presumably have no direct territorial dispute or strategic clash of interests. Rivers of blood, on the other hand, separated Germany from France and England. Moreover, with the former there was the eternal debate over Alsace-Lorraine; and with the latter, the more recent world-wide rivalries of commerce and naval power. The Emperor Charles of Austria had already tried, and woefully failed, eighteen months before, to remove the Alsace-Lorraine obstacle in his direct secret soundings with France. As for England, only during those past few weeks she had again used her powerful influence with neutral Holland to block von Hintze's attempts to start up serious mediation via The Hague. The path to peace in Europe seemed unnegotiable. Wilson's Fourteen Points may still have appeared very tricky in parts; but, by the autumn of 1918, they seemed to offer Germany the only solid plank in sight which might lead the army and the nation out of the quagmire. Von Hintze accordingly set out with a programme already drafted by his officials 'to approach President Wilson at the appropriate moment with the request to set about the securing of peace'. That also fitted well with the Kaiser's latest thinking, which was strongly influenced by German industrial tycoons and amateur diplomatists like Albert Ballin, who were spinning all the threads they could across the Atlantic.

---

* Those seemed by now to be going to pieces. He himself admitted to four of his officers on the evening of 25 September that, 'like a drowning man clutching at a straw', he had been placing great hopes in rumours that the French army was being laid low by pneumonia.

But von Hintze left Berlin with something more in his briefcase than a peace move. He also took with him the outline of a government reform designed to go with it. Germany's bumbling Chancellor, Count Hertling, was clearly not the man for the hour. He was held – and rightly – both inside and outside Germany to be little more than a political extension of the High Command, a reputation which would hardly commend him to the Allies. Moreover, his own political stock had just sunk even lower after the flat reception which the Reichstag, the Berlin Parliament, had given to a major speech he had delivered there on the 24th. On top of all this came the fact that his own party, the Catholic Centre led by Matthias Erzberger, was itself a minority group, and for some time the demand had been growing for greater representation in the government for the predominantly Socialist parliamentary majority.

This demand was now turning fast into a crying need. At least in appearances Germany would have to be democratized before she appealed for help to the most prominent democrat in the world. The reality of this so-called 'revolution from above' (which was supposed to pre-empt the more normal and more disturbing variety of a revolution from below) went little more than skin-deep, with such proposals as the attachment of Socialist State Secretaries to the various ministries. But Hertling, who was incapable even of recognizing the necessity for change, let alone of carrying much change through, had recoiled in fastidious horror at the mere suggestion of installing what, to him, were little better than emissaries of Beelzebub in his government departments. So, on all counts, he would have to go. That week the German press was full of demands for his resignation. But nothing was more characteristic of the way German politics – in stark contrast to Allied politics – still operated than the way the news was officially broken to him. On 28 September Colonel von Winterfeldt, a senior staff officer of Hindenburg's, called on the Chancellor of Germany to inform him that, in the opinion of Supreme Headquarters, 'a reorganization of the government or its expansion on a broader national base had now become necessary'. At that the astounded Chancellor, who had seemingly been oblivious of the fact that his office chair was folding up beneath him, hurriedly packed his suitcase and set off, in the wake of von Hintze, for Spa. The imperial train was also now heading for the same destination, despite the Kaiser's reluctance to leave the bedside of his sick wife. By the 29th all the leading actors had thus assembled again in the little Belgian watering-place for another, and more searching, look at Germany's balancing act between peace and war.

By then, of course, the Western Front was also in flames, though in a talk Ludendorff had with Hindenburg on the eve of the conference, in which the need for an armistice was agreed by both men, the Quartermaster-General still had his eyes anxiously fixed on the East. ('The situation could only get worse, on account of the Balkan position, even if we held our ground in the West.') With so much agreed in advance by the military, and with so many changes already under preparation on the political front, things moved quickly when the two sides got together again around the Field Marshal's operations table in the Hotel Britannique at 10 a.m. on Sunday 29 September. Hertling had not yet arrived, which gave von Hintze a chance to speak the unvarnished truth without the embarrassing presence of his Chancellor. Everyone agreed that a peace move to Wilson abroad, coupled with the famous 'revolution from above' at home* was the best strategy to adopt; but there were differences over the timing. After more than six weeks of humming and hah-ing, of promising, but never producing, that 'strategic defensive' on the battlefields on which the politicians could base their peace moves, it was Ludendorff who was calling for an armistice without a moment's delay. Hintze wrote later:

> 'In front of me sat the two warriors who had carried Germany's sword with such glory ... Now they were as good as saying to me, "Everything is lost except our honour: save whatever can be saved!"'

Hintze tried to explain that a new government was an integral part of the peace plan, and that an effective plea to Wilson could only

---

* Hintze produced, as a strange alternative, the setting up of a political dictatorship in Berlin. Ludendorff would have none of this; he, if anyone, was Germany's dictator already.

come after a different Chancellor had been installed. And, in any case, he pointed out, too abrupt a transition from 'fanfares of victory to grave-side lamentations of defeat' could have an unsettling effect.

The head of that dynasty reached Spa himself that same morning, and soon after 11 a.m. he joined and presided over the talks. Both as Emperor and, even more, as Germany's Supreme War Lord, William again cut a passive, almost pathetic figure at Spa. To begin with, as his military aide makes clear, it was only after arriving at Supreme Headquarters that he learned of the decision already taken to sue for peace. Yet he asked no questions and uttered not the mildest word of rebuke. Then, after listening to another gloomy analysis of the military outlook (delivered this time by Hindenburg) and Hintze's proposals for an armistice appeal to Washington coupled with government changes in Berlin, he approved the entire programme as it stood, 'with controlled emotions and regal dignity' as Hintze politely put it. As always, the Supreme War Lord was reduced to a decorative puppet when flanked by his famous generals.

By midday on the 29th Hertling himself had arrived – just in time to offer his resignation, which was promptly accepted by the Kaiser. At first William hesitated to carry out the change of government immediately, influenced by Ludendorff's argument that this would only delay, if only by a few days, the vitally important peace move. But the draft of the royal proclamation dismissing Hertling and welcoming the greater participation in government affairs of 'men who enjoy the trust of the people' had already been placed on the ruler's desk. Hintze caught his sovereign at the door as he was walking, still undecided, away from it. A few urgent words of persuasion and the Kaiser turned round, went back to the table, and signed. Hintze called up his Foreign Office and instructed it to inform Vienna and Constantinople, the two remaining allied capitals, that Germany was about to sue for peace on the basis of President Wilson's Fourteen Points.

All that now remained was to find the right person to head that government, the 'Peace Chancellor' which the hour demanded. How vital that change was Hintze discovered yet again from one

207

among a pile of telegrams awaiting him on his desk in Berlin, to which he returned on 30 September. The message was from the German envoy in Berne, Prince Hohenlohe, through whom the contacts with Washington were made. It read: 'America's aversion to the government leadership has further deepened considerably, and I regard any discussions as useless until our political system has been changed.'

After a hurried scrutiny of other possible candidates (the former Chancellor Prince Bülow was briefly considered; also, at greater length, the current Vice-Chancellor Payer who, however declined) the choice for Germany's new man fell naturally on a name which had been increasingly mentioned during the final weeks of Hertling's eclipse: Prince Max of Baden, cousin to the reigning Grand Duke Frederick II, and heir to the Grand Duchy.

This princely amateur had a number of personal qualifications for the unenviable job. Himself descended from the ancient house of Zähringen, he had married in 1900 Princess Marie Louise of Brunswick, who, as daughter of the Duke of Brunswick, was also a Princess of Great Britain and Ireland. In a Europe in which (it was still fondly hoped) all the surviving dynasties would somehow continue to reign, that direct link with Buckingham Palace might be considered useful. Another bonus lay in the Prince's war work among interned belligerents – Allied as well as German – in Switzerland, which would surely commend him as a humane person to the Entente powers. But the greatest hopes of all, in view of the Allied leader to whom Germany's peace appeal was to be sent, were placed in Prince Max's reputation as a man with liberal ideas. There was, for example, his speech of 14 December 1917 (a time when Germany still seemed invincible) in which he had declared: 'Power alone cannot secure for us the position in the world which we believe to be our due. The sword cannot tear down the moral resistance which has been raised against us.'

That those hopes, though over-optimistic, were not ill-founded, was shown by some of the reactions to his nomination in the enemy camp. A former American ambassador to Berlin declared in New York, for example:

'The Prince is one of the few high Germans who seem to be able to think like an ordinary human being ... [his appointment] means to my mind a very definite attempt to seek peace and an abandonment of the pan-German policy.'

And from London came the comment:

'A man of some personal charm and wide international connections, an orator whose speeches are believed to have found favour in pacifist circles abroad and a reformer who quotes Kant and Plato, Prince Max may well appear cut out for the part which now seems assigned to him.'

In appearance as well as in reputation, that lean-faced, slightly balding grandee of fifty-one years, whose languid well-opened gaze reflected the man whose pleasant lot in life it had always been to issue instructions rather than to receive them, seemed to fit the bill well enough as moral champion for the beleaguered House of Hohenzollern. The drawback was his lack of practical experience of any politics of note. As a Prince of his house he had served for the past eleven years as President of the Baden Upper Chamber which met, very leisurely, only every second year, to hear one of his cultured and 'progressive' orations. To be catapulted at one go from Grand-ducal affabilities in Karlsruhe straight into the big league of national and international politics, and all this at a historic turning-point in world affairs, was asking a lot. His uncle the Grand Duke, for one, clearly felt it was asking too much. His formal permission had to be sought and when, on 1 October, the Kaiser pressed him to agree, in a personal telegram dispatched from the imperial train, Frederick II did so in a manner which displayed both perplexity at the choice and misgivings about the outcome. ('I cannot understand why it has to be Max who should give his name to such a [peace] offer ...')

However, during the next three days, while the way was being cleared for his appointment, 'Bademax', as he had been nicknamed by his officer comrades, showed that he was made of sterner stuff than Hertling when it came to dealing with Ludendorff. The

Prince had arrived in Berlin on 1 October determined not to be rushed by the High Command into over-hasty action. The idea of an immediate armistice appeal to Wilson seemed to him a desperate step not justified by the admittedly serious military situation. It also seemed bad negotiating tactics. Ideally, he would have preferred to have waited anything up to a fortnight and have delivered a major speech to the Reichstag, separating the two concepts of cease-fire and peace conditions. Even if this was asking too much, he was resolved not to make any move with Washington until his new Coalition government, which was the moral guarantor of such a move, was formed.

Thus, for the first time, Ludendorff felt his sabre ringing against another sabre in Berlin; for the first time, the politicians were not scurrying to obey his orders like soldiers on a parade ground. The result was an unprecedented campaign of pressure from Spa. Two officers, Count Roedern and Major von dem Bussche, were dispatched to the capital with the specific task of hastening things up. The latter, on 2 October, gave a special briefing on the military situation to the leaders of all German political parties which, from all accounts, dropped among them like a hand-grenade. For the first time they too heard, virtually from the mouth of Ludendorff, what only a handful of civilian ministers had heard before. ('The collapse of the Bulgarian front upset our arrangements completely ... mighty attacks in the West ... did not find us unprepared ... the large part of our troops fought excellently and achieved superhuman results ... Despite this, the Army Command has had to acknowledge that ... there is no longer any prospect of forcing the enemy to seek peace ... No time should be lost. Every twenty-four hours can make the situation worse ...')

Of the politicians listening Vice-Chancellor Payer was the only one who had heard the truth before. The others were dazed by the realization that their military colossus was crumbling. Of the two key Socialists present, Ebert 'went as white as death'; Stresemann 'looked as if he had been struck'; while the Prussian minister von Waldow left the room muttering, 'The only thing left to do now is to put a bullet through one's head!' As Prince Max commented, on being given these reports, the spark of panic 'now leapt across to the people at home'.

Still, he held out a little longer against Spa. On 1 October, the day when Germany was effectively without a government, Ludendorff, hiding behind Hindenburg's name on a telegram, graciously consented to postpone the appeal to Wilson for twenty-four hours 'if it is certain that by seven or eight o'clock tonight Prince Max von Baden is forming a ministry'. Even by the Junker-ridden standards of Wilhelminian politics, it was an impertinent intrusion into the civilian domain. Phone call after phone call followed from Spa on the following day, as Prince Max was striving, not without difficulty ('Why take part in a bankrupt enterprise?' the Socialist Scheidemann had at first objected), to form his peace Cabinet. But it was the arrival in Berlin on that same day of the Kaiser, accompanied by Hindenburg, which decided the issue.

The Field Marshal, unlike his Quartermaster-General, was not seeking to play politics. He says in his memoirs that he had come to the capital simply to be near his Emperor, in case of need, and he can be believed, for it is in the character of the man. (No less a judge than Foch, asked after the war by Lloyd George to opine on his two great German opponents, distinguished between Ludendorff as 'a good soldier' and Hindenburg as 'a good patriot'.) Now, Hindenburg, gravely and calmly confirming the need for immediate action, carried far more weight with Prince Max on the spot than the excitable Ludendorff, cabling and telephoning from Spa. And when, at a conference on 2 October, the Supreme War Lord put himself squarely behind the military, chiding Prince Max (who was his own cousin) 'You have not been brought here to make difficulties for the Supreme Council,' there was little that the unfortunate Chancellor-designate could do. A series of five searching questions which he put to Hindenburg on 3 October to reveal the unvarnished truth about the military outlook produced only general replies, and the rest of that day was spent on completing the peace government and on finalizing the text of the peace appeal. To have delayed further now would have meant Prince Max resigning the office that he was just about to take over.

That same night, the note was sent off to the German mission in Switzerland, for onward transmission to the White House. It read:

'The German Government requests the President of the United States of America to take steps for the restoration of peace, to notify all belligerents of this request, and to invite them to delegate plenipotentiaries for the purpose of taking up negotiations. The German Government accepts, as a basis for the peace negotiations, the programme laid down by the President of the United States in his message to Congress of 8 January 1918, and his subsequent pronouncements, particularly in his address of 27 September 1918.

'In order to avoid further bloodshed the German Government requests the President to bring about the immediate conclusion of an armistice on land, on water, and in the air.

(Signed) Max, Prince of Baden,
Imperial Chancellor.'

The die was thus cast. In view of later German recriminations about 'civilian capitulation', it is worth stressing once more that it was Ludendorff, and not the recently deposed Chancellor nor his successor (in other words, the army and not the government), who had insisted that the die be thrown now, and so hurriedly. The politically-minded Prince who had reluctantly signed that telegram still had the same misgivings about the precipitate move when he woke up for his first day in office the next morning. 'I felt,' he wrote, 'like a man who has been condemned to death, and had forgotten it in his sleep.'

9

Home Fires

WHEN, LIKE AN AUTUMN WIND, these whispers of peace began
to move across Europe in early October, they stirred, at first, more
scepticism than hope. There had, after all, been so many false
dawns during the four dark years that had passed. General
Debeney, commander of the First French Army now fighting in
the St Quentin sector, told an American visitor that his own poilus
were even getting exasperated by the rumours, as they had already
geared themselves mentally for a campaign that would last through
the winter. 'It was important that their hopes should not be raised
... only to be dashed by a rejection of offers unacceptable to the
Allies.'

More difficult to gauge was the mood of the French nation at
large, which was part actor and part bystander in the conflict. What
was undeniable was that France had suffered far more than any
other of the major Allied combatants. Ever since 1914, ten of her
northern *départements*, areas covering about twenty-five thousand
square miles, had been occupied and largely devastated by the
enemy. More than a tenth of her soil, including some of her finest
orchards, vineyards and arable land, had been torn up by the rake
of war. Some four hundred thousand houses had been levelled to
the ground. Hundreds of her factories were either out of commission or, even worse, working for the invader, including key
industries like textiles, sugar and metallurgy, to say nothing of the
coalmines and heavy plants of Longwy and Briey.

Two preoccupations dominated everyday civilian life: fighting
cold and fighting hunger. All forms of fuel were both rationed and
scarce. The frantic hunt for coal was graphically summed up by a
top Paris jeweller who displayed a lump of it in his shop window in
place of his usual array of diamonds and emeralds. By now, the
liberation of the mines at Lens, which used to produce three

million tons a year, had raised hopes that the flooded and dyna-
mited galleries might yield up at least a few thousand tons of the
precious stuff. But no Parisian doubted that, if the war were to drag
on until 1919, it would be another winter of shivering in one's
apartment, with the family overcoats on, and huddled into one
room for most of the time. In that glacial setting social life tended to
freeze over. An invitation to dinner (a rarity in itself) was no more
welcome than an invitation just to sit by a fire.

The food problem was not, in practice, so severe – though acute
and distressing enough for a people with such veneration for their
stomachs. The vast lush countryside of France which stretched
south of Paris, untroubled by the war, down to the Atlantic and
Mediterranean oceans, knew few serious privations. Even in the
cities, the perpetual queueing for everything that was unrationed
was a commoner hardship than outright privation. Serious
shortages did, of course, occur. *Le saucisson*, so beloved of the
Parisians, had been in such short supply that the sausage dealers of
the capital had been closed three days a week throughout that
summer, and prospects did not look much brighter when they had
met to review the situation on 5 October. This fifth autumn of the
war had also brought a dearth of potatoes. Yet, as regards bread, the
main complaint in Paris concerned quality rather than availability
– 'In one quarter of the city dark brown; in another heavy and
golden like Indian corn; in another white as bread ever was.' The
prospects for drink supplies were even promising: 1918 had seen an
excellent vintage of wine, while beer was now declared to be better
and more abundant than for some time past.

Restaurants flourished. This was partly because they ignored
the food regulations and partly because, since they provided
warmth and light as well as a meal, it often worked out cheaper to
eat in them, despite the stiff prices, than at home. France strove to
remain true to its gastronomic heritage. The Food Commissioner,
M. Borel, insisted that all French restaurants should provide both à
la carte and table d'hôte menus, and warned proprietors to treat
both classes of customer equally well. The autumn had also seen
the opening of a chain of municipal restaurants where the working
man could buy himself a square meal for only 1 franc 65 centimes

(little more than one English shilling). Nobody, in short, was starving, and money could buy any delicacy.

More important for the nation's morale was the feeling that, with the great Allied summer advance from the Marne, the German grip around the throttle of Paris had been shaken off for good, however long it might still take to free Picardy and Flanders. The best token of this easement was the liberation of Crépy, just south of Laon, during the September fighting. There, on a railway siding, had crouched those huge 210 mm German guns, each a hundred feet in length and weighing over three hundred tons, which, at 7.16 a.m. on the morning of 23 March, had hurled the first of their shells into the north-western suburbs of Paris, a staggering distance of seventy-four miles away. These monsters, now driven from their lair, could, surely, never return.*

With their menace removed (and that of the Zeppelin and Gotha bombing raids as well as the proximity of the German army itself) many of the half-million Parisians who had left the capital in the spring were filtering back. 'Stations which a little while since were busy with departures are almost as busy with arrivals,' one observer noted. Moreover, shops and theatres were re-opening and the famous fashion houses were stirring into life again. The 1918 autumn models still reflected the shadows of war. Black, the colour of mourning, was prominent in the collections. An abundance of very long gowns and furs took note of the fuel shortage. The hats even included 'a helmet-shaped erection made of a metallic cloth with little plumes sticking out of it'. But though the associations may still have been military, the revival of the luxury trade itself pointed hopefully towards peace.

Above all, the French had now regained confidence in their own leaders. There had been a thorough, if belated purge of the defeatists in their ranks in 1917, the year when France, wracked by political scandals and mutinies in the army, had stood within a few tottering paces of collapse. In the spring and summer of 1918, most of the principal culprits were brought to justice after public trial. Louis Malvy, the former Minister of Interior, had been sentenced

---

* The siding can still be traced today but all that remains of the great guns are the mounts for the base plates.

to five years' banishment, having only just escaped a heavier penalty on charges of incitement to mutiny. Some of his principal henchmen in the same game (financed by German money) of spreading subversive pacifist propaganda were less fortunate, and had ended up before the firing-squad. The most illustrious defeatist of them all, the former Prime Minister Joseph Caillaux, was still in jail awaiting trial – which was not to come until February 1920 – for 'plotting against the security of the state abroad'. He was the black conscience of war-time France. But Georges Clemenceau, the seventy-six-year-old radical Republican who had stepped into that disgraced office on 17 November 1917, had soon become her talisman of hope. Nothing conveyed the transformation better than the phrase now often heard in Paris: 'If Clemenceau says that victory is in sight, then it must be.' In short, by the autumn of 1918 France, though more exhausted and bled whiter than ever, was no longer prostrate.

Her principal ally, Britain, had known neither the political traumas nor the personal degradations of military occupation suffered by the French. Yet, because she lacked the enormous home-grown agricultural resources of France – depending instead on sea-borne convoys which, for the past five years, had been running the hazardous gauntlet of German U-boats – Britain's food problem had, if anything, been graver. However, as the fifth war winter approached, the hallowed British breakfast, amid signs that the enemy's naval blockade was beaten at last, had certainly been assured for the months ahead: bacon and ham were declared coupon-free, due to the arrival of supplies from America 'sufficient to meet any possible demands for a considerable time to come'. Other meats were severely restricted under the nation-wide ration-book system which had been introduced in the summer – a comprehensive scheme which had left only tea, cheese and bread on free sale. 'Eat slowly. You will need less food,' was one of many rather despairing official slogans coined to meet the emergency.

Food and the fighting-fronts were already linked again by the annual operation of organizing Christmas parcels for the troops. 'It is not too early,' the authorities warned on 8 October, 'for people to make their arrangements.' The Americans, whether supplied from depots in England or France, or directly from the United States, had, not surprisingly, devised the most businesslike system of spreading a little seasonal cheer over the mud of the trenches. They had designed standard gift tins, four inches wide by nine inches long and three inches deep, each containing three pounds of food, and it was estimated that, a full month before Christmas, two million of these parcels would already be on their way to American soldiers on all battle-fronts. British plans were less lavish, and also less standardized, but it was nonetheless hoped that, as last year, every Tommy everywhere would somehow receive his bit of plum pudding by 25 December. That the Christmas of 1918 would already have brought its own most precious gift to all was not visualized. The coming winter still seemed one of struggle.

Serene as a great ocean liner – and apparently as unsinkable – the class system of Old England rode high through all these tribulations. It was reported, for example, that 'a number of well-to do people had decided to live off luxuries, leaving necessities for the poor'; while the famous writer, H. G. Wells, publicly supported the view that all who could afford wine should keep off beer, which was 'practically a necessity for many open-air workers'.

As in France domestic heating was one of the nation's acutest problems. The British people were approaching the winter with their domestic allowances of coal, gas and electricity drastically reduced by another twenty-five per cent; the fuel demands of the war industries, and the recruitment of another seventy-five thousand miners into the armed forces to meet the acute shortage of reserves, had left the authorities no other choice. It was going to be hard to keep the home fires burning in the literal sense of the words, and all manner of economy measures were being suggested for the winter ahead: mix coal with coke; use fire-bricks; don't use the poker; burn all rubbish; don't make up at night, and so on, through a long list of official tips. In his search for fuel savings the Coal Controller had fixed even on the six gas lights needed to illuminate each billiard table in the public saloons. In the winter ahead, he decreed, all such billiard saloons would have to close at 10.30 p.m. which, he loftily added, was anyway 'a reasonable hour for that amusement to cease'.

It was in the official attitude to outdoor, rather than indoor sports, that British tradition was seen battling its hardest against austerity. Not surprisingly, horse-racing proved one of the doughtiest fighters. It had survived a great debate in 1915 as to whether or not features such as the Ascot and Derby meetings should be banned as wasteful and frivolous or maintained as national morale-boosters. Then, in the black days of 1917, the Jockey Club had been obliged to suspend racing altogether on direct instructions from the War Cabinet. The University Boat Race, the regattas of Henley and Cowes and even the Football Association Cup Final all followed it into temporary oblivion. Yet, by the autumn of 1918, the race-courses were back in limited operation again. There was to be no steeplechasing in the coming winter. On the flat, however, a substitute St Leger was run at Newmarket (instead of Doncaster) and so the same papers which, in September, had reported the great Allied advances in France, Palestine and Macedonia, carried, on their sporting pages, the eternal speculation about a Classic winner. Indeed one paper carried the news that the Cambridgeshire had been won by a head by Zinovia slap alongside a column of war hero citations headed by a quote, 'Stick it, men – VC Colonel's Battle Cry'. The two reports were of roughly equal prominence. One felt that even the VC colonel might well have read the sporting item first.

Two official measures announced that same month revealed the depth and strength of Britain's racing following and equine lobby. The first was an attempt by the government to reduce horse-feed through a new Hay and Straw Order. The Jockey Club immediately dug its spurs into the 'Horse-Breeding and Racing Committee of the House of Commons' and the invidious order was duly rescinded a few days later. The second measure was a War Cabinet decision to ban all so-called 'flapping' meetings, which were unrecognized race gatherings springing up all over the country, largely for betting purposes. As Britain's bookmakers did not have the political punch of the Jockey Club, this order went into effect unchallenged.

Shooting, on the other hand, flourished unchallenged as the new season opened, its *raison d'être* being its contribution to the nation's larder. Rabbits and hares had been declared ration-free to what were termed 'self-suppliers', though all sportsmen were now supposed to surrender one coupon from their new ration-books to eat one brace of pheasant or two brace of partridge. A similar obeisance to the emergency was made on the Scottish grouse moors. The sport there had opened six days early that year, in what was mysteriously described as 'a war measure'. The coveys were plentiful and strong and the guns quelled any moral pangs they may have felt by sending most of the early bags to local military hospitals. Consciences were probably also eased by the feeling that the sporting traditions of the nation must somehow be preserved even against the Kaiser and his terrible war. That, at any rate, was the sentiment reflected in the press when the second great day in the sportsman's calendar for 1918 came round: 'Partridge shooting on the 1st of September remains an institution in England.'

But if in the autumn of 1918 those traditions still survived – reflecting, among other things, the conservatism of country life – the social face of Britain was in other ways changing fast, particularly in the cities. Mass mobilization (the Military Service Bill enacted in the spring had raised the recruitment age to fifty, withdrawing, in the process, thousands of professional and occupational exemptions) had jumbled all classes together, even if certain basic distinctions remained and were to survive. It was women, rather than workmen, who, after four years of war, were enjoying the greatest emancipation. For them the munitions factories were no 'satanic mills' of Mars but rather palaces of King Midas where undreamt-of wealth could be scooped up in brown wage packets. One incident is typical of many recorded at this time: 'A girl employed at some metal and munitions works went to a shop and asked for a sealskin coat, a real one. There was one other genuine sealskin coat in stock besides the one she took. "Put that aside for my pal, she will buy it", she said.' It was no coincidence that, as the final phase of the war opened up on the battlefields in October 1918, a debate was announced in the House of Commons 'on the principle of making women eligible for election'.*

* The bill giving women the right to vote had already been passed by a large majority at the beginning of the year.

The shape of Britain's future (in this case, a dark shadow) was also beginning to appear in the field of industrial relations. Paradoxically, the nation's workers, who had given the authorities relatively little trouble during the dark years of war, had grown restive almost as soon as the tide turned. Victory after victory on the battlefields was now matched by strike after strike on the home front. First, thirty-five thousand Midlands engineers came out, followed by eleven thousand London tram and bus staff, and after them the Yorkshire miners, the cotton-spinners and the railwaymen. Almost unbelievably, London's fourteen thousand policemen, the entire metropolitan force, also caught the fever and downed their batons for three days in a demand for better pay and union recognition. An eye-witness wrote:

> '... The most topsy-turvy occurrence witnessed during the war years was the sight of Downing Street, usually so well-guarded, being invaded by its guardians. The policemen good-humouredly but resolutely took possession of the street as their deputation went into No. 10 to see the Prime Minister ... Police minstrels, perched on the Prime Minister's walls, sang songs to while away the time. From midnight on Thursday to ten o'clock on Saturday there were no police in an enormous area stretching from Epsom in the south to Barnet in the north, from Dagenham in the east to Staines in the west ... It was well that many burglars were in the armies ...'

A highly intelligent fifteen-year-old English schoolgirl wrote this prim reprimand in her diary entry for 30 September 1918:

> 'I am sorry to say that our country is being disgraced by strikes just at the moment when all help is wanted to win the war. In most of the cases the men are striking for a minimum wage of £5 per week ... They say they are working for eight hours a day, but during that time they take meals and often work slackly ...'

To some extent, this was the legacy of four years' strain. As a leading journal wrote at the time of this same phenomenon: 'The general war-weariness of the hour has made serious inroads on our solid British temperament.' But the agitation can also be seen as the stirring of a work-force which, however tired, was just beginning to feel its industrial strength and to use that muscle to hang on to wages and living standards which, by now, surpassed anything in pre-war experience. Trouble often comes for governments not when things are at their worst, but when they begin to get better.

The emancipation of women, the wider spread of money, the new boldness of workers and the general throwing together of classes were not the only forces to disturb established social patterns. Another factor was the massive presence on British soil of the representatives of an alien if English-speaking way of life – American troops who, by the autumn of 1918, numbered scores of thousands on their way to or from the battlefields. British papers had begun to carry American baseball results for the benefit of these guests, some of whom had already started up regular sessions of the game themselves in Hyde Park.

That was one exact foretaste of a World War still to come. Another was the delicate question of providing sex for these virile crusaders so far from home. That autumn saw a heated exchange in newspaper correspondence columns on the subject. One writer complained that London's street-women were menacing America's 'clean-blooded and strong-limbed soldiers' (almost inferring that the pavement ladies were somehow on Ludendorff's pay-roll). That drew immediate retorts that such an accusation was 'hogwash'; that the doughboys were no more 'clean-blooded' than the average British Tommy; and that if any of them were falling for the 'toothless and bedraggled charms' of these women, they must be 'exceedingly anxious' to poison themselves. The argument reached a pitch where the government felt constrained to point out that the police, under an old act of George III, had 'very little power in the matter'.

Of direct relevance to the peace-making mood in the autumn of 1918 was the nation's attitude to another foreign element in its midst – the Germans, prisoners of war and civilians, not all of the latter being yet interned. The British people were showing a bewildering ambivalence in the matter. On the one hand, a violent xenophobic storm seemed to be sweeping all before it, at least in the capital, where demands resounded to wind up enemy banks, exclude enemy aliens (or even neutral aliens) from government offices and review all naturalization certificates issued during the war. The high point had been an 'Intern them all' campaign in which a petition bearing over one million signatures was borne from a mass demonstration in Hyde Park and handed in at Downing Street. No one seemed to be spared examination. The suspects ranged from 'naturalized aliens' still on the Privy Council, like that financial colossus from the Edwardian world, Sir Edward Cassel, to German or Austrian professors and scientists belonging to the London Institute of Hygiene, all of whom now had their names formally expunged, by a unanimous vote, from that body's register.

Yet, when mass agitation was absent, at home, as on the battle-front, common humanity often prevailed, and there were frequent instances of kindness and fraternization in defiance of all the regulations. An example of the latter was the terse announcement that a public footpath in Bishops Stortford had been closed 'to stop girls throwing cigarettes to interned German prisoners'. An example of the former was the sentencing, on 1 October at Banbury in Oxfordshire, of a railwayman named William Boscott to three months' imprisonment with hard labour. His offence had been to smuggle a food bag containing bacon, cocoa, bread and cigarettes into the cook-house of a local German prison camp. Passing sentence, the Mayor of Banbury made the significant observation that this sort of thing was happening all too often and that 'the Bench were determined to stop it'. Many individuals, it seemed, were already making their peace, whatever the authorities might say or do.

In Germany itself, the approach of the fifth war winter was seen by those same ordinary people as nothing less than a protracted nightmare which they would somehow have to stumble through wide-awake. The warm weather had eased a little of that earlier gloom, caused by the bread crisis at home and by the disconcerting war news from the Western Front, which had hung over the August anniversary. But by the autumn, the news was going from bad to worse on all fronts, while the low-fat civilian diets which one might scrape by on in the summer were dangerously inadequate for the bitter cold ahead. In any case the effects of malnutrition, being cumulative, were heaping up with every month that passed. After the war, German statisticians attempted to set out in figures and percentages the toll which the Allied naval blockade had taken on the life and health of the nation. They took as their yardstick the 3,000 calories a day diet which Allied experts, meeting in Paris in the spring of 1918, had laid down as the minimum health standard for any man of normal weight working an eight-hour day. Contrasted with this the Germans put the nutrition value of their own rationed food as low as 1,344 calories per head per day as early as the autumn of 1916 and estimated that, two years later, it had dropped to 1,000 calories or below. The flour ration by now represented exactly half of the normal quota for the last year of peace – 160 grammes a day compared with the 320 grammes of 1913. Fat consumption had dropped to one-third of peace-time levels, and that of meat to less than one-seventh. The consequences were inevitable, and grim. According to these same calculations, the average body weight of the German town-dweller had dropped by twenty per cent after four years of war – from sixty kilos to forty-nine. The death-rate, compared again with 1913, was thirty-seven per cent up, with fatalities from some diseases, such as tuberculosis, having more than doubled.

Statistics can be misleading at the best of times, and the cynic might argue that this batch was, if anything, designed to mislead. It could also be claimed that, as regards body-weight, the average German of 1913 had plenty he could safely lose; and further, that, so far as war-time calories were concerned, there were many ways of supplementing the ration-books with ingenuity or money or both. But when all such allowances have been made, these figures still rest on a bleak reality. The German people had come to suffer far more privations of every sort than any of their principal foes. Their position at the heart of the continent gave their generals all the well-known advantages of compactness and interior lines. It also meant, however, that the country was easier to isolate and to squeeze. By the autumn of 1918 Germany was like a citadel under siege, whose outer ramparts were falling and whose life-lines were being cut one by one.

It was not just for food and fuel that the defenders were desperately scratching (though these were, of course, their main concerns). Almost every manifestation of that solid prosperity which had made Germany the envy of the pre-war continent had vanished. The cobblers had no shoe leather and many of their clients were walking around in sandals or wooden clogs. The chemists had no drugs; the dentists no gold for fillings; the bicycle shops no tyres. Almost hardest of all for many Germans to bear, the tobacconists (or so it was announced on 17 September) would run out of tobacco altogether by the end of the year. The acute shortage of cloth of all sorts was setting the government on a collision course with the nation. Curtains and tablecloths were made liable to confiscation as unnecessary decorations which could be made into garments for the needy. A call had gone out for a million men's suits to be surrendered voluntarily to clothe miners, factory-hands and farm workers; and the authorities made it plain that, if need be, they would search private homes and take what was needed from the bedrooms.

It is significant that, though all the warring nations stretched their ingenuity to the utmost to manufacture substitutes for peace-time wares, only in Germany did the process leave behind it a permanent pejorative in the vocabulary: Ersatz. Ersatz was in all the food – bread adulterated with peas and beans; cakes with chestnut; tea with assorted forest leaves; pepper with ashes; butter with starch powder and so on with every item in the larder. It had also taken over the wardrobe. Women's dresses (only two were officially permitted) were made of nettle and willow fibre fortified by small quantities of cotton. New overcoats contained more heavy paper fabric than wool.

The only substitute for the vanished or inadequate buses and trams of Germany's major cities was to walk. Private motor-cars were by this time almost unknown; bicycles (due to the tyre shortage) were also scarce; while any civilian horse not needed for farm work had probably ended up in the butcher's shops long ago. The railways, once the pride of imperial Germany, were slowly collapsing under the combined effects of excessive loading and insufficient maintenance. Yet the ramshackle network was still expected to conform to Prussian discipline and the Germanic sense of order. The Transport Minister, Herr von Breitenbach, had recently circulated to all his railway staff a special memorandum on how the mounting chaos on Germany's trains should be mastered. Particular attention was to be paid to the growing number of travellers who used the inescapable overcrowding as an excuse to journey in greater style than their ticket entitled them to. All conductors now received strict instructions to admit third-class passengers to second-class compartments 'only when every seat in the lower category was filled'. First-class travellers who would be largely army officers, senior officials and other members of the ruling caste – were given the special protection to which their status entitled them. Only when the train was crammed were they to be disturbed, and even then only to the extent that their compartment 'could be occupied by six instead of only four persons'.

It was the life of the privileged, and particularly of the new moneyed élite of war profiteers, which by now was having a dangerously corrosive effect on the nation's unity, eating like acid through the old ties of respect and loyalty. Berlin's famous hotels, like the Adlon or the Esplanade, were gastronomic wraiths of their former selves. But, once through their portals, one still entered a different world of thick carpets and chandeliers from the drab, dark and empty streets outside – a world which was indeed preserved with official approval, in order to persuade neutral observers living in the capital that Germany was not yet economically on her knees. In another attempt to fool the outside world (as well as giving the Berliners themselves something to enjoy)* race-meetings of all sorts were actively encouraged. It makes strange reading to go through the files of such Berlin papers as survive from September and October of 1918 and see the tips for the horse-racing at Grünewald follow the evasive comments on the military situation or the confused reports about peace-making and domestic politics. In view of what was to happen that month, there is an especially ironic entry on 6 October. The horse Prunus is confidently selected

---

* The same applied to other major cities, such as Hamburg and Leipzig.

for Grunewald's big race of the day, the 'Ludendorff Stakes' over a distance of 2,200 metres with a prize of 60,000 Marks to the winner.

In Vienna too, often even more desperately hungry than Berlin – to which it more than once appealed for emergency food supplies – horse-racing continued, though in an exiguous fashion, at the famous Freudenau track on the Prater. And the capital of music had its special way of pretending that life went on as usual. On 13 October the composer Richard Strauss arrived in Vienna to conduct the premiere of his opera *Salome*, and there was talk of a contract 'beginning in December 1919' whereby the great man would spend six months a year at the opera house on the Ringstrasse, to take over its 'artistic direction'.

Even the double-headed Habsburg eagle, which had cruised above the Danube's banks for six and one half centuries, still seemed to be flying on somehow. After a serenely happy Harvest Festival trip by river steamer to the Slovak capital of Pressburg (Bratislava to the Slavs and Posony to the Magyars) the Emperor Charles and his wife, on 23 October 1918, went to Debrecen in southern Hungary to open the new university there. It was to prove the last peaceful episode in the reign of the ill-fated young couple but the citizens of Debrecen made it unforgettable – and phantasmagoric, in view of the military and political clouds that already hung so menacingly over the whole Empire. They stepped out of their royal train into a richly hung ceremonial tent which had been erected in the Station Square, where choirs sang national anthems, peasant girls handed over posies and the mayor and the rector read loyal addresses. This was followed by a ride around the town in the famous old Debrecen town coach, drawn by its five horses; and then, after the formal opening of the university, *sub auspiciis regis*, came the finest gala dinner which Hungary could provide. Indoors and outdoors, there was not one discordant note – nothing but loyal *Eljen* shouts from officials and people alike. No ruler of the Dual Monarchy visiting his subjects in the depths of peace and contentment could have wished for more.

The Empress recalls:

'As we got back aboard the royal train and the problems

confronted us again in the urgent despatches that had accumulated during those few hours, we asked ourselves: "Is it all a dream?" The Emperor warned me against any illusions. The cheering had, he said, been as deceptive as it was genuine. Without peace and reform, the Empire simply could not go on much longer.'

At moments like that the old order still seemed intact. But it was already crumbling fast from within, and even faster in Berlin than in Vienna. Imperial Germany had symbolized physical strength and material prosperity. Now the strength was visibly ebbing and the prosperity was gone. Above all, that Germany of Bismarck's had symbolized military might and the virtues of war. Now that might seemed to be cracking and all that the ordinary citizen could see or feel of war were its horrors and sufferings. The very title of 'Supreme War Lord' – so resoundingly apposite in the heady days of victory – had begun to appear as an archaic obstacle to a hungry and exhausted people yearning only for peace. One of the first shouts of 'Down with the Kaiser' to be recorded in wartime Germany had been uttered two years before by a crowd of Hamburg rioters demanding more food. That cry, a lonely one in 1916, was to become a swelling chorus as this last autumn drew on; and the Hohenzollerns had far less history than the Habsburgs to hold up against it.

The Peace Broker

THE AUSTERE, MIDDLE-AGED LIBERAL in the White House to whom Prince Max had reluctantly sent his telegram was something of an enigma even to close contemporaries. Posterity has not grown much wiser about this man whom that telegram had turned into the peace broker of the world. But there are some things about Woodrow Wilson's make-up which bear clearly enough upon the way he now set about playing the role. Indeed, his political approach had been fashioned throughout by his personal character: withdrawn, self-contained, dogmatic, and ruled almost entirely from the head. His hatred of war itself was as much intellectual as moral, and his deeply-held ideals, such as the post-war League of Nations, emerged from this clinical fervour rather like algebraic formulae inside which, for its own good, mankind had to be encompassed. Sir William Wiseman, the remarkable young baronet who served as the British Government's special liaison officer to the President (and who got to know him in the process as well as any American) wrote aptly of 'the chill of the cloister' which hung about Wilson. Wiseman went on: 'Everything and everybody was either black or white. He either liked and trusted a man, or he disliked and distrusted him. When he disliked a man, his manner would be cold to the point of rudeness.' Such an uncompromising way of reacting to people, when it was carried over into the business of peace-making, became an extreme way of reacting to whole nations as prototypes of good or bad. This produced some costly distortions, especially when applied to the enemy camp.

Thus Wilson never fully realized that, though Germany and Austria-Hungary were both empires, both latent autocracies, both bonded together by language and culture and now, even more closely, by war, their defeat and the elimination of their dynasties would nonetheless signify totally different things, if only because their historic natures were so contrasted. Whether a Kaiser or a President ruled in post-war Berlin, Germany would survive (as France would, if she were to succumb on the battlefields) because the nation was homogeneous, and its territory compact. Countries like those could be temporarily occupied; they could be bled white economically; ostracized politically; pegged down militarily; and have their boundaries trimmed or chopped around the edges. But after all that, the map of Europe would still go on looking much the same. Yet if a multi-national state like the Habsburg Dual Monarchy went under and its crown – the only thing which gave such a hotch-potch of peoples a semblance of unity – were cast aside, then that European map would have to be completely re-shaped. Even less did Wilson realize what a mess would then be made of that map when a swarm of ministers and officials tried, in the space of a few weeks or months, to draw their new dotted lines across paths worn bare by the centuries.

The President's 'black or white' approach could be almost as unfortunate with America's own allies. Of Republican France, he warmly approved. Quite apart from past memories of Washington and Lafayette the current prototype was right. It was another story altogether with Britain, where, quite apart from memories of George III, the current prototype was just as wrong. When war had broken out in 1914 the unpopularity of British imperialism was widespread. The Boer conflict still rankled and the battle for Irish Home Rule was at its height. Wilson never overcame his early suspicions that it was Britain's greed, and above all her commercial rivalry with Germany, which had played a powerful part in causing the war.

Events since 1914 had, if anything, fanned these suspicions, making him fear that the British would try to project their own economic ambitions into the post-war order, mostly at Germany's expense. There had been the ruthless enforcement of the Royal Navy's blockade against neutral ports and shipping, for example, which America herself had smarted under until her own entry into the war. There were the resolutions of the Paris Economic Conference of June 1916, which Wilson regarded as 'a blueprint for Entente, and chiefly British, world economic domination'. Subse-

229

quent speeches by Lloyd George and other British politicians proposing that, after the war, Britain should arrange the control of raw materials 'so as to prevent former enemies organizing a corner in them' added insult to injury, especially when coupled with suggestions that Wilson's pet project, the League of Nations, should be made the official instrument of such discrimination. Even the common effort of landing and equipping Pershing's great expeditionary force in France produced private misgivings which rankled under the surface of all the official euphoria. Wilson lent a ready ear when his Cabinet ministers accused Britain of profiteering from the sale of supplies to the American army and even of over-charging for the transport of American soldiers across the Atlantic. The Allied flare-ups which now lay ahead over armistice terms can only be understood against that back-cloth of White House distrust.

There were other, and more immediate pressures which bore down on Wilson when the Swiss Minister in Washington formally presented him with Prince Max's note on 7 October.* He was within a month of standing for re-election as President of the United States and so, not for the last time in American affairs, crucial world issues became entangled in the miasma of domestic politics. Wilson's Republican opponents immediately mounted the bandwagon of 'unconditional surrender'. The day the President received the German note James McCumber, a Republican from North Dakota, introduced a resolution into the Senate demanding that 'there shall be no cessation of hostilities and no armistice until the Imperial German Government shall disband its armies and surrender its arms and munitions, together with its navy ...' Mr McCumber also wanted the Senate to insist that Germany would pay the cost of 'rebuilding all the cities and villages destroyed by its armies', as well as 'make proper compensation for every crime committed by its soldiers'. Finally, to ram the same point home again, he demanded that Germany should 'repay every dollar and the value of all property exacted from the people of every territory invaded by it'. Other Republican senators like Borah of Idaho,

* The parallel Austrian plea for peace was delivered in Washington the same day by the Swedish Minister.

Thomas of Colorado and Reed of Missouri came out against the very idea of negotiating a peace with Germany in the first place; and that call from the Westerners and Southerners was taken up by their colleagues in the East. Some of these, like Theodore Roosevelt, even wanted Wilson's Fourteen Points* to be repudiated altogether by the Senate as a peace-making platform because they only 'confused the issue'.

The press joined in this chorus of hawks almost with one voice. 'No peace with the Hohenzollerns,' cried the *New York Times* of 7 October. 'If Germany wants peace, let her do away with her braggart and irresponsible Kaiser.' 'War to the limit, war until the now humbled Emperor hands over his dishonoured sword,' demanded the *Washington Post* of the same day. 'Germany can have the peace that came to Bulgaria – a peace of utter surrender,' said the *Cleveland Plain Dealer*. 'Those who are fighting in France,' observed the *Chicago Herald*, 'have their eyes on Berlin and nowhere else ... They are not anxious for a Kaiser-made peace.' Nor did the spokesman for the nation's workers lag behind. A message to Wilson from the American Federation of Labour called on him to 'batter away at enemy lines until the road to Berlin is cleared'. The private letters and telegrams which were pouring into the White House from all classes of American citizens carried, overwhelmingly, the same uncompromising message.

The political agitation had indeed found a popular echo whose strength Wilson seems at first to have under-estimated. Eighteen months of unremitting anti-German propaganda had, by now, done their work. It had been largely a poster campaign, the virulence of which comes out when some of the most famous specimens are seen re-assembled side by side. 'Hun or Home!', 'Remember Belgium!', 'Save Serbia!', 'Wake up America!', 'Destroy the Mad Brute!' were typical themes for these illustrations of slavering Huns carrying off diaphanous white maidens in their hairy arms. Occasionally, during the final phase of the war, the theme on the posters had been reversed, with terrified German dachshunds scuttling away before fierce Allied bulldogs. But it was the gorilla, not the

* For full text of the Fourteen Points of 8 January 1918, and subsequent elaborations of Wilson's peace programme, *see* Appendix A.

dachshund, that America was remembering now, especially in those obsessive references to the Kaiser.

Shutting his ears to most of this clamour, the leader of the only unexhausted major belligerent in the war (a position of which the President was fully aware, and one which he was determined fully to exploit) settled down to compose his reply to Berlin. Colonel House, his *confidant* in foreign affairs, and the man who was soon to become his plenipotentiary for peace-making, was summoned from New York to Washington to submit advice. The two men had already been in touch over the weekend as the first unofficial news of the German approach was received. House had struck a distinctly cautionary note. He telegraphed the President:

> 'I would suggest making no direct reply ... A statement from the White House saying "The President will at once confer with the Allies regarding the communication received from the German Government" should be sufficient. I would advise that you ask the Allies to confer with me in Paris at the earliest opportunity. I have a feeling that they will want to throw the burden on you but ... they should accept their full responsibility.'

As will be seen, the good colonel's 'feeling' about the Allies was grotesquely wide of the mark; furthermore, as he discovered for himself when he arrived at the White House on Monday, the President was totally ignoring his advice to send Prince Max no direct reply. Indeed, with a little assistance from House and the Secretary of State Robert Lansing, he spent most of the following thirty-six hours drafting and re-drafting the response, spurning suggestions that he should relax at the golf links for a while. The text seems to have been sharpened considerably overnight, after he had studied the fierce line being taken in both the American and Entente press, and at 4 p.m. on Tuesday, that final version was published in Washington while on its way to Berlin. It was, as Secretary of State Lansing observed when handing the text out to the newsmen, 'a query, not a reply'. Germany was asked to state categorically whether she accepted the Fourteen Points and the President's later elaborations on them as the basic peace terms;

whether she was ready to withdraw her forces from all 'invaded territory', a requirement on which 'the good faith of any discussion would manifestly depend'; and, finally, whether the Imperial Chancellor was speaking 'merely for the constituted authorities of the Empire who have so far conducted this war'.

That final thrust, oblique and gentle though it appeared, was to become the real thunderbolt for Berlin and Vienna. It reflected the contempt which this elected autocrat felt for all hereditary auto-crats – as much perhaps because they had been born to power as because they had abused it. When presenting the note to his Cabinet (his colleagues had barely ventured to discuss the text, let alone amend or object) the President, who entered the room whistling cheerfully, soon struck a sombre note: how could America 'have correspondence' with a Germany under autocracy? It would be unthinkable, he went on, for American troops to march in and set up themselves a German government to their own liking; yet unless there was a change in Berlin, 'We might witness bol-shevikism [sic] worse than in Russia.' This theme, lethal in its ultimate extension, appeared in this 8 October note as little more than a philosophical aside. The heart of the message was that if Germany accepted the Fourteen Points and withdrew inside her own boundaries, Woodrow Wilson was ready to talk peace.

The note disappointed all the President's American critics, and many of his own supporters, for whom it was far too soft. But their reaction was mild compared with the barely-suppressed anger of his allies in Europe. Britain and France were appalled by what seemed to them an utterly ham-handed approach. The Fourteen Points were an American blue-print for a new world order about which they had certain reserves but which was anyway something for a peace conference, not for an armistice, to decide. Either deliberately or naively, Wilson had tied together two processes which belonged apart; while his only military condition – the evacuation of occupied territories – was hopelessly inadequate as the basis on which the triumphant Entente forces could accept a cease-fire. But America's allies were angry most of all for the simple reason that the President had neither informed them nor consulted them over his actions. And that was the way Wilson intended to play his hand for another whole fortnight. It was an almost unbelievable situation. America, barely eighteen months in the war and only recently blooded in battle, was serenely negotiating peace terms over the heads of her European partners who had been fighting the common enemy for four and a quarter years.

The irony was that the Entente had known all about Prince Max's peace bid even before President Wilson. The French had cracked either the German or the Swiss diplomatic codes and had thus decyphered the German note to Washington while it was still on its way from Berne during the night of 4–5 October. Clemenceau never dreamt that France was about to be excluded from the exchanges between the White House and Berlin. But he instinctively feared the worst if this remote American moralist were to be allowed to re-shape a Europe of which he knew little and probably understood less. Moreover, the immediate issue, an armistice, was one for soldiers on the spot to decide, rather than politicians three thousand miles away. On the day he received the de-cyphered German message, therefore, the French Prime Minister asked his Generalissimo to draw up a paper on the subject. Foch (who, in his memoirs, characteristically claims the idea was his) had the memorandum ready three days later. Only one clause – the obvious one requiring the German army to withdraw from all invaded territories – was covered in the note which the American President had dispatched to Berlin that same day. Foch's other 'conditions for the Armistice' put the basic military case which Wilson had ignored, namely the requirement that the German army should now be rendered incapable of resuming hostilities, whatever ground it stood on. Thus Foch demanded three large bridge-heads on the right bank of the Rhine; the occupation of the left bank territories as 'security for reparations payments'; and a blanket undertaking that the Germans would leave behind undamaged all war material, military installations, factories, railway lines and equipment in the areas they evacuated. Foch was rightly concerned about ending a war, not building a post-war world.

Similar ideas had occurred to the British, the moment they got wind of Prince Max's peace move. For them, the post-war surrender of Germany meant, above all, the destruction of the German fleet, just as the peace-time challenge of Germany had been embodied in the fast-growing power of that fleet. Whereas Foch had confined himself entirely to the affairs of the Allied armies, in London it was the First Sea Lord, Admiral Wemyss who, on 6 October, started drawing up the requirements of the Allied navies. This division of interests and responsibilities between France and Britain seemed so natural that nobody had even thought of formalizing it.

But if the Admiralty went calmly about its age-old business of ensuring that Britannia ruled the waves, whatever the White House might get up to, the President's studied neglect of his allies had really raised the temperature at Downing Street. After a War Cabinet meeting held to discuss Wilson's reply to the Germans, the Chief of Imperial General Staff, Sir Henry Wilson, wrote in his diary:

'It is really a complete usurpation of power of negotiation. He practically ignores us and the French . . . I am certain we (British, French, Italians) ought to get together and put the truth baldly before Wilson. He is now taking charge in a way that terrifies me, as he is only a super-Gladstone – and a dangerous visionary at that.'

The great South African leader, Field Marshal Smuts, who also sat in the War Cabinet, was even more emphatic. He told a civilian colleague:

'Wilson is an autocrat in America and, as time goes on, will be an autocrat in Europe too, if he is allowed. One cannot but recognize that, with our superhuman efforts this year in the field, our Armies and the French are greatly exhausted, whilst the Americans are rapidly growing so that, next year, if things go on till then, Wilson might be in a position to dictate a peace to France and ourselves which we might not find acceptable . . .'

He might almost have been talking of an enemy, not an ally.

Fortunately, that British-French-Italian 'get-together' of which Sir Henry Wilson had spoken was already taking place in Paris. It so happened that the three Prime Ministers had convened in the French capital on 5 October, intending to discuss the crumbling situation in the Balkans in the light of Bulgaria's surrender and Turkey's imminent collapse. Their sessions, prolonged over the next four days, concentrated instead on the German peace move and Wilson's cavalier behaviour in handling it. If the Allied generals of Europe felt disturbed that the President was ignoring their case, the Allied statesmen were, even more worried that he was actually pre-empting theirs. Maurice Hankey, Secretary to the British Cabinet, who had accompanied his Prime Minister to Paris, reflected both concerns in his diary. His trumpet, as always, is clear, despite being discreetly muted:

> 'Lloyd George is irritated with Wilson for replying without consulting us. Not only because, in asking if the Germans accept his fourteen points, he almost seems to assume that we do accept them (although as a matter of fact we totally reject the doctrine of the freedom of the seas) but still more owing to the statement that withdrawal from the occupied territories is an indispensable condition of an armistice. Lloyd George agrees that it is an indispensable condition, but, of course, many other conditions are indispensable, and he fears that the Huns will try to assure that it is the only condition ...'

The extraordinary situation thus arose that two entirely separate, and indeed rival sets of Allied deliberations were now in progress on opposite shores of the Atlantic. While the President was pondering his reply to Berlin, the three European Prime Ministers were working out the very different and far more detailed conditions which they desired to impose on Germany. They first spelt out the overall evacuation programme required, extending it from the Western Front to Serbia and Montenegro and even including those parts of the Austrian Empire south of the Brenner secretly promised to Italy. They then charged their military experts to work out all the technical arrangements needed on the ground to execute this programme and, at the same time, to draw the teeth from the German armed forces in each and every battle arena they were evacuating. General Bliss, the American Representative on the Allied Council, followed his President's cue and absented himself from all the meetings, though he was solemnly handed the texts of the various agreements for transmission to Washington. In that way Mr Wilson's allies were hoping to hear, in return, something of what was going on in his mind. Indeed, on 9 October, the three Prime Ministers appealed directly to the President in two notes which pleaded respectively for closer political consultation and for the involvement of military experts.

The enemy, of course, was even more curious, as well as far more anxious. The special armistice commission appointed by Ludendorff as soon as the appeal to Wilson was decided upon had held its first session at Spa on the morning of 7 October. If confirmation were needed that it was Foch, and not Wilson, who had his finger on the German military pulse, the findings of that meeting provided it: they placed absolute priority on preserving the German army as an effective war machine throughout every stage of the cease-fire process. The two key sentences were, first, 'The evacuation must be executed in such a manner that we are always ready to fight'; and, second, 'The cessation of submarine war must certainly be granted but its resumption must be assured.'

When Wilson's reply reached Germany on the morning of 9 October, the staff officers at Spa must have breathed a huge sigh of relief. No timetable had been set out for the expected evacuation requirement and no military demands whatsoever had been made which might cripple the German army as it moved back. Even Prince Max had to admit, when he was handed the text, that 'the note seemed to justify the optimists'.

What the new Chancellor was chiefly concerned about now was whether the pessimists among his advisers could really justify their gloom. From the moment Supreme Headquarters had started to bombard Berlin with telephone calls and telegrams demanding instant peace moves and his own immediate installation, the Prince had felt in his bones that Ludendorff was playing to the gallery of German history – exaggerating the military plight of the nation in order to saddle a civilian with the onus of ending the war. But this particular civilian was no ordinary bureaucrat or politician who lived in awe of his general staff. Prince Max was, in his own right, the colonel of a crack German regiment; moreover, as the heir to a Grand Duchy and a kinsman of the Supreme War Lord himself he certainly suffered from no inferiority complex in front of the modestly-born Quartermaster-General. The day before Wilson's reply arrived he had dispatched (rather than submitted) to Ludendorff a list of fifteen crisp questions on the current state of the army and the prospects of further resistance. But the Chancellor's aim – to pin the military down to something concrete and categorical with which to justify their renewed pressure for an armistice – was again frustrated by the evasive set of answers which Ludendorff handed him over when the general arrived in Berlin for consultations on 9 October. Thus, one of the Chancellor's key questions – 'Assuming the present peace moves break down and the allies we still have left fall away from us, could we continue to fight on by ourselves until the spring?' produced only the delphic response: 'We need a breathing space and then we can consolidate our positions again.' All that Prince Max had to go on from the army, as he weighed his reply to Wilson's note, was sombre vagueness. Those vital assets for any negotiator, an elastic time-scale and a set of options within which to manoeuvre, were both denied him. What worried the new Chancellor most of all however was that he was lending his own name to this armistice for which the generals were clamouring. It was his status as a civilian which concerned him as much as his dignity as heir to a grand duchy. He felt an injustice, and also, perhaps, sensed some deeper mischief in the way the German Supreme Command refused to take public responsibility for ending the war which it had fought and had now declared to be lost. 'I am already being called "the pacifist Prince",' he rebuked Ludendorff at these Berlin consultations. The Quartermaster-General was as bland as the Chancellor was bitter. 'I thank your Grand Ducal Highness in the name of . . . the army,' was all he replied. The Prince's misgivings that he was being trussed up as an offering to posterity were spelt out plainly in an editorial printed that week in Germany's leading liberal newspaper. All talk that the current peace moves were being inspired by pacifists on the home front should, it urged, be squashed. Such ideas, the paper warned prophetically, 'could develop into a dangerous legend'.

Once the Chancellor had agreed, yet again, to military pressure for immediate action, there were few problems between Berlin and Spa over the actual wording of Germany's second note to Wilson which was dispatched on the afternoon of 12 October. It breathed eager, almost grateful compliance. The Fourteen Points were accepted as 'the foundations of a permanent peace' with only 'the practical details of application' to be agreed upon. The evacuation of all occupied territories was also accepted without demur. In both cases, Austria-Hungary associated herself with the German position. As for that awkward little dig of Wilson's about the credentials of the new team now negotiating from Berlin, the German note pointed to the large Reichstag majority which had voted for the peace move, and concluded hopefully: 'The Chancellor, supported in all his actions by the will of this majority, speaks in the name of the German government and the German people.' Of the Kaiser and Supreme War Lord, there was not one word.

So the Rubicon was crossed. The two great enemy powers had accepted not only the President's conditions for ending the fighting, but also, lock, stock and barrel, his philosophy for framing the peace. The shape of the post-war world, as well as the conclusion of the war itself, had been placed in his hands. For the first time even the placidly confident Woodrow Wilson seemed unnerved by the weight of this awesome responsibility he had striven for, and which was now his to carry. 12 October was a Saturday, and he had received the first news of Germany's acceptance at the Waldorf Hotel in New York, where he was dining before attending the Italian Fête at the Metropolitan Opera House. (In the event, the real fête of that evening was the tumultuous reception which the audience, who had also heard the news, accorded their President.) He did not begin working on his answer until after breakfast when back in Washington on the Monday. Colonel House, who was with him, wrote:

'I never saw him more disturbed. He said he did not know where to make the entrance in order to reach the heart of the thing ... It reminded him, he said, of a maze. If one went in at the right entrance, he reached the centre, but if one took the wrong turning, it was necessary to go out again and do it over ...'

As he was composing his reply, the now familiar pressures from his political opponents re-asserted themselves. Roosevelt again thundered for 'unconditional surrender' and this time, thanks to an obscure twenty-two-year-old German U-boat commander prowling around in the Irish Sea, the call fell on even more receptive ears. The arrival of Prince Max's note coincided with the news that the *Leinster*, a 2,646-ton mailboat which plied between Dublin and Holyhead, had been torpedoed without warning when in sight of land, and that 450 of the 687 passengers on board, including some Americans, had lost their lives when the vessel sank, within minutes, like a stone.

But if, to many of his domestic critics, the Fourteen Points were too soft as a basis for peace, to Wilson's allies over in Europe, they appeared steadily more rigid and uncomfortable the further the President progressed with his solo diplomatic act. On 14 October three separate telegrams from the British Foreign Secretary Arthur Balfour were handed in at the White House. Two of them touched again on the military arguments already transmitted to Washington from the Allied Council in Paris the previous week. The third went to the core of Britain's anger and concern at having the politics of peace-making determined over her head by a self-appointed guru from the other side of the Atlantic. The Fourteen Points, this third message from London pointed out, had never been discussed between 'the Associated Powers'. They were open to many interpretations and to some of them the British Government was bound to protest sharply. Immediate steps, the message urged, should be taken to negotiate all these doubtful questions, so that the Allies could present a united front at any peace conference.

When, later that same day, Wilson had completed his reply, it revealed concessions to some of these complex pressures. The sinking of the *Leinster* and the German army's 'scorched earth' policy during its withdrawal on the Western Front were coupled together as 'direct violations of the rules and practices of civilized warfare' which must cease forthwith if any negotiations were to go forward. More significant was an indirect admission that the single military provision of his first note – the demand for evacuation of all occupied territory – was inadequate as a programme for winding down a long and complex war. 'It must be clearly understood,' he now wrote, 'that the process of evacuation and the conditions of an armistice are matters which must be left to the judgement and advice of the military advisers of the Government of the United States and the Allied Governments.' He went on to echo the principal point which the Supreme War Council had been hammering at him, namely that all such arrangements must guarantee 'the present military supremacy of the armies of the United States and of the Allies in the field'.

But if the voices of the Allied generals in Paris had been heeded by Wilson, those of the Allied statesmen were blandly ignored. The President had decided, after only a few hours' reflection, that 'the heart of the thing' which he had to find in order to give the right reply was, quite simply, the existence of all autocracies on the continent of Europe. The correct entrance to that maze he had talked of to Colonel House was, therefore, the entrance emblazoned with ancient coats of arms. At the maze's centre were thrones waiting for him to topple.

He saved this revelation for the end of his reply. He referred first to a passage in his Fourth of July address, delivered at Mount Vermont three months before, in which he had dedicated himself to 'the destruction of every arbitrary power anywhere that can separately, secretly and of its single choice disturb the peace of the world'. Then came the withering sermon on his text:

'The power which has hitherto controlled the German nation is of the sort here described. It is within the choice of the German nation to alter it. The President's words just quoted naturally constitute a condition precedent to peace, if peace is to come by the action of the German people

241

themselves. The President feels bound to say that the whole process of peace will, in his judgement, depend on the definiteness and the satisfactory character of the guarantees which can be given in this fundamental matter ...'

With those four sentences – two of them plain, two of them ponderous – Woodrow Wilson from Washington wrote the final death sentence of the Hohenzollern and Habsburg empires. The formulation was his, and his alone. His Cabinet colleagues who were brought in to discuss the reply neither added nor altered anything of substance. His allies, the Entente Prime Ministers of that Europe he was re-shaping, were not even informed,* let alone consulted, of the momentous step he was taking, in his own name but also in theirs, by proxy. As a usurpation of power, it was as unique in its arrogance as it was doleful in its effects.

When the news of these exchanges between the lofty gentlemen sitting in Washington and Berlin reached the ordinary German soldier in the field he reacted with a mixture of bitterness, nostalgia, and resignation. Corporal Kurt Raschig wrote to his girlfriend Rosa Ney in Mannheim:

'I don't need to tell you that we all feel a great longing for peace. But can we accept all Wilson's conditions? After all, we are not yet defeated, so there is no need to abandon all hope. If only one could speak to all our soldiers at once and put back in them all, just for one day, the courage and enthusiasm of 1914 ... But, as it is, each one of us feels exhausted in the face of the enemy's ceaseless attacks ...'

Corporal Casper of the 12th Artillery Regiment was seized with fury. 'Wilson's negative reply,' he wrote to a friend in Chemnitz, 'should rouse us to throw everything in a final struggle to save our homeland. I feel sick when I even repeat his drivel. No true German can ever forgive him this journey to Canossa ...'

But Lieutenant Werner Stephan, a company commander serving in the 69th Reserve Infantry Regiment, showed little of the

* It was not until 23 October that Wilson officially transmitted to his allies the details of his exchanges with Germany.

corporal's heroics in the letter he sent home that week. 'The dream of German world conquest has been quickly dreamt away,' he wrote. 'Perhaps it wasn't such a beautiful dream, after all.'

In the Chancellery of Berlin, where Wilson's reply arrived at 5.20 a.m. on the morning of 16 October, there was only one reaction: shocked dismay. When Prince Max hastily summoned his Cabinet together to discuss this unexpected turn for the worse, he found one of them, the newly appointed Foreign Minister Solf, 'completely broken up'. The most dreadful thing about Wilson's message, Solf complained, was its tone. 'This is not the language of a man who is seeking a just peace but that of the leader of an alliance that is out to destroy us.' Another colleague reported on the reaction of public opinion. 'Wilson's note has exploded like a bomb,' he told his Chancellor. 'Only now do the people realize the true gravity of the situation, for Wilson speaks like a man who is expecting Germany's capitulation.' He added that the pointed references to the position of the Emperor had caused general consternation, and that the possibility of abdication was now being discussed openly in the streets.

Abdication: it was a startlingly new question for the ordinary patriotic German,* but the thought had already crossed the minds of both the Emperor himself and his ministers while the decision to address Germany's peace appeal to a democratic President was being made. As the first German note was being prepared, the outgoing Chancellor Count Hertling was asked, on the steps of the Berlin Chancellery, what would happen if Wilson should include abdication in his demands. Hertling told his questioner: 'The Kaiser asked me that last Sunday and I told him "Your Majesty, I don't believe Wilson will do that, but if such a demand should come, then we shall simply have to resume the battle."'

Hertling's successor saw things more clearly. Before the President's reaction was even known, he had sent secret appeals to Washington through the Danish envoy in Berlin, Count Karl Moltke, urging that America should not use the peace talks to

---

* Leaflets had appeared in Berlin during the previous winter with the slogans: 'Down with the Kaiser! Down with the Government!'; but these represented the views of what was still a radical minority.

interfere in Germany's internal affairs. And though he kept this step from his colleagues, he asked them point-blank whether they would join him in resisting such interference over the question of the monarchy. Their response was fairly encouraging. Erzberger, the leader of the Catholic Centre Party, was predictably robust: a republic would spell the destruction of the State. Even the Socialist spokesman, Scheidemann, assured the Chancellor that he personally would join in opposing American pressure, though he added sombrely: 'If the question is put to us, continue the war or give up the Hohenzollerns, then the people would choose peace, even at this price.'

Now the question had been put, obliquely in Wilson's first note; bluntly and brutally in his second. The Kaiser himself was under no illusions as to what the American President was driving at. 'That's aimed straight at the overthrow of my house and at abolishing the monarchy altogether!' he exploded when the text was brought to him at his Berlin palace. His wife chipped in with prim astonishment 'that this upstart on the other side of the ocean should presume to so degrade a royal house that could look back on centuries of bounteous service to the people and the fatherland'.

At their Cabinet meeting of 16 October Prince Max and his ministers tried, without overmuch conviction, to put a less drastic light on Wilson's meaning: perhaps he only meant that the Emperor himself should go, to be succeeded by his son, or even his grandson, who would then continue to rule as a strictly consitutional monarch on the lines of the Scandinavian kings? All agreed it was anyway senseless to enter into such political debates with the American President until the military position was clearer. The army on the Western Front was still retreating, and, far away to the south-east, other Allied forces were still advancing steadily towards Belgrade and Constantinople. How much time did the Supreme Command give the government to play with, if it came to a poker game with Wilson, and what military cards did Berlin still have left?

The following day, at a long session of the War Cabinet, the politicians made one final attempt to get some unequivocal answers to these familiar questions out of Ludendorff. Prince Max himself approached the meeting with little confidence. The night before, at his Chancellery desk in the small hours, he had penned a desperate letter home to his cousin, the Grand Duke of Baden:

> 'I send you these lines in a sleepless hour after midnight . . .
> The total collapse of the old Prussian order first became
> clear to me when I arrived here. I wanted to draw back in
> despair, for I realized that my policies could no longer be
> backed by military strength and that on the battlefield we
> were bankrupt . . . I thought I was coming on the scene at
> five minutes to twelve, but realize I was only summoned at
> five minutes after twelve . . .'

Now, in the sober light of day, the First Quartermaster-General proceeded to confuse matters further by fiddling about with the minute hand once again.

The War Cabinet meeting in Berlin on 17 October 1918 has been described as 'one of the most dramatic and moving events in German history'. As regards the actual proceedings (of which, fortunately, a full official protocol exists), that is pitching it a little high. Indeed, considering that the leaders of the nation were sitting, while they talked, on the crossroads of its destiny, their debate over which path to take is remarkably free from personal outbursts or emotion of any kind. The drama lies deeper. This conference marked the end of that arrogant stranglehold which the military had exerted over the civilian power in Berlin ever since the creation of the Prussian state. Only two days before, as part of the hasty cosmetic surgery being undertaken to make Germany's face more acceptable in Washington, the Kaiser had issued a decree stipulating that, henceforth, he would only issue orders to the Supreme Command after consultation with the Chancellor or his representative. That, for the first time, gave formal sanction in law to the supremacy of the civilian authority. Prince Max now translated that supremacy into practice by hearing all Ludendorff's arguments and demands, and then ignoring them. The Quartermaster-General, whose accounts of this conference are highly selective, unwittingly made the rejection easier by contradicting himself so thoroughly in his own statements.

The government had presented him with still more detailed queries designed to get an honest, unvarnished picture of the military outlook against which the proper peace strategy could be drawn up. There were twenty-one questions in the list, but the key ones were the first and the last. Those ran: 'How long can the war be conducted so as to keep the enemy away from Germany's borders?' and 'Will our military position be better or worse by next spring than it is now?' Prince Max, in other words, was again asking how much time he had to play with.

As they went through the list, Ludendorff proceeded on many points to display such optimism that anyone present who had heard his cries of hopeless despair uttered in the Crown Council meetings on 13 August and again on 29 September must have wondered whether this was really the same man. Army morale, for example, though still threatened by contamination from the home front, had apparently greatly improved since the black day of 8 August; and Ludendorff cited as evidence the 41st Infantry Division which had collapsed completely in the battle of Amiens but which was now 'giving a splendid account of itself on the east bank of the Meuse'. A few minutes later, he went so far as to declare that 'If the army can get through the next four weeks until the onset of winter, then we are on safe ground.'

Nothing approaching such a clear and positive verdict had been heard from Ludendorff's lips at any of the crisis talks of the past three months. In his memoirs he justifies his sudden change of heart by some estimates of maximum replacements given to the meeting by the new Minister of War, Major-General Heinrich Scheuch.* In answer to a question which Ludendorff had previously submitted to the government on what help the home front could give the army, Scheuch had declared that, by pre-empting all future recruitment and ignoring the manpower demands of industry, he could scrape together for the army 'one single strong reinforcement' of six hundred thousand men. Yet the minister went on to make it clear that, in the short term with which all present were concerned, only a fraction of the six hundred thousand would be ready for the front. The rest would have to be plucked from the

* He had succeeded General von Stein the week before, on 9 October.

farmers' fields and the factory benches, then trained as soldiers, and then transported to the battlefield. 'I wouldn't want to estimate too short a time,' he commented cautiously and vaguely. Ludendorff was, in fact, snatching hopefully at shadows. Indeed, even had the whole six hundred thousand appeared by Christmas, on his own argument, repeated again at this meeting, that would only have sown six hundred thousand more seeds of unrest and disaffection on the battlefields. If, as he had maintained throughout the summer and autumn, it was the manpower replacements from a mutinous homeland which were weakening his army's morale, why pin any high hopes on the promise of these last concentrated scrapings from the bottom of the recruitment barrel Scheidemann, the Socialist spokesman present, told the general as much.

There were similar contradictions, explicit or implicit, as Prince Max probed around the other questions on his list. He reminded Ludendorff that when the government was being hustled along into launching immediate peace moves – against the Chancellor's better judgement – the Supreme Command had prevailed by insisting that a military catastrophe could overwhelm them at any minute. What had happened to the catastrophe? In tones worthy of the oracle at Delphi, Ludendorff merely replied: 'The day before yesterday, things went well for us; they can also go badly.'

Prince Max had no better luck when they turned to the projected build-up on the enemy's side. Even if one considered only the enormous and steady expansion of the American forces, he pointed out, the Entente powers would have 1,100,000 more men in the field by the spring of 1919, nearly twice General Scheuch's 'once-only' reinforcement. Would, therefore, Germany's position by then be better or worse? Ludendorff gave the astonishing reply: 'It will be no worse as regards the figures,' and instantly turned the talk to the grave effects of further withdrawals on Germany's industrial output. (He was now, with the war as good as lost, coming round to the idea of building tanks, and hoped to start catching up on enemy construction during the winter.)

A few minutes later, while accepting that precise predictions were difficult, the Prince made his final effort to get a military spade called a spade, and not an entrenching tool. 'Can we,' he asked the General, 'end the war under better conditions next year than now?' Ludendorff merely parried the question. 'Every exertion that we make at the moment will improve our position,' he replied. Even that ambivalence was perhaps more helpful than the inexplicable confidence shown by the Chief of the Naval Staff, Admiral Reinhard Scheer, when the Chancellor pressed him with the same query. 'Our position will improve because that of the enemy will get worse,' the Admiral answered. 'That is why they want to finish things off this autumn.'

Scheer, who in 1916 had been one of the keenest advocates of unrestricted submarine warfare, was just as emphatically against abandoning it now, as Wilson's second note had clearly, if indirectly, demanded. In this Ludendorff, categorical for once, had supported him. The two war leaders finally got up from the table feeling that at least on this issue, their advice could scarcely be disregarded and that, in general, the German reply to Washington would neither expose their country to any harsh ignominy, nor preclude its armed forces from resuming hostilities at any moment that might be opportune during the negotiations ahead. As Ludendorff wrote of the conference in a memorandum penned, under dramatically changed circumstances, a fortnight later: 'I stressed the need to reply to the Note in a dignified way which would do justice to our interests. Abandoning the U-boat war could not even be considered . . . I returned to Spa in good spirits.'

Those spirits, which had no real reason to rise, were soon to sink again. Though, outside the cabinet room, Prince Max at last managed to extract from Ludendorff a clear 'yes' to his insistent question as to whether Germany's military position would be better, rather than worse, in six months' time,* the Chancellor still had no faith in the prediction. Things were, in his eyes, still not as black as Ludendorff had painted them in the most recent of his panic moods less than three weeks before; but neither was the light on Germany's horizon any brighter. On all counts – men, war material, reinforcements, industrial output and morale – and on all

---

* Neither in his memoirs nor in his memorandum of 31 October does Ludendorff mention this private exchange.

fronts, the enemy had an unassailable lead which was lengthening further with every day that passed. It was simply no use relying on Ludendorff's latest mood of bland fatalism, which the general was later to sum up, in his own words, as 'Part of war is luck, and luck may again come Germany's way.' Indeed, after that marathon but inconclusive discussion on the 17th, the Chancellor came to the conclusion that it was no use relying on the First Quartermaster-General for anything any more. As he wrote: 'At this conference, I lost faith in Ludendorff as a person. He should have faced up to the situation ruthlessly, without any concern for his personal prestige. Only a heroic frankness could help . . .'

That same day, therefore, the Chancellor decided that the peace action with Washington had to go forward, and that meant that some of Wilson's clear if unspoken demands would have to be met. As the Prince was not yet prepared to sacrifice Germany's dynasty, it followed that he would have to sacrifice her submarines. He was strengthened in that conclusion by the arrival back in Berlin on the 18th of one of his most trusted unofficial diplomatic advisers, the German banker, Carl Melchior. The banker had come from The Hague, where he had managed to hold direct talks with an official from one of the enemy's embassies there on the peace strategy as seen in the Entente camp. Wilson (in contrast to the vengeful Foch) is striving for an honourable peace, Melchior, somewhat misleadingly, reported. The President's *sine qua non* however (apart from the 'democratization' of Germany, which Prince Max imagined he had already carried out) was an immediate end to the unrestricted U-boat campaign which had just produced the scandal of the *Leinster* sinking.

That same day, Prince Max's advisers had a draft ready which sought, among other things, to meet this point by confining German submarines henceforth to so-called 'cruiser warfare'. A hard battle faced him. Even with some amendments, he failed to carry his cabinet on the 19th. A furious Admiral Scheer then tried to mobilize both the Supreme Command and the Supreme War Lord in opposing the concession. Ludendorff jumped in willingly with a strong telegram of protest from Spa: by abandoning the U-boat weapon without getting anything in return, Germany was treading the path of capitulation 'before the supreme effort had been made'. (Where was this supreme effort, the Chancellor asked himself, when Ludendorff had raised the white flag in despair three weeks before?) But the generals, on this occasion, stayed in Spa, and the Kaiser, at the Chancellor's urgent pleading, came alone to Berlin. There, reluctantly, he gave his consent to the revised draft. The Prince could only extract it by the threat of his resignation; 'and if I go, the Cabinet will fall apart and then comes the revolution.' By now, that dreaded word loomed larger for the Emperor than all his submarines put together. And so, in the last days of the Hohenzollern dynasty, a civilian in the Prussian capital had won a vital argument about the conduct of war against the combined opposition of the country's military and naval leaders.

The Cabinet having by now united under the provocation of that telegram from Spa, the way was clear for Germany's third note to be dispatched, and it left for Washington via Berne soon after midnight on 20–21 October. The central concession on U-boats was clearly enough expressed, the complicated technical concept 'cruiser warfare' having been abandoned for the formula Melchior had brought from The Hague. 'In order to avoid anything which might hinder the cause of peace,' the reply now read, 'the German government has sent orders to all its submarine commanders which will preclude the torpedoing of passenger ships.'*

For the rest, the note was a rambling and provocative affair. It assumed that arrangements for the agreed evacuation of occupied territories and the armistice conditions 'should be left to the judgement of the military advisers' (which might have been acceptable to Foch providing it was his advisers who did the judging); but then went on to suggest that the basis for such agreements should be 'the current balance of strength at the fronts', a quite unrealistic proposal which implied that Germany's parlous position should somehow be disguised beneath a rifle count. At the end came another rather laboured defence of Germany's newly-created political purity. Hitherto, the note admitted, 'the people's repre-

---

* The order ran: 'Return at once. Because of negotiations now in progress, every kind of mercantile war prohibited. Submarines returning home may only attack ships of war in daytime.'

sentatives had had no constitutional role in shaping decisions about war or peace'. But all this had just been changed. President Wilson could now rest assured that Germany's peace offer 'was coming from a government which, free from any arbitrary and irresponsible influence, is supported by the approval of the overwhelming majority of the German people'. Of the House of Hohenzollern, and what powers still remained to it, there was, again, not one word.

This was something Woodrow Wilson now set about remedying. Two factors helped persuade him to move from political fencing to concrete military talks, and, as he did so, to put the sword right against the throat of imperial Germany. The first was that his own presidential elections were now less than a fortnight away, and his opponents had seized on the latest German reply to return to their campaign theme of 'unconditional surrender'. Indeed, the day after Prince Max's third note arrived in Washington, the Republican Senator Poindexter declared that the President ought to be impeached if he continued such exchanges with Berlin until Germany was both conquered and disarmed. Moreover, that same day, he introduced in the Senate a longwinded resolution to that effect.

The second factor which persuaded the President that it was time to stop talking and get down to brass tacks was the growing surge of resentment and unrest among his allies at being excluded from this crucial dialogue. Even the aloof and Olympian Wilson could, by now, feel this rising tide lapping at his feet. Indeed, one very rough wave came across the Atlantic as he was pondering how best to deal with Berlin once and for all. All that weekend in London Lloyd George and his principal ministers, plus the First Sea Lord, Admiral Wemyss and Field Marshal Haig, who had come over from France, had been in urgent discussion over the armistice terms which they wanted to present before Wilson ran too far ahead of them; they resumed their talks at a marathon session of the War Cabinet on Monday 21 October and half-way through this, the text of Prince Max's third note came in. They reached the same conclusions that Marshal Foch had come to, studying the same note as his new headquarters at Senlis, namely that the German attempt to base armistice conditions on the relative strengths of the two sides could prove a trap over the whole evacuation programme and that, in any case, America's allies simply must break in immediately on these dangerous bilateral exchanges. Maritime Britain had a special concern of her own: apart from the dialogue over submarines, the Prince and the President were saying nothing about naval terms. This was one point raised in a 'Very Urgent' telegram sent to Washington that same day by the Foreign Secretary, Mr Balfour. On this and other vital matters, the message urged, they hoped President Wilson would consult his allies before making any commitments.

Increased consultation was now the order of the day in Washington, and for the first time since Berlin opened the exchange more than a fortnight before, the President asked for the views of his whole Cabinet, who met with him for two hours on 22 October. Their views were generally hawkish. They were also rather too vague and rhetorical for a man who had started off in that vein himself but who was now moving in for a clean kill. Again, the reply was his, and his alone. When he and his colleagues met again the following afternoon, he waited only long enough to assure himself that the great majority supported the idea of an armistice on the general lines of the exchanges thus far. He then pulled from his pocket a typewritten memorandum containing his reply. He called it a 'tentative draft' and said he would be happy to receive 'suggestions regarding any changes'. But apart from one proposal to amend one single phrase (which the President brusquely rejected) the reply was approved word by word as it lay on the table. On peace-making, Woodrow Wilson had a rubber-stamp Cabinet.

The reply at last brought in America's allies,* with whom the President now declared himself ready to take up, on Germany's behalf, 'the question of an armistice'. But the passage which followed ruled out any suggestion of negotiations being based on relative battlefield strengths or indeed on anything else, for it ruled out any dialogue at all. The Entente's military advisers were now to draw up 'necessary terms ... as will ... ensure to the Associated

---

* The actual phrase used was 'the powers associated with the United States', to reflect the distinctive legal basis on which America had entered the war.

Governments the unrestricted power to safeguard and enforce the peace to which the German Government has agreed'. Moreover, as the President made plain, the only arrangements he was prepared to endorse were those which would 'make a renewal of hostilities on the part of Germany impossible'. This was as near as one could go to 'unconditional surrender' without actually spelling the words out.

Wilson then turned the same blow-torch on the House of Hohenzollern itself. Recent constitutional changes in Germany were welcome enough, he conceded, in so far as they boded for a better future; but they did not affect the present war. He concluded:

> 'It is evident that the German people have no means of commanding the acquiescence of the military authorities of the Empire in the popular will; that the power of the King of Prussia to control the policy of the Empire is unimpaired; that the determinating initiative still remains with those who have hitherto been the masters of Germany. Feeling that the whole peace of the world depends now on plain speaking and straightforward action, the President deems it his duty to say, without any attempt to soften what may seem harsh words, that the nations of the world do not and cannot trust the word of those who have hitherto been the masters of German policy, and to point out once more that in concluding peace and attempting to undo the infinite injuries and injustices of this war the Government of the United States cannot deal with any but veritable representatives of the German people who have been assured of a genuine constitutional standing as the real rulers of Germany. If it must deal with the military masters and the monarchical autocrats of Germany now, or if it is likely to have to deal with them later in regard to the international obligations of the German Empire, it must demand, not peace negotiations, but surrender. Nothing can be gained by leaving this essential thing unsaid.'

Whether Britain, herself a constitutional monarchy, and ruled by a

253

sovereign who was of pure German extraction,* might not at least have considered the option of establishing another genuinely constitutional monarchy in post-war Germany was not even considered by Wilson; or conceivably, it was considered and its rejection was part of his motivation. One way or the other, he had committed his allies to imposing republics on their enemy-states as a pre-condition for even a cease-fire. It was a grotesque distortion of the concept of armistice. But, at any rate, the Allies were now in the game. On 23 October, the same day Wilson's third note was dispatched to Berlin, all nineteen powers with whom America was 'associated' in the war were sent copies of all the exchanges the President had had with Germany, with the hope expressed that they would 'acquiesce and take part in the course of action' which the American notes outlined.

The Allies were only waiting for the signal to take part. Forty-eight hours after Wilson's correspondence was received in Paris, Marshal Foch called together the Commanders-in-Chief of his three main national armies at Senlis to ask them for their proposals on the armistice conditions. There was a marked difference in sentiment. Haig, who at times over the past few weeks had spoken as though the war was as good as won, now reverted to extreme caution. The German army was still capable, in his view, of offering serious resistance, especially if drawn right back against its own frontiers. On the other hand, his British army was fifty thousand under strength in infantry, whereas the French were exhausted and the Americans not yet fully organized. Therefore, he was for moderate conditions: nothing more than the evacuation of occupied France and Belgium; the handover of Alsace-Lorraine with Metz and Strasbourg; and the return of French and Belgian rolling stock with the repatriation of their prisoners.

That was an armistice even Ludendorff might have leapt at. By the same token, Foch rejected it as too mild, and so did his other commanders. Pétain wanted to cripple the German war machine by establishing bridgeheads on the right bank of the Rhine and an

---

* George V's father, Edward VII, spoke with a slight German accent to the end of his life. At the court of his grandmother, Queen Victoria, German was spoken as much as English.

Allied occupation of the entire left bank, with the surrender of five thousand German locomotives and a hundred thousand trucks thrown in for good measure. Pershing, who had the most to lose personally by an early end to the war, was for even tougher conditions. Foch took note of them all, and added a few of his own, in a memorandum which he handed over to Clemenceau in Paris on 26 October. The Allied conference on the armistice, soon to hold its first meeting, now had something to bite on, though, as we shall see, a lot of agonized chewing lay ahead.

The immediate impact of the note in Germany was paradoxical. Though Wilson's aim was levelled only at the King of Prussia by name, he first struck down another and more powerful target at the sovereign's side, none other than Ludendorff himself. The First Quartermaster-General seemed almost to welcome this strong reply to what he called Prince Max's 'cowardly note'. His reaction now was a further swing back to toughness: 'In my view there could no longer be any doubt anywhere that we must go on fighting.' From Spa, he realized, he could achieve little in such a fast-moving situation. And when he heard, on 24 October, of a looming crisis in the capital over the Kaiser's position, it was to Berlin, he announced, that he and Hindenburg were coming to continue that fight. He had sown the seeds of his downfall. Prince Max, determined to prove to Wilson that it was the civilians who were now in command in Berlin and that the government were no longer negotiating as marionettes of the military, demanded (as opposed to requesting) that the generals should stay away. Even a month before, such behaviour by a German Chancellor would have been unthinkable.

The two war leaders reacted as though it were still unthinkable. They blandly ignored the Chancellor's order and turned up in the capital early the following morning. Prince Max's wrath was directed almost entirely at Ludendorff, whom he probably suspected as being the prime mover in this defiance. It was not only that, after the experience of the Cabinet meeting the week before, he personally had written off the Quartermaster-General as being the wrong man for the moment. He knew that, by now, all his colleagues were coming to the same conclusion. Indeed, when the question of

Ludendorff's future had been raised at a Cabinet meeting on 24 October, nobody had challenged Erzberger's brutal verdict: 'The defeated War Lord should resign!' The Chancellor determined to bring this about the moment he heard of Ludendorff's arrival. He later wrote:

> 'One thing was certain in my mind. This journey could only end with the dismissal of General Ludendorff. His arbitrary behaviour was only the immediate cause. The desire to ease our situation at home and abroad played a role, but the decisive factor was the lost trust.'*

Defiance seemed compounded by outright rebellion when, on the afternoon of Ludendorff's arrival in the capital, the Berlin papers published the text of a proclamation, which had been issued the evening before in Spa over the signatures of both Hindenburg and Ludendorff. That astounding document, headed 'For the information of all troops', rejected Wilson's latest armistice demands out of hand as 'unacceptable to us soldiers'. In what amounted to a call to break off all peace negotiations, the message went on: 'Wilson's reply can therefore only constitute a challenge for us to continue fighting with all our strength.'

This Order of the Day was both the climax and the conclusion to the long and doleful history of the German army's meddling with politics. It was, on the face of it, so scandalous an interference that even Ludendorff later attempted to dissociate himself from it, as far as was possible. He had queried the text, he claimed, when it was put before him to counter-sign, and had only added his signature when assured by an aide that it was 'in harmony with the views of the government'. It is not a very convincing story in view of the glaring breach between Spa and Berlin which Ludendorff himself had declared after the dispatch of Germany's third 'cowardly note' to Washington.

But whatever the truth about the origin of the proclamation, what mattered more was the transformed political climate into

* Ludendorff in his memoirs makes no mention at all of the Chancellor's insistence that he should not come to Berlin.

Above: The French Prime Minister, Georges Clemenceau, talking to Field Marshal Haig (centre) and other Allied officers, October 1918. Despite his battered hat and shapeless old raincoat, the 'Tiger' still manages to look fiercer than his generals.

Right:
A diminutive and badly wounded Tommy takes his cheerful German prisoner out of the war with him. A scene near Epéhy, September 1918.

A mule in a limber team just struck down by a shell splinter near Remy, September 1918 —one of the million four-legged casualties of the war.

Before the tide turned: the Supreme War Lord flanked by his two legendary commanders, Field Marshal von Hindenburg and General Ludendorff.

Right: Hindenburg Line loot: a Canadian souvenir hunter emerges from a captured dug-out at Cambrai with a whole hat-stand of German helmets.

Across the St. Quentin canal. The familiar but indispensable picture of British troops (137th Brigade) massed happily on the steep eastern bank at Riqueval Bridge which they stormed on 29 September 1918. Their VC commander, Brigadier-General J.V. Campbell, congratulates them from the shattered parapet.

Aerial view of Salonika, 1918, 'a sort of Balkan Marseilles'.

Left: Lloyd George. The huge losses in the West drove Britain's war leader to press for thrusts on the other fronts.

The Irish Sergeant-Major Flora Sandes, probably the most remarkable of all the polyglot members of the 'Allied Armies of the Orient', on convalescence in Salonika after she had been badly wounded during hand-to-hand trench fighting with Serbian troops against the Bulgarians.

Australian soldiers of Allenby's advance guard in Damascus, October, 1918.

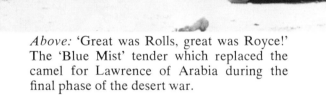

Above: 'Great was Rolls, great was Royce!' The 'Blue Mist' tender which replaced the camel for Lawrence of Arabia during the final phase of the desert war.

Palestine's vital links. German soldiers, with Turkish and Arab civilians, roughing it on the main Baghdad line.

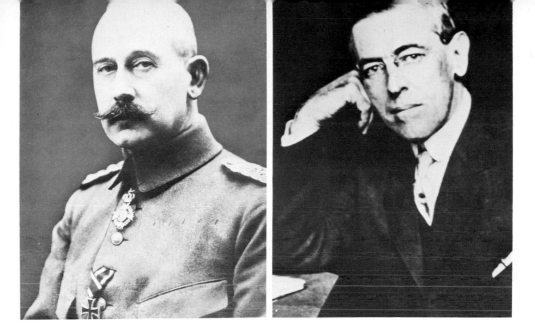

Left: Prince Max of Baden, the 'German gentleman' with liberal leanings and British connections, installed at the eleventh hour as German Chancellor with the hopeless task of saving the empire and the Kaiser, his own cousin.

Right: The American President, Woodrow Wilson, who, without consulting his allies, dictated peace terms to the defeated European empires from the other side of the Atlantic.

Struggling to clear a pass near the Monte Marmolada in the Italian Dolomites, some of the worst fighting terrain of the whole war.

The rake of war: an Italian mountain village in ruins after the fighting.

Left: British soldiers issuing a change of linen to their Austrian prisoners, who had been fighting in the same shirts and underwear for weeks.

Left: Defence lines across the broad River Piave, the obstacle forced by British troops in October 1918 to start the Allied offensive in Italy rolling.

Revolution strikes down two empires: *Above:* 11 November, Berlin—armed sailors take over a government building. *Below:* 12 November, Vienna—the 'Republic of German-Austria' is proclaimed from the Parliament steps.

Jubilation back home—cheering WRAF girls in London.

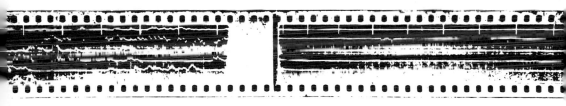

The great moment recorded by a British sound-ranger on the Western Front. The small breaks in the silent minute's graph after 11 a.m. are thought to have been pistol shots.

Opposite: Forest of Compiègne. The only known armistice picture of Marshal Foch (second from right) and (on his right) the chief British delegate, Admiral Wemyss, taken shortly after the signing in the Marshal's special train.

Overleaf: Sombre celebrations at the front—an armistice ceremony behind the lines at Wignacourt.

which it had been launched. That most flagrant of all public acts of military defiance had come at a time when the civilians were, at last, on top, both in law and, to some degree, in force of character. It had come, moreover, at a stage when Ludendorff's head (though not that of his much more widely respected Field Marshal) was already half on the platter as an offering to Wilson. The President's last note had inveighed against 'the military masters and monarchical autocrats' as the unacceptable rulers of Germany. Perhaps a sacrifice of the former might improve the latter's chances of survival.

That, without much doubt, was not far from the mind of the Supreme War Lord himself when, on 26 October, the Kaiser received Ludendorff for the second time in Bellevue Castle, berated the general for the army order of 24 October and instantly accepted his proffered resignation.* Prince Max had made it clear enough that the Emperor would have to choose between him and the Quartermaster-General. One can believe Ludendorff, who had become his own worst enemy, when he wrote that this audience with his Emperor brought 'some of the bitterest moments of my life'. Others thought differently. Prince Max, just stricken down by influenza, was talking things over with a group of colleagues at his bedside when the door burst open:

> 'Colonel Haeften suddenly rushed into the room, shouting with great excitement, "General Ludendorff has been dismissed!"
> "And Hindenburg?"
> "He remains."
> Everyone present jumped to his feet and cried, "Thank God."'

There were also those in the German army for whom, evidently, Tannenberg and its heroes were now light years away. Corporal Ludwig Schroeder, for example, of the 162nd Infantry Regiment, heard the news while his unit, on the move in France, was enjoying

---

* The official announcement said simply that General Ludendorff had been 'placed on the unattached list'. As a somewhat ludicrous gesture, it was also announced that the Lower Rhine Infantry Regiment No. 39 should henceforth bear his name.

a brief roadside rest. He wrote that same day, 27 October, to his parents:

> 'It was as though we could all breathe again, and most of us murmured a "Thank God" that this man, who for so long as a soldier has made German policy, this barrier to peace who has now brought us to the brink of the abyss, has disappeared himself into oblivion.'

It was not only among the soldiers in the field that the magic of Tannenberg had dimmed. One of the favourite 'railway jokes' back in the homeland that autumn ran in the form of this riddle:

> 'Why are Hindenburg and Ludendorff like the sun?'
> 'Because they rise in the East, and set in the West.'

At last – and too late – the German nation was shaking off the spell of its two military titans. What that spell had once meant is illustrated by a story told by Ludendorff's own wife, Margarette. In the middle of the war, the small daughter of a friend came into the room where she was having tea with some ladies, and was presented to her. The child's face had immediately fallen: 'Oh, so that's what you are like! I thought you would be wearing a little golden crown!'

The day after Ludendorff's departure to Spa to pack his bags, the Cabinet, still under the direction of the feverish and bed-ridden Prince Max, approved its fourth note of the month to Washington. Wisely, the Chancellor now abandoned his battle of rhetoric with that past master of the wordy art in the White House. The new message was brief, dignified, and resigned. There was still no mention of the crown. The President's armistice proposals which, by definition, were to make it impossible for Germany to resume the war, were now simply 'awaited'. Berlin had given in.

As for Ludendorff's vacant post, this was allotted, without the new incumbent even being asked, to General Groener. The man who had been put in the shoes of the tarnished legend was even further removed than his predecessor from the standard model of the Prussian Junker leader. He was a fifty-one-year-old Württemberger who had worked his way steadily up the military ladder from the humble social origins of an NCO's son. *Nur net hudle* ('Just don't rush things'), the peasant saying of his Swabian fatherland, was typical also of the man: solid, methodical, unimaginative and blunt. Perhaps those were the qualities most needed to wade through the chaos ahead. Certainly, Groener's general staff background made him an appropriate choice. He was, above all, a railways expert, and had masterminded the formidable transport and supply side of the 1914 mobilization. Now, four years later, the main task which faced him was to bring that much-changed German army back home.

Landslides

THE POLITICAL TUG-OF-WAR which had gone on throughout October – increasingly slithery at the Berlin end of the rope, increasingly sure-footed in Washington – had, at least, been a two-way affair. On the battlefields during those same autumn weeks, the armies of the Central Powers went only one way – backwards. In some cases, their retirement was more or less voluntary and controlled. Ludendorff's overall plan in the West, for example, (the last he was to direct), called for a slow withdrawal to the Meuse, where a prolonged stand was to be made. This river line, which screened the centre and south of his long front, indeed offered good prospects for defence. The plains of Flanders, which stretched up to the English Channel two hundred miles to the north, held no such hope. When, therefore, on 14 October, the Flanders Army Group of King Albert (to which the British Second Army was still attached) resumed their general offensive, they found themselves pushing at a slowly-yielding barrier. After forty-eight hours with their shoulders held against the door (during which time Roulers, Iseghem and Thourout were evacuated after tough rearguard fighting) the German Fourth Army, on orders, suddenly gave way.

On 17 October, as Ludendorff was leaving Spa for Berlin to attend the War Council debate, he ordered General Sixt von Arnim, the Fourth Army's commander, to pull right back to the River Scheldt, thus abandoning some eight hundred square miles of the Flanders battlefields, including the whole of the Belgian coastline. Ostend was entered by the Allies that same day; Zeebrugge two days later. Inland, the beautiful city of Bruges, whose citizens gave the triumphant King Albert a rapturous welcome, hoisted the Belgian flag again. Not all of von Arnim's men and material had got away: his army left behind some six thousand prisoners and three hundred and fifty guns in this coastal sector alone. But far more important than booty was the strategic dividend. Germany's Channel U-boat bases were now gone for good, while, on the political front, Belgium was taking shape again as an independent kingdom after four years of subjugation.

The British Second Army, fighting on the right flank of the Flanders Army Group, had a similar tale to tell. There the prize was the great manufacturing town of Lille, occupied by the Germans ever since the first weeks of the war. Had they fought to hold it now, or practised 'scorched earth' demolitions before withdrawing, one of the key-stones for France's economic recovery would have been destroyed before recovery even began. But the great punch delivered by General Plumer's divisions in the first forty-eight hours of the general offensive had threatened to encircle the city entirely, and the threat proved enough.

As an observer with the Second Army wrote on 17 October:

'In Lille, the first news of the enemy's flight was received by our airmen today, who saw people signalling to them with their handkerchiefs, waving frantically to give some message. Our airmen guessed that it was joyful news, and could only mean one thing. After that a civilian came over to our lines and said "You can go in; the enemy has gone in the night." Our patrols fell forward and encountered no opposition.'

Lille had escaped lightly. It was a different story at Douai, forty miles due south, which troops of the British First Army occupied the same day. They saw scenes that seemed to have been copied from the most lurid propaganda posters of the wanton Hun. Douai was a pillaged ghost town. All its inhabitants had been carted off eastwards and the only human being who crawled forward out of the carnage to greet the liberators was a deserter from the enemy's rearguard. Everything of value that the Germans could carry they had taken off with them. Most of what remained had been smashed, from the crockery and furniture in the houses to the reeds of the cathedral organ, torn out for scrap metal and then abandoned in a heap on the stone floor as too cumbrous.

Courtrai had suffered a fate between these two extremes. The

Second Army found, in the streets of a damaged but not devastated town, some twenty-five thousand of the civilian population waiting to greet them; though, given the fact that the Germans were still bombarding the town, their welcome was somewhat restrained. A splendid exception was a seventy-year-old Irish lady named Mary Cunningham who had lived since 1906 in a tiny house opposite the cathedral. When an English officer visited her he was received in her parlour as though she were a chatelaine dispensing peace-time hospitality. Her only concession to the German shelling, which was shattering glass and stone-work all round the cathedral square, was to ask: 'Do you mind shutting the door, my dear? I don't like those bombs coming in.' She turned out to be a cousin, on her grandmother's side, of Woodrow Wilson, which made this icy contempt of the Germans very appropriate.

But whatever the Flanders towns were suffering, it was again the centre of the line which saw the toughest fighting, and once more it was the British Third and Fourth Armies, which had led the way across the Hindenburg Line the month before, who bore the brunt. Pushing eastwards from Cambrai, which fell on 9 October, they drove the enemy back to, and then across, the line of the River Selle. The week-long battle in this key sector only ended on the 24th, the day Ludendorff left Spa for his second and last visit to Berlin to plead his defiantly muddled cause. In all, twenty-four British and two American divisions had pushed back thirty-one German divisions, several of whom had fought stubbornly for every yard of ground before leaving twenty thousand prisoners behind. (During that one month of October Marshal Haig's forces suffered a hundred and twenty thousand battle casualties, ample evidence of the fight they still had on their hands.)

Even tougher was the enemy resistance against the hapless Americans pinned down in the forests of the Argonne. The beginning of October, it will be recalled, had seen Pershing's advance lagging far behind his aspirations, and, just as galling, far behind the breakthrough achieved by his allies moving through easier terrain to the north. Though the terrible 'Mountain of the Falcon' had eventually been stormed in the initial American assault, the main defences of the Hindenburg Line – smashed or turned almost everywhere else on the Western Front – had not yet even been tackled down here. On 4 October Pershing mounted his next general attack, aiming at the Cunel Heights on the right of his front and the Romagne Heights in the centre, two more of those formidable natural barriers around which the Germans had built their defences. It was a bloody slog forward, reminiscent more of those early bogged-down days on the Somme than of this 'Tally-ho!' of the final victorious pursuit. It took the First Army* and its French supporting formations nearly a fortnight to storm those key heights and make good the strong-points behind them. That meant an average advance in this central sector of barely eight hundred yards a day – niggardly on the map but still costly in men, thanks largely to the formidable concentration of enemy fire-power. One hill, taken after six assaults, was found to hold no fewer than two hundred and thirty machine-gun nests, one to every seven of the defenders. Despite this, the Germans, legalistic to the end, found time to lodge a formal protest after they had captured some American infantry carrying repeater shot-guns with six cartridges: fowling pieces, the German High Command pointed out, were contrary to the Hague Conventions on warfare. (In reply, the Americans asked sardonically what the inventors of flame-throwers were complaining about.)

As in the earlier engagements, Pershing's commanders proved, in action, to be a mixture of adequate, inadequate and unconventionally dashing. Two of the second category (the generals commanding the 3rd and 5th Infantry divisions) had to be summarily removed in the middle of the attack and replaced by brigadiers from a more successful formation. Elsewhere, quality told – emphatically, even prophetically. There was, for example, the affair of the Côte de Chatillon, a precipitous height held by good German troops which the American 42nd Division (the crack 'Rainbow' formation) came up against on 15 October as it was

---

* On 16 October immediate command of this army was handed to the capable General Liggett, hitherto of I Corps. The other corps commander, Bullard, took over the newly-formed American Second Army. Pershing himself moved up to the position of Army Group commander.

battling its way through the Romagne woods. The obstacle had to be cleared, and quickly. 'Give us the Côte de Chatillon or report five thousand casualties!' was the grim order sent down the line from V Corps Headquarters to the 84th Brigade facing the height. 'We'll take it or report "No Brigade",' the even tougher reply went back. That particular American brigade commander was called Douglas MacArthur.

By 26 October, the day Ludendorff was dismissed, the Americans had finally pierced their sector of the Hindenburg defences and were fighting in the streets of Grandpré. This meant that, by the time the First Quartermaster-General disappeared from the scene, both basic requirements for his 'orderly withdrawal to the Meuse' – holding the British on the River Selle and the Americans on the Kriemhilde fortifications – had disappeared with him. There was no direct link between these happenings, for it was with a political spade that Ludendorff had dug his grave. Nonetheless, the conjunction of events was apposite. That vision of the 'strategic defensive' which he had been holding up, in various guises, before the eyes of the confused Berlin peace-makers ever since August, had evaporated at last like the mirage it always had been. Far behind the evacuation zone there was still, of course, the Rhine, and the possibility of one last stand along that great river to guard, not foreign soil, but the fatherland itself. Yet, by the end of October, all such military contingencies were rapidly being outpaced by the plummeting morale of the German nation and outflanked by the stampede of political events.

Those last weeks on the Western Front brought an odd mixture, on the Germans' part, of ferocious hand-to-hand fighting and almost resigned languor, a contrast which comes out well in the diaries of the advancing Allied troops. In some sectors the Germans were still at their familiar game of booby-trapping everything – including the dead – to delay the advance. A captain in a French anti-aircraft battery, hurrying forward in mid-October near Tionville to catch up with his infantry who were 'marching with the steps of giants', noted that traps had been laid in every evacuated building. 'Sometimes it's a rifle, sometimes a helmet which a thin strip of wire links up with the charge of a fat grenade.

It's an excellent precaution to begin by cutting every piece of wire in sight.'

But a British officer advancing that same week through the 1916 'land of crosses' east of Péronne found only hastily-scraped graves in ditches all along the German line of retreat with not a booby-trap in sight. The enemy had found time, however, to leave some memorials behind to some British dead. One such mound of earth was crowned with the rough inscription: *Hier ruht Smith*, as though that very name, just as commonplace in either language, had about it the aura of a universal unknown warrior.

A British war artist moving behind Haig's forces at Cambrai recorded an even odder sight as he rode past fields 'full of dead Boche and horses':

> 'In one spot in the mud at the side of the road lay two British Tommies who had evidently just been killed. They had been laid out ready for something to take them away. Standing beside them were three French girls, all dressed up, silk stockings and crimped hair. There they were, standing on the dead Tommies, asking if we would not like "a little love" ...
>
> 'They themselves might be blown to eternity the next moment. Death and the dead had become as nothing to the young generation ...'

As for the languor, where that prevailed, mostly in the deep pockets of this strange battlefield, it seemed as much induced by talk of peace as by sheer physical exhaustion. On 11 October, for example, many prisoners from the 8th German Division were taken without resistance because they had read the latest exchanges between Prince Max and President Wilson to mean the end of fighting. 'Men of the 2nd German Cyclist Brigade went to sleep at Fresnoy with these dreams of peace and were captured while sleeping.' In one of his last first-hand surveys of the Western Front, Ludendorff himself noted (after meticulously recording the 'extremely inconvenient' loss of a number of de-lousing stations) that: 'The armistice offer had had an unfavourable effect on the men's spirits, and war weariness had increased.'

Even the Allies had to keep the seductress of armistice at bay, in case she took men's minds prematurely off a task still unfinished. The famous historian of the Irish Guards in France records that, on 10 October, a special Order of the Day was issued to all units from Fourth Army Headquarters laying down that 'all peace talk must cease'. And the diary of a guardsman in the Grenadiers showed, even in a crack regiment, how necessary the precaution was, if the fighting spirit was to be kept up to the last:

> 'Everyone was fearful of a bad wound [he wrote] or blinding or death so near the end. The reckless ones became cautious, taking no risks.'

The airmen on both sides seem to have spurned such caution; at least, the references to it either in operational orders or in private diaries are as good as non-existent. In some technical aspects, the dwindling and despairing German squadrons were still ahead of their opponents. A young British pilot flying his Sopwith Dolphin over the German lines accounted for an enemy machine and later wrote of the engagement in his diary:

> 'I will never forget my surprise ... in seeing a German jumping out of his aircraft and float down in a parachute.'

No parachutes, it seemed, were yet in use with the Royal Air Force, and their planes also lagged behind in the matter of self-sealing petrol tanks.

In numbers of operational machines, however, the Western Allies now had a commanding lead. A French general, leading his 162nd Infantry Division against the Hunding fortifications (one of the last reserve positions of the Hindenburg Line still to be taken on French soil) wrote of his advance on 27 October:

> 'My motor-car is bracketed with two shells, one to the right and the other to the left which showers me with earth. But we hardly take any notice of the incident with such a joyful . sight in the air above us. The sky is covered with our squadrons; I count 120 machines flying in well-ordered formations towards the enemy. That has the real smell of victory about it!'

Three days after that French diary entry, the young British airman who had been so astounded at the sight of an enemy parachute in action described in his log-book what was, in his experience, the decisive air battle of attrition on the Western Front. On 30 October 1918, he records, sixty-seven German aircraft were destroyed. British losses on that same day amounted to forty-one machines shot down, three pilots being killed, eight wounded and twenty-six declared missing. As the Englishman commented: 'There was certainly plenty of fight left in the German Air Force.'

So much for the key Western Front as Ludendorff abruptly and unceremoniously bowed out; it was crumbling steadily and there was not enough cement left, moral or material, to fill the widening cracks for long. Yet that battered structure, as seen from the Allied side, still somehow held together, prompting Field Marshal Haig to opine, as late as the eve of Ludendorff's dismissal, that the German army 'was by no means broken'. Indeed, said the British Commander-in-Chief, if the enemy Supreme Command, instead of pulling back in pockets, would only shorten its lines at one go by a clear one hundred miles and thus save seventy divisions in the process, it could still present a challenge.

The Allies now had no such fears, and the Central Powers no such prospects, on the secondary fronts of the Balkans and Asia Minor. On those fronts, it will be recalled, the armies of the Entente had started the last full month of the war with Bulgaria already knocked out of the reckoning altogether by General Franchet d'Espèrey, and Turkey facing a similar capitulation under the pressure of General Allenby's imperial forces advancing steadily up the coast from Palestine. Belgrade was now the Frenchman's prime target, Constantinople the Englishman's. But all manner of complications intervened, both as between the commanders and their campaigns on the ground and as between their political masters fighting for their national strategies in London and Paris. England, her eyes, as always, on the gateways to the great oceans, was determined to settle with the Turks by herself, to avenge the humiliation of the battle-cruiser *Goeben*'s exploits four years ago and to anchor the British fleet again in the Dardanelles. The problem was how to force the approaches to the Turkish capital. Allenby, moving up the railway line from Damascus in the first week of October, duly took Homs on the 16th, Hama on the 21st and Aleppo on the 26th. But from there the railway line, and the high road to Constantinople, swung westwards, with one thousand miles of the tough country of Anatolia and the Taurus Mountains between him and his goal. It only made sense, if the final blow against the Turks was to be delivered by land, to allot the task to forces drawn from d'Espèrey's Army of the Orient, who could make the much easier approach across the plains of Thrace. But which forces?

D'Espèrey, a visionary always drawn forward through faith in his star, had now, with that star riding high and seemingly immovable in the firmament, become semi-Olympian in his pretensions. His biographer records a letter which the general wrote home to a friend on 2 October 1918, when the advance into Serbia was gathering momentum:

> 'With 200,000 men I can cross Hungary and Austria, assemble my forces in Bohemia and then march on Dresden. Should the Boches cling to the Rhine, this would be the least costly way in human lives, and above all French lives, of prising them loose. There's no doubt that my appearance in Bohemia would cause a collapse all round.'

The irrepressible Frenchman was even dreaming of appearing, in proxy at least, in Constantinople. Lloyd George and his advisers had set out for Paris on 4 October for top-level Allied discussions on the situation with the firm intention of making the final swoop into Turkey an entirely British affair. If Allenby was prevented by the terrain from leading it in person, then General Milne, whose divisions had played that thankless and bloody supporting role in the Macedonian victory, should detach himself from d'Espèrey's force and undertake the operation under the overall command of Allenby from the other side of the Aegean. The irritation of the British Prime Minister can be imagined when, on arriving in Paris, he discovered that the French wanted to concentrate everything on the Serbian campaign (roping Rumania in on the way) and leave Turkey to stew disconsolately in her own juice for the time being.

But he became 'absolutely furious' when, two days later, Clemenceau produced an alternative plan for dealing with Turkey which he had just received from the Commander-in-Chief of the Orient Armies. This certainly matched Lloyd George's view that Turkey ought to be knocked out at once and not merely 'isolated'. The trouble was that d'Espèrey proposed to do the knocking out himself. Of the army of five divisions proposed by him for the march on Constantinople, three would be French, one Greek, and only one British. Needless to say a French officer, General Anselme, was to be in command. Under this arrangement, General Milne and the bulk of his forces were to move north-east and occupy the already capitulated Bulgaria – a task almost as humdrum as Milne's long siege of the malarious Struma Valley had been unhealthy. After Lloyd George's flat refusal of any such scheme, a face-saving formula was eventually devised: Milne would undertake the land operation against the Turks, though still acting under d'Espèrey's overall command.

It might have helped a little if these august statesmen debating the fate of whole armies and nations had always used adequate maps to work from. Lloyd George and Clemenceau, together with Orlando, their Italian colleague, were discovered at one of these Paris sessions planning their joint strategy for the Balkans 'on a small hand-atlas map, the whole page of Europe being about eight inches by six inches!' But the real trouble, of course, was political, not topographical. As one French historian of the Balkan campaign put it:

> 'The Entente possessed no military direction. Its governments did not base their decisions on the plain principles of strategy and the obvious operational imperatives of warfare, but solely on their political designs, which differed from state to state.'

These differences stood out even more sharply when the war leaders in Paris next considered the parallel operation to a land advance on Turkey, namely a massed descent by the Allied navies on Constantinople. Though the commander of all the Allied fleets operating in the Mediterranean was a Frenchman, Gauchet, the

269

naval forces in the Aegean were now under a British Admiral with the resounding name of Gough-Calthorpe.* His fleet was the obvious one to carry out the task; moreover, Britain, in Lloyd George's view, was the obvious nation to preside over the capitulation of Turkey, having done so much – in Gallipoli, Mesopotamia, Egypt, Arabia, and now Palestine and Syria – to bring that surrender about. The fur really flew when Clemenceau, pointing to General Milne's appointment as the land forces commander against Constantinople, insisted that it must be a French officer who should command the naval operations.

As the warships of England, France, Italy and Greece – more than a hundred in number and ranging in size from giant Dreadnoughts to nimble patrol boats – gathered at Mudros, the port of Lemnos Island, the argument over command dragged on inconclusively at Paris. Though adamant with Clemenceau, Lloyd George was, for the most part, polite. But the final exchanges occasionally became heated and sarcastic, as at the point, recorded even in the official minutes, where the fiery Welshman exploded with astonishment at the 'lack of generosity' which the French were showing. After all, he pointed out, the British now had some five hundred thousand men on Turkish soil. They had captured three or four Turkish armies and had incurred hundreds of thousands of casualties in the process. Compared with this, the British Prime Minister continued somewhat offensively: 'The other governments had only put in a few nigger policemen to see that we did not steal the Holy Sepulchre! When, however, it came to signing an armistice, all this fuss was made.' The fuss, not surprisingly, was settled to the Welshman's satisfaction.

As the warships assembled and the statesmen debated, General Milne's three British divisions, with one French division and some Greek and Italian elements in support, accordingly started off on their long slog eastwards across Thrace. It was all to be in vain, as this personal account of a historically-minded British soldier mar-

---

* He had been rushed out to the area because he outranked the senior French officer in the Aegean, Admiral Amet. With Calthorpe had come powerful Royal Navy reinforcements.

ching with the 98th Brigade Royal Field Artillery describes:

'We got our marching orders about 10 October ...

'The country through which we were to pass was an area in which for centuries time had almost stood still. In ancient times the Romans had built a paved highway from Salonika through Philippi to Constantinople; this was called the Via Egnatia and it was along this highway that St Paul travelled from Neapolis (Kavalla) to Philippi, and thence by Amphipolis (near the Struma mouth) to Thessalonika, as described in the Acts of the Apostles; traces of this road still remain, quite a long stretch near Kavalla ... As a student of the classics I felt rather excited at the thought that another army had traversed this route though in the opposite direction – the great army which Xerxes, King of Persia, led against Greece in 480 BC and which was to suffer near-defeat at Thermopylae and final defeat at Salamis and Plataea.

'The first part of the journey was uneventful and took us through pleasant country by Lakes Beshik and Langaza, through Stavros and over the River Struma. We had the sea on our right, with the mountainous island of Thasos in the near distance and Mount Athos about thirty miles away. One of our night camps was in almost Arcadian surroundings; after a hard day's march involving steep ascents for the horses, we came in the valley of the Ilijedere. Here were clear running streams, pleasant woodlands and rich pasture; it was a joy to turn the tired animals out to graze and then ourselves to relax in the warm autumn sunshine ...

'Our spirits went up as we took stock of our position. Here at Dedeagatch we were within a few miles of enemy Turkey, the hills of which rose behind us to the north-east. Away to the south-east, some thirty miles away, a long spit of land on the horizon was the Gallipoli peninsula which was to have been our objective. But now ... there came to us over the water, from the direction of the Gallipoli peninsula, a distant rumble which was at first thought to be a cannonade but later turned out to be the blowing up by our mine sweepers of the minefields blocking the Dardanelles ...

'Alas, we were not to go to Constantinople after all. We were to return to Macedonia – Macedonia the place which none of the troops wanted or expected to see again – and we were to travel, not by sea or by rail, but by road, the way we had come – and carrying all our unfired ammunition.'

What had happened was that the ever pragmatic Turks, realizing that their hour-glass was almost empty, decided to tilt it for comfort towards the Royal Navy. They released General Townshend, the ill-fated British commander at Kut (who had been their prisoner ever since the fall of that Mesopotamian garrison two and a half years before) and dispatched him as their official peace emissary to Mudros, where he arrived, doubtless like a man in a daze, on 20 October. It was with the British, Townshend told Admiral Calthorpe, and not with the French, that the Turks wished to deal. The War Cabinet in London could not have been more delighted with the news, which corresponded with diplomatic feelers they had been receiving for several days from Constantinople. On 22 October, Calthorpe was accordingly instructed to go ahead.

The admiral conducted himself with both the aplomb of a Royal Navy grandee and the astuteness of a professional diplomatist. The Turkish delegates who duly arrived on the 26th at Mudros (headed by Raouf Bey, the Minister of Marine) were anyway at a massive psychological disadvantage as, from the portholes of their comfortable cabins on HMS *Agamemnon*, they gazed along massed ranks of Allied warships lined up the length and breadth of the harbour as though for a Spithead review. An even greater handicap was that, from their British man-of-war, they were unable to establish direct wireless contact with Constantinople and so were thrown back on their own nervous resources. The upshot was that, with the French brusquely excluded from the proceedings, Calthorpe, after only three days of talks, persuaded his visitors to sign an armistice which conceded in full practically all of the twenty-four clauses drawn up hurriedly in London three weeks before. The main provision called for the immediate re-opening of the Dardanelles and the Bosphorus, with access to the Black Sea; the return of all Allied prisoners; the disbandment of the Turkish army with the exception of security and police units at levels to be separately fixed; the occupation by the Allies of any and all strategic points considered necessary; the control by them of all Turkish communications and railways; the expulsion of all Germans and Austrians and the breaking-off of Turkish relations with both Central Powers; and, of course, the sweeping and demolition of all mines which had blocked the Straits. It was the 'distant rumble' of their destruction which the British troops resting at Dedeagatch before setting out on their final march to the Dardanelles peninsula had mistaken for a cannonade of some unresolved battle. It was in fact the drum-roll of the Turkish surrender.

Together with Allenby's victories in Palestine, which had prepared the way for this moment, the Mudros armistice entrenched British power and influence in the Eastern Mediterranean throughout the post-war decade. For France it had been a humiliation. Throughout the last ten days of October, Lloyd George had successfully employed in Paris every argument and prevarication to keep a French naval representative from joining Calthorpe in the ward-room of the *Agamemnon*. (Amet, the senior French naval officer in the Aegean, had to wait until the great Allied naval display put on before Constantinople after the armistice to show his country's flag.) In the Balkans, it was a different story. There Franchet d'Espèrey continued to fight his battles and to dream out his dreams. It was his own government, and not any challenge by his Allied commanders, which put successive curbs on both.

On 7 October he received orders from Clemenceau which not only, as reluctantly agreed by the 'Tiger', allotted the march on Constantinople to British forces. They also announced the appointment of another French commander, General Berthelot, to take over the entire task of luring (or snatching if need be) Rumania from the German grasp. Clemenceau and his military advisers clearly feared that d'Espèrey was planning on too bold a scale for the broader unity of the Entente to bear, and getting too big for his boots in the process. But even with two operations on the right flank now removed from its immediate control, the Army of the Orient still had the glittering task ahead of liberating the whole of Serbia and of confronting the enemy on, and then with luck beyond, the Danube Line itself.

Glittering, but exhausting. For while d'Espèrey re-grouped his divisions for this central thrust, so the Central Powers were doing what they could to prevent disaster becoming a débâcle in the Balkans. One device was a change of command. The admirable von Scholtz was switched to the Rumanian front and the defence of Serbia was entrusted to Field Marshal von Kövess, the Austro-Hungarian general who had driven those same Serbs southwards along these same valleys in 1915. But this time the Serbs were not alone, and they were advancing to liberate their own soil. As for the enemy reinforcements they faced,* these looked more substantial on paper than they proved on the ground. They had arrived at different times and places, scraped up from various battlefields; some, like the German troops transferred from the Western Front, were already exhausted by weeks of continuous fighting.

Nonetheless there were some tough battles ahead for the Entente armies before their last breakthrough; and Nish, lying roughly half-way between Skopje and Belgrade, was the toughest. It was also the most vital. There, the main north–south railway line to Salonika met up with the other strategic line running south-eastwards to Sofia and Constantinople. Immense dumps of stores, guns and ammunition of all types guaranteed the defenders all the military supplies they needed. A force of three German and two Austrian divisions was now in position alongside the regular garrison with orders to hold the town to the last man. The First Serbian Army, which arrived in front of this formidable barrier on 9 October, had already, with French cavalry and infantry units in

---

* Reinforcements which had now arrived in the Balkans battle area by land or sea included the German Alpenkorps from France; the 50th Landwehr from Minsk; two more low-grade occupation divisions from southern Russia, the 217th and 219th Infantry, and elements of other regiments. The Austrians had rushed across from Italy their 9th and 25th Divisions.

support, advanced some seventy miles over the past six days. They had far outrun their supplies – provided mainly by a fleet of five hundred light Ford lorries driven by the British up roads that heavier vehicles simply could not negotiate – and they were now down to handfuls of rounds per weapon. Their strength in actual rifles was barely ten thousand ragged and half-famished men – about a quarter the number of their amply-provided opponents. Their strength in spirit proved irresistible.* Prince Alexander, again in person at the key point of action, decided to send in his three decimated divisions immediately. By 12 October they had duly driven the enemy out, after first fighting their way up to the heights which dominated the city from the south. It was a triumph of the moral over the material which Napoleon had always prized as the surest foundation of victory. After Nish, a few stubborn rear-guard skirmishes still lay ahead, but the road to Belgrade was now open. On 19 October the 76th French Division, pushing up through Bulgaria, reached the loop of the Danube at Vidin and thus cut, by water also, the links between the Central Empire and their eastern allies. On the last day of October, after sharp clashes at Parachin and Stoinik, the Serbians were on the hills of Topcider, overlooking Belgrade itself. The next day they re-entered their capital. The enemy garrison scurried back across the broad confluence of the Sava and the Danube in every vessel they could muster, heading, in reverse direction to August 1914, for the relative safety of the Hungarian shore. Serbia, from where the great conflict had erupted four summers before, was now out of the maelstrom.

But why had the Austrian Emperor Charles and his Chief-of-Staff, General Arz, not been able to rush more of their own troops

---

* This numerical inferiority of the attackers at Nish was strictly local and tactical. An official French count of the Orient Army in October 1918 gave its ration strength as 209,000 French; 138,000 British; 119,000 Serbs; 43,000 Italians and 157,000 Greeks. With the Bulgarians now virtually out of the war, this total of nearly 670,000 men far outnumbered the retreating Austro-German forces. The losses suffered by the various Entente belligerents during the whole campaign showed clearly enough however, the extent to which d'Espèrey had relied on the Serbs to free their own homeland. They suffered 45,000 killed and 133,000 wounded – more than the losses of all their allies put together.

across the Adriatic to try and hold Belgrade and the Danube Line? The river was, after all, the great strategic and economic waterway which both screened and linked the twin Habsburg capitals of Vienna and Budapest. The reason lay in an even greater military challenge on the empire's southern front. That same last week of October which had seen, on the Western Front, the storming of the Selle by British troops and the smashing of the Kriemhilde fortifications by the Americans; and, on the Eastern Front, the surrender of the Turks at Mudros and the capture of Belgrade, had also brought, in the south, the last bitter round in the struggle with Austria's arch-rival. On the night of 23–24 October, the Italians, this time with powerful British, French and American support, launched their long-dreaded general offensive from the Piave line to which they had been driven back in such ignominy a year before. The Italians were after spectacular revenge, and they were to get it; but the seeds of their coming triumph had been sown for them by their enemies, and they had been sown far from the battlefield.

Throughout the first fortnight of October, the Emperor Charles had been following with growing dismay the exchange of notes (to which, as Germany's principal ally, he had formally subscribed) between Berlin and Washington. As already described,* at his own Crown Council meeting held in Vienna in the immediate aftermath of Bulgaria's collapse, there had been a general call for emergency action, both at home and abroad, to stave off the threat, now looming up in the Danube Basin itself, to the existence of the Dual Monarchy. Charles himself had summed it up by calling simultaneously for 'energetic pressure on Germany in the peace question' and for 'the speediest start on the internal reconstruction of Austria'. The young ruler was now face to face with the dilemma – summed up by that one word 'simultaneously' – that had baffled his own conscience, as well as all his own counsellors, throughout his brief two-year reign. How could one carry out a fundamental reconstruction of a sprawling, multi-national empire, with all the ethnic and political wounds that such surgery would inflict, and hope to keep together the imperial army, drawn from the soldiers of those same eleven peoples, still standing

* See pp 147–48.

shoulder to shoulder as a fighting force? Surely, such vast reforms could only be carried out, if indeed at all, in the calmness of peace? And yet, as Wilson was making it ever plainer to Berlin, political reconstruction was itself the price of peace. There had, as yet, been no personal threat to the Habsburg dynasty to match the reproaches and menaces being levelled directly at the Hohenzollerns. But the American President's refusal to accept an unreformed Dual Monarchy had been clear ever since 8 January 1918, when Number Ten of his Fourteen Points had called specifically for 'the peoples of Austria-Hungary to be accorded the freest opportunity for autonomous development'. Since then, the recognition on 3 September by America and England* of the Czech exile movement as the *de facto* Czecho-Slovak authority, showed the ominous turn the wind was taking, and by mid-October, this *de facto* government had become a Provisional Government, residing officially in Paris, with Dr Beneš as its 'Secretary of State for Foreign Affairs'.

Irrespective of any effect on his army, Charles now had to act – at a few minutes to midnight and still standing right in the cannon's mouth – to federalize his dominions. The irony of it all was that, in his own Habsburg way, his views on this had been both clear and positive long before they had been taken up by an ambitious American politician called Woodrow Wilson. In April 1911, three years before the assassination of his uncle Francis Ferdinand (which both started the fuse of war to splutter and also placed him as new heir-apparent on the steps of the throne) the young Archduke Charles had talked about the future of the Empire when walking in the woods of St Jakob in Styria with the Bourbon princess who had just become his fiancée.

> 'The only solution' [he told her] 'is a truly federal one to give all the peoples a chance ... Every nation must have its freedom within the state as a whole ... It wouldn't even matter if one or the other wanted to declare itself a Republic in the process; after all, the three Hansa towns are republics within the German Empire. The essential thing is that whatever constitutional form they choose, the nations

---

* Followed by France on 28 September and Italy on 3 October.

should maintain their link with the monarchy and their identity within the state as a whole.'

That was the reverse of a political campaigning speech. Moreover, it was made in an age when both Mr Wilson – and Dr Beneš for that matter – would not only have doffed their hats and bowed to whoever sat on the Habsburg throne but would have regarded him – as would the leaders of England and France – as the best hope there was of keeping the lid on the Balkan powder keg. Stability was then the name of the game; and, in any case, what the Empire's own nationalists were after, in that era, was no more than a fatter share of the imperial cake.

But when, as a prematurely-aged Emperor seven and a half years later, Charles moved 'to give all the peoples a chance' (and his own dynasty, of course, with it) there was one immovable obstacle: his kingdom of Hungary. The Magyars, heirs to a thousand-year-old Christian history whose unity and antiquity surpassed any common memory or tradition which the German-speaking Austrians of the empire could muster, had always put their own cause first, and the imperial cause second – despite the fact that their leaders owed to the Habsburg crown not only, in most cases, their lands and titles, but also, in all cases, their dignity as citizens of one of the five great powers of Europe. Since the so-called 'Compromise' of 1867* their own status had grown, especially as regards the internal government of their half of the empire, a half which they refused to democratize, even up to the limited standards introduced by Vienna. In his own solemn oath, pronounced after his coronation on 30 November 1916 in the Gothic Cathedral of Mathias Corvinus at Buda, the freshly anointed and crowned King Charles IV of Hungary (for such he was to the Magyars) had sworn 'by the living God ...

---

* After Austria's disastrous defeat, in 1866, in the fratricidal war with Prussia, engineered by Bismarck to establish the supremacy of Berlin in the German-speaking world, the Hungarian nationalists, early the following year, pushed through their Dualist agreement with Vienna. Though foreign affairs, defence and finance remained under Vienna's centralized control, Hungary regained complete independence in internal affairs.

that we shall not alienate the boundaries of Hungary and her associated countries ... shall not reduce but as far as possible increase and extend their territories'. (Had he succeeded to the throne in peacetime, he would have postponed this fatally binding coronation – as his murdered uncle Francis Ferdinand had intended to do – using the postponement as a lever to secure social and political reforms in the Magyar-ruled territories. But instead, it was wartime, and his authority as crowned king of Hungary was legally necessary to administer and prosecute that war.)

The Hungarian dilemma, which would have bedevilled all Charles's blue-prints for post-war federal reconstruction after the war, blocked any clear-cut formula now. The moment they sniffed what was in the air, the Hungarian Prime Minister Wekerle, together with his great predecessor Tisza and two other political leaders, Andrassy and Appony (Counts one and all, it is superfluous to add), hurried in alarm to Vienna. There they filled the Emperor's ears, and the air in general, with cries of Hungary's 'thousand year rights' over their own Slav subjects, and notably the Croats who, for generations, had looked in vain to the crown for deliverance. As a result, when, six days later, federalism was finally proclaimed in the Dual Monarchy (Charles himself being the driving force amid his band of wrangling ministers) it had to be publicly proclaimed that – to adapt a famous phrase which was to be coined twenty years later by a British writer – some subjects were going to be more federal than others.

The vital passages of the historic 'People's Manifesto', issued from Schönbrunn Palace over Charles's signature in the early evening of 16 October, read:

'Following the will of its peoples, Austria shall become a federal state ('*Bundestaat*') in which each racial component shall form its own state organization ...

'To those peoples on whose rights of self-determination the new Empire will be built, my call goes out to implement the great work through National Councils which, composed of the parliamentary deputies of each nation, shall represent the interests of the peoples with each other and in contact with my government.'

But the proclamation had to contain one stultifying, nullifying sentence: 'This reconstruction shall in no way affect the integrity of the lands of the sacred Hungarian crown.' This one pledge* ensured that the 'new empire', its life already gravely threatened in advance by the rising authority and pretensions of the émigré governments, should come into the world still-born. Before the month was out, the Emperor's peoples had taken the independence proffered but thrown away the federalism and, with it, the crown. Czechs, Slovenes, Poles, Rumanians, Ukrainians and Croats (breaking away from Vienna as well as from Budapest) led the procession of newly-independent states – republics in intention though not at once in name. Hardly a drop of blood was spilt. Not even the multi-national British empire was to be wound up in such a legal, peaceful way.

For the 'Peace Emperor', that remained, to the day of his premature death in exile three and a half years later, a permanent balm. Just as well, for his Manifesto brought him nothing at the time. Though it matched Number Ten of the 'Fourteen Points' on self-determination, President Wilson soon made it clear that, in politics as in war, circumstances alter cases. The White House spent four days digesting the contents of the Manifesto and then spat them out. The eagerly-awaited American note, sent to Vienna on 20 October 1918, pointed out that, as the Czecho-Slovak National Council was now 'a *de facto* belligerent government' on the side of the Entente, and as America also now 'recognized in the fullest manner the justice of the nationalistic aspirations of the Yugo-Slavs', the mere offer of autonomy just made to these peoples could no longer be accepted in Washington 'as a basis for peace'. The Habsburg Empire was being drowned under its own life-belt. What now of the military outcome?

In contrast to the violent fighting and the surging Allied

---

* To ensure its insertion Dr Wekerle had threatened to cut off all supplies of Hungarian food to Austria.

advances which had lit up the other battle-fronts throughout the summer and early autumn of 1918, the entire line in Italy had remained stationary since June. That month, in an attempt to match the mighty German offensive in the West, the Austrians had launched their own offensive in a bid to drive the Italians from the Piave River line, take Treviso and even Padua. After a week of swaying fortunes, it fizzled out ignominiously, leaving the Austrians more or less where they had begun, holding the northern bank of the Piave and the Asiago Plateau up in the mountains which tower up inland above the Venetian Plain. After repeated proddings from Marshal Foch, General Diaz, the Italian Commander-in-Chief, at last wound up his mixed forces* for an autumn counter-attack. As the mountains dominated the plain (and the Austrians were renowned above all for their artillery prowess) the Italian offensive would have to try and push the whole of the enemy's front back in unison. An initial thrust was thus mounted up in the Monte Grappa, to dislodge the Austrian Eleventh Army from the peaks of this commanding high ground, while the main attack was reserved for the river line, concentrating on the junction of the Austrian Fifth and Sixth Armies. Thus the defenders in the mountains, the so-called Tirol Army Group, were to be separated from the defenders in the plain, while the forces of the Army Group (commanded by Field Marshal Boroevic) were to be split from each other by an axe-blow aimed at the vulnerable suture where their two armies were joined. Preparations were completed on 25 September, the day King Ferdinand announced Bulgaria's sudden capitulation.

General Diaz was not counting on any such rapid capitulation here. To begin with the Austrians held good defensive positions, both on the broad-flowing lower Piave and up peaks and ridges of the whole Trentino-Tirol-Asiago area. Furthermore, though more than a thousand guns weaker in artillery (6,030 guns to the attackers' 7,700) they were moderately stronger in manpower. Finally, they knew that this offensive was coming, and had

---

* His army comprised fifty-one Italian divisions, three British, two French plus one exile Czechoslovak formation and one US infantry regiment tacked on to show American solidarity.

a pretty exact idea when and where it was coming.* But they suffered from two grave disadvantages, at the extent and effects of which General Diaz and his Allied commanders could only guess. The food and general supply situation of the Austro-Hungarian forces at the front was appalling; while, far behind the front, their common homeland was bursting apart into its racial fragments, an explosion whose tremors reached right out to the trenches.

The physical plight of the Emperor Charles's soldiers in Italy was touched on when surveying briefly the morale of all the combatants as the fifth year of fighting opened. Since August, things had gone from bad to near catastrophic. Problems of food and clothing obsessed even the officers, as shown by these autumn extracts, taken almost at random from the unpublished diary of a Czech army captain serving with the 16th Infantry Regiment (the so-called '*K.K. Peterwardeiner*') up in the mountains:

> 'There's a bonus for anyone collecting stinging nettles (for soup) ... When we bury our dead no linen can now be spared for wrapping the corpses in the coffin, unless it's a question of contagious disease ...
>
> 'Expert smugglers have been exempted from military service in the field so that they can bring supplies across the Swiss border – and are even awarded decorations for bravery as well ...
>
> 'One soldier, who's a good angler, is stationed permanently at Percha, near Olang and his sole duty consists of supplying Army Group Headquarters at Bozen with 20 kilos of trout a week ...
>
> 'All further supplies of underclothing cancelled. We're cutting up our white snow capes instead to make just one set for each man ...'

---

* Indeed, on the very eve of the attack, the Emperor Charles, warned by his general staff that an Italian offensive was imminent, had sent a personal message to the Pope, appealing to the Vatican to intervene and get the operation cancelled 'on humanitarian grounds'. The appeal was just as unpractical as it was desperate.

There were some officers of the old regime who, even in these desperate circumstances, still managed to put appearances – or rather the example of appearances – above everything. Such a one, serving on the Monte San Danielli, was the young artillery lieutenant, Count Albrecht Dubsky. A fellow nobleman and junior officer serving in his battery wrote admiringly in his private memoirs of how the lieutenant dealt with the one litre per man water ration which was brought up each night by pack-horse from the valley, and had to serve all the next day's needs. When he received his litre Count Dubsky would first call for a bowl and carefully wash and shave himself with a goodly part of his ration. Only then would he use the rest for drinking. His admirer, even younger at the time, could only thank God that, as his beard had not yet begun to grow, he had no need to follow the lieutenant's lead.

But more important than the supply situation which was re-ducing the so-called Isonzo Army of the Austrian Empire to a mass of hungry scarecrows were the political earthquakes rending the fields which these scarecrows were supposed to be protecting. The Bulgarian débâcle, which preceded the Emperor's October Manifesto by three weeks, had done damage enough – there as everywhere in the Austro-German camp. The general command-ing the 27th Austrian Infantry Division in Italy wrote, for example, of the general mood among his men at the end of September:

> 'Bulgaria had already collapsed and even the German army in the west, considered so invincible, could no longer stand up to superior odds and was engaged in constant and costly retreat. What was there to hope for for us in all this? Was there any point in further fighting and more shedding of blood – especially now, when ... there was already talk of an armistice ...'

After 16 October, the talk was no longer primarily of Bulgaria nor even of armistice, but of loyalty. What was the sense of risking your life for a Dual Monarchy that had just proclaimed its own dissolution? Where did your duty lie in this rapidly darkening imperial twilight – to the crown which had now granted legal independence to all its constituent peoples, or to whichever of those separate peoples you happened to belong? The centuries-old pull of the past – symbolized by that famous battle-cry sent to the Emperor's multi-racial army the century before in this same northern Italy: 'In your camp stands Austria!' – was weakening with every hour. Against it tugged a nationalism now sanctified by the crown itself. The Austro-Hungarian battleline was torn in two where it mattered most, in the hearts of the soldiers themselves.

Desertions had been growing from their ranks ever since the failure of the June offensive for, nationalism and cowardice apart, the deserter knew he could live better off fruit and berries in the woods than by queueing up with his comrades at the meatless regimental field-kitchens. Yet, however the numbers had mounted during the summer (and one senior officer estimated that there were no fewer than thirty thousand deserters, some of them armed, at large across the Adriatic in Croatia and Dalmatia) these were still individual decisions. On 22 October, five days *before* the Italian offensive was launched, came the first desertions of whole units, in the form of outright mutiny. Two Croat regiments, the 25th and 26th, serving in Hungarian divisions, refused *en bloc* to move from their reserve positions and relieve their comrades in the line. A battalion of regular Hungarian Honved infantry managed to arrest some of the ring-leaders, but was helpless against such superior numbers who refused to be persuaded or bullied. Eventually the remnants which remained of the two rebellious units, after a few hundred men had simply melted away, were moved even further from the front.

It was no surprise that the first gaps in the empire's battle-line should have been blown by the Croats. A week before, the representatives of the so-called 'Yugoslav Parliamentary Club' in Vienna had declared that they would only support the Emperor's peace moves if, among other things, he recognized that the Croats, Serbs and Slovenes were 'an indivisible people, wherever they lived'. Moreover, these parliamentarians had also demanded that their national groups should conduct their own negotiations with the enemy, as the Austro-Hungarian Monarchy was henceforth only competent to speak for 'the Germans and the Magyars'. Three days later the Czecho-Slovak exiles in Paris had given the lead to the other Slavs of the empire by formally breaking with the Habsburg crown and declaring their peoples, over the signature of Thomas G. Masaryk as 'Prime Minister and Minister of Finance', to be 'a free and independent nation'. The Croats, who had to free themselves from Budapest as well as Vienna, then led the way inside the empire itself. On 24 October, the 79th Croat Infantry Regiment at Fiume disarmed the local Hungarian army garrison and stormed the main buildings of the town. Troops were rushed up from Albania in an attempt to quell the uprising, but it was an empty military gesture: the National Council of the Croats was about to be formed in Agram to shouts of 'Down with Austria' as well as 'Down with Hungary'.

Budapest itself, the twin capital of the Dual Monarchy, was also in ferment and, as usual, the Hungarians were striving to snatch the best of both worlds – the old world of imperial privilege and the new world of nationalist chaos – for themselves. In the wake of the October Manifesto, political leaders like the veteran Count Tisza had joined Wekerle himself in demanding total independence from Vienna;* yet, at the same time, they were hoping to preserve their non-Magyar provinces like Croatia 'within the community of the Hungarian state'. Incredible though it seemed that the thousand-year-old crown of Hungary, the historic symbol of Magyar unity, should itself be threatened, there was growing talk of a Republic. Count Michael Károlyi, leader of the left wing Independent Party, was emerging as the man of the hour: the Messiah of a new Magyar Jerusalem in the eyes of his followers but, in the eyes of his sovereign and most of his fellow aristocrats, little better than a Bolshevik saboteur in the pay of the Entente. We shall have a closer look at this tragic dupe – destined to be both a traitor to the old regime and then a victim

---

* His concept was a return to the so-called 'Personal Union' only – i.e. a link through the common crown but separation from Vienna in all other fields, including defence and foreign affairs.

of the new – later on. But even this glance at developments in Budapest will explain a message which Field Marshal-Lieutenant von Nagy, commander of the 40th Honved Infantry Division in Italy, had already sent back to his headquarters. The critical passage read: 'In view of the political separation of Austria from Hungary which has now begun, no one can guarantee that the Hungarian troops will remain at the front and fight on at the side of their Austrian comrades.' That ominous warning was passed right up to Army Group command, with the suggestion that the Emperor himself should demand of Count Károlyi, 'the leader of the Hungarian opposition and probably the next Hungarian Prime Minister', that he call on Hungary's soldiers 'to fight on until the battle was ended'. A clearer indicator of those shock-waves which were now passing between the home and battle-fronts of the empire could not have been given. The tremors were now coming from the other direction as well. Shortly before von Nagy sent back his gloomy report, the Italian, British and French divisions launched their combined offensive. Despite torrential rain, the day could not be missed. 24 October was the exact anniversary of Italy's disaster at Caporetto the year before.

To begin with the defenders fought back almost as though they were a still united army protecting a still united fatherland. Down in the plains, for example, where the main attack unfolded on the third day, the British and Italian divisions of Lord Cavan's Eighth Army had to master fierce enemy resistance, as well as the broad Piave, before they could throw their vital bridgeheads across. The spot chosen for the crossing was the Grave di Papadopoli, where a large shingly island, held as an outpost by the Austrians, bisected the river – here nearly a mile and a half wide and in spate after the continuous heavy rain. It was British troops, the 22nd Brigade of the 7th Infantry Division, who were given the tricky job of storming the island. For the operation, twelve flat-bottomed boats, not unlike gondolas in appearance, had been concealed in the brushwood of the left bank. Each could carry only seven soldiers at a time, apart from the 'crew' of two Italian watermen; surprise and silence were thus essential. That meant a night operation. After a reconnais-

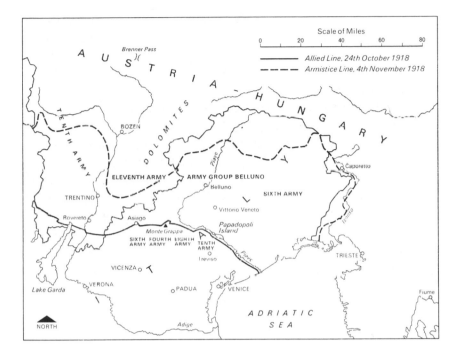

Vittorio Veneto, Italy; Armistice, 4 November 1918

sance, the tiny invasion fleet began its ferrying operations in pitch dark at 8 p.m. on the evening of the 24th.

The twenty-seven-year-old British lieutenant-colonel whose battalion, the 2nd HAC, spearheaded the crossing (and who was soon put in overall command of this crucial operation, which won him a bar to his DSO) somehow found time to scribble a daily diary of events. He wrote of this first night:

> 'The beach was very small and the greater part of the Bn. were on it and the 12 boats were right along side the shore. The moon was getting up and the stream looked particularly unprepossessing. However, all went fairly well to start with and about the first half of the first company got across without much trouble though some

287

boats were swept down. Then suddenly the [enemy's] SOS signal was sent up. It was a rocket bursting into four red balls, which remained in the sky for quite half a minute. We had not long to wait. In about five minutes the shells began to fall. Absolutely in amongst us, only the soft sand of the shore prevented us having awfully heavy casualties ... I have never felt I wanted to get on with things as much as I did then and was delighted when the turn of my boat arrived, the river, and even the unknown on the other side of it, being preferable to the shell-fire!'

The roar of the current over the Piave's pebbled bed made it impossible to detect the whine of the oncoming shells, and, to make matters worse, the clouds broke and the moon silhouetted the black scurrying shapes of men and boats. But the crossing continued imperturbably under the control of British beach-masters with an Italian captain commanding the invaluable '*Pontieri*'. By a miracle, not a boat was sunk (though two had been swept away by the current) as the remainder of the eight-hundred-man assault force was brought across.

The British now fanned out through the scrub to clear the whole island. 'It was just like putting hounds through cover,' that same British officer laconically recorded. By dawn most of their initial objectives had been reached. Before the island was completely secured some of the garrison managed to escape across to their bank of the river; but in one tough engagement alone fifty of their dead were counted on the ground before the remainder surrendered. It was a brisk and auspicious start. The same applied to the engineering feat which was launched the following night – the construction of a bridge to span the entire river, using the island as a half-way house. British pontoons were not designed for anything faster than five knots and here the current was flowing at twice that speed. The generals insisted on their bridge, for the main force which was to advance up the Venetian plain had to be across the Piave by the 27th. The engineers doubted whether the anchors would hold, even given skilled Italian help in the laying. The High Command inevitably prevailed over the technical rule-books and, by the 26th, the vital bridge was in position.

Just how vital was to be seen two days later. It was still, on the 28th, the only solid bridgehead across the whole of the lower Piave; and General Caviglia, commanding the Eighth Italian Army on the left flank, wisely, on Lord Cavan's suggestion, detached half his forces to make use of it, join up with the Tenth Army which had already crossed, and move forward together. It was a decisive manoeuvre in the battle.

High up in the mountains inland, an even fiercer contest was now reaching its climax. Mountain troops of any nationality are an élite to themselves, and, even for the ordinary soldier fighting with them, there is something far more personal about a peak from which, for months past, you have been surveying the granite world around and below than there ever could be about the anonymous charge of a trench dug in the plains. The personal note is intensified when, as in the case of the artillery lieutenant or the machine-gun sergeant, one particular gun emplacement or rocky nest had been his and his only to live in and defend, often in isolation from his comrades. Thus it was that, despite all their hideous shortages and discomforts, the Austrians up in the key Monte Grappa gave as good as they got in the four days of hand-to-hand fighting which were touched off by the massive Italian artillery bombardment at 5 a.m. on the 24th.

There were three principal strongholds to be seized by the Fourth Italian Army in this area, the Asalone, Pertica and the Solaroli; and over each objective the battle swayed to and fro as the heights changed hands in attack and counter-attack. One Italian battalion, the Levanna, suffered no fewer than six hundred and ninety-two casualties in its first vain attempt to take the Solaroli, while a single company of its sister battalion lost one hundred and fourteen men. The Austrians had comparable losses and, to staunch the blood-letting, they threw ten more battalions and the whole of the crack 'Edelweiss' Division into the battle on the 25th. But that last frenzied effort of the Dual Monarchy in battle simply could not be sustained, for, all the while, its strength was being drained away as much by mutiny and mass desertion in its own ranks as by the attackers' bullets.

The day the 'Edelweiss' division was sent into action, for example, its Chief-of-Staff recorded in his war diary how a gaping hole had suddenly appeared elsewhere on the front:

> 'At five o'clock in the afternoon, General D. telephoned to tell me that in the Eleventh Army three Honved* Infantry Divisions, the 27th, 50th and 38th, had declared in the bluntest fashion that they were not going to fight any more but demanded to be sent back to their homeland to protect it. Army Group Headquarters issued orders to scrape together whatever was possible.'

That feeble reaction from Army Group echoed the helpless despair that was seizing the Austrian High Command as it saw its forces simply melting away beneath its eyes. Indeed, by the time the battle had reached its height, the task of enforcing discipline against rebels had more or less been abandoned. As the commander of an Austrian infantry division noted on 28 October:

> 'An instruction from Army Group that came in this afternoon gave one a lot to think about. It advised us that, as a general rule, it was now no longer considered practicable to suppress cases of mutiny by force. The means were simply not available as every reliable man was needed at the front.'

By now it was reckoned that of forty-nine regiments at the disposal of one of the two Austrian Army Groups, eleven had mutinied almost in their entirety and, of the remainder still obeying orders, three were considered doubtful. While the defence was bleeding itself to death like this, the attack was steadily gathering in momentum. Though, up on the Grappa Massif, the Austrians, in a counter-attack on 27 October, had even managed briefly to regain the Monte Pertica, down on the plains the main British and Italian forces were advancing along a twenty-five-mile front. By the 28th, three armies – Lord Cavan's Tenth, plus the Eighth

---

* i.e. Hungarian army.

and Twelfth Italian – were across the Piave and were pushing forward against rapidly weakening opposition. That same day Field Marshal Boroevic telephoned back to his Supreme Headquarters in Baden in the darkest language. The resistance of his troops, he reported, was now weakening at an alarming rate, thanks above all to the fast-spreading waves of mutiny and desertions among all but the German-Austrian regiments. There was no military answer to this, as the last sentence made plain:

> 'It is of the greatest importance' [his message ended] 'to be clear about the future and take decisions which will bring about political changes if anarchy is not to set in – and with it a catastrophe of unpredictable results both for the monarchy and the army.'

That same evening, one of his armies, the Sixth, issued orders for a general retreat, moving its headquarters from Vittorio Veneto (the name that the Italians were to choose to take into history with them) to Pordenone. Its GOC, Prince Schönburg-Hartenstein, moved much further back. He handed over the army to one of the corps commanders, General Hadfy, and transferred himself all the way to Vienna. It was not just a case of the lower-deck rats leaving the empire's sinking ships; one of the captains had gone as well from the bridge.

Meanwhile, back in Vienna, those far-reaching decisions to ward off anarchy for which Field Marshal Boroević had pleaded were being taken with a vengeance. As the Emperor Charles's troops were deserting his armies, so he now deserted the German alliance, in one last eleventh-hour bid to secure a direct peace with their common foe. It was not the grave situation on the battle-fronts so much as the even graver situation in his own home front which had decided him. His realm, unlike that of the German Kaiser, was already falling apart. There was no time and no sense in trying to keep in step with Berlin over joint approaches to Washington. From Budapest – where he had spent a frantic four days trying to save his Hungarian crown from the cauldron – Charles, on 26 October, had warned his fellow Emperor of his 'unalterable resolve to seek a separate peace and an immediate armistice within the next twenty-four hours'. Despite the German Kaiser's telegram of protest, the fateful telegram was dispatched to President Wilson on the night of 27–28 October, soon after the exhausted Austrian Emperor had got back to Vienna. It accepted without reservation all the conditions and principles laid down in the President's earlier messages and asked for a cease-fire on all Austro-Hungarian fronts and the opening of direct peace talks between the Dual Monarchy and the Entente 'without awaiting the results of other negotiations'. That last phrase effectively toppled the Austro-German alliance which had stood ever since 1879, the oldest of all military pacts between the major belligerents. Ironically, Count Julius Andrássy, the newly-appointed Foreign Minister* of the Monarchy, over whose name the telegram had been sent, was the son of the Hungarian statesman who had forged the pact with Bismarck nearly fifty years before.

On the crumbling Italian front – the only battlefield where he could act independently – Charles set the wheels in motion without awaiting further reaction from Washington, let alone from Berlin. The upshot was that, at 6 a.m. on the morning of 29 October, an Austrian staff officer, Captain Ruggera, climbed up a railway embankment north of Serravalle in the Adige Valley waving a white flag and moved nervously, through a ragged curtain of artillery and machine-gun fire, to the outposts of the 26th Italian Infantry Division. The Italian armistice talks – which were to cost Austria more in both men and prestige than she had lost in the battle itself – had begun.

* Charles had dropped the faithful Burian in an attempt to give a new peace profile to his government. For the same reason Professor Lammasch had replaced Hussarek as Prime Minister.

'Finis Austriae'

THERE WAS A DOUBLE PARADOX about the happenings of 29 October 1918. Captain Ruggera's white flag, wobbling along the railway embankment at Serravalle, had signalled the capitulation of the third, and by far the most important, of Germany's allies. But the same morning which saw the alliance of the Central Powers fall completely apart militarily also saw the leaders of the Entente assemble in Paris for a debate so violent that, at one point, it threatened to fragment their own alliance politically. Moreover, the Entente, assuming that their deep divisions were known to the enemy, suspected him of trying to drive a wedge between them to widen the rift still further. In fact the Chancelleries of Berlin and Vienna had no inkling of the angry disputes which were flaring up between President Wilson and his European partners, and imagined any debate to be confined merely to differences over the military terms of surrender. Thus, with only a fortnight of the war still to go, the combatants continued to stumble out of it, like men with blindfolds tied around their heads.

Colonel House, by now appointed Wilson's personal representative in the Allied Supreme War Council, had arrived in Paris with one overriding aim: to persuade England, France and Italy formally to accept the Fourteen Points as the basis for armistice negotiations. So far, this acceptance had been very tentative. The three European powers, still smarting anyway under Wilson's bid to settle with the common enemy over their heads, had grave doubts about his crusade to construct a post-war world, complete with League of Nations, before the guns of war had even been silenced. As we have seen, they had even graver doubts about his attempt to turn his dream-like vision of the future into the foundation stone of the cease-fire itself. Yet, on this general issue, there was relatively little that they could do. From the start of his exchanges with Prince Max, Wilson had made acquiescence with his Fourteen Points the *sine qua non* of entering into talks of any kind, and both Berlin and Vienna had already fallen in with this demand before the President had deigned to bring his own allies into the exchanges. Short of demanding a complete re-negotiation of the armistice conditions, with all the delay and confusion that would cause, Wilson's European partners would be obliged in the end to accept his cart-before-horse approach. But this did not mean that all of them accepted every aspect of that approach. The worst of the head-on collisions that now loomed up in Paris was between Lloyd George and Wilson, and it centred above all on one issue – the Freedom of the Seas, as proclaimed in the second of the President's famous Points.

Just as he was going to bed on the night of the 28th, House had been visited by that trusted British intermediary, Sir William Wiseman, to warn him of the trouble ahead. The Cabinet, Wiseman reported, had been having 'some stormy sessions' in London over Wilson's peace terms and were refusing outright to accept the controversial Point Two. Colonel House, who knew, of course, that this obstacle would lie in his path, tried to steam-roller it out of the way at once. In language quite extraordinary for one Anglo-Saxon spokesman to be addressing to another on the eve of their common victory, House declared that he:

> 'did not believe the United States and other countries would willingly submit to Great Britain's complete domi-nation of the seas any more than to Germany's domina-tion of the land, and the sooner the English recognized this fact the better it would be for them; furthermore our people, if challenged, would build a navy and maintain an army greater than theirs.'

America had the advantage in manpower, money and natural resources to do all this, he added, and such a programme would, moreover, be popular with the American people. That was the language of that awakening military giant which was already spawning Pershing's vast army of five million men. Yet, as House discovered when he sat down to lunch with the Allied leaders the following day, it had made no impression at all on Lloyd George. The British Prime Minister immediately made it clear that in no circumstances was he prepared to hand over the power of blockade (for that was the sanction which Wilson's Point Two would have taken away from the Royal Navy for good) to the trusteeship of some nebulous and as yet non-existent body like the League of Nations. If England were again fighting for her life nobody, he declared, would prevent her from again employing this weapon 'which had been used with so much success by the Allied fleets, including that of the United States'.

There may have been an element of political calculation in all that. Lloyd George knew that in the general election he would most probably be facing somewhere between the armistice and the peace-making, there were few better campaigning slogans for a nation flushed with victory than the proud old cry of 'Rule Britannia'. Indeed, while these debates were unfolding in Paris, the prestigious Navy League, in what looked like an orchestrated burst of propaganda, was holding public meetings in London to denounce the Freedom of the Seas concept in all its aspects. 'The proposal made by President Wilson,' Admiral Lord Beresford told one such gathering, 'means that the British fleet was going to be under international control. That would never be allowed.' But politics apart, naval power was far too deeply embedded in both the war strategy and the national honour of Britain to be prised out and cast aside at the whim of some transatlantic dreamer. Moreover when, after lunch, House accompanied Lloyd George to the Quai d'Orsay for a general conference, he found the other Allied leaders ranged against him as well. War, Clemenceau observed, would simply not be war if there was freedom of the seas. Baron Sonnino expressed his objections in more abstruse zoological terms. 'Nations, like animals, had different weapons. One animal had teeth, another tusks, a third claws.' Without going into Italy's speciality, he maintained that every country had the right to defend itself in its traditional way.

The longer the discussion dragged on, the more heated it

became. Things threatened to boil right over when House, faced by a continued refusal of the European leaders to accept all Fourteen Points as they stood, hinted that, as President Wilson had been negotiating with the enemy all along on the basis of acceptance, he might now have to proceed alone with Germany and Austria.

Clemenceau interjected: 'That would amount to a separate peace between the United States and the Central Powers.' 'It might,' Colonel House replied.

The three Allied Premiers may well (as House telegraphed to his President that evening) have been 'excited' by that reply; but they were certainly not over-awed. Whether the colonel was bluffing or not Lloyd George, for one, was ready to call his cards. He would be sorry, he replied calmly (and with some understatement), if the United States were to make a separate peace; but that would not affect Britain's attitude. The blockade weapon, which had enabled his country to survive, could not be abandoned. 'As far as the British public is concerned, we will fight on.' 'Yes,' interjected Clemenceau.

It was a strange confrontation, genuine and artificial at one and the same time. Genuine because, after all, America had gone to war with England in 1812 and with Germany in 1917 on the question of her rights at sea; Wilson's resolve to have his way was thus as deeply-rooted in popular sentiment and national tradition as was Lloyd George's determination to oppose him. Yet also artificial because for the Allies to go their separate ways now, when the path they had trod together had led them to the very threshold of victory, was unthinkable. Moreover, as the real sticking point concerned only one of Wilson's Fourteen Points and Five Principles, a compromise would almost inevitably be found. After four more days of haggling, huffing and puffing, it was in fact Lloyd George who finally produced the magic formula. The Allies, he told Colonel House, 'were quite willing to discuss the freedom of the seas in the light of the new conditions which have arisen in the course of the present war'. The colonel immediately glimpsed retreat with honour in those words. At his request, Lloyd George put them down in writing and the conference, having sorted out its own quarrels, turned to deal single-mindedly with the enemy.

Though their main concern here was to hammer out armistice terms with Germany, it was Austria who presented the Allies with a more immediate as well as a far simpler task. The Italian Prime Minister Orlando, who joined the conference on 30 October, arrived with exciting news for his colleagues. While his train had stopped at Turin, the Italian Commander-in-Chief, General Diaz, had telephoned him to say that an Austrian officer had crossed the lines asking for an immediate cease-fire and the opening of negotiations. At the same time the text of the Emperor Charles's own peace telegram became known, in which the beleaguered sovereign had called for the cessation of hostilities in order that the evacuation of Italy's 'well-cultivated plains with their rich crops could take place without any damage whatsoever to the country'. Orlando seemed to suspect some deep Habsburg trick in this transparently pathetic message; but both Clemenceau and Lloyd George urged him to take up the offer without a moment's delay. The British Prime Minister pointed out what an advantage it would be to them all if Austria could be settled with completely before Germany had to be tackled. Moreover, as they and their military advisers were all in session together in Paris, terms for an Austrian armistice could be produced by the Allied generals on the spot without any more of those frustrating transatlantic solo acts which had bedevilled the initial contacts with Berlin.

> 'I propose' [he said] 'that terms be submitted straight-away to Austria. As soon as Austria is out, Germany will capitulate at once. Therefore we ought to act before President Wilson has time to answer.'

Despite this unflattering reference to his chief Colonel House fell in with the idea. Thus the Allied Supreme War Council was able to feel itself really supreme as regards the capitulation of Austria. But what, meanwhile, had been happening to that officer whose dawn mission had started it all?

The Austrian armistice, which was to develop into one of the

most muddled and controversial episodes of the entire war, got
off to a suitably confusing start. Captain Ruggera reached the
main Italian lines at 8.30 a.m. on the morning of the 29th, having
endured a few bullets whistling past the ears of himself and his
two trumpeters on the way – a mistake for which apologies were
duly made. From the front of the Italian 26th Division he was
conducted to the headquarters of XIX Italian Army Corps,
where his dispatch asking for an immediate cease-fire and the
opening of negotiations was formally received and passed back to
the Italian Supreme Command. Claiming that, like every other
member of the Austrian Armistice Commission, he was individually authorized to speak for it, Ruggera then proposed himself as
an intermediary with the Italian Commander-in-Chief. The
claim, though technically accurate, was a foolish one to pursue,
for no full general of any army on the eve of victory would be
prepared even to discuss a cease-fire along the whole of a major
battle/front with a mere enemy captain escorted by two trumpet-
blowing privates. Ruggera was kept kicking his heels impatiently
for twenty-four hours (a delay which was even harder on the
nerves of his superiors waiting on the Austrian side of the lines)
before, at 9 a.m. on the 30th, the Italian reply was handed to him
to deliver, simply as a courier.

The Austrian Armistice Commission itself, to whom the
captain duly handed the message three hours later, had by then
taken up forward quarters at Rovereto. It had been in existence
ever since 4 October, the eve of the first peace appeal to Wilson,
under the presidency of Major-General Viktor Weber von
Webenau. It may sound harsh to say that Weber was scarcely fit
for the task before him, since that task was, in itself, so bitterly
hopeless. But, unhappily, he does emerge, from the accounts of
his own subordinates, as one of those typically Austrian figures
who can muddle up even the straightforward ('Why do it simply
if there's a complicated way?' is an ironic national saying). His
performance in the treacherous maze he was now entering needs,
therefore, little imagining.

The general had two principal assistants, Lieutenant-Colonel
Seiller from the Austrian Fifth Army Headquarters in nearby

Trient, and Colonel Karl Scheller, who had been Chief-of-Staff of the élite Edelweiss Division fighting up on the Monte Grappa. Scheller had just been plucked from the front line – partly because he spoke Italian and partly because he was anyway an experienced staff officer – and it is to his unpublished diary of the week's events that we owe many revealing details of the fiasco ahead. He describes, for example, a sobering experience in Rovereto while the commission was still awaiting Captain Ruggera's return. Before lunch, General Weber had outlined to his colleagues the speech he proposed to deliver to the Italians when given the opportunity. The colonel's heart sank deeper the more he listened to his chief. The proposed speech was far too long – more like a bishop's sermon than a general's appreciation – and quite misplaced in its tone. Thus, Weber proposed to speak of Austria's 'unshaken front', which was an obvious nonsense, and to stress how his soldiers 'yearned for an end to the mass killings', which was true enough but quite irrelevant for a technical discussion. Scheller's spirits were not subsequently improved by a night spent in a cheerless military hotel which was 'so freezing cold that one could only exist in a great-coat or in bed'. The Italian reply which they now had to consider was equally frigid.

In the first place the Italian High Command rejected the credentials it had been shown as insufficient. General Diaz did not propose to deal either with Major-General Weber or his subordinates until they produced properly authorized plenipotentiary powers issued by the Austrian Supreme Command in their name. Then came an ominous sentence that ought to have given some warning of the dangers ahead. The Italian authorities would not in any case enter into talks 'which would have as their aim the interruptions of the operations currently in progress'. Captain Ruggera had not exactly helped matters by unsealing and reading the document himself. This meant that General Weber, to whom it was addressed, had no option but to respond in person. In fact, within a few hours, the response was made for him in an order from Austrian Supreme Headquarters back at Baden: General Weber was to leave at once with his commission for the Italian lines and 'must bring about a cease-fire at all costs as things are going very badly along the Piave'.

Off they set within half an hour of receiving the order, following Captain Ruggera's route along the railway embankment into No-Man's-Land, with Colonel Scheller carrying the white flag himself. After some excellent hospitality at two Italian Divisional Headquarters *en route* (which had the effect of delaying their progress) they travelled via Avio, Verona and Vicenza to the prescribed meeting point. That was the Villa Giusti near Padua, which they finally reached in time for another excellent meal (but still no sign of negotiations) at 8 p.m. on the 31st. No talks, they were told, could begin until the next day.

Whether or not the Italians were also following some purpose of their own in this drawn-out approach, the Italian Commander-in-Chief, General Diaz, really had no option but to keep the Austrians at arm's length because he himself was still awaiting his armistice terms from the Supreme War Council in Paris. Not that that august body can be accused of dragging its heels over the matter. On the 30th, the day General Weber and his party were *en route* to the Villa Giusti, the British Chief-of-Staff Field Marshal Wilson loftily wrote in his Paris diary:

> 'Another squeal from Vienna this morning, begging for an armistice ... Lloyd George asked me what terms we should offer. I wrote on a bit of paper: "Demobilization down to ? divisions; retire to the line of the London Pact; free use to Allies of all roads, railways and waterways; occupation of strategic points, as Allies may decide on." Lloyd George put the paper in his pocket and bundled off to meet Tiger and House. Was telephoned for at 2 o'clock to the Embassy. Lloyd George told me my 4 points had been passed unanimously. Hankey being there, I added another – repatriation of prisoners and civilians ...'

And the next day, when the Supreme Council met, the British Field Marshal was able to make an even crisper entry: 'Our last night's Austrian armistice proposals passed with minor alterations. Then naval ditto passed ...' The 'naval ditto' provided for the surrender of all Austrian submarines completed since 1910, plus the hand-over of six battleships, four cruisers and nine destroyers. The Austrian army demobilization figure which Wilson had left blank was set at a peace-time strength of twenty divisions, and that was that. It all went to show how swiftly the Supreme War Council could operate when it was dealing solely with the mechanics of an armistice, unencumbered by philosophical visions of a post-war world: a military man's scribble on the back of an envelope, endorsed within a few hours by the politicians, and the Dual Monarchy on the battlefield was disposed of. As a result Austria and Germany were henceforth set on different paths to peace. Like Prince Max, the Emperor Charles had also sought to end the war on the basis of President Wilson's Fourteen Points; yet though those had underpinned all the exchanges with Berlin they were not even mentioned in the terms now telegraphed to Padua. This was to complicate the settlement of the former Habsburg domains at the post-war conferences. In those last days of the war, however, the doomed dynasty had other complications to contend with.

Clemenceau commented, when he and his colleagues saw the Austrian armistice conditions drawn up by the Allied experts: 'They have not asked for the Emperor's trousers, but that is about all.' Alas for that Emperor, it was not all. During the first five days of November Charles was destined to lose his trousers as well in the plains and mountains of northern Italy. Again, chaos on the home front inter-acting with chaos on the battlefront was partly to blame.

By the time the Austrian delegation sat down for its first armistice session at the Villa Giusti, the ruler they represented had been abandoned not merely by most of his Slav peoples. In both capitals of the Dual Monarchy the National Councils conjured out of the ground by his October Manifesto were also heading for republicanism and independence. General Weber was negotiating for an army-in-being, but he was no longer negotiating for an empire-in-being.

In Budapest an explosive power vacuum had existed

throughout the last week of October. The Hungarian National Council, formed around the enigmatic figure of Michael Károlyi on the 25th, was a government in name though not in title. The formal chain of imperial command had snapped, with hardly any of the regular army units, for example, obeying the orders of the King-Emperor's newly-appointed garrison commander, General Lukasics. Yet the street mobs and the odd band of idealists, demagogues and opportunists they shouted for were still neither sufficiently bold nor sufficiently organized to take over. In a country so permeated with the concept of monarchy, their ultimate sanction–like their initial impetus – had to come from the crown.

That sanction was finally given by telephone from Vienna at dawn on 31 October. Faced by a mounting tide of violence in Hungary and the prospect that the end of his reign there would be drowned in bloodshed – the one disaster he had, above all, striven to avoid – the distraught young Emperor bowed to the seemingly inevitable and appointed Count Károlyi Prime Minister. Károlyi's first act was to form a government based on a suspicious marriage of convenience between his own Independent Party and the more radical Social Democrats. The Defence Minister in this uneasy Coalition was a left-wing Colonel of artillery, Béla Linder. Károlyi's second act – despite the fact that, only a few days before, he had promised Charles that he did 'not want a republic' – was to prepare the way for one: on 1 November, again over the telephone with the Emperor in Schönbrunn Palace, he demanded and got absolution from his loyalist oath of allegience.* Hungary's slide into anarchy, which was to culminate, six months later, in the red terror of Bela Kun's dictatorship of the proletariat, had begun.

For those soldiers of the disintegrating monarchy who were

---

* There was a direct link with the Italian campaign in the manner of all these changes. The Archduke Joseph, who had strong Hungarian links and sympathies, had been commanding an Army Group in the mountains when the Italian offensive began. But when both the domestic and battle-fronts started to crumble he hurried back to Budapest and got Charles to appoint him *homo regius* in Hungary. It was in that capacity, as intermediary, that he appointed Károlyi Prime Minister and secured his release from his oath.

still fighting on, that slide into anarchy was, however, immediate. The moment he got to his desk in the Hungarian War Ministry Colonel Linder telephoned the Army Group in Italy direct and ordered all Hungarian soldiers in its ranks to lay down their arms immediately. The Supreme Command in Baden, who had been by-passed altogether by this move, attempted to re-assert its authority by preventing Linder's 'orders' from being passed down. Instead, Hungarian troops were to be told to await the results of the armistice talks which had already started. Only after insistent pressure from Budapest was Colonel Linder's order finally issued, on the Emperor's authority, on the evening of 2 November, after which the wave of Hungarian desertions became a flood.

Meanwhile Vienna itself was slipping into a political vortex of its own. The Emperor's October Manifesto, with its call for each racial component to form 'its own state organization in its territory of settlement' had forced the Emperor's seven million German-speaking Austrians to look at themselves, for the first time, fairly and squarely in the mirror of history. For centuries they had been able, and very content, to avoid the issue of their own identity. Their mission had always been to administer the supra-national Habsburg empire as though they were the stewards, butlers, grooms and gamekeepers who ran a vast feudal estate. The price of this privilege was to endure political castration: was there such a thing as an Austrian, as opposed to a was to the dynasty, not to themselves.* But now, with the estate breaking up fast, the staff had to look after themselves. Befuddled and bewildered by the crash they now faced the question: was there such a thing as an Austrian, as opposed to a German-speaking inhabitant of the Habsburg lands? If so, what sort of constitution would provide the best roof over his head?

The first attempt to find an answer had come only five days after Charles had issued his Manifesto: the German-speaking members of the expiring imperial Parliament gathered together at

---

* The classic expression was the remark of the Emperor on hearing one of his subjects praised for his patriotism: 'Is he a patriot for me?'

the seat of the Lower Austrian Provincial Government in Vienna and declared their resolve to create 'an independent state of German-Austria'. Initially, the 'Provisional National Assembly', as it was styled, sounded more racial than national in its aim, proclaiming sovereignty, for example, 'over the entire German area of settlement and especially the Sudeten lands'. At its next session on 30 October that strange body, with its pre-Hitlerian pretensions, turned itself formally into a new government, and 'German-Austria' was born. It had a name, yet everything else was still obscure about the infant-state, including the legality of its parentage and its future place in the world. But though a federal link with the other new states of the Empire was not ruled out nor even – as Charles had fondly hoped – a link through some de-sanctified crown, the tide of republicanism, swollen by street demonstrations, was steadily mounting in Vienna as in Budapest. 'Long live the republic! We need no Emperor!' was the cry which drowned all other cries, both from the benches of the Provincial Assembly, and from the mobs outside.

The political *dénouement* of all that belongs to a later chapter; what concern us here are the effects on the front-line army and its armistice negotiators struggling away in Italy. For the Emperor's military commanders, the near-certainty that Vienna too would now be swept along in the socialist torrent called into question for the first time the loyalty of the only troops who had hitherto stood like rocks: the Austrian regiments drawn from the old heartlands of the empire. Things were not improved by frantic attempts made by the Supreme Command to use its soldiers in the field as 'voters' to prevent the Provisional Assembly in Vienna from taking too drastic a decision at its second meeting of 30 October. The general commanding the 29th Austrian Infantry Division in Italy wrote this in his diary for that same day:

'An order which arrived around 11 a.m. this morning threw a sharp light on the political confusion at home. It ran:

"The National Councils are seeking to promote the republican form of state in the political systems under construction. The army in the field is not being consulted about this despite the fact that it comprises men aged between 18 and 55 and so really represents the people. Details are required by telegram of troops and formations of all nationalities which, without any pressure from their officers, declare themselves in support of the dynasty and the monarchy ... Very urgently needed are such reports from German-speaking units, as the National Council in Vienna is holding its crucial meeting at noon on the 30th."'

Quite apart from the fact that that instruction arrived far too late in the day, it was totally counter-productive. The mere attempt to use the soldiers of the empire to prop up its political structure only brought home to them all how wobbly that structure was, as well as touching off damaging debates about its future. As the infantry general commented. 'So it's come to this! There's no doubt that this order is going to have the direst effect on the troops' morale.'

He could have said the same for the wretched Armistice Commission. When General Weber left for Padua he was still acting for only one constitutional authority above the Supreme Command, that of his Emperor. But after the formation of 'German-Austria', two administrations were pedalling away in ludicrous tandem, for the new Provisional Government promptly placed its own State Secretaries in each of the imperial ministries. Those gentlemen were prepared to share everything except responsibility. Indeed, they made it quite clear that, though they intended in due course to remove the double-headed eagle from its perch, that exhausted bird still had a lot of unfinished business to wind up for them first. That meant, above all, the ending of the war. Repeated pleas to them to shoulder their share of authority were to fall on deaf ears. The monarchy had started the war, they replied, so the monarchy, alone and unaided, must bring it to a close. General Weber was thus already written off by the new men in both sister-capitals of the empire before he sat down for his first formal session with the Italians. That took place, as scheduled, at 10 a.m. on the morning of 1 November. General Badoglio, who was to win both renown and notoriety as the conqueror of Ethiopia, took the chair as Deputy Chief-of-Staff for the Italians. That same blend of fame and controversy which followed him later is attached to the victory he won at the negotiating table of the Villa Giusti.

Proceedings began on a tentative note. The Italian Staff Officers had been up all night taking down, on a shaky telephone line from Paris, the terms just agreed by the Supreme War Council. This process lasted from 1.50 a.m. to 6.15 a.m., for though the actual text was relatively brief, it contained a plethora of place-names, each one of which was vital to identify precisely. The notes based on that laborious telephone dictation were all that Badoglio could hand over to begin with; an officer, he said, would arrive from Paris by train the following day bearing the official French text.

Weber's fears were confirmed when he was given this early on 2 November, for the differences between the verbal version and the written one turned out to be trifling. Points One and Two, which called respectively for the immediate cessation of all hostilities and the total demobilization of all Austro-Hungarian forces in the field, were much as expected. Point Three spelt out in remorseless detail what Vienna had hitherto only known about in outline, namely, the extent of that vast territorial bribe by which England and France had induced the Italians to enter the war three years before. The Italians were, of course, reaching out for their coveted *fino al brennero*, the frontier along the Brenner Pass, for which they had been clamouring for decades, and many a familiar German name fell along and behind the line the Austrians were now called on to evacuate for good – the Rhetian Alps, the source of the River Eisach, Mount Reschen and the crests of the lovely Ötz and Ziller Valleys of Tyrol. All that, plus the Adriatic basin and Dalmatia, with many of its off-shore islands, was to be abandoned and all the military and railway equipment the areas contained left behind *in situ* and undamaged. It was a bitter pill to swallow, and may even have been a little larger than the Austrians dreaded, though they had always known that, once defeated, swallow it they must.*

It was the demands made in Point Four which caused Charles the most anguish, for they put the dagger right against the spine of the ally he had just abandoned. Elaborating on Field Marshal Wilson's impromptu jottings made in Paris three days before, this clause gave the Allies 'free movement over all road, rail and waterways in Austro-Hungarian territory' as well as the right to 'occupy such strategic points in Austria-Hungary at such times as they may deem necessary to enable them to conduct military operations or to maintain order'. That turned the Brenner Pass not only into the new political frontier of Italy but also into an Allied military spring-board against a German army that now, in those last days of the war, was struggling on quite alone.

For two days† after receiving these demands Charles wrestled both with his own conscience and with the twenty State Councillors of German-Austria. The former yielded reluctantly; the latter not at all, despite pleas and warnings from General Arz that agreement to this clause as it stood would almost certainly mean the occupation of the Tyrol by either Italian or German troops.†† When, at five minutes past ten on the morning of 3 November, Charles finally gave the order to sign the armistice, all that he could offer his long-time ally was an empty gesture of loyalty. Acceptance of Point Four was made on the understanding that it would not lead to an attack through Austria against Germany. Then (as it was realized that this was precisely what it probably *would* lead to) came the pathetic gloss: 'Though such a move cannot be prevented, the most energetic protest must be raised against it.' Charles followed that gesture up with a mourn-

---

* For full text of Austria armistice terms, *see* Appendix C.

† General Weber had already telegraphed the provisional text to Supreme Headquarters at Baden on 1 November.

†† German troops from the Second Bavarian Corps of General Krafft von Dellmensingen did indeed occupy Innsbruck and even probed south beyond the Brenner during the last few days of the war.

ful telegram of condolence to the Emperor William, the last personal message he was to send to the German ruler. Their last steps in the gigantic conflict, he pointed out with sorrow (and a measure of under-statement), 'could not be taken in common'.

But the biggest tragedy over the Villa Giusti peace, which duly led to the bitterest controversy, centred not on the conditions of the cease-fire but on its timing. The Austrians had already made one muddle over that, entirely on their own, during the small hours of 3 November. While General Arz was in Vienna, driving backwards and forwards between Schönbrunn Palace and the Parliament building on the Ringstrasse in his vain attempts to persuade the new State Council to back up the crown, his deputy, General Waldstätten, was left in charge at Baden. Throughout the day Colonel Scheller of the Armistice Delegation had been bombarding him with telephone calls pressing for immediate acceptance of the terms in view of the rapidly crumbling situation along what was left of the Austrian front. Time and time again Waldstätten had to plead for patience: His Majesty was still trying to get some sense out of 'the representatives of German-Austria'. At one point he exploded: 'I know exactly how critical the whole thing is but I can do no more than ring up Schönbrunn every half an hour!'

Under that pressure; in the expectation that the armistice would anyway be signed at some point that same day; and in the hope that one last midnight session in the Parliament building would produce an agreed policy Waldstätten was authorized, at 1 a.m. on 3 November, to send a telegram to the forces in Italy ordering the immediate suspension of all hostilities. It had barely been dispatched before Arz arrived back at the palace with the news that his talks in Parliament had been inconclusive, and that another session would have to be held after breakfast. There was nothing for it but to cancel the cease-fire just issued. That countermanding order reached one Army Group just in time, but came too late for the Eleventh Army, whose commander decided to let things ride, as to do otherwise 'would certainly lead to a catastrophe'. That confusion in the early hours of 3 November was all the Austrians' doing. Their precise share in the greater and costlier confusion which set in later that day is a matter for some debate.

The final, and irrevocable, order to General Weber to sign the armistice terms as they stood was telephoned by Arz from Vienna at a few minutes after 10 a.m. (the State Councillors had meanwhile opted out of the decision-making altogether by simply failing to turn up at their appointed meeting with him). There was silence for a couple of hours and then, around noon, two messages arrived from Padua. The first was a request from the Italians for an unabbreviated text of Austria's acceptance, as the telegraphic version was considered insufficient. That request, which smacked somewhat of procrastination, was considered reasonable and was promptly complied with. But the second message, which reached Vienna in a roundabout signals route via the Austrian naval base Pola, on the Dalmatian coast, and Budapest, burst like a bomb. The Italians, Weber reported, would only end hostilities twenty-four hours *after* both sides had accepted the terms. That opened up for the Emperor a new nightmare prospect, namely that his entire forces in Italy, which had now been finally stood down on his orders, would be scooped up by the enemy as they sat by their stacked rifles and unmanned guns. The fatal Point Four of the armistice already gave the Allied forces unrestricted use of all Austrian communications and the right to move where they chose behind the cease-fire line. Not realizing that this clause had originated not from the Italian General Staff in Padua, but from the impromptu suggestions of a British Field Marshal in Paris, General Arz suspected the worst. What must also have dawned on him, rather too late, was that, bloody and chaotic though the last few days of fighting had been, a botched-up armistice might well cost the empire even dearer.

Yet there was nothing he felt he could do about it now: the stuffing, it seemed, had been knocked right out of him and his army. So Arz confined himself to a weary telegram of protest (which was not even strongly worded) to Padua and a message to his Army Group commanders in the south calling on them in turn to protest (but not resist). It was the flabbiest of reactions though, as we shall see, some Austrian officers on the ground were made of sterner stuff than their totally demoralized Supreme Command.

The Austrian protest, very naturally, cited as justification Clause One of the armistice text, which called for all hostilities to cease immediately, and this has, ever since, been the backbone of the Austrian case that they were shamefully tricked into surrender. Yet the unpublished diary of Colonel Scheller (who was not only an experienced staff officer but also an Italian-speaker) casts a rather more ambivalent light on General Weber's performance at the Villa Giusti. Under the heading 'Interesting details about the armistice signing', he gives this first-hand account of the crucial exchange at the opening of the 3 November session:

Badoglio: 'On the basis of the conditions laid down yesterday, hostilities will cease twenty-four hours from now.'

Weber: (takes note of this statement and orders hostilities to be stopped in twenty-four hours' time – tomorrow 4 November at 3 in the afternoon on the part of the Italian army. Requests a pause so that he can issue the orders immediately.)

Badoglio: (declares himself ready to inform the Austro-Hungarian Army Command that hostilities will only cease as from 3 p.m. tomorrow.)

Weber: (makes the point that our Army Command has considered itself obliged to bring about an immediate cessation of hostilities, as this is laid down in Point 1 of the agreement.)

Badoglio: "At our discussion yesterday Weber agreed that it is the moment that we express acceptance which counts as the beginning and that hostilities will end twenty-four hours afterwards. These twenty-four hours were laid down so that the order should reach all the troops."

(The declarations of Weber and of Captain Witowski* are recorded in the protocol. Badoglio then asks whether Weber considers yesterday's meeting to be legally binding.

* Austrian naval delegate at the armistice talks.

When Witowski again raises an objection, Badoglio
threatens to withdraw the cease-fire order altogether.)'

That threat was clearly sufficient to silence the Austrian delegation. But what is most significant, and – on the face of it – most
damning about Scheller's on-the-spot notes is that they make no
mention whatsoever of General Weber disputing Badoglio's as-
sertion that the twenty-four hours' delay had, as the Italian
claimed, been agreed between the two men the day before. If the
head of the Austrian delegation could have denied that, surely he
would, if only for the record; and, by the same token, his general
staff colonel sitting next to him would have registered that
denial in his diary. All in all, the objective observer cannot help
feeling over this famous affair that if any deliberate deception
was practised by Badoglio it was more than matched by the
native 'Schlamperei' (which can best be rendered as easy-going
negligence) of General Viktor Weber von Webernau. And in
that case, the fiasco of the Villa Giusti can only be seen as a lethal
blend of two national characteristics – Italian cunning and
Austrian muddle.

Just how lethal the next controversial twenty-four hours were
to show. The immediate result was an unholy confusion as,
everywhere along the front, Allied soldiers, still fighting a war for
one more day, sought to engage and press back Austrian soldiers
who thought the war had just ended. The chaplain of the 7th
British Infantry Division (the formation which had led the Allied
advance across the Piave the week before) describes this comic
opera scene, for example, when the division pursued the retreating Austrians across the Tagliamento River line on the morning of
4 November:

'Almost an entire Austrian division had laid down their
arms on the far side of the Tagliamento, and the officers
in it were only intent on arguing that they should be
allowed to retain their swords. As soon as the divisional
commander crossed the river he was spotted by the
Austrian general and his staff, and before he knew where
he was he found himself completely surrounded. The

Austrians, who were all armed, were full of protests. They produced a large paper which they urged the general to sign. This paper was to the effect that they had not surrendered but had merely allowed the Italian cavalry to pass through, and that therefore none of them were prisoners of war. General Shoubridge merely remarked that his orders were to kill or capture every Austrian he encountered till 3 p.m. that afternoon, that he had a whole division across the river (in point of fact it was near two companies), and that the Austrians could take their choice! He added, with a smile, that he had been soldiering too long to sign anything on the battlefield, whereupon they joined in the laugh too. General Shoubridge then rode on, the Austrian general running after him shouting "protest" and waving the paper in the air.'

The unfortunate Austrian general involved in that episode was hardly to blame, for he was only carrying out to the letter the orders he had received from Supreme Command to register his protest if confronted by force; yet, undeniably, it made for a miserable and distinctly unsoldierly farewell to arms. Some of his colleagues, however, reacted in a more robust fashion, regardless of what their instructions might have been. One Austrian corps commander, whose troops were also lining the Tagliamento, sent out this order on the afternoon of 3 November:

'There is clearly great confusion over the beginning of the cease-fire. We have begun immediately, the Italians apparently at a later time. If the enemy attacks, therefore, he is to be resisted.'

One of the divisions in that corps, the XXIV, did indeed engage the enemy throughout the night when the Italians attempted to force the river. The commander of a neighbouring division, the 26th, took the law into his own hands when day dawned and there was still no end to the attacks. He dispatched an Italian-speaking officer through the lines to the nearest Italian headquarters at Udine bearing with him a copy of the Austrians' own cease-fire order and also a crisp threat: unless the Italian forces in the area stopped their offensive operations forthwith, he would surround the town with an entire artillery brigade and open fire on it with every gun. Even during those last flickering hours of Austria's resistance her artillery still commanded deep respect, and the threat worked.

There were occasions when Allied soldiers, embarrassed by this gratuitous advantage they had been presented with over the enemy, themselves did their best to warn him of the situation. On 3 November, for example, a plane landed behind the Austrian lines at Campoformido and three officers (two Italian and one British) alighted to explain that their side was being allowed to fight on until the following afternoon; the message delivered, the plane returned to base again, without engaging any targets on the way. But for the most part the Allied armies in general, and the Italians in particular, concentrated whole-heartedly on exploiting the opening they had been given. Specially organized flying columns of Italian cavalry and motorized infantry sliced through the soggy, disorganized mass of enemy forces facing them and raced as far north as they could get in the time available. By 3 p.m. on the 4th they had reached a general line running from the Stilfserjoch to Salurn in the mountains down to Pontebba in the plains and finally Grado on the Adriatic coast. Every soldier of the Dual Monarchy found south of this line was declared a prisoner.

For those soldiers the great scramble for home now began. Those north of the line were able to organize themselves – as far as flagging discipline would allow – and tackle the long slog in formation and on foot. One such enormous procession which set out from Bruneck comprised the remnants of no fewer than thir-teen Austro-Hungarian divisions, 'one of the largest march columns in military history', claimed an officer who took part. But most of them, and especially the thousands who had abandoned or been cut off from their units, just made for the railways. The empire may have been collapsing, its armies routed and its dynasty reeling, but still its trains, wheezing and clanking, somehow managed to run. This was the night-time scene at one station south of the Brenner:

> 'The soldiers left their horses and waggons simply stand-
> ing and settled down in the dark to wait. When a train
> appeared, everyone – including those from well outside
> the station – rushed for the carriage and mocked any
> attempt by the railway staff to maintain any order. They
> were surging with a mad haste to get home as their fore-
> fathers in the crusades had once pressed to reach the
> Holy Places. No thought of waiting, not an hour, not a
> minute to lose ... And so these witless people clambered
> up on the roofs of the carriages, rode on the buffers, or
> crammed on to the engine platforms. From a distance,
> the trains looked like moving swarms of bees. On one
> day, over a hundred people were reported to have killed
> themselves travelling like this through the numerous
> tunnels leading up to the Brenner.'

A few managed the journey in greater leisure and comfort. That aristocratic young artillery lieutenant, for example, whose private diary has been quoted before, used his own coat of arms as a magic carpet. He describes how, soon after the cease-fire, he found himself standing in the lovely market square of Bozen – as we can still call it – alone and without a penny in his pocket, for he had divided up all the cash the battery had left among the men. His was a typical predicament. For a while he was unde-cided whether to march with the Czech soldiers back to Ronsberg, where his family had an estate, or with the Austrians back to Vienna, where he also had a house. Finally he opted for the latter; but where was help and money to come from? Then he remembered that Count Toggenburg, the imperial governor of the province (who was still, theoretically, in office), was an ac-quaintance as well as a fellow-nobleman. He continues:

> 'So I rang at the door of the Toggenburg palace and
> asked if I might speak to their excellencies. The countess
> received me, heard my request and then simply took out

a green-bound copy of the *Almanack de Gotha* from the bookshelves and put me through an interrogation: parents' date of birth; names and birthdays of my brothers and sisters, aunts and uncles. After I had passed the examination, she became very friendly, apologized for her initial mistrust (so many charlatans were turning up these days) and invited me to take tea . . .'

The count duly lent him some money and, after a few days in Bozen watching the Italian take-over, the lieutenant made his way back to Vienna.

Not many had that luck, and not all that many escaped in any fashion from the noose the Italians had drawn round the neck of the Austro-Hungarian army. The Allied count of enemy prisoners taken leapt from over one hundred thousand on 3 November to three hundred thousand by the time the cease-fire had come into effect on both sides the following day. In twenty-four hours the Dual Monarchy had lost some two hundred thousand men, nearly all to its most hated enemy and in the most humiliating way. The peace of Villa Giusti was another large sharp nail driven into the Habsburg coffin. Ironically 4 November, the day of the disaster, was the Emperor Charles's name-day and throughout the disintegrating empire special masses were still held in celebration.*

The final outcome at sea was just as doleful for the empire as on land. In an attempt to forestall his navy falling into enemy hands (as was indeed prescribed in the separately issued naval terms of the armistice) Charles had, on 31 October, handed over the entire fleet to the newly emerged state of the Serbs, Croats and Slovenes. So, on that day, in the main Adriatic naval harbour of Pola, down came all the red-white-red flags from the masts of the Emperor's ships and up went the unfamiliar red-white-blue

---

* The Emperor Charles had in fact already handed over the supreme command to Arz in the small hours of 3 November – partly out of reluctance to conclude personally an armistice which might damage his German ally but mainly because the refusal of the new Austrian State Council to co-operate left him, as constitutional monarch, in a limbo.

flags of Yugoslavia. From the deck of the *Viribus Unitis* the last imperial Commander-in-Chief, the Hungarian Admiral Nicholas Horthy, gave the signal for the hand-over as, at four-thirty in the afternoon, he left his flagship with tears in his eyes and his personal banner and the ship's silken ceremonial ensign under his arm. The vessel was not to survive his departure for long. At 6 a.m. in the morning of 1 November two Italian officers slipped into the now unguarded harbour and planted a delayed-action mine below the ship's waterline.

There now came an episode of tragic farce, that combination which hovers so closely around all things Austro-Hungarian. As the Italian intruders were swimming away, their mission accomplished, they were spotted in the water by a petty officer of the ship's complement who pursued them in a boat and had them brought back on board as prisoners. Beside themselves with agitation they insisted on being taken immediately to Captain Vukovic, the Croatian naval officer who had taken over the fleet from Horthy, and explained to him that, thanks to their exploit, his flagship was about to be blown up. The captain responded in the approved naval tradition. He ordered the whole crew, and the two Italians, to row or swim for safety as fast as they could, and then went up on the bridge to await the explosion. He went down with the 20,000-ton battleship in minutes.

The final irony of it all was that the daring saboteurs had, in fact, only succeeded in robbing their own fleet of a valuable acquisition. Italian warships soon appeared in all the harbours of Istria and Dalmatia and, a week later, hoisted their flags on every former enemy vessel they could find.

On both land and sea the proudest symbols of the empire had now been wiped out together with its armed force. *Inseparabiliter ac indivisibiliter*, 'Inseparable and Indivisible', the pledge on the Habsburg double eagle, had been finally broken by Colonel Linder's order from Budapest on 1 November recalling all Hungarian soldiers from the combined army. And the flagship which sank that same day in Pola harbour had borne for its name the personal motto of the legendary Emperor Francis Joseph. The vessel had never brought the dynasty much luck. It was on board the *Viribus Unitis* that Archduke Francis Ferdinand had sailed down the Dalmatian coast *en route* for Sarajevo in June of 1914, on that last journey of his which touched off the great conflict that was only now ending.

The Padua armistice had its little epilogue, played out in a chilly, dimly lit villa in the newly-liberated Serbian capital of Belgrade. That episode is especially intriguing for the contrast between the two colourful characters who took part in it – General Franchet d'Espèrey, flushed with his victories of the past six weeks and thirsting for even greater laurels, and Count Michael Károlyi, already sobered rather than uplifted by the problems that only a few days of high office had already piled on his shoulders. Apart from the fact that both were of noble blood, the contrast between them could hardly have been greater. The Frenchman was very much the professional soldier; a master of his craft and a believer in those traditional values he had sought to defend. (He had no time, for example, for President Wilson's liberal pacifism.) The Hungarian was the epitome of the amateur politician, totally untrained and unequipped* for the role he had now assumed, yet determined nonetheless not to preserve but to overturn almost everything he had been born and brought up to believe in: a Magyar Count Tolstoy, with even more of the idealism but absolutely none of the genius. It was Károlyi's doing that the meeting took place.

Before the Italian offensive started, he had declared to the Budapest Parliament: 'We have lost the war. What is important now is that we should not lose the peace.' And not losing the peace meant, for every Hungarian, whether count or cobbler, republican or monarchist, retaining every yard of the historic 'lands of St Stephen' he could cling on to. When he learned that armistice talks had started in Italy, Karolyi at first wanted to go to Padua himself and plead Hungary's case. The speed of the settlement, the question of credentials and the chaotic state of communications had all ruled that out; and so, at the Villa Giusti, General Weber, in signing for the Dual Monarchy, had signed for

---

* He was no orator, for example, and a cleft palate which had been operated on when a sickly child of fourteen had anyway left him with a permanent speech defect.

Hungary as well. Yet surely, Károlyi reasoned, the Emperor's representative could not act for the newly-independent state which had sprung out of the withered loins of that empire? Constitutional niceties apart there was the military emergency on Hungary's southern border to be reckoned with: Serbian troops under d'Espèrey's command had already crossed the River Save, and that by itself suggested that the Italian armistice was not being applied to the Balkan theatre. The only remedy was to open direct negotiations with the Commander-in-Chief of the Allied Orient Armies, and so, at 11 a.m. on 3 November, while the last controversial meeting at Padua was still in session, two Hungarian lieutenant-colonels presented themselves in Belgrade with a request for separate negotiations.

D'Espèrey telegraphed to Paris for instructions and, at the same time, transmitted his own programme of action to Clemenceau. That was the last flowering of his old dream to march with twenty divisions through Budapest and Vienna into Bohemia and there, sitting at the cross-roads of the continent less than one hundred and fifty miles from Berlin, to dictate surrender terms himself to the German army. Clemenceau and the Supreme War Council would have none of it, preferring, if needed, the direct thrust over the Brenner and into Bavaria; yet it was realized in Paris that talks with the new Hungarian government would usefully plug a gap in the Entente's planning. They had allowed the Dual Monarchy fifteen days in which to evacuate all German troops and personnel from their territory, but had made no provision whatsoever for any rival movements of the former imperial forces within that territory. Accordingly d'Espèrey was instructed to regard the Villa Giusti armistice as valid also for the new Hungary but to round it off with a separate military convention which would avoid all delicate issues such as political boundaries. The stage was thus set for one of the strangest encounters of the war.

Károlyi arrived by Danube steamer from Novisad, apprehensive of the welcome he would receive both from the local Serbs (whom Hungarian troops had driven from their capital four summers before), and from this formidable French general for whom the Serbs now fought. His fears on the first score were allayed when his steamer, a white table-cloth from the dining saloon hoisted as a flag of peace, anchored at dusk on the quay-side to welcoming shouts of '*Zhivoi!*' from the large crowd that had gathered. (It was doubtless the table-cloth, even more than the radical Hungarian nobleman, they were cheering.) Franchet d'Espèrey, who arrived at 17.30 hours the next day – as fit as a fiddle despite an exhausting seventy-two-hour journey from Salonika – lived up to Károlyi's worst premonitions. 'We were the "burghers of Calais",' he wrote of his fears before the encounter, 'to be sacrificed for the errors of our predecessors.' More than just sacrificed, they were to be crucified.

The meeting took place only an hour and a half after d'Espèrey's arrival, at No 5 Rue de Theâtre (the Belgrade streets were marked in French and Serbo-Croat), the handsome home of a Serb professor recently evacuated by the Austrian garrison commander, and later destined to become the French embassy.

> 'The small and chilly sitting room' [Károlyi wrote] 'was heated by a log fire and lit by petrol lamps in majolica vases. There we stood and waited for Franchet d'Espèrey's arrival. His entrance was that of a victorious General on the stage; I felt he had rehearsed it beforehand. He wore a light-blue uniform and top-boots and had a row of decorations on his chest. A bulky, medium-sized man with broad shoulders, sparkling dark eyes and a small, turned-up moustache, he came straight to us with a sprightly martial walk . . . After being presented to the general, I introduced the members of my delegation . . .'

It was during these introductions that d'Espèrey began to vent his feelings. He gave no reaction when greeting Deszö Bokányi, the President of the Workers' Council, or Oskar Jészi, one of Károlyi's ministers without portfolio. But he winced when the visibly Jewish Baron Hatvány was presented and he stopped short in horror when it came to Imre Csernyak, a primitive rabble-rouser who had founded the first revolutionary Soldiers' Council to be formed in the Hungarian army, and who now appeared in a fantastic uniform designed by himself. '*Vous êtes tombés si bas?*' the general demanded bitterly of Károlyi. For all the new Prime Minister's socialist persuasions, the shaft probably went home. He had had heated political arguments by the score with his fellow-aristocrats in Hungary. This was the first reproach levelled at him across the battle-lines from a representative of the old European order. It was not a promising start.

D'Espèrey then took up a somewhat theatrical stance – back to the fireplace, left elbow lightly resting on the mantelpiece, right arm free for gesturing – as Károlyi read out his memorandum. It sounded rather like those encomiums of President Wilson to Prince Max produced in reverse. The war had been the doing of the old feudal monarchy, allied with Prussian militarism, the statement said. But now a new Hungary had arisen, representing the true will of the people and seeking an honourable peace of its own with the Western democracies, for it was no longer their enemy but had become a kind of neutral. This new Hungary, however, was plainly just as keen as the old to safeguard the historic lands of St Stephen which, for nine hundred years, the crown had symbolized. Would it be possible, Károlyi asked, for French, Italian or American troops (and not Serbs, Czechs or Rumanians) to be used if any occupation of Hungarian soil became necessary?

Ignoring his instructions to avoid anything which smacked of domestic Danubian politics, d'Espèrey rode clear over Károlyi's entire apologia and delivered in reply a history lecture of his own. Ever since the Hungarians had achieved near-parity with Austria in 1867, he said, Hungary had done nothing but oppress the non-Magyar peoples placed under its rule. Now, naturally, these peoples were its enemies, which he could unleash against it by snapping his fingers. As for the war, Hungary had marched with Germany and would be punished alongside her. In any case, the offer of Hungarian neutrality came too late. 'A fortnight ago I might still have needed it, but not today, now I am in Belgrade.' And at that, he handed Károlyi the typed sheets bearing the Allied Armistice terms and went off to dine with the French and Serbian officers of his staff, leaving the glum Hungarian delegates to their own devices.

His abrupt disappearance was a shrewd psychological blow. His visitors had been counting on an invitation to dine with the general and to discuss their brave new world with him; some had even brought with them postcards which they had wanted him to sign as souvenirs. As it was, the only souvenir they had to take back to Budapest with them was a set of eighteen very stiff cease-fire conditions. Most of those were a re-statement of the central provision of the Padua armistice – the right of the Allied armies to move freely across enemy territory and occupy all strategic points considered necessary – as applied to the Hungarian half of the vanquished monarchy. The new state was to provide everything to facilitate such movement – railway rolling stock, river craft, repair work-shops, lorries, twenty-five thousand horses, and so on. It was a military *Diktat* imposed on a vanquished foe and not an amicable convention with a would-be neutral.

After a mournful dinner in their hotel the Hungarians returned to the villa at 10.30 for a final confrontation with the Frenchman who held all the cards. Károlyi did what little he could to ward off the menace from Hungary's hostile neighbours. He persuaded the general, for example, to drop a clause giving the Entente powers (who now included those same hostile neighbours) the right to occupy any parts of Hungary which had become 'areas of disturbance'. And in a telegram to Clemenceau which d'Espèrey, after some argument, agreed to dispatch to Paris, he declared that Hungary's acceptance was only given 'on the condition that the integrity of the Hungarian state is guaranteed until the conclusion of a peace treaty against all attacks – whether from the Austrians, Germans, Czechs, Rumanians or Jugoslavs'. But that was merely a cry into the teeth of a storm. Without even waiting for Károlyi's National Council to ratify his acceptance, French and Serbian armies, already across the Danube, moved up through southern Hungary to occupy everything that the South Slavs wished to incorporate in their new state of Yugoslavia. Simultaneously, on Hungary's eastern flank, the agile Rumanians executed another of their political somersaults,* re-entered the war in its last hours as the allies of the Entente, and gathered the huge and lovely province of Transylvania as their prize. The Hungarians were tasting not merely the bitterness of military defeat but also their humbling as a self-appointed master race.

---

* Previously allied with the Western powers, they had concluded a separate peace with Germany six months before.

The encounter between d'Espèrey and Károlyi had been one between the conqueror and the conquered. Yet, ironically, for both men alike, the Hungarian armistice they had concluded was the beginning of the end. The French general had lived his last moment of glory, leaning against the mantelpiece of that dimly-lit room. There was to be no march on Bohemia for him and, as a telegram which now arrived from Clemenceau made clear, whatever limited operations he embarked on were henceforth to be under the orders of the Allied Supreme Commander, Marshal Foch. So, though d'Espèrey later consoled himself with the thought that, alone of all generals in the war, he had occupied two enemy capitals, Sofia and Constantinople, the grand design of his life remained unfulfilled. Károlyi's grand design – to achieve true socialism in his own country and, ultimately, a democratic federation of all the East European peoples – was also doomed to failure and, as far as Hungary was concerned, the causes went back to that same treacherous armistice. On 20 March of the following year Károlyi, by then President of an officially constituted Hungarian Republic, was handed a demand by the Entente representative in Budapest ordering the evacuation of still more Hungarian territory for the Rumanians to take over. He refused and resigned and power fell unexpectedly into the lap of Lenin's Bolshevik agent, Béla Kun, whose five-month dictatorship of the proletariat was succeeded by the twenty-four years of Horthy's dictatorship of the right.*

All that lay in the future. What mattered as the first week of November 1918 drew to a close was that every arm of the Central Powers' alliance had now been cut away from the trunk in Berlin. Bulgaria had gone in the French residence overlooking Salonika Bay; Turkey in the ward-room of a British warship in Mudros; the old Austria in an Italian villa near Padua; and, finally, the new Hungary in the house of a Serb professor in Belgrade. Only the tottering Leviathan, Germany itself, remained on its feet.

---

* The rule of Admiral Horthy only ended in October 1944 when he was forced out of office by his suspicious German allies. As Horthy had ruled as Regent of a theoretical monarchy he had himself restored, one can say that it was Adolf Hitler who destroyed the last surviving remnant of the Habsburg empire.

November Nightmares

WHEN WE LEFT PRINCE MAX in Berlin he had just taken to his bed with influenza when, on the afternoon of 26 October, the news was brought to him that the Emperor had finally screwed up the courage to dismiss Ludendorff. That removed what, in the Chancellor's eyes, was a major obstacle to the peace negotiations he had embarked upon. Now a far more daunting decision had to be faced. Had not the Emperor himself become an even greater obstacle lying across Germany's exit path from the war? That question raised others. Would it be enough for President Wilson if William II simply stepped down from his throne and handed over to the repugnant Crown Prince? If the Crown Prince were equally unacceptable, would a younger brother fit the bill, even as Regent? If the imperial title had to go, could the Prussian monarchy as such continue? This arrangement might provide the other three kingdoms,* six grand duchies, five duchies and seven principalities of the 1871 empire with some prospect of individual survival; and the Chancellor was, first and foremost, heir to one of those grand duchies himself. But before any of those other questions could be considered, the immediate problem was to 'enlighten the Kaiser' (Prince Max's own phrase) about the delicacy of his position and to establish whether Germany's Supreme War Lord was, in fact, willing to hand over his crown to anyone. It was a tricky task for any Chancellor to tackle, and it was not made any easier by the fact that, for the next five days, Prince Max had to conduct it, together with the rest of Germany's business, from an office that was virtually a sick-room.

The abdication drama began with a procession of reluctant marionettes across the Berlin stage. The first was General Oscar von Chelius, a Badener, like Prince Max, but also a former aide-de-

---

* Bavaria, Saxony and Württemburg.

camp of the Kaiser's and an ex-commander of the imperial life guard regiment of Hussars. When, on 28 October, this loyal officer and courtier arrived in the capital from Brussels (where he was serving with the German military government) and informed the Chancellor that abdication was now the only hope of saving both the country and the dynasty, Prince Max felt that fate had sent him the ideal messenger of doom. He immediately dispatched the agitated general to the eighty-year-old Count August zu Eulenberg who had been in the personal service of his royal master, as Crown Prince and Emperor, ever since 1866, and was now the so-called 'House Minister' of the court. Surely, between them, Max reasoned, the two men could get the message across. For good measure, he handed Chelius a letter he had just received from Prince Hohenlohe-Langenburg in Switzerland, in which the case for abdication, as seen from his neutral post, was argued with anguished fervour by the envoy. Finally, the Chancellor tried to mobilize the chief court chaplain, Ernst von Dryander, by asking him, as keeper of the imperial soul, to plead with the Emperor to renounce worldly dignities for the common good.

All these emissaries funked it. Late that same evening a reply came from Eulenberg returning Prince Hohenlohe's letter and suggesting that the Chancellor should forward this himself to the Emperor 'as a private communication for information only'. The chaplain had already declined in writing to undertake his mission, but the greatest blow came when General Chelius reappeared in the Chancellor's room the following morning, an utterly changed man. The Emperor, he declared, must on no account renounce the throne, for this would bring about the dissolution of the army as well as the empire. As for himself, the general protested, he had only spoken otherwise the day before 'under the Chancellor's influence'. Prince Max must have wondered for a moment whether his own high temperature was making him delirious.

Any doubts that the All-Highest intended to cling to his pedestal were removed by a draft proclamation sent over from the palace in which William II tried to get his own person and the dynasty publicly anchored to the new constitution. 'The office of the Emperor means service to the people,' this belated populist ploy

concluded. Confronted by such stubborn illusions from the court
and by the refusal of all his emissaries to break out of, or into, this
fantasy world, Prince Max realized that he would have to do the
enlightening himself. It was indeed high time. By now the clamour in
the streets, fanned by the left-wing press, was almost all for
abdication. In Parliament the Independent Socialists had already
declared that there was no sense in Germany clinging to the
monarchy 'at a time when crowns were rolling in the dust', and even
the more moderate majority Socialists, though more restrained in
public, were already thinking much the same in private. Moreover
the framework of the German empire, never too securely bolted
together at the best of times, was being shaken dangerously loose by
the political crisis. Catholic Bavaria, by far the most important* of
Prussia's subordinates was, as usual, also the most restless. The
delivery of President Wilson's third note, with its uncompromising
language about the imperial dynasty, had decided the Bavarians once
and for all that the Hohenzollerns would have to go if a reasonable
peace were to be secured and if Munich itself were to stand any
chance of remaining a royal capital on its own. The Bavarian Cabinet
had said as much to the Prussian envoy, von Treutler, who had
passed the baleful message on to Prince Max in Berlin. The threat of
outright secession thus ranged itself alongside all other domestic
pressures.

But by leaving it until the last minute to act himself, the
Chancellor had left it a minute too late. At five o'clock on the
afternoon of 29 October, as Prince Max was steeling himself to
request an audience, he was brought the news that the Emperor had
decided to leave that same day for Supreme Headquarters at Spa.
Incredulous at first, and then horrified, the sick Chancellor dispatched his Foreign Minister, Solf, to the palace to get the move
cancelled. Then, realizing that Solf would probably never penetrate
the screen of protocol which Eulenberg had erected around his

*The special privileges accorded to the kingdom of Bavaria in the 1871 constitution
included, for example, the permanent chairmanship of the Confederation's Committee of
Foreign Affairs; the right to represent the empire abroad should the accredited envoy of the
empire be unable to discharge his duties; and the right to send its own delegate to any peace
negotiations.

master, Prince Max telephoned the Emperor himself. The All-Highest did not set very lofty standards of rectitude in the long conversation which followed.

He began by claiming that the Supreme Command were suddenly pressing him to come to the battlefield, which was at best a half-truth, for though Hindenburg had, three weeks before, expressed a desire to see his royal master at Spa again, this was in no sense an urgent invitation. The Emperor next asserted that even his wife had been taken aback by his decision, whereas in fact the Empress Augusta had been urging it on him for days past. Then, when Prince Max begged to be received in person to discuss vital matters of the moment, the Emperor took refuge in his doctors who, he said, had warned him against the danger of catching his Chancellor's influenza. It was like trying to pin down an eel.

The Emperor, probably uneasy himself about this slippery performance, dispatched the following telegram to Prince Max that same evening:

'As important discussions are being held in Spa tomorrow
. . . I am travelling there to attend them . . . In order to make
things easier for you, Ludendorff had to go. His departure
means a severe loss in military terms for the army. It is my
duty to make up for this loss and to see his replacement settle
in, and that is why I am leaving this evening . . . You will have
received my suggestion concerning England.'*

It was a transparent attempt to justify what was simply a panic flight. The Supreme War Lord was talking as though his power and prestige lived up to that resonant title, whereas everyone knew that he hardly opened his mouth before his generals at Spa and then, almost always, only to agree with them. On that appropriate note of comic posturing, William II left Berlin that night and was never to return, as Prince Max had already sensed. His departure provides a final

---

* This is a reference to the idea (which in fact stemmed from Prince Max and Dr Kurt Hahn of Salem School fame) of seeking a last-minute understanding with England. The Emperor had now adopted it as his own, believing that resentment over America's growing influence in Europe could be exploited in Germany's favour. It was a precursor of similar eleventh-hour illusions cherished by Hitler when Germany faced an even greater military catastrophe a generation later.

measure of contrast between the two German-speaking empires and their rulers. When flash-point was reached in the political crisis in Austria-Hungary the Emperor Charles was to be seen journeying incessantly between his twin capitals in an attempt to resolve it with new governments and new concessions, and he actually handed over the military command in order to free his hands as sovereign. But when fate started knocking at the door of the Neues Palais in Berlin, William promptly abandoned both his ministers and his capital, and fled to the army which he rashly hoped would prove his salvation.

Ironically, the Bolshevik régime in Russia, which was busy releasing the famous pre-war 'Willy-Nicky' correspondence between the German Emperor and the Tsar, chose that juncture to publish some stern advice which William II had penned to Nicholas in 1905, when the Russian empire was in ferment after its disastrous defeat in the war with Japan. In that epistle (duly reprinted in the German papers) William urged the Tsar to 'enact a great personal deed to re-establish power and save the threatened dynasty'. And the deed he had in mind was that Nicholas should 'address the people from the balcony of his palace at the Moscow Kremlin and speak to them like a father – the mass of the people to be surrounded by the clergy in their full vestments and crosses, by the nobles and notables, and by the troops'. Willy, as every German newspaper reader must have concluded, was better at advising heroics than at practising them. But, if the truth be known, it was probably the fate of that same Nicholas II twelve years later which prompted his fellow-Emperor to take to his heels now. William was always convinced that, if the Tsar had taken refuge with his army early enough in 1917, instead of lingering on in his Petrograd palace to be taken by the rebels, he would have escaped his terrible end.

But whatever the motivation the damage was done as soon as the royal train steamed westwards out of Berlin. In Spa, which was to prove his political tomb, he achieved absolutely nothing of military significance. General Groener, the successor to Ludendorff whom the Supreme War Lord was grandiloquently proposing to introduce to his task, had just got to Spa himself when, at four o'clock on the afternoon of 30 October, the royal train pulled in. Groener recalls the astonishment at headquarters at the Emperor's arrival which, he was assured by Hindenburg, was none of the Field Marshal's doing. Nearly thirty years later, the last Quartermaster-General of imperial Germany wrote:

'To this day, it is not clear who caused the Emperor to make this journey which was undertaken at the most unfavourable time. In view of the threat to his empire and to the monarchy as such, his presence in Berlin was far more important than at Headquarters.'

Prince Max was trying to get the same message across at the time. He chased the Emperor to Spa with a personal telegram begging his royal master to return to his capital at once; otherwise, the Chancellor warned, rumours that a military coup was being planned to sweep away the new constitution and establish a dictatorship would only strengthen. And, in any case, he added, when decisions had to be made on which the future of Germany depended, the crown, the Chancellor and the government had to be together to take them. All he got back the next day by way of answer (and that only signed by Clemens von Delbrück, the former Prussian Minister of Interior who had been appointed head of the Emperor's own 'Civilian Cabinet' a fortnight before) was that 'urgent military affairs, closely connected with the questions of armistice and peace, make the presence of the All-Highest absolutely indispensable here'. Bitterly, Prince Max realized that this dismissive telegram symbolized more than the distance between Spa and Berlin. An even wider gulf of mistrust now yawned between the Chancellor and his Emperor. He would have to soldier on as best he could alone.

The next day, 31 October, he left his sick-room for the first time in nearly a week to attend a full session of his Cabinet again, and immediately broached the subject of abdication. He found his ministers sharply divided, though the scales were tipped, on balance, against the monarch. Those who argued that the Emperor must go if a Wilsonian peace were to be reached included the Vice-Chancellor, von Payer (a Württemberger); the Minister of Interior, Wilhelm Drews (a Prussian); the Foreign Minister, Solf (another Prussian); and, of course, the Socialist State Secretary Scheidemann, who was at pains to point out that it was not primarily the workers who were demanding the monarch's head:

'The demand [for abdication] is not being raised so much by the working class as by the bourgeoisie, especially in Bavaria, where separatism is growing stronger . . . What has surprised me most is the similar attitude of government officials. I would never have dreamt that such people would simply fall right over backwards. Quite a number of officers have called on me to express similar views, officers up to the rank of colonel. They were all very sorry about it but they felt that the position of the fatherland was even more important than that of the Emperor. And they are right . . . He must accept the consequences of defeat and step down voluntarily.'

To ram his point home Scheidemann indicated that he might step down voluntarily himself from the Cabinet unless the Emperor went.

Those against the abdication included the War Minister, Heinrich Scheuch, who maintained that if the Supreme War Lord were uprooted, the army would be destroyed with him; and the leader of the Catholic Centre party, Matthias Erzberger who, in an emotional speech, cited everything from arousing the contempt of foreigners to courting the dangers of Bolshevism as reasons for keeping William on his throne. Finally, though everyone was clear that whatever the outcome, the Emperor should only go of his own free will, nobody was at all clear as to what would happen after that. The imperial constitution of 1871 made no provision for a Regency. Prussia, however, had such provisions. Did that mean that a Prussian Regent would automatically rule the empire?

To try and cut through the tangle Prince Max asked half a dozen of his key ministers to meet him again back in his office at the Chancellery that afternoon. 'Our decisions,' he admonished them, 'must come from the head, not the heart.' Then came the only oblique reference Prince Max ever made to his colleagues as to how difficult it was for him, a kinsman of the Emperor and heir to a Grand Duchy, to shut his own heart out from the debate: 'I don't need to tell you what it means for me that I even have to broach this subject.'

But his six ministers remained as divided in private session as they had been at the full cabinet. One thing stood out from the recital of arguments and counter-arguments, and that was the impressive way in which Drews, the epitome of the loyal servant of the Prussian crown, fought his way with anguish to his conclusion:

> 'I admit that abdication will have no good effect on the army . . . But my eyes are on the domestic front. If the workers and wide circles of the middle classes see the figure of the Emperor as a stumbling-block to peace, then I don't see how we can go on with the defence of the country.'

That was precisely the conclusion Prince Max had reached himself, and as they parted company on the staircase – where Drews almost collapsed with emotion – the Chancellor asked him to go to Spa that evening and, as Prussian Minister of the Interior talking to the King of Prussia, to present the blunt facts. As reinforcement, Prince Max tried to mobilize, first Count Lerchenfeld, the Bavarian envoy in Berlin; the Prince August William, the fourth son of the Emperor; then the Grand Duke of Hesse; and finally Prince Frederick Charles of Hesse, who was the Emperor's brother-in-law. Draft proclamations were drawn up and a special train was ordered to stand by. But when it came to the point Frederick Charles joined all the others who had declared themselves unable or unwilling to undertake the task. At one point, when asked why he did not go to Spa and tackle the Emperor himself, Prince Max pleaded his own delicate position as the heir to the throne of Baden. Even he, deep down, was funking it. Yet, as imperial Chancellor and presumptive Grand Duke combined in one person, he was the only man in Germany who had both the prime duty to 'enlighten the Emperor', and some faint prospects of succeeding.

As it was, more mundane things intervened to keep him in Berlin. At the end of two exhausting, inconclusive days of wrestling with the abdication crisis, the Chancellor was in even worse shape than the tormented Drews. The fever, which he had never properly shaken off, claimed him again, and the doctors decided this time that what Prince Max needed above all else was a good rest. Either they overdid the dose, or the patient was in such a weakened state that he responded abnormally to the sedative. At all events, the doctors succeeded in knocking the Chancellor out cold for more than thirty-six critical hours. Prince Max closed his eyes on the night of Friday, 1 November, and did not open them again until the afternoon of Sunday the 3rd.

It would be too much to say that he was aroused, like some political Rip Van Winkle, into a different world. He resembled rather an opera-goer who has dozed through one entire act of a work he has never heard before and awakes to find a lot of new twists to the plot unfolding, *fortissimo*, on the stage. Almost the only fully expected development to greet him was the failure of Drews's mission to Spa, where Prince Max's envoy had had a terrible time of it. The Emperor had first heard his message in private audience at the Villa Fraineuse,* and brushed it contemptuously aside. How could a descendant of Frederick the Great simply renounce his throne? And in any case, how could a Prussian official who had sworn the oath of loyalty to the crown, bring himself to advocate such a step? Next, the Emperor summoned Marshal Hindenburg and General Groener, each of whom sharply attacked Drews in turn for his suggestion. Driving away from the villa, the Emperor was in such transports of joy over this support that, when he spotted his aide, Major Niemann, walking by, he stopped his car, blew on the horn, and waved him over to hear about it.

> 'You should have seen how the Field Marshal stood by his Emperor!' [he shouted]. 'And to think that the placid Groener could get so worked up! He really rubbed it into Drews where the main threat to the fatherland lies – not in the greater strength of our enemies, but in divisiveness and opposition at home. It really did me good to see a south German general backing up the Emperor and the King of Prussia like that!'

William II would have been far less enthusiastic about his new Quartermaster-General had he known what that officer had done

* A small residence formerly used by the late Queen Marie Henriette of the Belgians and now requisitioned for the use of William II.

next. Groener, privately shaken to the core by Drews's mission (which evidently had the backing of both the Chancellor and the government in Berlin), promptly took the Emperor's Prussian adjutants on one side and suggested to them that the right place for the Supreme War Lord now was with the fighting troops, right up in the front line. 'If he should be killed or wounded,' the down-to-earth Swabian pointed out, 'this would be an honourable end and would only strengthen monarchist sentiment among the people.' The adjutants gave him no reply.

The negative report which Prince Max got from Spa, though not surprising, was as gloomy as could be. Even more disturbing were three other items of bad news he was given on returning to his senses that Sunday afternoon. The first concerned the armistice which had just been signed on the Italian front – not just the fact of Austria's surrender, but the alarming evidence that her delegates seemed to have made such a hash of the cease-fire agreement that yet another powerful enemy army was now advancing, unopposed, on Germany's back door from the south. Troops had to be scraped together from somewhere to bolt that door, and as it was too complicated and dangerous to bring them from the east, there was nothing for it but to strip the already decimated Western Front of one Bavarian and one Prussian division and rush them down to the Tyrol. Austria-Hungary was no longer an ally, so there was no need to ask in Vienna for permission.

The second complication arose from the first. The prospect of Entente forces crossing the Brenner and moving on Munich had fanned the already lively flickers of Bavarian separation. Bavaria's War Minister, von Hellingrath, was all for dynamiting the Brenner tunnel and, in the general panic, there was much talk of Bavaria following the Austrian example of a separate peace. But it was the third disturbing development which was swiftly to overwhelm all others. Also on 3 November the Chancellor was given preliminary, and as yet vague, reports of serious unrest in the German Navy. Among other things, Prince Max had re-awoken to a revolution.

One of the greatest ironies of the collapse of the German

Empire was the manner in which the earth just subsided beneath
it. For months past the Supreme Command – and, above all,
Ludendorff until his dismissal – had been berating the civilian
front as a germ-carrier of defeatism, which was gradually infect-
ing Germany's stout-hearted fighting men with its bolshevik
bacillus. Yet, in the event, it was the stout-hearted fighting men
(and many of them veterans at that) who started the fuse of
disaffection spluttering up and down the country. Germany's
November Revolution – if that is the right word for such a
haphazard series of explosions – began with an old-fashioned
mutiny.

It was hardly surprising that the trouble should have begun
below decks on the warships anchored in the northern harbours.
The German army had always been active, even if it was only on
the endless skirmishing engagements and artillery duels which
stretched between the great advances and retreats. But the High
Seas Fleet had lain bottled up in its ports for four years, and that
meant that the thousands of its four-year peace-time volunteers
who would normally have completed their terms of service
during 1914 and 1915 had, by now, been seven or eight years in
uniform, away from their wives and families. Only naval action,
however bloody or indecisive, could have alleviated such prolonged frustration. The Emperor Persius of old had stressed the
dangers to morale of a high seas fleet being cooped up too long in
harbour. Admiral Tirpitz, creator of the Emperor William's
navy, had pointed to the same danger after the first mutinies
among his sailors had broken out in 1917.

The trouble now was even more understandable, as well as
far more serious. Ever since the pressure of the peace negotiations had obliged Germany to abandon U-boat warfare, her admirals, who had only swallowed that decision through their
gritted teeth, had been planning one last spectacular foray to
throw their entire battle fleet against England. How far their
motives were purely professional (to go down with guns blazing
rather than surrender meekly or scuttle), or partly political (to
sabotage the armistice talks by starting up a fight to the finish), is
hard to determine. The final plan, which had been drawn up a

fortnight before the 1918 mutiny by the Commander-in-Chief of the High Seas Fleet, Admiral Hipper,* was bold enough to encompass either aim. The Royal Navy was to be lured out into the North Sea by probing attacks launched by light units against the Thames estuary. Once drawn out in pursuit, the British Grand Fleet would be lured into minefields and submarine 'ambushes' laid off the Frisian Islands, and then – with luck in a much weakened state – be engaged and blown out of the water by Germany's battleships. Whether this *Götterdämmerung* of the German admirals would have worked out so neatly in practice is highly dubious. It is also irrelevant. The ordinary seamen, who were not to be let into the secret until anchors had been weighed, got word of this 'death cruise', and prevented the fleet getting out of Cuxhaven and Wilhelmshafen for the planned assembly under Hipper's flagship in the nearby Schillig Roads. At first it was only the stokers who failed to turn up for duty; then power supplies were cut and equipment was sabotaged; finally there was open rebellion on deck and even the threat of ship firing upon ship in harbour. The sailors, who had anyway long since lost the feel of battle, found the prospect of an early peace far more alluring than that of eleventh-hour heroics. Their constant refrain, when interrogated afterwards, was: 'We have done our duty as long as it seemed to make any sense. But now that the war is as good as over, why should we go to the bottom of the sea, instead of back to our wives and children?'

All that had been taking place in the foggy northern harbours during the last five days of October, and Prince Max seems to have known nothing at all about it – neither the Admirals' secret plan, nor the way it had been frustrated. Indeed the paradox was that the whole affair really exploded after the operation itself had been abandoned. On 1 November the good people of Kiel were puzzled to see warship after warship steaming through their famous canal into harbour. They were units of the Third Battle Squadron, mutinous like the rest, which had been sent back to its home base in the belief that a little shore leave would improve

---

*He had succeeded Admiral Scheer in the post the previous August, Scheer moving sideways to become Director of Naval Operations.

morale and discipline. That proved to be one of the most disastrous and far-reaching miscalculations of Germany's war. Kiel was a hotbed of strikes and political agitation. The unworldly admirals had now tossed dynamite into the fire.*

During the weekend of 2–3 November (while Prince Max in Berlin was lying insensible under his sleeping drugs) uproar grew in the streets of Kiel as the sailors of the warships mingled with the civilian demonstrators like two angry waves surging together in tumult. The workers demanded the release of all the naval mutineers who had been caught and put in irons; military patrols sent out to round up more delinquents just melted into the crowds. Like some daemonic djinn popping out of a bottle, an unknown stoker named Artelt emerged as the main demagogue at open-air meetings which met and dissolved without plan or programme. Radical republicanism was the only theme discernible through this confusion. 'Down with the Kaiser!' became a background chant to all other demands. Finally, on the Sunday, the first blood was shed as troops and armed demonstrators exchanged shots outside the naval prison where the captured mutineers were being held.

That was the crisis Prince Max found staring him in the face when he opened his eyes again that afternoon. He acted with speed and common sense by dispatching to Kiel the following morning the Socialist deputy Gustav Noske who, as his party's specialist in naval affairs, was the best man to talk to the sailors. A State Secretary, Konrad Haussman, accompanied him as a direct representative of the Chancellor. The sailors, for their part, proved grateful to have somebody to talk to who was both congenial and in authority. Artelt was already operating through a 'Workers and Sailors Soviet' by the time Noske got to Kiel on the Monday evening; but he and his comrades were clearly overwhelmed by the task which was falling to them of administering a great city trapped, in utter chaos, between the old order and the new. Red flags were fluttering in triumph everywhere,

---

* Despite prophetic warnings of trouble sent out by one of their colleagues to the Governor of Kiel, Admiral Souchon, hero of the *Goeben*'s historic adventures in the Mediterranean in 1914.

including on all the Third Squadron's ships in harbour,* but the revolutionaries had no idea how to feed the people, let alone maintain some semblance of order. They asked Noske to take control, which he did, selecting for his 'Council' half-a-dozen of the least ruffianly characters out of a batch of fifty who were offering to assist him.

And so, in the first of the Emperor's cities, imperial rule had come to an end, and it had ended with a whimper which, to amend the poet's phrase, was louder than any bang. None of the rebels had been disciplined let alone arrested. That kid-gloved approach conformed fully with the declaration, signed by Prince Max, which Noske had brought with him – full of appeals for patience and co-operation and assurances that the notorious 'death cruise' had been just a monstrous rumour. ('Nobody would even think of putting the lives of our fellow-citizens, fathers of families, at risk for no purpose.') Noske demanded a formal amnesty for the mutineers whose release from jail the rebel mob had already secured. Though there was some desultory discussion in Berlin about refusing this demand, and even of dispatching troops to the city to restore the government's authority, the amnesty was duly granted and the troops, needless to say, never marched.

Looking back on those events Prince Max wrote: 'Without Kiel, no revolution; without revolution, no capitulation on 11 November.' The verdict is no less misleading for being so frequently cited. The popular tumult which swept across Germany in the autumn of 1918 was driven mainly by a war-weariness converted into fury by the belief that only the old order now stood in the way of an immediate peace. Nothing could have stopped that tumult erupting into armed violence somewhere and at some time. And the same applies to Germany's capitulation. The complete disintegration of the Central Powers' alliance and the collapse on all the battle-fronts had already put that beyond doubt at some stage in the immediate future before the first shots were

---

*The battleship *König* had held out till last, still flying the imperial standard on the night of 4 November. Its captain shot a sailor who tried to raise the red flag instead, whereupon he was killed himself.

fired in Kiel. What was achieved by the mutiny – or rather, by its passive acceptance on the part of the government – was to advance the date of surrender, and to ensure that Germany could not resist the severest terms. Respect for *Obrigkeit*, or superior authority, which had always bound the Prussian kernel of the state tightly together, had also been shattered. At Kiel the empire had publicly kissed the rod of revolution, thus baring its own back for the violent, haphazard blows which swiftly fell from other quarters.

Just how desperate Germany's military position had become was to be outlined to Prince Max by Groener, who had arrived in Berlin at the Chancellor's urgent summons on the 5th. The war maps showed, clearly enough, how the Entente armies were encircling the fatherland from all sides. General Diaz was already on the Brenner; General d'Espèrey was across the Danube in southern Hungary; and, in the West, the last great Allied offensive, launched by Marshal Foch on 1 November, was making giant strides towards Germany's frontier. French and American troops attacking north of the Argonne had cleared the last remnants of the Hindenburg Line still in German hands, and their advance guards were even threatening Sedan, more than twenty miles from the starting point of the attack.* In the centre of the line the British First and Third Armies had turned the defences along the Scheldt, taken Valenciennes, and were rolling forward, on a thirty-mile front, across the very ground where British troops had first assembled in France four years before. Nineteen thousand prisoners and four hundred and fifty guns had been taken in that one advance alone.

Groener's last act before leaving Supreme Headquarters for

---

*An appalling mix-up ensued as to whether French or American troops should take Sedan itself. In view of its almost traumatic emotional significance for France, Foch had arranged the general boundaries of the advance so that the city lay in the French sector. But, tempted by the slow progress of the French Fourth Army in that area and by Foch's overall directive that the prime task now was to attack the enemy, Pershing tried to snatch the honour for himself, and on 5 November ordered his First Army to race for Sedan. The farcical free-for-all which ensued ended with the French threatening to shell American troops in their path to the target. In the event the fortress town held out until the armistice.

Berlin had been to yield to Foch's relentless pressure by ordering a general retreat to the shortened so-called 'A-M Line', the final semi-fortified defensive system in occupied territory which ran from Antwerp to west of Brussels and so through Charleroi down to the Meuse. But, as the Quartermaster-General now explained to the Chancellor and his War Cabinet, even that major withdrawal offered little hope of respite. The 'A-M' defences themselves were still incomplete; the military supply and communications problems were getting steadily worse; and, above all, the German army in the West was fighting against overwhelming odds. Foch had started his last grand offensive with more than ninety-six divisions in reserve, compared with the fifty-six available to Hindenburg. Even those figures, the general indicated, did not show the really dark side of the picture. In actual battalion strengths, in or out of the front line, the German army had sunk to an average of five hundred men, compared with six hundred for the French, seven hundred for the British and twelve hundred for the Americans. Despite that it might be possible to achieve a vital fourteen days' breathing space. Groener ended his exposé with what had, by now, become the almost ritual tribute to the bravery of those divisions which were still giving a good account of themselves and with the (equally ritual) Supreme Command complaint that 'bolshevik subversion' was an even greater menace than the enemy. Given the bald statistics he had just produced, it was asking a lot to expect any civilian to believe that.

The next day, Wednesday 6 November, Groener was far gloomier. In an hour's talk with Prince Max in the Chancellery gardens, he revealed something which he had kept to himself at the War Cabinet meeting. The Emperor, he said, had told him at Spa that the situation could only be saved by taking 'the direct route from army to army', in other words, by going over, uninvited, with a white flag to the enemy in order to speed up the cease-fire. This, the Quartermaster-General said, was now his own view. At this alarming remark, the following exchange took place:

Prince Max: 'But surely not before eight days' time?'
Groener: 'That is too long to wait.'
Prince Max: 'Not before Monday then?'
Groener: 'That's also too long. Saturday at the latest.'

The Quartermaster-General had evidently caught the Ludendorff germ from his predecessor, for the symptoms were precisely the same – a gloomy but not entirely hopeless military appreciation followed by an unexpected shout for peace tomorrow. Groener sought to justify his sudden change of heart to the horrified Chancellor by pointing to the progress the American forces were making on the Western Front and the progress the bolsheviks were making on the home front. That was quite irrational. Nothing had happened overnight cither on the battlefield or inside Germany itself to justify such total despair. To have sounded convincing he should have waited a day or two longer.

At noon the leaders of the Socialist party and of the Trade Unions came, by appointment, for a meeting with Groener, with whom they had always worked cordially during the war. The cordiality was still there, but there was no longer a shred of common purpose. Ebert urged the immediate abdication of the Kaiser – 'at the latest by tomorrow' – as the only measure which would quieten popular unrest. This need not mean the end of the monarchy. True, the Crown Prince was too widely hated by the public to succeed his father, but one of the Emperor's younger sons might 'represent' him. Groener retorted that, if only in the interest of holding the army together, the Emperor's abdication was unthinkable and, in any case, he was authorized to say that all the royal princes would refuse to step into their father's shoes.

Two things cut short those circular, inter-linking arguments as to whether the Emperor should stay on his throne and as to how the armistice could best be speeded up. The meeting itself was interrupted by Scheidemann, who burst in with a white face, shouting:

'There's no point in arguing any longer about abdication,

339

the revolution is on the march. Sailors from Kiel have now seized power in Hamburg and Hanover ... We don't even know whether we shall still be sitting on these chairs tomorrow.'

When the Chancellor made enquiries he found that the situation in Hanover was still so confused that, from Berlin, it was impossible to tell what was going on. The news from the Northern Front, however, was more precise, and it was all bad. Hamburg-Altona was indeed in the hands of the mob, led by sailors who had occupied all the railway stations to prevent any troop reinforcements coming in. The local garrison had refused to open fire on the rebels and its acting commander had fled. Moreover, also on 5 November, both Brunsbüttel, which commanded the mouth of the Elbe, and Lübeck had been taken over. The old Hanseatic town had been seized by a form of pirate invasion: four warships, packed with mutineers, had simply appeared in the harbour and discharged gangs who had taken possession of the post office, the munitions store, and other strategic points. As Prince Max drily commented: 'A new front, the North Front, was forming.' That may well have been so. However, the point to note is that, by that time, both the south-eastern and the southern battle-fronts had collapsed beyond repair, while Germany's Western Front was deemed to be in such an irreparable state that the white flag was being unfurled. The revolution did indeed stab the German army in the back. But that colossus was already mortally wounded when this last dagger went in. To use sportsman's parlance, the rebels had shot a dying bird.

As for those proposals – floated by the Emperor in Spa and formally launched by Groener in Berlin – of an 'army to army' surrender to the Allies in the West, they were overtaken by a radio bulletin from Washington received during that same afternoon of 6 November in Berlin. In that fourth and last communication, the official text of which was received from Berne the following day, President Wilson informed Prince Max that America's allies had now concurred with all his previous notes but had reserved their own positions over freedom of the seas and had demanded full compensation 'for all damage done to the civilian population of the Allies and their property by the aggression of Germany by land, sea or air'. Whatever their import for the future those, at the moment, were merely phrases to Prince Max. The message he was really waiting for came at the end: 'Marshal Foch has been authorized ... to receive properly accredited representatives of the German Government ... to communicate to them the terms of an armistice.' With that one sentence, the greatest of Germany's November nightmares – fighting and bleeding further in a hopeless struggle – was banished.

Two questions remained to be settled. Who was to carry out Germany's capitulation; and, whoever the unfortunate man was, would he be surrendering for an empire or a republic?

Flight and Surrender

IT WAS A BAND of Kiel mutineers who gave the government the first unsolicited advice as to how Germany should surrender. An officer had boarded the strike-bound battleship *Thüringen* at dead of night in an attempt to talk some naval sense into the rebels. As he groped his way in the dark along the deck to the crowd of men gathered around the forward gun battery, he paused and called out to them: 'Tell me what it is you want!' The expected answers demanding an amnesty, shore leave, or the abandonment of the 'death cruise', failed to materialize. Instead, after a long pause, a shrill voice cried out: 'We want Erzberger!' And, at that, there was a roar of applause from his comrades, who started to bang their metal drinking-mugs in approval.

It seemed extraordinary that these sailors, whose persuasions now lay somewhere between republicanism and outright bolshevism, should call for such a champion – a Catholic, a Conservative and a monarchist, and the epitome, therefore, of everything they were bridling against. Yet Matthias Erzberger was no ordinary man. The Centre Party leader had started the war, conventionally enough, as yet another of those firebrands who could be found in 1914 in every one of the belligerent capitals, prophesying early and total victory and proclaiming surrender terms for the enemy almost before the first battle had been joined. Indeed, a memorandum which Erzberger presented to the German Government (as *rapporteur* of the Reichstag's Military Affairs Committee) when the war was less than a month old, reads almost like the blue-print Adolf Hitler was to draw up for his Thousand Year Reich a generation later. Victory, Erzberger wrote, would establish Germany's dominance over Europe 'for all time'. Some of her neighbours, like Poland and the Baltic states, were to be incorporated outright into the German empire. Others, like Belgium and northern France, would be held under permanent military occupation. England's 'intolerable hegemony' was to be ended, though her colonies, unlike those of France and Belgium, were not to be seized – another precursor of the Hitlerian scenario which saw Germany running the European continent and an acquiescent England contented with ruling the world overseas.

Five months later Erzberger wrote this in a leading Berlin newspaper:

> 'The greatest ruthlessness in war is ... the greatest humanity. If one could destroy the whole of London, that is more humane than to allow one fellow-countryman to bleed to death on the battlefield, because such a radical cure most speedily leads to peace ...'

That was written after the great German offensive, which was supposed to end the war in a matter of weeks, had first faltered and then frozen into the rigid mould of trench warfare, and Erzberger's final words reflect the deadlock. In the years that followed he changed colour more and more, to match the increasingly sombre military scene, and also changed shape, as the eagle became a dove. From 1916 onwards the frock-coated figure of this coarse, dumpy, fidgety little Swabian ('Why, he looks like an ornamental beer-cork!' exclaimed a Hungarian countess after meeting him) was to be found wherever there was talk of peace or moves for peace – in The Hague, at the Vatican, in Switzerland, and, above all, in Vienna at the court of the young 'Peace Emperor', Charles. If his political opponents, and even some of his colleagues, questioned his motives, the people at large cared little whether he was an opportunist, an idealist, or just a plain realist. By the autumn of 1918 he had become the symbol of what they were all yearning for; hence that shout from the gun battery of the *Thüringen*.

Yet on 6 November, when the peace he had been labouring for was within grasp, Erzberger proved to be neither an automatic choice for the task, much less a willing one. At first it was assumed that General von Gundell, the infantry officer who had presided over the Armistice Commission ever since its formation in early October, would also preside over the actual surrender. But even before President Wilson's final note arrived in Berlin Prince Max's colleagues – and especially the Social Democrats – had begun to press for a civilian to be put in charge. They needed to demonstrate to Washington that it really was the new democratic government in Berlin and not the old Junker caste, exemplified by the Supreme Command in Spa, which was in charge of Germany's destiny. They needed also to symbolize the fact that, thanks to the character of those exchanges between Prince Max and the White House, the armistice had become more a political act than a military capitulation. Finally there was the fear that, if any general were given plenipotentiary powers, he might use them to delay negotiations, or even break the contacts off. For their part the Supreme Command were, by then, glad to slide out of the entire business, as General Groener's comment showed: 'I could only welcome it if the army and the army command remained as little involved as possible with these unfortunate negotiations, from which nothing good was to be expected.'

It was Groener who, in a talk in the Chancellery garden, persuaded Prince Max to pick Erzberger for the unenviable job, rather than the other suitable civilian candidate, State Secretary Haussmann.* According to the general, the Centre Party leader turned 'pale with shock' when he heard he had been chosen. But, bustling as ever, he lost no time. Erzberger left for Spa together with his sponsor that same afternoon, having received full powers signed in blank by the Chancellor just as their special train was pulling out of the station. Never in history, said the breathless messenger who brought him the document, had such an instrument been drawn up. Never in history, Erzberger replied, had there been such an end to such a war. The experience ahead of him was to bear that verdict out.

They arrived at Spa at 8 a.m. on the 7th, having halted at Hanover to send a radio message to Marshal Foch at Senlis,

---

* Konrad Haussmann, also a Swabian, was a founder of the so-called 'Progressive Peoples Party' in the Reichstag. His attempts to bury the hatchet with France dated from before the war when he had organized meetings of German and French parliamentarians. Ever since 1914 he had campaigned for the autonomy of Alsace-Lorraine and for the so-called 'peace of reconciliation'.

advising him that the German armistice delegation was already on its way. From his carriage Groener had seen groups of sailors hanging around the station in an unfriendly fashion and, though they made no attempt to approach the train, the mere sight of those undisciplined bands was depressing enough. At Supreme Headquarters the party took on its final shape. General von Gundell's name was removed from the list altogether (on the advice of von Hintze, who was now in Spa as the permanent representative of the Foreign Office), thus formally installing Erzberger as first plenipotentiary. The political character of this strange delegation was reinforced by the inclusion of a career diplomat and close friend of Erzberger's, Count Oberndorff, who had recently held the hapless post of German Minister to renegade Bulgaria. The uniformed element was reduced to the two officers who had been working under von Gundell in the preparatory commission. That meant that the German Admiralty and High Seas Fleet were represented by a mere naval captain named Vanselow, while the spokesman for the mighty German army was one Major-General von Winterfeldt. Winterfeldt had the advantage of speaking fluent French, having served before the war as military attaché in Paris. He had the grave disadvantage, however, of possessing a father who, in 1870, had helped to draw up the terms for France's humiliating surrender at Sedan. As one of the British armistice delegates was later to comment: 'I wonder why they sent him.' Hindenburg came to wish the party good luck and, eyeing the somewhat unimpressive figure of Erzberger, observed that this was probably the first time in the annals of war that a military armistice was being concluded by civilians. The Field Marshal added, in another revealing comment from the Supreme Command, that he personally had no objection to the arrangement, given the fact that his headquarters 'no longer had responsibility for political directives'.

After lunch the delegates, accompanied only by an interpreter and a stenographer, set off in five staff cars – a mixture of high-backed saloons and open tourers, all emblazoned on their side panels with the imperial arms. The convoy got off to an ominous start. It had barely cleared the streets of Spa when the leading vehicle, with Erzberger and Oberndorff on board, failed to negotiate a curve and crashed against the side of a house; the car behind promptly ran into it, injuring nobody but knocking both vehicles out of commission. Rather than return ignominiously to head-quarters so soon for fresh transport, they all piled into the three remaining roadworthy cars and made their way slowly across the crowded roads of eastern Belgium towards the appointed rendez-vous with the French army at La Capelle.

As darkness fell a drizzling fog came down, adding to the ghostliness of this journey into history. They finally cleared their own lines near Trelon at 9.20 in the evening and as they moved off into No-Man's-Land, Erzberger hoisted two white flags the size of small tablecloths on poles fixed to the running boards and also got out the trumpet he had brought with him for this most tricky part of the operation. The last compatriot he spoke to before jolting forward into the unknown turned out to be a soldier from his native Swabia. The man was dumbfounded when Erzberger, now seated in the front car with only one other delegate, told him they were on their way to sign the armistice. 'What!' the reply came back in thick dialect, 'just the two of you are going to do that?' Erzberger must have been wondering about that himself.

After they had travelled a hundred and fifty yards – with a short warning blast on the trumpet accompanying almost every turn of the wheels – the first French soldiers loomed up out of the mist and guided the cars into the battered village of La Capelle. The French had only taken it that same afternoon, and had had no time to remove the usual disciplined forest of German military signs, simply hoisting the tricolour over the building still marked *Kommandantur*. Everything had been efficiently prepared, how-ever, for the arrival of the delegates, who were now transferred to five waiting French cars, one for each plenipotentiary, with a French liaison officer allotted to each vehicle. Erzberger's guide turned out to be Major de Bourbon-Busset, a French prince serving on the staff of General Debeney's First Army, into whose sector the armistice delegation had crossed. The prince proved a practical fellow, and he made himself immediately useful by explaining precisely how Marshal Foch pronounced his Breton name. (Erzberger, for all his diplomatic aspirations, spoke no

French, which, for the international society of the day, made him seem almost a barbarian.) After a plain supper – soup, salted meat and peas – taken *en route* in the presbytery at Homblières which served as Debeney's headquarters – they moved on through the night, heading for the railway line.

Though he and his colleagues had not been blindfolded nor humiliated in any way, Erzberger was by now exhausted and irritable. His stiff hat had been dented by the incessant jolting; he had lost his spectacles; and still nobody would tell him where they were bound. At last, at four o'clock in the morning, they pulled up outside the ruined shell of a railway station. Nothing else could be seen.

'Where are we?' Erzberger asked his guide.
'At Tergnier.'
'But there are no houses.'
'True,' the prince replied reflectively, 'but there was once a town here.'

They left their cars and picked their way across the rubble to the special train which was waiting to carry them on the last stage of their journey. As a means of transport it was in marked contrast in comfort to anything the delegates had experienced since leaving Spa in another world fourteen long hours before. Hooked up behind the engine were a dining-car, a sleeping-car, and the saloon coach that had once belonged to the Emperor Napoleon III, still resplendent in its green satin upholstery and emblazoned with his monogram of initial and crown. As they boarded for a welcome glass of brandy a company of riflemen presented arms on the torch-lit platform. The French were not forgetting their manners in that night of triumph.

Three hours later, at 7 a.m. on 8 November, the train halted. Peering through the carriage curtains, which up till now had been kept firmly drawn, the Germans at first saw nothing but a marshy clearing between belts of bare autumn trees dripping with rain. Then, through the dawn mist, they made out another train, stationed on a parallel stretch of track about a hundred yards away. But where were they? It was not until Erzberger, like a good

347

Catholic, asked where he could hear Mass, that the sleeping-car attendant, who had been denying all knowledge of the neighbourhood, provided a vital clue. That would hardly be possible, the man replied, because Marshal Foch had already gone to the church at Réthondes and the priest would only be holding one service. That confirmed Erzberger's calculations. The armistice was to be signed in the forest of Compiègne.

Senlis, the headquarters of the Commander-in-Chief, would have been the normal *venue* for the ceremony of German surrender. But Foch had ruled against it on several grounds. To begin with it was both too close to the capital and too widely-known. Floods of sightseers and journalists would have descended on the place, rendering security difficult and tranquillity impossible. Moreover Senlis had suffered cruelly after its capture in 1914 by the Germans, who had shot the mayor and several other citizens as hostages. Ugly demonstrations might therefore be expected if the representatives of that conquering army were to appear in the town now as humbled spokesmen for the vanquished. Those objections were obvious enough. But there was another reason for choosing instead a remote forest glade which Foch probably did not mention to his staff, and that was his own sense of personal grandeur which subordinates had watched swelling up inside him as victory had followed victory during the heady weeks of late summer and early autumn. One of his leading generals, for example, had written this bitter comment in his diary during the great Allied advance:

> 'Pétain and the Army Group commanders are dropping out of the war reports and there remains only Foch ... This is not happening by chance. This man manipulates the press very well. He wants to raise up himself alone.'

The final triumph was now at hand and Foch wanted to savour that rendezvous of his with destiny as far as possible alone, like a lion dragging off its prey to its secret lair, there to be devoured in isolation.

Had it not been for the seas which lapped around the battle-fields he, as the Supreme Commander of all the Allied armies, might well have had the forest of Compiègne all to himself – as indeed he has it in the restored armistice site today, where his statue, with just the four letters of his name carved on the base, dominates the glade, unchallenged by any monument to, or even mention of, another commander or army.

But, in 1918, England's Royal Navy spoke with a voice that was even more authoritative than that of Marshal Foch, as well as being far more venerable. So, though no American, Italian or Belgian representatives were included (a fact which surprised the Germans), two British admirals had, as a matter of course, made the journey with Foch to Compiègne; the First Sea Lord, Admiral Wemyss, and his deputy, George Hope. Together with General Weygand, the Marshal's Chief-of-Staff, they made up the small party of victors, a notable contrast in rank and importance to the delegation of the vanquished. Foch, Erzberger and Weygand have all given their much-quoted accounts of the first encounter between the two sides. A less familiar version is provided in a letter, only recently published, which the then Rear-Admiral Hope wrote to his wife on that Friday 8 November, headed 'A train in Compiègne Forest':

'The Bosches [*sic*] ought to have arrived at midnight but only got here at 7 a.m. in a train similar to ours, which pulled up on a siding about 100 yards away.* As soon as they arrived Weygand went to their train and intimated that, if they wished to see the Marshal, he would be disposed to receive them in his train at 9 a.m. exactly. The party consists of four plenipotentaries and two officer interpreters ... The Bosches evidently wish to make it principally a civilian affair, and the French and we are very angry with them for only sending military and naval officers of a rather subordinate rank.

At 9 a.m. the party approached us in single file and got into the conference carriage where, with the exception of Foch and Wemyss, who remained in the Marshal's saloon, we received them stiffly but courteously. The Bosches

---

* The two parallel sidings were in fact spurs of track intended for long-range railway guns.

looked most uncomfortable and rather nervous. Weygand then said he would announce their arrival to the Marshal and went to fetch him. Foch and Wemyss then entered and exchanged salutes and we lined up on each side of the table.

'Foch then asked the reason for their visit and they said they had come to hear the Allies' propositions for the creation of an Armistice. The Marshal then said he had no propositions to make so Oberndorff read an extract from President Wilson's last despatch. That would not do for Foch and he asked them definitely to state if they had come to ask for an armistice. On their saying such was the case, Foch asked for their credentials and he and Wemyss retired to examine them . . . Erzberger was very nervous at first and spoke with some difficulty, the general awfully sad, the diplomat very much on the alert, and the naval officer sullen and morose . . .'

The nervousness, sadness and sullenness steadily increased when – the credentials accepted and formal introductions completed – the Allied armistice terms were read out across the table. There was dead silence in the railway carriage but for Weygand's voice going through the long schedule of the thirty-four clauses, in French. Wemyss toyed with his monocle as the list was read out; Foch sat as still as a statue except when he moved up his hand to give an occasional brisk tug on his moustache; tears began to trickle down the cheeks of the emotional Captain Vanselow. The only genuine bystander at this stage was Erzberger himself. As he 'did not have the French', he was unaware of Germany's precise fate until the translation which followed.

It was Clause Five which had worked most on the tear-ducts of Captain Vanselow; not surprisingly, since it put the enemy on the soil of the fatherland. Allied garrisons were to be established at the principal crossings of the Rhine* (Mainz, Coblenz and Cologne)

* The Allies, and especially the French, had long ago determined on the need for this. Foch, talking of how victory should be used, had once said to a friend: 'This time, we must go to the limit . . . We must go as far as the Rhine, otherwise our young generation will have to start this business all over again.'

350

and, to protect them, military bridgeheads were to be set up at all three points extending to a radius of thirty kilometres from the right bank. Away from the bridgeheads, a neutral zone ten kilometres wide was to run all the way down the river from the Dutch to the Swiss frontiers. All German districts on the left bank of the Rhine were to be evacuated completely and placed under Allied military government.

That was one of two issues which had led to sharp differences in the Allied camp when the armistice terms were being hammered out by the Supreme War Council in Paris the week before. Pershing, his vast American army increasing by tens of thousands almost every day, yet still with no spectacular strategic victory to call his own (St Mihiel had been a promenade; the Hindenburg Line a slow and costly slog), would have been quite happy to fight on and, accordingly, was demanding almost unlimited conditions of surrender. But the real argument, in practical terms, had been between the British and the French. Haig, arguing yet again for caution and moderation, questioned the need for bridgeheads, or indeed any advance beyond the left bank of the Rhine. Pétain, on the other hand, had not only insisted that the river should be crossed but had proposed that a zone fifty kilometres wide should be occupied on the far side. It was only after much discussion that Lloyd George had agreed to the formula now presented to the Germans, which was a compromise leaning strongly on the side of severity.

The other lively argument in Paris had been over the naval clauses drafted by the British, who found themselves – with the boot on the other foot – being accused in turn of excessive harshness by the French. Just as Foch, the spokesman for the continental land power, was determined to crush the German army which, for decades, had menaced France's frontiers, so Vice-Admiral Wemyss, spokesman for the island empire, was resolved to break the threat of the German High Seas Fleet which challenged England's might on the oceans. Long disputes had resulted as to how many German ships should be surrendered and how humiliating the actual process of surrender should be, with Foch having to submit more than once to a lecture on the realities of naval power.

(Characteristically, Clemenceau had got the point more readily. 'There will be no place in the Society of Nations,' he had observed, 'for a country with thirty-two Dreadnoughts!')

The compromise, this time leaning heavily towards the British approach, was embodied in the Clauses 22 and 23 as now read out in the railway carriage. All German submarines in existence were to surrender at specified ports. Of the surface warships, six battle-cruisers, ten battleships, eight light cruisers and fifty destroyers were to be disarmed 'and thereafter interned in neutral ports, or, failing them, ports to be designated by the Allies'. That was the wretched fate which Admiral Hipper's 'death cruise' had been intended to pre-empt. The new High Seas Fleet, in some ways an even more remarkable proof of Wilhelmenian virility than the traditional German army, was to be castrated by the enemy in public.*

Compared with the unpleasant shock of the Rhine bridgeheads and the dismantling of the fleet, the military and general clauses of the text must have been roughly what the German delegates expected.† It was obvious that all occupied territories would have to be evacuated and all inhabitants repatriated. Inevitably too, large quantities of war material, transport, and rolling stock would have to be handed over (though the exact figures were perhaps arguable). Even the financial clause requiring 'reparation for damage done' was not unexpected and may, at first hearing, have sounded encouragingly vague to the Germans. As for the time-table, once the conditions had been accepted and the instrument had been signed, all hostilities on land and in the air would cease six hours afterwards, and the struggle would be ended. However, in the brief discussion which followed the reading of the clauses, Foch laid down a strict limit for acceptance. The longest he was prepared to wait for the armistice to come into force was 11 a.m. on the following Monday. That meant that, at the latest, the actual signing would have to take place before dawn of that same day. As it was

---

* At the Scottish base of Scapa Flow, where the doomed ships were eventually directed, the German caretaker crews on board managed to avoid this humiliation by scuttling their own fleet.

† For complete text, *see* Appendix. D.

now nearly 10 a.m. on 8 November the German delegates were thus left with little more than sixty hours to haggle as best they could in Compiègne and get the final results approved both at Spa and in Berlin. Erzberger's first problem, as he walked back across the duck-boards to the German train, was, therefore, one of communication.

He had brought no cyphers with him and, in any case, the encoding and decoding of such a long text would have eaten up too many valuable hours. Foch had offered him a radio link, both to the German Chancellery and to German Supreme Headquarters, but had forbidden the armistice terms themselves to be transmitted in clear. There was nothing for it but to send the text by hand back along the tortuous rail and road route to Spa. Though Erzberger had failed to get any general suspension of hostilities while the discussions were in progress (Foch, rather surprisingly, had asked Clemenceau in Paris for a ruling on this), the cease-fire was to remain in force along the French First Army's corridor to the German lines. At one o'clock, three hours after the morning meeting had ended, Captain von Helldorf, the officer-interpreter of the German delegation, started back along that corridor by car with the armistice text in his brief-case. He also bore a verbal message to Hindenburg from Erzberger that it seemed hopeless to expect any concessions of principle or substance out of Foch and that the most the German delegation might secure at Compiègne were mitigations in detail such as reductions in the deliveries of war material demanded.

While Helldorf was on his way (being held up for an infuriating five hours outside his own lines by German troops who, for some reason or other, continued, despite the cease-fire, to 'fire like the devil') Erzberger's colleagues doggedly pursued these mitigations all that afternoon in a series of separate technical discussions with General Weygand and Admiral Hope. It was hard going, but Erzberger was sufficiently emboldened (despite what he had told Hindenburg) to include a request for the suppression of the Rhine bridgeheads and the immediate lifting of the Allied naval blockade in his counter-proposals. Those were drawn up and formally presented to Marshal Foch on the morning of Saturday

9 November. There was nothing for the German delgation to do now but wait.

Early that evening a French captain approached the German train bearing a written message for Erzberger. It turned out to be something very different from the expected Allied reply, and far more startling than anything even Foch could have devised. Erzberger found himself staring at a telegram from Prince Max announcing that, earlier on that same Saturday, the Emperor William had abdicated and the Crown Prince had renounced the throne after him. While Erzberger had been engaged at Compiègne in affairs of seemingly unparallelled significance, events in the fatherland itself had turned 9 November 1918 into the most momentous and dramatic day of German history.

It was on Friday 8 November, that the political torrent sweeping the Wilhelminian Empire to destruction turned into a maelstrom which nothing and nobody could withstand. What Prince Max had called 'the Northern Front' of rebellion now spreading to all points of the German compass as Brunswick, Stuttgart, Cologne and Munich all fell in the hands of 'Workers and Soldiers Councils'. The revolution was simply extemporizing, and not unfolding to any co-ordinated plan. There was a great deal of shooting, but hardly any fighting; a great deal of rhetoric but hardly any thinking. Mob leaders popped up from nowhere and most of them, like the sailor Artelt who had found himself in charge of Kiel the previous weekend, sank back into obscurity as rapidly as they leapt into prominence. What, until a few months before, had been the greatest and most disciplined military power on earth was being blown away in shreds like a dandelion's head by those with the strongest lungs. Nonentities those wreckers may have been, with few exceptions. But behind them was the elemental force of a nation determined on peace at almost any cost, and sick at heart with an old order which was associated now only with suffering and defeat. Equally important, in front of them was a vacuum, for that old order had also lost faith in itself, with its leader to all intents and purposes a refugee already, skulking with his generals in a Belgian watering-place.

The triumph of mob-rule in Munich was by far the gravest of

all these blows to the dying empire: not only because it concerned the capital of the Bavarian kingdom which ranked second only to Prussia in the imperial order; not only because it brought about the first abdication and flight of a German sovereign; but above all for the grotesque ease with which King Ludwig III, the last of the thousand-year line of Wittelsbachs, was sent packing by his subjects. To add insult to injury his own ministers had unwittingly helped in the process. Kurt Eisner, the Socialist journalist and writer* mainly responsible for the coup, was a Galician Jew who had only drifted to Munich in October, more or less invited there by the Bavarian Cabinet which had secured his release from a Leipzig prison in the strange belief that he would act as a calming influence on the Munich population. Eisner's true influence was shown on the morning of 8 November when he turned an open-air Socialist meeting held on the famous Theresienwicse into a mass demonstration to proclaim the 'Democratic and Socialist Republic of Bavaria', with himself as its first Prime Minister, despite the fact that he had not a drop of Bavarian blood in him. With a deed to match his own, silly-sounding name, the outgoing Prime Minister, Otto von Dandl had thus appointed his own political executioner, as well as that of his sovereign.†

The novelist Thomas Mann, then living in Munich, wrote in his diary that evening:

> 'Several shops plundered ... the women take a fur coat store by storm. The barracks empty, the soldiers sell their arms and equipment and go home ... Munich, like Bavaria, is ruled by Jews from the literary world. How long will it take that lying down?'

In what was still the capital of what was still an empire the *Berliner Tageblatt* of 8 November had pointedly drawn attention to the fact that the Emperor was lingering on at Spa and 'seems to be in no hurry to return to Berlin'. The paper demanded his immediate

* He was a former editor of the Socialist newspaper *Vorwärts* and his books included one on Nietzsche and another (prophetically) entitled *The End of the Empire*.
† It is worth recalling that the egregious von Dandl came out much the better in the end. He survived the débâcle to become President of the Finance Offices of Würzburg and then Munich itself from 1919 to 1933. Eisner was murdered in the streets of the city in February 1919.

return to the capital. Prince Max had already given up that hope. Indeed, in the light of the news from Munich and other key cities, the Chancellor was now determined not so much to urge the Emperor's return to the hub of events as to remove him from the political scene altogether. Earlier in the week he had fought off an ultimatum from the two Socialist leaders, Ebert and Scheidemann, for the Kaiser's abdication to be announced by noon on this same Friday; only his own threat to resign had held the decision up. But now there was no baulking the issue if Ebert and his moderate Socialists were to prevail over the extremists and if William II were to have any empire left to renounce. Prince Max drew up a formula intended to achieve both ends and told the head of his Chancellery staff, Arnold Wahnschaffe, to read it over the telephone to Spa. The essence of the plan was that the Emperor should immediately declare his 'firm resolve' to abdicate, leaving a final decision on the future political form of Germany to a newly-elected Constitutional Assembly. Until that decision was taken, a 'representative' nominated by the Emperor would deputize for him. In this way, Prince Max pointed out, the crown would not be capitulating to any Socialist ultimatum; the awkward problem of a Regency for the Crown Prince would be side-stepped; and, in any coming elections, 'monarchical sentiments would have the advantage over republican ones'.

That was simply whistling in the dark; indeed, the entire scheme, given the brutal facts of the situation, was but a legalistic fantasy. Perhaps, therefore, it was just as well for the Chancellor that the Emperor and his entourage brushed it aside. Within three hours a contemptuous answer came back from Spa that the proposals had been 'totally rejected'. At eight o'clock that evening (with the news resounding in his ears that, meanwhile, ten more major German cities had 'gone red') Prince Max resolved to make a fresh appeal himself to the Emperor over the telephone. Sheer desperation swept aside all formality. The heir to the Grand Duchy of Baden now spoke to his sovereign not as a Chancellor but as a fellow German prince and as a relative, pleading for the rescue of whatever remnants could be saved from the shipwreck of that old imperial order to which they both belonged. The familiar *Du* replaced the baroque humility of court language, with its plural, indirect style of address.*

'Your abdication has become necessary if civil war in Germany is to be avoided ... The great majority of the people believe that you are to blame for the present situation. This is a false belief, but it exists ... Today I can no longer hold my protecting hand before the wearer of the crown, now that the Social Democrats have made their ultimatum ... The demand contained in that ultimatum is echoed today in far wider circles ... The attitude of the troops cannot be relied on ... We are heading straight for civil war ...

'There are two possibilities. First, abdication, nomination of a deputy and the summoning of a National Assembly. Second, abdication, renunciation of the succession by the Crown Prince and a Regency for his son. Whichever course is chosen, it must be acted on with the utmost speed ... This is the final hour ... If abdication does not follow today, then I can no longer carry on, nor can the German princes protect their Emperor any further ...

'Such is the dreadful situation which forces us to speak out without glossing over anything. I hear people have been telling you that I am intriguing against you. That is a lie, as any one of my colleagues can prove. Had I not shielded you, the question would have become acute a week ago ... A voluntary sacrifice must now be made if your good name is to be preserved in history ...'

Never had the Supreme War Lord heard such blunt language. One cannot help thinking that it might have been far better had Prince Max used it the week before instead of indulging in his shielding operation. To reinforce his words now he dispatched a telegram – this time in full ceremonial style – listing the German princes who had already renounced their thrones, and warning the Emperor

---

* The full text of Prince Max's telephoned appeal was preserved, for the Chancellor had told his personal aide, Wilhelm von Prittwitz, to listen in and take down in shorthand everything he said.

that, unless he followed suit, his empire would be paralysed – without a Chancellor, without a Cabinet and without a majority in Parliament. The Foreign Secretary, Wilhelm Solf, followed this up with a telegram of his own to Spa, telling the Emperor that, unless he abdicated at once, the Socialists would quit the Government and 'then there remains only a military dictatorship'.

Neither the telephone call nor the telegrams seemed to make the slightest dent in the wall of resistance at Spa. The written messages were left unacknowledged. As for Prince Max's appeal, that had been swept airily aside by the Emperor, who informed his cousin that he was resolved not to yield. The Emperor then remarked ominously down the telephone that he intended 'to restore order in the country himself, at the head of his troops'. The necessary instructions for this 'had already been issued'. At the time, the Chancellor, absorbed with his dual problem of keeping the moderate Socialists in his Cabinet and keeping the extremists off the streets of the capital, seems not to have grasped the significance of those words. In fact, that day at Spa, the Emperor tried to embark on his last venture as Germany's Supreme War Lord, a venture more vainglorious than ever, and this time attended with the direst consequences.

The idea for it seems to have taken final shape during the walk in the grounds of the Villa Fraineuse which he took every day after breakfast with Major Niemann. As they paced up and down in the mist under the bare, dripping trees of the park, the Emperor talked ceaselessly to his aide of the 'rising flood of bolshevism'. It had, in his eyes, already engulfed Austria-Hungary, and now threatened, not just Germany, but the whole of Europe. 'It is my sacred duty,' he exclaimed, 'to build a dam against this madness.' And when Niemann commented that the army - the only stuff from which such a dam could be built – would itself be cut off from the homeland if the revolution spread along the Rhineland, his sovereign replied: 'Swift military action can master that·difficulty.'*

---

* In an agitated letter of 8 November to his wife, left behind in Potsdam, the Emperor developed the same theme: 'The people have all gone insane! . . . God be with you and us. I am gathering together all the troops from the front so as to march on Berlin with them . . . Our sons must protect you until we can come to your aid from here . . .'

And so it was that, a few minutes later, at the morning conference in the so-called 'Garden Room' of the villa (where Groener presented the gloomiest of reports, both on his Berlin visit and on the military position) the Emperor produced his bombshell. He proposed, he told his generals, to place himself at the head of his army on the Western Front, turn it around, take the rebellious Rhineland cities by storm and then march on the capital to restore order. The First Quartermaster-General was instructed to draw up plans straightaway for the operation.

His military chiefs dispersed, too flabbergasted and also probably too embarrassed to make any comment in front of this sovereign who, after four years of playing at war with the enemy, was now trying to wage it in earnest against his own people. But that evening, when they met for an hour together by themselves to discuss the plan,* they ruled it out, almost unanimously, as totally impracticable. Groener, with his unemotional recital of facts and figures, presented the unanswerable case against it: how was it feasible to detach and bring together the so-called reliable units from a battlefield stretching all the way from the Channel to the Swiss border and then march them eastwards three hundred and fifty miles through rebellious lines of communication to Berlin? Even if the front-line troops were willing to undertake such a mission (which he doubted) the problems of supply and transport would alone render it impossible. Hindenburg, who was sinking more and more into the role of an anguished but passive spectator of the tragedy, gave his reluctant agreement. Only Count Friedrich Schulenburg, Chief-of-Staff of the Crown Prince's Army Group and the seventy-seven-year-old General Hans von Plessen, who had served as the Emperor's principal adjutant ever since 1892, dissented. Surely, the latter pleaded, it should not be impossible for the Emperor and his army to control 'a handful of revolutionaries?' That last phrase was enough to show his colleagues that the white-haired courtier, for whom unquestioning loyalty to the throne had

---

* It was a measure of the Emperor's real authority at Spa that though he had ordered, at midday, plans to be drawn up immediately, the idea was not even discussed until 9.30 that evening.

long since become a Pavlovian reflex, was out of touch with both the mood and the dictates of the hour.

Just how far out of touch was to be demonstrated at 9 a.m. the following morning, when thirty-nine weary and travel-stained officers gathered in the large dining-room of the Hotel Britannique for what was surely the most extraordinary meeting that even Supreme Headquarters – the scene of so many dramatic conferences – had ever witnessed. These men were all fighting officers, Commanders of regiments or divisions in the three central Army Groups* and they had been ordered to Spa the previous day by Groener to give a front-line verdict on their Supreme War Lord's latest plan. Of this they had, as yet, no inkling. Indeed, cut off as they were at the front from up-to-date news (there had hardly been any deliveries of mail or newspapers in their Army Groups since the beginning of the month) they lived mainly on rumours, and the most persistent rumours of late had been of an imminent armistice. This, they presumed, was what they had been brought here to discuss – some of them having travelled more than two hundred miles in open cars through the night. They were frozen, unwashed, unshaven and also unfed. Almost as though he had wanted to have them questioned at their lowest level of vitality, the First Quartermaster-General had not even provided breakfast for his visitors – a lapse which, as he later admitted, was to be somewhat on his conscience.

On that Saturday morning in Spa, however, Groener did not even appear before the exhausted guests. Instead, soon after nine, Hindenburg himself, accompanied by Colonel Wilhelm Heye, Chief of Army Operations, came into the dining-room to explain the real purpose of the meeting. For many of those thirty-nine officers, and especially the more junior ones recently promoted to command the decimated German regiments in the West, this was the first glimpse they had ever had of the hero of Tannenberg. And for junior and senior commanders alike, such was the awesome reputation of that legendary figure that, if he had only uttered a few

---

* Crown Prince Rupprecht, German Crown Prince and Gallwitz. In all, fifty had been summoned (five from each of the ten armies concerned) but eleven of them arrived too late for the meeting.

words of encouragement or guidance, it would have raised their spirits more than the most copious of breakfasts. But, after thanking them for all they had endured and achieved in the battle, the Field Marshal presented the situation in its starkest form. Revolution had broken out in the homeland and the demand for abdication had been made. The Emperor, for his part, was now proposing to take personal charge of his army and lead it back to Berlin to secure his throne; that journey would, however, have to be made on foot, as the railways could not be relied on, which would mean a march of two to three weeks, with skirmishes and supply problems all the way. At that, the Field Marshal took his leave and handed over to Colonel Heye, without even mentioning, let alone appealing to, the officers' sense of duty or loyalty.

That lack of any recommendation was itself recommendation enough, when it concerned this pillar of patriotism and most revered figure in German uniform. The response to the two questions which Colonel Heye then put to the front-line officers, perhaps predictable in any case, now became a foregone conclusion. To the first question – 'What is the attitude of the troops towards the Emperor; is it possible for him to reconquer the homeland by force at the head of his army?' – only one of the thirty-nine officers present (Major von Kretschmann, Adjutant of the 36th Infantry Division) gave an affirmative answer. Fifteen thought it 'more or less doubtful' whether the army would follow the Emperor, and the remaining twenty-three were quite certain it would not. Colonel Heye's second question was, 'What is the attitude of the troops towards bolshevism and would they actually take up their arms and fight against it in the homeland?' To this, eight replied with an emphatic 'No'; nineteen thought it was doubtful; and the rest felt that, for there to be any prospect of such a fight, a lengthy period of rest and indoctrination would be needed first (a verdict which, in the circumstances, amounted to rejection).

A few weeks before, the widely syndicated Dutch cartoonist Louis Raemakers had produced a drawing showing a cynically grinning German Kaiser being borne on his throne across a field of corpses by half-a-dozen wounded soldiers, their eyes bandaged. The caption was: 'They will go on carrying me as long as they are

blind!' On 9 November, in the dining-room of the Hotel Britannique at Spa, the Emperor's soldiers had appeared and acted
without the blindfolds. Their refusal to carry their sovereign any
further across the field of corpses was probably even more emphatic than anything Hindenburg or Groener had reckoned with. For
the Emperor it was a mortal blow, for it went far beyond the
rejection of that one hare-brained scheme of his. The unquestioning loyalty of each German (and, above all, each Prussian) officer to
the Supreme War Lord was based on a personal oath of allegiance
whose roots went right back to Teutonic mythology and its traditions of obedience to the tribal chieftain.* All that had now been
openly trampled in the dust in the War Lord's own headquarters.
Destroyed with it were the Emperor's fond hopes that Hindenburg
and Spa could give him the security that he had failed to find in
Prince Max and Berlin. It is hard to think of a crasser case of a man
being in the wrong place at the wrong time at a crucial moment in
history.

While his thirty-nine executioners had been reflecting on and
then pronouncing their verdicts in the Hotel Britannique, the
Emperor was passing another anguished morning at the Villa
Fraineuse, discussing the situation with members of his personal
staff and the Supreme Command, represented by Hindenburg and
Groener. The Field Marshal, who had clearly already written off
any real prospect for the dynasty's survival, began by ominously
informing his sovereign: 'What I have to tell Your Majesty I cannot
say without having first taken my leave.' But that thinly-disguised
offer of resignation was not accepted and the Field Marshal then
lapsed painfully again into silence. Groener, who was reluctant to
take over the task of 'enlightening the Kaiser' (a job, in his eyes, for
one of the Prussian generals of the entourage rather than for a mere
Swabian), confined himself to repeating all the military objections
to the Emperor's plan.

Soon afterwards the Prussians did indeed speak up, but with
unhappy consequences. Schulenberg, supported by Plessen,
argued that it ought surely to be possible to gather together some

* Adolf Hitler was to revive it with deadly effect in the *Führereid* which bound each
officer of his 'Thousand Year Reich' to follow him unquestioningly.

reliable army units and 'after giving them a few days' rest, lead them against the rebel cities of the Rhine'. He then threw in the idea that the Emperor might renounce only his imperial throne but stay King of Prussia and command the rescue operation as such. To a south German like Groener, such a notion simply meant that the threat of a republican civil war tearing Germany apart would be overtaken by the certainty of a dynastic one. When he saw that the notion was gaining some support, his patience snapped, and he uttered the fateful words:

> 'The army will march back into the homeland peacefully and properly under its own leaders and commanding generals but not under Your Majesty's orders, since it no longer stands behind Your Majesty.'

At last, the Chancellor, the Field Marshal, and all the Prussian aides and courtiers had found someone to do their job for them.

Describing the scene afterwards, one of those aides did his loyal best to preserve his master's image as a cardboard hero. 'The Emperor's eyes,' he wrote, 'flashed with anger, and his body stiffened.' But what mattered at this instant was not what the Emperor looked like, but what he did. Instead of throwing his newly-promoted First Quartermaster-General out of the villa for his treacherous presumption, the Supreme War Lord merely strode up to him and demanded confirmation of the statement in writing.

Around noon the Crown Prince (who had been summoned to Spa the night before by his father, and not by the Supreme Command) arrived at the Villa Fraineuse from the Hotel Britannique. He describes the picture he saw:

> 'In the middle of a group, the Emperor was standing in the garden. I shall never forget this scene of half-a-dozen people in their grey uniforms against the background of the late autumn flower-beds, withered and drained of colour. Apart from them, not a soul in sight and no sound disturbed the silence. All around only the rising circle of wooded hills, their pale colours of green, red-brown, yellow and red shining gloriously through a mantle of autumnal mist.

'The Emperor stood there as though he had just halted with the others from his agitated pacing up and down. He was talking to Groener and von Hintze, who were next to him, with vigorous, expressive gestures of his right hand. In between, his gaze sought out the aged General Plessen and the Field Marshal, who just nodded silently and gazed into the distance ... While the Emperor went on speaking by himself, the others listened, bowed and heavy-hearted, as though frozen into silence because they saw no way out. Catching sight of me, my father beckoned me over and moved a few steps forward to greet me. Only now, when I was facing him, could I see how distraught he looked and how his face, grown so sallow and emaciated, twitched and shook ...'

The Emperor then gave this weedy, dissolute son and heir of his a resumé of the seemingly hopeless situation, ending with the remark that if, as seemed likely, he would have to abdicate, he would hand over the supreme command to Hindenburg. The Crown Prince was more concerned over other dispositions. Surely, he asked his father, even if an abdication as Emperor was unavoidable, he would remain, come what may, King of Prussia? 'Naturally,' the firm reply came back.

It was, by then, anything but natural. Soon afterwards Colonel Heye appeared at the villa and delivered his report on the two questions he had put to the thirty-nine front-line officers and the way they had responded. Even after hearing the shattering news Count Schulenberg tried to keep a flicker of monarchist hope alive. Surely, he protested, the great majority of the troops, as he knew them at first hand, would not break their military oath and desert their Supreme War Lord in his hour of need? Once again, it was left to General Groener to dampen down any illusions. 'Oath of loyalty? War Lord?' he answered. 'Those are just words; they are no more than an idea, when it comes down to it.'

At that point von Hintze burst in with another message from Berlin. Prince Max had just been on the phone to him to say that the situation in the capital had now become so menacing that, unless the Emperor abdicated at once, there was no chance of saving the monarchy in any form. That Prince Max had got through on the telephone at all was something of an achievement. There were two lines installed to separate instruments in the Villa Fraineuse but, as he later complained, one appeared to have been taken off its hook altogether and the other was almost constantly engaged. Nonetheless, various messages had been exchanged earlier that morning between the Emperor's entourage in the Ardennes and the Chancellery in Berlin, which was under greater immediate pressure than Supreme Headquarters. At 9.15 von Hintze had got through to report that the Supreme Command were ruling out any idea of the armed forces fighting under the Emperor's orders in a civil war. That message, which seemed to point plainly to abdication, was passed to Ebert, with the plea that he should now call off the threatened left-wing demonstrations. 'Too late,' the Socialist leader replied, 'the die is cast. One factory has already taken to the streets.' (His colleague Scheidemann had placed his resignation in front of the Cabinet only a few minutes before this exchange, as he had been threatening to do since dawn unless the abdication were announced.)

Then, between ten and eleven, Prince Max had reported at length to Spa on the rapidly deteriorating security situation i the capital* and demanded an immediate decision on the dynasty, 'for it is now a question of minutes, not hours'. He had been fobbed off with assurances, first that the decision was 'about to be made'; then, that the Emperor had definitely decided upon abdication, but that the actual wording would not be ready for another half an hour. After those thirty minutes had expired without result and after all last-minute attempts to talk to the Emperor personally had failed, Prince Max – at the end of his tether both mentally and physically – took his sovereign's decision for him. Shortly before 1.30, as they were sitting down to a glum lunch in the Villa Fraineuse, the Chancellor had this message relayed to the streets of

* Though it had looked, at the beginning of the day, as though the three battalions of the Berlin garrison would be able and willing to maintain order, the situation was transformed when the most trusted of them, the Naumburger Jäger, went over *en bloc* to the demonstrators.

Berlin through the Bureau Wolff, the official German News Agency:

> 'The Emperor and King has decided to renounce his throne. The Chancellor will remain in office until all questions have been settled concerning the Emperor's abdication, the Crown Prince's renunciation of the imperial and Prussian thrones and the setting-up of a Regency. He intends to propose to the Regent that the Reichstag Deputy Ebert be appointed Chancellor and that a draft bill be drawn up calling for immediate general elections to a German constitutional National Assembly. This body would then be responsible for finally determining the future form of state for the German people ...'

About half an hour after this statement had been given out, von Hintze, still unaware of what had just happened in Berlin, came on the telephone from Spa to read the long-promised statement. In it, William II, 'in order to save further shedding of blood', agreed to abdicate as Emperor of Germany, but not as King of Prussia. Among the reasons he gave for holding on to this Prussian crown was that, were he to renounce it, 'most of the officers would fall away, and the army, left leaderless, would dissolve'. To the last, the Emperor was living out the legend of the Supreme War Lord which had lured him to Spa the week before – that, despite the demonstration he had just been given that the ordinary army officers in the field, Prussians included, had fallen away from him already. The Emperor's decision, impatiently awaited in Berlin for days, and pressed for continuously all that morning, was thus irrelevant by the time he had braced himself to make it. When one of the Chancellor's aides dismissed it as a 'constitutional nonsense', nobody tried to contradict him. And now, as the Chancellery had got von Hintze on the line, they read over to him the text of their own abdication communiqué which was about to make its way round the world. Prince Max came to the phone himself to assure the flabbergasted Hintze that the proclamation was indeed official. If the truth be told, it was another 'constitutional nonsense'; but, unlike the Emperor's, this one could take immediate political effect.

Prince Max freely admitted afterwards that he had no legal right to declare an abdication on his sovereign's behalf without the formal approval of that sovereign. As a German prince his moral responsibility for dethroning his emperor was even heavier. But by midday of 9 November in Berlin, law and morals had become the same as oaths of loyalty in Spa – mere words. Prince Max, the exhausted helmsman of a fast-sinking ship, had simply taken to the life-boats; and as he, thanks to his fugitive master, had been left in charge on the bridge, he could fairly claim that the decision when precisely to abandon ship belonged to him. He had still, after all, left the monarchist colours flying on the wreck, though he must have known in his heart that they would soon be hauled down.

At Spa the tragi-comedy reached its height as soon as the Wolff Bureau communiqué became known. Von Hintze evidently could not bring himself to be the messenger of doom. Instead, it was the Emperor's senior military adjutant, General von Gontard, who brought the text into the drawing-room of the villa 'breathing heavily, his teeth chattering as though in a cold sweat, and tears streaming down his cheeks', as one eye-witness wrote.

William II responded to this final crisis of his life as he had responded to all the others – with a blend of strong words and weak action, bombast combined with indecision. 'Treachery, monstrous and unashamed treachery!' he exploded, as the communiqué ending his reign was read out to him. Never, he declared, would he knuckle under to such betrayal. The Crown Prince must return immediately to his Army Group and announce this to his soldiers. Meanwhile, the Berlin announcement would be denounced – and the Emperor promptly sat down and 'covered one telegram form after another' with his proposed rebuttal.

The rebuttal, however, soon became a mere protest against the *fait accompli*. As for what was to happen next, it was the Supreme Command, and not the Supreme War Lord, who now decided that. At half past three the generals met in Hindenburg's apartment to review the new situation. There was no point, they agreed, in trying to force the government to go back on the published abdication; that would have necessitated the march on Berlin which had already been ruled out. That meant, quite bluntly, that they had an ex-Emperor on their hands to dispose of (though the polite formula used throughout for removing the encumbrance was 'to ensure His Majesty's safety'). Should it be Switzerland or Holland for the neutral asylum? Hindenburg preferred Holland. It was a monarchy and might, therefore, show more sympathy; moreover, the border was so much closer, with a direct rail link. The Emperor was ending up as a military movement order.

The whole party repaired to the Villa Fraineuse where, between four and five o'clock in the afternoon, the generals went in separately or together to present their views. Hindenburg, as always, was received with affection and respect and formally appointed Germany's Commander-in-Chief for the last forty-eight hours of the war. Groener, on the other hand, got short shrift. 'You are a Württemberg general,' his former sovereign snapped at him, 'and as I am no longer Emperor, I have nothing more to do with you.'

It was not until the early evening that the Emperor decided to fall in with the idea of seeking asylum in Holland. To the bitter end he went on behaving true to his special quality of Europe's imperial clown. Having agreed to go he could at first not go soon enough, and promptly dispatched mountains of baggage and most of the members of his suite to the imperial train. (This despite the fact that he had originally announced his intention of spending the night in the villa, ordering extra arms and ammunition to be brought there in case of 'bolshevik attacks'.) In the event William II spent his last night among German troops on his train in Spa station, receiving officers who sought to resign their commissions now that Germany was no longer imperial. He also penned his two last letters as Emperor to his family. To his wife, a bewildered and sick woman, helplessly watching the torrent of events engulfing her in the Potsdam palace, he wrote:

> 'If I am not allowed to stay among those who remain loyal, then I must go with you to a neutral state, Holland or elsewhere where a merciful haven may permit us to eat our bread – in exile. God's hand lies heavily upon us! His Will be done! So, on Hindenburg's advice, I am leaving the army, after fearful mental struggles ...'

The second letter, to his eldest son, reached an exhausted Crown Prince soon after he had regained his Army Group Headquarters at Vielsalm. It ran:

'My dear boy,
As the Field Marshal can no longer ensure my safety here and is not prepared to guarantee the dependability of the troops, I have decided, after a heavy inner struggle, to leave my disintegrated army. Berlin is totally lost in Socialist hands ... Until the army can march back into the homeland, I suggest that you stick it out at your post and hold the troops together. May we meet again, if it is God's will.
Your deeply bowed father,
William.'

The Crown Prince was given little chance to follow these last instructions. He was removed from his command only a few hours later.*

The Emperor's vacillations continued to the bitter end. By the time he sat down to dinner the idea of flight appeared to have been given up altogether. It was unheard of, he told his perplexed aides, to abandon the army like this. He would stay with his troops and stick it out to the last, even if it meant sacrificing his life. But a joint message from Hindenburg and Hintze sent to the train two hours later melted his new-found resolution in a trice by warning him that rebel troops were now marching on the Headquarters itself and that he must seek safety at once. The Emperor delayed another seven hours; then, at five o'clock in the morning of 10 November, he suddenly ordered the train to head for Holland without replying to Hindenburg's message. The first that the Field Marshal knew of the departure was when he was told after breakfast that the special siding at Spa station was now empty. His royal master had gone without even saying goodbye.

The Dutch Government had been warned the previous even-

---

* The Crown Prince followed his father's example by turning up at the Dutch Frontier on 12 November and asking for asylum. This was granted, but frostily, and he was assigned to a derelict parsonage on a bleak island of the Zuider Zee.

ing that the deposed ruler of Germany might be descending on them at any time; but when the imperial party reached the border at Eysden soon after dawn (having, for security reasons, transferred to motor-cars *en route*) no final decision over his reception had been made. The ex-Emperor was thus obliged to pace up and down Eysden station and wait in its guard-room until the afternoon when, the Cabinet having meanwhile met in The Hague to grant asylum, a deputation of ministers arrived to welcome him to Holland in Queen Wilhelmina's name. As he bade farewell for ever to German-occupied soil, still in Prussian uniform, he unbuckled his sword and handed it over. It was an appropriate exit from the world stage for the man who had brandished that sabre over Europe for the past thirty years.

Meanwhile, as their ex-sovereign was chaffing restlessly in the No-Man's-Land of Eysden, his former subjects were having their first weekend of republican rule. On the Saturday, almost at the same time as the Chancellor had issued his statement on the Emperor's abdication, Ebert had appeared in his office to present a formal demand that the Socialists should now take over the government. Prince Max was only too relieved to shed a burden he had never sought and one which had brought him the five most agonizing weeks of his life; five weeks, moreover, which were to agonize him throughout the rest of that life. But any faint hopes he still nurtured that, under the moderate and patriotic Ebert, the monarchy as such might be preserved in Germany, were dashed during the brief process of hand-over. When Ebert was asked by the Foreign Minister Solf whether he was prepared to operate within the constitution, and 'even within the monarchist constitution', the Socialist leader gave the evasive reply: 'Yesterday, I would have given an unconditional yes to that question. Today, I will first have to consult with my friends.' And when Prince Max intervened to say that surely the matter of a Regency had to be settled, there was a chorus of 'Too late, too late' from Ebert and his colleagues – a chorus which none of the others sought to challenge.

And so Germany received her first republican Chancellor – not appointed by any head of state because, by then, no such figure existed – but simply nominated on demand by his own predecessor. The republic itself was born in a similar vacuum of power. Scheidemann, the leader of the Independent Socialist faction, is credited with launching it by proclamation at two o'clock in the afternoon of 9 November from the steps of the Reichstag building. But he seems to have begun by merely shouting 'Long live the Republic', which had been the battle-cry of the left wing for weeks past, and events swept him on from there. Like that stoker-demagogue at Kiel, or Kurt Eisner on the Theresienwiese at Munich, all he had to do was to touch the tiller and the rudderless ship, already drifting his way, came willingly under his hand.

Ten days before, as anti-monarchist feeling was mounting throughout the country, some wags in the town of Duisburg had placed a soft civilian hat on the stone head of the town's statue of the Emperor and had wedged an overnight travelling bag between its stone hands. At the foot of the statue, they had daubed the words 'Pleasant Journey'. So it seemed during this first weekend of republican Berlin: William II might have been just another distinguished guest who had checked out of the Hotel Adlon rather than the last of a line of Prussian kings before which, for three centuries, all heels had clicked and all necks had bowed.

For the servants of that crown sheer disbelief almost outweighed horror as they watched the mob taking effortless control of the streets. Princess Blücher, for example (American-born and therefore doubly *ancien régime* after her marriage), wrote, 'more dead than alive', in her diary as night fell on 9 November:

> 'Through the dense masses of the moving crowds large military lorries made their way, packed with soldiers and sailors flourishing red flags, shouting wildly and clearly trying to provoke the strikers to violence. What struck me as characteristic of the whole thing were the cars crammed with young people ... who kept on jumping out to force officers and soldiers walking by to tear off their uniform badges – and did it for them if they refused ... The Hohenzollern dynasty has succumbed tragically.'

Indeed what stood out above everything else over that weekend was the sudden friendlessness of the Hohenzollern dynasty, once it had started to topple. The passivity of the Prussian officer corps, always so proud to worship a throne which had made them the unchallenged élite of German society, was most astonishing of all. As one of them said during the long post-mortem into the empire's collapse:

> 'I myself am one of those officers who, like all the rest, should not still be here today, if, on 9th November 1918, they had showed the conviction which their duty demanded of them, to defend the old order with their lives.'

In the event, only one officer is recorded as having made that sacrifice during this traumatic weekend in the capital – a captain of the Guards Fusiliers who refused to abandon his post and was shot by the insurgents. All those other peacocks from crack Prussian regiments who had once been so eager to fight duels if the honour of the monarchy were as much as questioned, were not now even prepared to resist as their epaulettes – the symbols of that monarchy as well as the feathers of their own plumage – were ripped off their shoulders in the streets. They cannot be accused of mass cowardice so much as mass demoralization. They had always followed blindly but the leader himself had now vanished. Where indeed was that ruler of whom Bismarck had written, in his famous letter of 5 January 1888, that he would 'rather fall on the steps of his throne, fighting for the rights with his sword in his hand, than yield'? Pacing the platform of Eysden railway station.

Ironically the most blatant public demonstration of loyalty to that absent monarch on the streets of Berlin had come from a civilian. On the afternoon of 9 November, as the crowds of workers were flooding down the broad Unter den Linden, shouting their republican slogans, a small, well-dressed gentleman kept pace with them on the pavement, and was observed to lift his black top hat at regular intervals, crying out as he did so, 'Long live the Emperor!' His name was Professor Schiemann and he was not even a German, but a Balt.

Everything about England, the land of his own mother, always fascinated William II, for he had an uncomfortable feeling that the

English probably understood him better than his own subjects. He would therefore have been interested to have known that the most sympathetic summing up of his situation at this terrible time had come from a fifteen-year-old English schoolgirl, who wrote in her diary for that week:

> 'They say Germany is in revolution and that the Kaiser and Crown Prince ... have run away ... They are cads about the Kaiser. They worshipped him while they were winning, and now they are beaten they pretend it is all his fault ...'

On a more elevated plane this was how the Emperor Charles reacted in Vienna to the news of his fellow emperor's flight, as recalled many years later by the Empress Zita:

> 'The Emperor Charles was not surprised at the news, including the choice of Holland, though, to put it mildly, it wasn't considered exactly an inspiring example. But as we always knew that he was under the thumbs of his generals this, after all, seemed the natural end. They had just packed him off. Even in this, he was typical!'

For better or for worse, however, the Emperor was gone; so was the dynasty; and so was Prince Max, whose last act after handing over office on the Saturday had been to decline Ebert's offer to stay on himself as a sort of Regent, in order to provide some semblance of political continuity. Ebert's prime task on the Sunday, therefore, was to supply the legitimacy for himself. So far, he had merely, in the words of his own proclamation appealing for support, been 'entrusted with the responsibilities of Chancellor' by his imperial predecessor, 'with the approval of all the State Secretaries'. What he needed now was a Cabinet. It would have to include the left-wing Independent Socialists, but if Germany was not to slide into anarchy, it would have to keep out if possible the extremist Spartacus group (led by the Communists Rosa Luxembourg and Karl Liebknecht) who were trying to ride into power on the backs of the Soviet-style workers' and soldiers' councils. The issue was decided that afternoon in the incongruous setting of a Berlin circus, the Zirkus Busch, where delegates from all interested groups had been summoned. For once, moderation triumphed over demagogy. After a tense debate Ebert's proposal for a bi-socialist government, to be formed only by his own majority group and Scheidemann's Independents, was carried. The Republic had moved off the streets into the council chambers.

One person had almost been forgotten in all the excitement of the abdication, Prince Max's resignation and the struggle to instal a new political entity in the capital – Matthias Erzberger, sitting glumly in his train in the forest of Compiègne and awaiting instructions from whoever was there to issue them in Berlin. That could only be Ebert, and, in the early afternoon of 10 November, despite the fact that he still had no properly constituted Cabinet, the new Chancellor summoned his own party colleagues and some members of Prince Max's outgoing government to hear the full text of the armistice conditions as relayed by Erzberger, read out to them. Accompanying the text was a telegram from Supreme Headquarters at Spa urging that the Allied terms should be agreed 'immediately and without modification'. Ebert and his harassed little gathering in the Chancellery needed no urging. With the exception of General Scheuch, who was still functioning as War Minister despite Socialist attempts to replace him, they were all civilians, and he too recommended that they bow to the inevitable. After a brief discussion, a historic message of one sentence was radioed direct to Erzberger:

> 'The German Government accepts the armistice conditions put forward on 9 November.'

The stage was thus set for the day which was to end the greatest war which man had known.

11 November 1918

HISTORY BEGAN TO BE MADE soon after midnight on this long day, and the first of its many arenas was the forest clearing in Compiègne. By then, Erzberger, waiting impatiently in his train, had received two telegrams, dispatched from Berlin and Spa* the previous afternoon, authorizing him to conclude the armistice. One message concluded with a four-figure group, 3084, which had been pre-agreed as a mark of authenticity. The other signed itself off with the word 'Schluss', signifying in German simply that the message was finished. The French interpreter, puzzled, asked Erzberger whether that was the name of the man just appointed as German Chancellor. He cannot have been a very good interpreter; for that matter, Herr Ebert cannot have been very well known outside his own country.

In addition Erzberger had received from his new Chancellor a plea to do something about securing emergency food supplies for Germany, while from Hindenburg had come a long coded telegram listing nine other alleviations he should try to achieve. Several of the Field Marshal's points had already been raised by the German delegates, either in formal counter-proposals or informal conversations. But the Field Marshal's last instruction was both novel and dear to Erzberger's theatrical heart. If satisfaction was refused, the message from Spa had ended, a 'fiery protest' should be delivered. Erzberger and his colleagues spent most of the two hours after midnight drafting this protest and then, at 2.05 a.m., sent word across that they were now ready. Ten minutes later, they were all in their places again in the Wagon-Lits Company's carriage 2419D

---

* Supreme Headquarters had dispatched a message of its own, urging Erzberger to try for better terms before signing.

which served as the office of the Allied train.*

That final session lasted nearly three hours. Considering he held the poorest of hands without a single trump card, Erzberger did not do too badly. In the clauses covering war material, he got the number of machine guns to be handed over cut from thirty thousand to twenty-five thousand; the airplanes reduced from two thousand to seventeen hundred; the lorries from ten thousand over fifteen days to five thousand in thirty-six days and so on. His colleague, the naval delegate, did not fare so well with Admiral Wemyss when it came to arguing the fate of the High Seas Fleet. The only German surface ship on the surrender list that England relinquished her claim on was the *Mackensen*, for the good reason that it was found to be no longer in service. As regards the dreaded German submarines, the British Admiralty got what it had always been after, namely, the lot. Wemyss had originally demanded a hundred and sixty, having backed down, at his own Prime Minister's insistence, from demanding the entire force. To his surprise and delight Vanselow now informed him that 'there were not nearly a hundred and sixty to be had' – at which Wemyss promptly inserted the words 'all submarines' into the text.

Throughout, Captain Vanselow seems to have been considerably more affected than effective. He certainly got on the nerves of the British Admirals, one of whom wrote loftily:

'Vanselow showed a captiousness which was tiresome and quite unavailing. He made the remark: was it admissible that their fleet should be interned, seeing that they had not

---

* This carriage was to have a bizarre history. For a while after the war it was allowed to revert to its humble role as an ordinary dining-car on the French railways. The government then made amends by withdrawing it from service and installing it in the courtyard of the Invalides in Paris, where it was intended to remain as a permanent monument to victory. However, in the summer of 1940, after the German occupation of Paris, the carriage was brought back again to the forest of Compiègne where, on the exact spot it had rested twenty-two years before, Hitler's armistice terms were read out in it to the vanquished French. Carriage 2419D was then moved as a trophy to the German Chancellery in Berlin, where it was meant to stay for the life of the 'Thousand-Year Reich'. It was destroyed during Allied bombing raids in 1943. The present carriage at Compiègne is a duplicate.

been beaten? – the reply to this was obvious and it gave me a certain amount of pleasure to observe that they only had to come out!'

Count Oberndorff got the same short shrift when, perhaps rashly, he questioned the humanity of the Allied blockade and used the English word 'fair'.

'Not fair!' exploded Wemyss. 'Remember that you sank our ships quite indiscriminately!'

It was Erzberger, plodding doggedly along, who continued to save for Germany fragments of advantage or honour from the wreck. Thus, by arguing that the creation of a thirty-kilometre neutral zone all down the right bank of the Rhine would only 'increase the danger of bolshevism' in that heavily industrialized area, he got the zone reduced to ten kilometres (though he could do nothing about the three Rhine bridgeheads). He did battle for more than an hour on Clause 26, which dealt with the blockade, and though, at the end, he failed to get it lifted, he at least managed to insert into the text an Allied undertaking to 'consider supplying Germany with food, to the degree considered necessary', during the thirty-six day period for which the armistice was to last. Oddly enough the main issue of military honour concerned, not Europe at all, but East Africa, where the German Commander-in-Chief, General Lettow-Vorbeck, had fought a brave campaign, thousands of miles from his fatherland, which had aroused the professional admiration of all. Foch agreed that his original Clause 17, which called for the 'unconditional surrender within a month of all German troops fighting in East Africa', should be softened to a requirement that they merely 'withdraw' over an unspecified period. For Foch, it was a cheap concession: East Africa, after all, had never impinged greatly on the Generalissimo's imagination.

It was at twelve minutes past five that they disposed of the last of the thirty-five clauses. Fifteen minutes later,* they began the signing in duplicate though, at Foch's suggestion, the time of signature was entered as 5 a.m., to give a clear six hours before the

---

* Foch puts the signature ceremony at 5.10 a.m., not 5.20.

pre-determined moment when the armistice was to take effect.

When they had all put down their pens Erzberger rose, cleared his throat and, having politely asked permission, delivered his statement. It proved to be more a glow of righteous indignation than the 'fiery protest' Hindenburg had wanted. Speaking for his whole delegation, Erzberger acknowledged that the Allies had made certain concessions, but pointed out that, with the best will in the world, it might prove impossible to carry out all the conditions laid down in the short time specified. Indeed, he went on, if the terms were to be carried out as agreed, 'the German people will be plunged into anarchy and famine'.

He ended on a note of plaintive pride:

> 'In view of the declaration which led up to the armistice, we might have hoped for terms which – while assuring complete military security to our opponents – would have ended the sufferings of the women and children who took no part in the war. The German people which, for fifty months, has held out against a world of enemies, will preserve its freedom and unity in the face of any violence. A nation of fifty millions may suffer, but it does not perish.'

Nobody spoke except for Foch, who uttered two words: '*Très bien.*' Erzberger seems to have taken this as a gesture of approval. Had he known even a little French, he would have realized that, depending on the tone, it could just as easily have been a non-committal acknowledgement or merely a curt way of indicating that their business was now over. At any rate, there was no shaking of hands as the German delegates departed and returned to their carriage. They had nothing to do there but glumly await their official copy of the armistice act, complete with map showing the exact evacuation zones. Once that was in their hands their train pulled out, the blinds drawn down again, heading for Tergnier and Spa by the same route they had travelled four interminable days before.

Foch had a happier task. As soon as the Germans had left he dispatched his famous Order of the Day by radio and telephone to the Commanders-in-Chief of every Allied theatre of war, beginning with the words:

'Hostilities will cease on the entire front on 11 November, at 11 a.m. French time.'

Early that same morning, while his army was being disposed of in a French railway carriage, its fugitive Supreme War Lord was moving on at last into exile. The ex-Emperor William had spent the night on his train just inside Dutch territory while a search was made for a landowner willing and able to receive the banished sovereign in suitable style. The choice had fallen on the partly English Count Godard Bentinck, whose castle, 'Huis te Amerongen' lay near the town of Maarn. It was drizzling when the special train reached Maarn station where the host was waiting with a motor-car to do the final stage of the journey. The ex-Emperor alighted – still wearing uniform, though now with all decorations removed – and was greeted on the platform by Count Bentinck, who tactfully introduced him to the Governor of Utrecht Province as 'William of Hohenzollern'. Most of the large suite who had travelled thus far with him took their farewells at this point, and then tried to raise one last cheer as his car moved off and was swallowed up in the November mist. But their shouts were blanketed by the hostile silence of a crowd of some three hundred Dutch locals who had turned up to witness the event. There were even a few hisses.

It was a depressing start and the ex-Emperor only recovered from it after they had crossed the drawbridge of Amerongen Castle. Sighing with relief at being back again in tranquil and congenial surroundings, he promptly asked for 'a cup of real, good, hot, strong English tea'. Count Godard did better than that. He had a Scots housekeeper at the castle, and soon William of Hohenzollern was enjoying the scones and shortbread he had first tasted as a small boy at Balmoral, on the lap of his grandmother, Queen Victoria. In one small way, at any rate, his life had turned full cycle. The self-righteous bitterness with which he looked back on that life – still unable to comprehend the major role he had played in his own downfall – comes out in a letter he wrote to his wife from Amerongen later that day:

'My reign is ended, my dog's existence is over, and has been rewarded only with betrayal and ingratitude.'

The path into exile which his fellow-sovereign, the Emperor Charles, was treading on that same November morning in Vienna was a very different one. Not for him a flight from Supreme Headquarters orchestrated by his own generals, or an abdication announcement read over the telephone as a *fait accompli* by his own Chancellor. The last of the Habsburg rulers had stayed on in his own palace in his own capital, trying to reason with both the new and the old forces around him and, at the end, deciding his own fate, without recrimination or self-pity, for himself.

What that fate would be, however, had been clearly foreshadowed during that same eventful weekend which, in Berlin, had seen the strange deposition of the German Emperor. Fittingly it was President Wilson, who had done so much to bring that event about, who now performed the last rites for the Habsburg monarchy. On 8 November the President had dispatched telegrams of greetings not merely to the new breakaway regimes in Budapest and Prague but also to the recently formed State Council in Vienna itself, expressing his pleasure that 'the constituent peoples had thrown off the yoke of the Austro-Hungarian empire'. That was tantamount to proclaiming an Austrian republic – from a distance of three thousand miles. Sure enough, the following evening, after the news of the Emperor William's abdication had reached Vienna, the Austrian Socialist leaders called publicly for the creation of 'a democratic socialist republic of German-Austria'.

Charles made one last effort to stem the tide by calling on those traditional props of the monarchy – the Christian-Socialists and the Catholic Church – for support. But it seemed that his crown had grown too heavy and sunk too deep for anyone to fish it out of the torrent. With few exceptions, those right-wing politicians who had recently pledged themselves to stand by their Emperor, were now only concerned how they could get out of their promise, and get him off his throne, with a minimum loss of dignity. The church had also decided that discretion had become the better part of valour. Cardinal Piffl who, only four days before, had celebrated a solemn mass at St Stephen's Cathedral for the name-day of His Apostolic Majesty (and, as that title signified, a ruler ordained by God and not by man) now advised the sovereign to forget about God and yield to man by 'putting aside his rights and placing the constitutional decision in the hands of the people'.

By an odd coincidence, it was at eleven o'clock on the morning of the following day, just as the general armistice was due to come into force on all the battle-fronts, that the long-awaited constitutional decision was presented to the Emperor. The republic was not swept along in Vienna, as it had just been in Berlin, by the violence of street mobs. Instead, its credentials were borne sedately out to Schönbrunn Palace by a motor-car carrying two members of the last imperial Cabinet – Dr Lammasch, the Prime Minister Charles had appointed a fortnight before, and the Minister of Interior, Dr Gayer. The formula, which had been worked out between the leaders of the old order and the representatives of the new, was an inspired and typically Viennese compromise which salvaged the consciences of the former while meeting the demands of the latter. Charles was to recognize in advance any form of constitution which German-Austria might choose and, in the meanwhile, agree to 'relinquish all participation in affairs of state'. The vulgar word 'abdication' was not mentioned. The Habsburg eagle was not being pushed off its perch; it was merely being asked to hop quietly aside. And, as with that muddled business in Schönbrunn the week before of concluding the Italian armistice, the new regime in Vienna left it to the old to take all responsibility.

The two representatives of that regime who had been charged with this task were beside themselves with agitation. Fifty years later, Charles's widow recalled the scene:

> 'The ministers pursued the Emperor in a panic from room to room demanding his signature. They had been promising to let him see this famous compromise for two days. Now ... they wanted it proclaimed within fifty minutes. At one point, the Emperor literally had to shake them off with the exclamation: "If you won't even let me *read* it, how do you expect me to *sign* it?"'

The Empress herself held things up for a while. When shown the document, she mistook it at first glance for an instrument of outright abdication and pleaded passionately with her husband:

> 'A sovereign can never abdicate. He can be deposed and his rights declared forfeit. All right. That is force. But abdicate – never, never, never! I would rather fall here at your side. Then there would be Otto.* And even if all of us here were killed, there would still be other Habsburgs.'

Charles withdrew with her and one personal aide to the calm of the so-called 'Porcelain Room'. Here he persuaded his wife, as he was already persuading himself, that the formula would both avoid conflict in his capital and preserve some freedom of movement for the dynasty in the future, particularly in other crown lands of the now fragmented empire.† He took out the metallic pencil he always carried with him and firmly wrote under the manifesto the one word 'Karl' which was to put an end to six and a half centuries of Habsburg rule.

There remained only the macabre ceremony of relieving the last imperial government of office. As Vienna, unlike Berlin the week before, still possessed a head of state at his proper post, it was the Emperor and not any of his politicians, who presided over it. Indeed, both protocol and gratitude prevailed to the end. The Prime Minister, Professor Lammasch, who had struggled through his farewell speech with tears dripping down his white beard, was presented with the Grand Cross of the Order of St Stephen to dry them on. Lesser orders were bestowed on the other members of his government, while two of them, who had reached retirement age, were each awarded pensions of 20,000 crowns a year. There had been particular competition for the honorary title of *Geheimrat* or Privy Councillor, which entitled the recipient to be called 'Your

---

* Eldest son and heir to the Emperor, then almost six years old and in Schönbrunn with his parents; now a well-known writer and member (for the Christian-Socialist Party of Bavaria) of the European Parliament.

† The technicality that this was a political rather than a dynastic renunciation was indeed to have significant effects, especially in Hungary which, legally, could revert to being a monarchy; as such it was the scene of two abortive restoration bids, led by Charles in person, in 1921.

Excellency' for life. The dynasty was winding up its affairs as though it had another six and a half centuries before it. But then the ministers left and, as one courtier put it, 'a strange quietness fell over Schönbrunn which almost hurt'.

There are two final contrasts to note between the exits of these two German-speaking Emperors, rulers whom, all too often, the outside world had lumped together as one. The first is that, ironically, the gentle 'Peace Emperor' was better served by his army than the fire-eating Supreme War Lord. The break-up of the Austrian army into its national components had, of course, reached right to Vienna. A whole Hungarian battalion of the 69th Infantry Regiment, which formed part of the palace guard force of the capital, had, for example, simply disappeared at the beginning of November. Even Austrian units, when not properly controlled by their officers, had a habit of melting away during the last days. Thus, a reserve battalion sent from Army Headquarters in Baden to replace the Hungarian unit was foolishly dispersed among several trains travelling to the capital instead of being concentrated in one. The result was that, of the thousand men who set out, only sixty, with fifteen officers, reported for duty at Schönbrunn the following day. But then the young military cadets from the academies of Wiener Neustadt, Mödling and Traiskirchen turned up to the last youthful warrior to fill the gap and defend their Emperor; and the many officers of all ranks and regiments in Vienna who volunteered for the same task were only turned away by the palace guard commander because he had no rations for them. One friend and former brother officer of the Emperor's, Count Waldendorff, simply turned up late one night in green loden shooting clothes with a sporting rifle under his cape to add to the palace armoury if needed.

Those were the acts of sentimental loyalty which have graced the downfall of most dynasties. On quite a different scale – and with a very different potential – was the rescue operation which had been worked out by Field Marshal Boroević, who had managed to extricate the bulk of his Isonzo army from the Italian débâcle and bring it home in good order and spirits, in twelve days. In that second week of November the Field Marshal stood with his force in

Carinthia, and, fanatical monarchist as he was (like most Croats), he now proposed to march it to Vienna and occupy the capital in the Emperor's name. That was no romantic gesture of a gallant sportsman but the sober plan of one of the most senior and distinguished field commanders of the empire. Moreover, Boroević had taken all possible precautions: any units he considered politically doubtful had been weeded out and shipped off elsewhere, and all the key railway junctions up to Wiener Neustadt had been surrounded by flying columns of reliable troops. Whether the operation would have worked is a matter for conjecture, but it was not the Field Marshal's fault that he was never given the chance to try. He twice called the Emperor from Klagenfurt offering his help, and twice the offer was politely declined in the Emperor's name. In fact Charles, who would have jumped at the offer, was never shown it. One of the officials who blocked the plan was General Dankl, the commander of the Vienna garrison, to whom the telegrams were referred. But the point to note is that whereas the front-line commanders of the German army, when asked to 'march against the homeland' in their Emperor's cause refused point-blank, an Austrian Field Marshal had volunteered and prepared for the same task.

The ultimate contrast between the reigns of these fellow emperors lay in the exiles which ended those reigns. William II headed for abroad. Charles headed for Eckartsau, a shooting lodge in Lower Austria close to where the borders of Austria, Hungary and Slovakia all ran together. As it was indisputably a private family property and not a State residence, the republic that was about to be launched had no legal title to it.*

When that German-Austrian Republic was duly proclaimed (with the ex-Emperor of Austria, his family and his suite still residing in the midst of it) the Viennese, compulsorily sobered anyway by a twenty-four-hour ban on alcohol, took it with remarkable calm. For example, when a pillar of the vanished order,

---

* Charles managed to stay on in Eckartsau until 23 March 1919 when he was obliged to leave for Switzerland, protected by a British officer and a small detail of British soldiers. His final place of exile was Madeira where he died on 1 April 1922, still only thirty-five years old.

Prince Franz Liechtenstein, went to his customary haberdasher's shop in the first hours of the republic to buy a pair of gloves, he found himself being politely shown the door with the beguiling remark: 'No, Your Highness, come tomorrow. Today is revolution!' The assistant was merely displaying a little of that instant pragmatism with which his city had greeted so many great upheavals in its life.

Vienna was unique among the main belligerent capitals in that the gathering in the forest of Compiègne held for it relatively little significance: for the Austrian empire the real war had already ended at Salonika and Padua. It was a very different story elsewhere, and especially in the victorious capitals, where 11 November 1918 was being celebrated as the most joyous day of the century.

Understandably, the explosion of delirium was greatest in Paris, the city which had lived for nearly five years with the enemy encamped outside its back door. Appropriately, the first of the government to hear that victory was sealed, signed and delivered, was the Frenchman who had done most to bring that victory about, the Prime Minister, Georges Clemenceau. A liaison officer at the War Ministry, General Mordacq, had been sitting by his telephone all night (like most of his colleagues) getting reports from Compiègne on the progress of the conference. When, at about 5.45 a.m., he was told that it was all over, he hurried immediately to tell Clemenceau the news. The 'Tiger' threw his arms around his messenger of joy and the two men stood thus, locked in a Gallic embrace, for several minutes, unable to speak for emotion. Mordacq then went on his pre-dawn rounds to tell the other French leaders, starting with the President, M. Poincaré who, though not usually a demonstrative man, began crying for happiness. (He was, after all, an Alsatian, and the return of Alsace-Lorraine to France was one of the armistice conditions which the Germans had just accepted.)

Colonel House had stayed up in his Paris house until midnight but was asleep when, at 5.30 a.m., he was awoken by an American aide and given first word of the signing. Mordacq arrived soon afterwards – on Clemenceau's instructions – and House was tactful enough to pretend that this was the first intimation he had received.

Still in his bedroom and still in his dressing-gown, President Wilson's peace plenipotentiary exclaimed: 'At last, our dead on the *Lusitania* are avenged!' It was a curious remark, considering the two hundred thousand men that America had lost on the battlefields of France since the summer, and also in view of the fact that America had waited from 7 May 1915 to 6 April 1917 to avenge those *Lusitania* victims.

Clemenceau spoke very differently when he stood up later that day to address a special session of the National Assembly in the Palais Bourbon. After the old man (who had stood in the same building and signed the protest motion when France capitulated to Bismarck's Germany forty-seven years before) had read out the clauses of the armistice one by one, he ended:

> 'Now that I have finished reading, my duty is accomplished and I should reproach myself for adding anything at this great hour, so solemn and awesome. But in the name of the French people ... I honour our magificent dead who have brought us this great victory ... Thanks to them, France, yesterday the soldier of God and today the soldier of humanity, will also be the soldier of ideals!'

At that rousing stuff the whole Assembly got up on its feet and broke into the 'Marseillaise' while, from outside, artillery salutes blended with the cheers of the crowds.

In London the House of Commons responded rather more phlegmatically to the great occasion, despite the fact that Lloyd George, to whom it fell to read out the armistice terms to the British Parliament, could be just as emotional and just as stirring with his oratory when he chose as Clemenceau. But on that occasion, having signalled the end of 'the cruellest and most terrible war that has ever scourged mankind', he ended simply:

> 'This is no time for words. Our hearts are too full of a gratitude to which no tongue can give adequate expression. I will, therefore, move "That this House do immediately adjourn, until this time tomorrow ..."'

But if the Prime Minister could find no adequate tongue that day, the British people had no such difficulty. The scene that is most often quoted is the one that the Minister of Munitions described from his office window in the heart of London after the first stroke of the eleventh hour had sounded from Big Ben – how, as the second chime sounded, the slight figure of a girl clerk dashed into the still empty street, gesticulating wildly, to be joined, within seconds, by streams of people pouring out of all the neighbouring buildings until, 'almost before the last stroke of the clock had died away, the strict, war-straightened, regulated streets of London had become a triumphant pandemonium'.

Many other accounts of that moment exist, however, which – though in plainer prose from far humbler pens – capture its quality even better, if only because they were written down before night had fallen rather than reconstructed years later for political memoirs. Thus, a seventeen-year-old English schoolgirl, deep in the English countryside, entered this in her diary that day:

'I was in the middle of an essay on Garibaldi and I just stopped and wrote ARMISTICE in big letters across the page ... I went over to our little church to which we had plodded Friday after Friday for "War Intercession" for four terrible years. One couldn't pray ... one's heart was just overwhelmed with a big "Thank God". We knelt there with guns booming, bugles blowing and church bells ringing and the whole air filled with great joy and thankfulness.'

Or this letter, written to her parents by a young student at a training college just outside the capital:

'I had been working and was just in Miss Anderson's room talking to her when I heard rockets and sirens. We went to the window and heard maroons so we tore up to the station. On the way, flags were being hung out of windows. Some terrified souls really believed, however, that it was an Air Raid! But a dustman over the road waved his hand to us and called out: "It's Peace all right this time!"'

On a farm deep in the Kent countryside, the father of that young airman who, three months before, had ferried the RAF's precious

Handley-Page bomber out to General Allenby in Palestine, wrote in his diary that evening:

> 'Went to my threshing gang (of five women land workers) and gave them the news. Great rejoicing. I asked the engine driver if he could get a whistle out of his engine. He said "Certainly!" It gave one flimsy screech and blew the whistle out. Then our Yalding village bells got to work, and rang a merry peal. It was all over. The wounded came up for billiards and tea and at 6 p.m. we all went down to Yalding Church for a special short service. Church crammed ...'

There were, of course, some bitter-sweet scenes amongst all the rejoicing. That night in London, as the Chief of the Imperial General Staff was walking home after a celebration dinner at 10 Downing Street, he came across 'an elderly well-dressed woman ... alone and sobbing her heart out'. When the Field Marshal asked if he could help in any way, she looked up and replied: 'Thank you, no. I am crying but I am happy for now I know that all my three sons who have been killed in the war have not died in vain.' It was a consolation denied to the millions of mourning mothers on the defeated side.

Across the Atlantic President Wilson, like Colonel House, was asleep when the news came through but, allowing for the five-hour time difference, he had even more excuse. It was, in fact, 2.25 a.m. when the armistice report reached Washington and, as they did not wake the President to tell him, he did not hear about it until breakfast. Not surprisingly (for it was, in the political sense, his peace) he then lost not a moment in celebrating it. He immediately declared a public holiday and drafted this characteristic announcement to the nation:

> 'Everything for which America has fought has been accomplished. It will now be our fortunate duty to assist by example, by sober, friendly counsel and by material aid in the establishment of just democracy throughout the world.'

It then fell to him, in turn, to read out the armistice terms to his legislators. He ended his speech to Congress in the same messianic vein as his announcement to the American people:

'To conquer with arms is to make only a temporary conquest; to conquer the world by earning its esteem is to make permanent conquest.'

And this, he indicated, was precisely what he now intended to do. For Woodrow Wilson, to invert the classic phrase, peace was to be the continuation of war by other means. Not for nothing had Colonel House exclaimed, in a rapturous telegram sent to his master in the White House that day: 'Autocracy is dead. Long live democracy and its immortal leader!'

It was natural that there should be such self-congratulation and rejoicing in the capitals of the victorious powers. But what is much more remarkable about this day of Allied triumph is the way in which, the closer one moves to the red core of the conflict, the cooler and greyer does the mood become.

For some, especially the veterans, that was partly induced by a dazed disbelief that the hideously abnormal, which had become so normal for them, had ceased; that after more than fifteen hundred days and nights rent by artillery fire, the skies had suddenly fallen silent. For some, especially those of the huge American army not yet blooded in battle, it may have been helped by a feeling of disappointment that this greatest adventure of their young lives was over before it had begun. And, for any soldier on any battlefield, there was the cost to be reckoned with, the evidence of which was all around them. By the time the last war communiqué was signed that day (Pétain, closing the French files, had written under his signature '*Fermé par cause de victoire*') the final Allied offensive which had started in midsummer had, by itself, cost some four hundred and thirty thousand British battle casualties, five hundred and thirty-one thousand French and more than two hundred thousand American. As for their enemies, the losses sustained by Germany and her allies over that same period were thought to have totalled no fewer than one and a half million men. In the cities of the homelands, the cheers could roll down the unscarred streets of the living. Here, they had to rise above heaps of rubble and death, piled layer upon layer over the years, like the fallen leaves which carpet a forest floor. Counting each casualty for a leaf, the twenty million dead or wounded which the war had cost in its entirety would, indeed, have made such a carpet.

Soberness in the face of all this sacrifice is first noted on 11 November well behind the front line itself. A nursing sister at the American military hospital at Villers Cotterets described how, though they drank champagne out of tin cups on hearing the news and decorated the wards with American and French flags, most of the sisters felt a sense of suspense rather than the joy and excitement they had looked forward to. It was, she wrote, as though, at that moment, they were thinking 'of those who would not return, and of the countless numbers they had nursed who must face life maimed . . .'

Another American Red Cross girl, stationed near Puy de Dôme, appears to have been almost disgusted when the great news arrived. She wrote in her diary:

'I was standing in the kitchen planning menus when the commanding officer came in and told me that the armistice had been signed. To me, everything stopped dead for a moment. Then went on the same. It all seems so ignominious . . . The whole thing seems to have petered out so – it began over nothing and it ends where it all began . . .'

A French baroness who had managed to keep her damaged château open to Allied officers throughout the war had a far loftier, but almost equally troubled, reaction:

'The Armistice! It seems a dream. At least the nightmare is passed. How shall we emerge from all this suffering – better or worse? Will the aftermath drive the world to greed and selfish pleasure-seeking? Danger produces noble deeds. Sometimes, idleness and cowardice flourish with security.'

On the long battle-front itself, there were, obviously, many individual outbursts of joy. The 'Marseillaise' must have been sung thousands of times in the French lines on that armistice morning, and one French soldier describes how, when his regimental band struck up the emotive anthem and started to march through the village, 'an immense and majestic crowd of *poilus* followed on – infantrymen, cavalry, artillery, engineers – twenty deep and arm in arm in fraternal triumph'.

An Australian gunner whose unit heard the news near the French village of Cappy recorded similar scenes of enthusiasm – steel hats thrown in the air up and down the column, and several of the drivers actually kissing their horses with emotion.

Yet the deeper, broader mood was one of chastened foreboding, and it seems to have been felt by soldiers of all nationalities, from the lowest rank to the highest. A Marshal of France entered this, for example, in his private diary that day:

> 'Joan of Arc said that though the warriors could fight the war, it was God who would give the victory. So it has come about and God has once more made us victorious. But will the people of France realize that it is indeed God who, yet again, has saved them?'

The general commanding the 27th American Infantry division not only found nothing to philosophize about on that morning but absolutely nothing to record. He wrote:

> 'The signing of the armistice caused not the slightest ripple of excitement among the American soldiers ... There were no cheers ... Everything went on as usual ...'

Certainly, the grim business of war itself went on as usual, right up to 11 a.m., and, at one or two points along the line, even beyond. Thus a captain commanding an English cavalry squadron which took the Belgian village of Erquelinnes wrote that morning:

> 'At 11.15 it was found necessary to end the days of a Hun machine-gunner on our front who would keep on shooting. The armistice was already in force, but there was no alternative. Perhaps his watch was wrong but he was probably the last German killed in the war – a most unlucky individual!'

Elsewhere on the British front an officer commanding a battery of six-inch howitzers was killed at one minute past eleven – at which his second-in-command ordered the entire battery to go on firing for another hour against the silent German lines.

But generally, any firing still going on ended on the last second of the tenth hour, sometimes with droll little ceremonies – as on the British front near Mons, where another and more fortunate German machine-gunner blazed off his last belt of ammunition during the last minute of the war and then, as the hour struck, stood up on his parapet, removed his steel helmet, bowed politely to what was now the ex-enemy opposite, and disappeared.

The British division on whose front that little incident took place had lost, during that one final week of the war, two officers killed and twenty-six wounded, and among the other ranks one hundred and seventeen killed, six hundred and ninety-three wounded and sixty-one missing. Small wonder that its historian recorded 'no cheering and very little outward excitement' as peace came. And it is above all in the regimental records and private diaries of British units that one finds the cost of that peace weighing more heavily than its arrival.

The historian of a British infantry regiment wrote:

'The most wonderful thing when the armistice came into force and all ranks "stood to" was the silence of the battle-fields. Here and there along the long line of battle-worn and weary troops a cheer broke the stillness, but the records show that when hostilities ceased Peace fell amidst a hush almost painful in its coming. If, far away from the line of muddy, dirty trenches in France and Flanders, across the Channel, in every city, town and village throughout the United Kingdom (even throughout the world) people went mad with joy and forgot everything but that the black pall of war had been lifted, no such happenings took place in the front-line. It was impossible to forget in a moment the four long years ... Impossible also to forget those brave messmates who had not come through, who in a soldier's grave somewhere between the Aisne and the tortured Ypres Salient lay silent for ever.'

392

Mor prosaically, that young artillery lieutenant whose description of the advance up to and through the Hindenburg Line has already been quoted, recorded this of the great moment:

> 'Some of the men started to cheer but their voices sounded as unnatural as the noise of the guns (firing blank ammunition) and they soon stopped. There was Silence. It had come to stay.
>
> 'We drifted towards the mess.
>
> '"Oh God, what a war," the major said. "Nothing to drink but lime juice! What a peace!"
>
> '"What on earth are we going to do with ourselves now?" someone said.
>
> '"Work, for a change," the major said.'

An officer of the Welsh Guards found the same thoughts preoccupying his men on that day:

> 'The quiet manner in which troops received the news of an armistice was most remarkable. Their attitude, their conversation, all expressed the question, "And what happens now?"'

And a famous war artist wrote:

> 'Yet, on this day, looked forward to for years, I must admit that, studying people, I found something wrong – perhaps like all great moments expected, something is sure to fall short of expectations ...'

That 'something wrong' was not simply that the fighting men, now no longer needed, had begun to worry about their individual futures. It was as though they sensed that, for the world at large, it was going to be harder to make a peace than to end a war, and harder still to keep the peace than to make it; as though they felt in their tired bones that Armageddon was to become a familiar of their twentieth century.

Source Notes

Chapter 1: Bombon

p. 18. l. 9.   'Morally, I am certain we can win.' Maricourt, *Foch*, p. 149.

p. 18. l. 24.   'Every step with divine help.' Liddell Hart, *Through the Fog of War*, p. 45.

p. 20. l. 7.   'The only way to bring the English along with you.' Raymond Recouly, *Le Mémorial de Foch*, p. 271.

p. 20. l. 15.   *Le gros ver blanc*, James Marshall Cornwall, *Foch*, p. 225.

p. 20. l. 19.   Pétain's advice 'to quit Paris', Weygand, p. 534.

p. 20. l. 34.   'The moment has come ... to pass over to the offensive.' Foch's proposals of 24 July given in full in Weygand, *Ideal Vécu*, pp. 582 *et seq.*

p. 21. l. 19.   Pétain's advice 'to quit Paris', Weygand, p. 534.

p. 21.   New British verb, 'to deb', Liddell Hart, *Foch, The Man of Orleans*, p. 346.

Chapter 2: Anniversaries

p. 24. l. 10.   'Peace just will not come.' Intercepted letter of Kanonier A. Baruch to Direktor Feist, reprinted in *Ursachen des Deutschen Zusammenbruchs* (henceforth cited as *Ursachen*), Vol. 5, p. 308.

p. 25. l. 37.   Emperor William's Proclamations translated from the *Vossische Zeitung* of Berlin, 1 August 1918.

p. 26. l. 22.   'German people, go into your church.' Undated early August edition of the Reichsbote, quoted in *The Times* of 23 August 1918.

p. 26. l. 32.   Napoleon's eye-glass. From a Berlin report carried in the Vienna *Neue Freie Presse* of 2 August 1918 (henceforth cited as *NFP*).

p. 27. l. 26.   Interview of Hindenburg and Ludendorff at Spa. Extracts from the *NFP* of 3 August 1918.

p. 28. l. 7.   General Ardenne and Captain Salzmann, quoted in *The Times* of 8 August 1918.

p. 28. l. 17. 'We do not ask for more.' *Le Figaro* of 4 August 1918.

p. 29. l. 5. 'Tribes of Germany fighting like dogs.' Bavarian Minister of Interior on food quarrels. Report in *Vorwärts* quoted in *The Times* of 7 August 1918.

p. 29. l. 15. 'We must face the fact.' From article carried in the *NFP* of 2 August 1918.

p. 29. l. 32. 'Complete helplessness ...' Letter to Kurt Hahn, given in Appendix to Prince Max's *Erinnerungen und Dokumente*, p. 635.

p. 31. l. 3. Lloyd George's message read out in cinemas etc. *The Times* and *Daily Telegraph* 5 August 1918.

p. 31. l. 17. Anniversary sermons etc. in St Pauls and St Margarets. *Ibid.*

p. 33. l. 17. 'Tricolour, Union Jack and Stars and Stripes.' *New York Tribune*, 4 August 1918.

p. 33. l. 24. President Wilson's proclamation quoted in *The Times*, 1 August 1918.

p. 34. l. 10. 'Dependence Day' telegram to Lloyd George quoted in *Daily Telegraph*, 5 August 1918.

p. 34. l. 21. Anecdote on the Crown Prince's teeth from *New York World*, 6 August 1918.

p. 35. l. 8. American manpower call up and statistics. Washington report quoted in *The Times* of 6 August 1918.

p. 36. l. 4. 'Queen of Peace' statue in Rome. Report in *Le Figaro*, 4 August 1918.

p. 36. l. 15. 'At this glorious hour ...' Clemenceau telegram to Orlando. Text in *Le Figaro*, 6 August 1918.

p. 38. l. 12. 'The greatest obstacle to peace ...' *NFP* quoted in *The Times*, 8 August 1918.

p. 38. l. 22. 'More people are starving ...' *Arbeiterzeitung* of Vienna, quoted in *Daily Telegraph*, 13 August 1918.

p. 39. l. 11. Count Gerolf Coudenhove handed one of four typewritten copies of his diary – *Achtzig Jahre* – to the author only a few weeks before his death in January 1979.

p. 40. l. 3. 'Another new month ...' Colonel Karl Scheller's stenograph war diary, only deciphered in 1978, and now in the Heeresarchiv, Vienna.

p. 40. l. 13. 'Nothing more for us to eat ...' Intercepted letters of complaint by Austrian soldiers on the Italian front, August 1918, and comments of censorship officer. All in Heeresarchiv, Vienna.

p. 41. l. 8.   'Confusion and muddle on the increase' and 'People are tired of the war.' Both from the war diary of Rudolf Binding, *Aus dem Kriege*, pp. 344–5, 348–9.

p. 41. l. 34. Captain Henry Lawson, letter of 4 August 1918. Peter Liddle Archives.

p. 42. l. 8.   *Ce qui Demeure* by Bonoist-Méchin (letter of Raphael Laporte), pp. 237–8.

p. 42. l. 22. 'I still seem to see those two Boches ...' Jacques Bouis, *Notes d' un Agent de Liaison*, pp. 99–100.

p. 43. l. 4.   'Our most unexpected discovery ...' *Ibid*, pp. 100–101.

Chapter 3: One Man's Black Day

p. 44. l. 20. 'I attack them' etc. Foch's monologue from Lt.-Colonel C. Repington, *The First World War*, Vol II, p. 377.

p. 45. l. 8.   'I am this parrot.' *Foch, The Man of Orleans*, by Liddell Hart, p. 350.

p. 45. l. 22. Captain C. G. Leland. *From Shell-Hole to Chateau*, pp. 40–41.

p. 46. l. 16. 'A tough, cheery gentleman.' *The World Crisis*, by Winston S. Churchill, Part II, p. 507.

p. 48. l. 12. '10,500 yards average advance.' This and other details of planning and order of battle from Sir A. Montgomery, *The Story of the Fourth Army*, pp. 11–26.

p. 49. l. 5.   For Allied deception plans see Major-General Sir F. Maurice, *The Last Four Months*, p. 106; also *Canadian Army Journal*, Volume 4, No. 8.

p. 49. l. 33. General Marwitz's report of 3 August 1918, from *Die Katastrophe des 8 August 1918*. Reichsarchiv, *Schlachten des Weltkrieges, Volume 36*. (Hereafter cited as *Katastrophe*).

p. 50. l. 15. Ludendorff Order of 4 August, quoted in Montgomery, *op. cit.* pp. 17–18 (footnotes).

p. 51. l. 3.   Intelligence warnings. *Katastrophe, op. cit.*, pp. 17–18.

p. 51. l. 13. 'One hundred enemy tanks.' *Ibid.* p. 19.

p. 51. l. 22. Prisoners' interrogations. *Ibid.* p. 40.

p. 51. l. 31. 'Glass steady.' *The Private Papers of Douglas Haig*, p. 322.

p. 52. l. 6.   'Up at the guns ...' Diary of Lt. P. J. Campbell RA. P/Es, British. Imperial War Museum.

p. 53. l. 25. Figures from *Canadian Army Journal* for January 1951, *The Battle of Amiens* and Montgomery *op. cit.* p. 51.

p. 54. l. 17. 'Each tank fought individually.' *Royal Tank Corps Journal*, July 1937, *The Battle of Amiens.*

p. 54. l. 19. 'Saurian Ghosts' etc. From Liddell Hart, *op. cit.* p. 349.

p. 54. l. 24. Visibility estimates. *Katastrophe*, pp. 98–9.

p. 55. l. 1. Carrier-pigeon. *Ibid.* p. 109.

p. 55. l. 18. Railway gun bombed. H. V. Jones, *The War in the Air*, Vol. 6, p. 438.

p. 56. l. 1. Somme air battle. *Ibid.* p. 441.

p. 56. l. 12. Goering in action. From Herman Goering, *Ein Lebensbild* by Martin Sommerfeldt, p. 32.

p. 56. l. 22. Bridge damage. Jones, *op. cit.* pp. 441–2.

p. 57. l. 21. 'A murderous artillery fire' etc. Diary of Lt. Albers, printed in *Katastrophe, op. cit.*, pp. 49–50.

p. 58. l. 27. 'One of the freshest divisions.' *Katastrophe*, p. 138.

p. 59. l. 6. 'I stayed with the infantry.' *Ibid.* pp. 146–7.

p. 60. l. 12. 'A glorious summer evening' etc. Campbell Diary.

p. 60. l. 28. Debeney 'much distressed' etc. Haig, *Private Papers*, p. 323.

p. 61. l. 7. Push to Roye. Foch, *Mémoires* Vol. 2, p. 183.

p. 61. l. 22. 'Home like one of ours.' Campbell Diary, p. 109.

p. 62. l. 16. Cavalry Corps failure. Montgomery, *The Story of the Fourth Army*, pp. 62–3.

p. 63. l. 6. 'Tanks are no bogey' etc. General Marwitz Order, Montgomery, p. 69.

p. 63. l. 20. Crown Prince Rupprecht's remarks. Rupprecht, Kronprinz von Bayern, *In Treue Fest, Meain Kriegstagebuch*, pp. 346–51.

p. 66. l. 3. Ludendorff Order of Day of 11 August. *Story of Fourth Army*, p. 16 (footnote).

p. 67. l. 26. Enemy divisions just as tired. Quoted in *Kaiser und Revolution* by Alfred Niemann, p. 40.

p. 68. l. 8. Lt. Herbst surrender. *Katastrophe*, op. cit., p. 82.

p. 69. l. 24. 'We must draw up the balance.' Niemann, *op cit.*, p. 43.

Chapter 4: Post-Mortems

p. 71. l. 14. 'Unadorned balance sheet ...' *Ursachen*, Vol. 2, p. 391.

p. 71. l. 16. Notable among the memoirs on the civilian side are those of the Chancellor, Count Hertling, the Foreign Office State Secretary, Admiral von Hintze, and his secretary von Vietinghoff; on the military side, those of Hindenburg and Ludendorff, and the Emperor's aide, Colonel Niemann. The memoirs of the Emperor himself are of little value on this and other episodes of the final phase. The principal official reconstruction of the whole period in Vol. 2 of *Ursachen*.

p. 72. l. 9.   'We should gradually paralyse ...' *Ursachen*, Vol. 2, Annexe 15, p. 388.

p. 72. l. 16.   'Termination of War.' Ludendorff, *op. cit.*, pp. 552–3.

p. 73. l. 8.   Ludendorff on Germany's allies. *Ursachen*, p. 389.

p. 74. l. 9.   'Let an old man go.' *Ibid.* p. 227.

p. 74. l. 29.   'The political leadership bows.' *Ibid.*, p. 228.

p. 75. l. 14.   'He is even more cowardly ...' Brook-Shepherd, *Uncle of Europe*, p. 255.

p. 75. l. 26.   This and all subsequent direct quotes from the protocol of the 14 August Crown Council from *Ursachen*, Vol. 11, pp. 237–41; also Hertling, p. 149; Niemann, p. 58; and Hindenburg, *Aus meinem Leben*, p. 364.

p. 77. l. 5.   'They would have liked it in Vienna.' General A. von Cramon, *Quartre Ans au G.H.Q. Austro-Hongrois*, p. 285.

p. 77. l. 19.   'The Emperor Charles had been sceptical' etc. The Empress Zita, in conversation with the author, 9 October 1978.

p. 79. l. 25.   Priority for Western Front. Cramon p. 286.

p. 79. l. 32.   'Would not fight on into 1919.' *Ibid.*, p. 287.

p. 81. l. 1.   'No man strong enough' etc. Lloyd George, *War Memoirs*, pp. 3239–40.

p. 81. l. 33.   Plea to Haig. Foch. p. 179.

p. 82. l. 3.   Wear and tear on tanks. Montgomery, pp. 62–3.

p. 82. l. 9.   Foch's modest plans for 1918. Calwell, *Field Marshal Sir Henry Wilson*, p. 121.

p. 82. l. 14.   War Cabinet meeting. *Ibid.*, p. 122.

p. 83. l. 16.   Emperor Charles on Spa. Empress Zita to author, 9 October 1978.

p. 84. l. 35.   'It is less the military situation ...' *Ursachen*, Vol. 5, pp. 304–5.

p. 85. l. 11.   Behaviour of German prisoners. War Dispatches of Sir Philip Gibbs, pp. 364–65.

p. 85. l. 30.   Scenes in Bapaume. *Ibid.*, p. 370.

p. 86. l. 17.   'They are great sign-writers, these Germans.' *Ibid.*, pp. 376–7.

p. 86. l. 34.   'No reason to doubt our victory.' *Ursachen*, Vol. 2, p. 236.

p. 87. l. 15. Von Hintze in Vienna. Cramon, p. 288.

p. 87. l. 20. Mediation by neutrals 'ineffective' etc. *Ursachen*, Vol. 2, Appendix 7, pp. 352 *et seq.* for this and subsequent details of the 5 September discussions.

p. 88. l. 26. 'Enemy's will not yet broken.' Cramon, pp. 289–90.

p. 88. l. 37. Austria's 'Cry to the World'. *Ibid.*, p. 291.

p. 90. l. 20. 'Four weeks of bickering' etc. See von Hintze's admission in *Ursachen*, Vol. 2, p. 397.

p. 90. l. 31. Balfour's rejection. *The Times* of 17 September 1918.

p. 91. l. 9. Wilson's rejection. Quoted in W. B. Fowler, *British-American Relations 1917–19, The Role of Sir William Wiseman*, p. 221.

p 91. l. 18. 'A more reasoned answer. *Ibid.*, p. 222.

Chapter 5: *'We Have Come to Die for You'*

p. 92. l. 20. 'A beautiful ride through Normandy in apple blossom time.' Claude G. Leland, *op. cit.*, pp. 20–22.

p. 93. l. 3. 'Can anyone who took part ... ?' Hervey Allen, *Toward the Flame*, pp. 1–3.

p. 93. l. 17. 'The little French tots followed us.' Unpublished Diary of Corporal Francis Duffy (27th U.S. division). Peter Liddle Archives.

p. 93. l. 25. 'I got lost in the dark ...' 2nd Lt. Curtis Wheeler, *Letters from an American soldier to his father*, p. 42.

p. 94. l. 5. 'A big adventure for them ...' Mildred Aldrich, *The Peak of the Load*, p. 90.

p. 94. l. 26. A.E.F. strength. W. B. Fowler, *British–American Relations 1917–1918*, pp. 129–30.

p. 94. l. 36. 'Many recruits ... had never even heard of the weapons.' Forrest C. Pogue, *George C. Marshall*, p. 165.

p. 95. l. 10. 'Americans ... suitably embarrassed.' John J. Pershing, *My Experiences in the World War*, p. 250.

p. 96. l. 12. Pershing's appointment. *Ibid.*, pp. 15–16.

p. 97. l. 18. Directive to Pershing. *Ibid.*, pp. 46–7.

p. 98. l. 9. Furore over British buttons. *Ibid.*, p. 283.

p. 99. l. 14. 'The time may come ...' *Ibid.*, p. 379.

p. 99. l. 20. Pershing 'very obstinate and stupid'. Haig Diaries, p. 307.

p. 99. l. 25. Crash programme of shipping etc. Pershing, p. 423.

Source Notes

p. 100. l. 21. Colonel Tyrrel Hawker (RA retd.). From war notes prepared at the author's request, 1979–80.

p. 101. l. 9. 'More Yankees came in last night' etc. C. H. Dudley Ward, *History of the Welsh Guards*, pp. 229–31.

p. 102. l. 17. '... their nickname of "Terrible".' *Histoire de la Guerre par les Combattants*, Vol. IV, pp. 384–51.

p. 103. l. 1. '... so much wine around.' *Ibid.*

p. 103. l. 3. 'Buck and Wing dance'. War Report in *The Times*, 21 September 1918.

p. 103. l. 8. 'Tea was ready.' Leland, *op. cit.*, p. 86.

p. 103. l. 13. 'Every day I feel more at home.' Mildred Aldrich, *op. cit.*, p. 90.

p. 103. l. 31. 'Hurry, here comes the King' etc. Will Judy, *A Soldier's Diary*', pp. 118–19.

p. 105. l. 4. 'Hernia of St Mihiel.' Maréchal Fayolle, *Cahiers Secrets de la Grande Guerre*, p. 302.

p. 105. l. 14. 'A tentative agreement by General Pétain and myself.' Pershing, p. 296.

p. 106. l. 2. 'Operation should be prepared without delay.' Foch, p. 165.

p. 106. l. 5. St Mihiel battle statistics from Pershing, pp. 581–2.

p. 107. l. 9. 'Put the Americans into battle at once.' Haig Private Papers, p. 325.

p. 107. l. 15. Foch 'in full agreement'. *Ibid.*

p. 107. l. 26. 'An entirely new plan.' Pershing, pp. 568–78 gives his version of the episode.

p. 108. l. 8. Pershing to regroup his forces, Foch, p. 202.

p. 109. l. 3. 'Pray for Fog!' *American Soldiers also Fought* by Lt. General Robert Lee Bullard, p. 82.

p. 110. l. 30. 'A long glacis ... much wire' etc. Col Repington Diaries, p. 397.

p. 111. l. 16. 'Six ... second class formations' etc. Pershing, p. 587 and Maurice, p. 120.

p. 111. l. 24. 'Keep enemy at arm's length.' Ludendorff, p. 572.

p. 111. l. 34. One million shells. Bullard, pp. 77–8.

p. 112. l. 5. 'Never engaged in offensive combat.' Pershing, p. 587.

p. 112. l. 26. 'As our first lines passed over the ridge' etc. Ernest L. Wrentmore, *'In spite of hell.'* pp. 98–101.

p. 113. l. 18. 'I'll keep it as a souvenir.' *Ibid.*

p. 113. l. 30. 'I'll be in Metz' etc. Liddell Hart, *Foch*, p. 360.

p. 114. l. 2. Battle casualties. Pershing, p. 591 (though, curiously, Pogue, in his *General Marshall* p. 193 puts the figure at 13,000).

p. 114. l. 14.   'Like election returns.' Harvey Cushing, *From a Surgeon's Journal*, pp. 439–40.

p. 114. l. 24.   'A strategical blunder.' Quoted in Liddell Hart, p. 361.

Chapter 6: The 'Gardeners'' Harvest

p. 117. l. 4.   Balkan battle strengths in 1915. Luigi Villari, *The Macedonian Campaign*, p. 23.

p. 118. l. 13.   'Never did one see such a collection of uniforms' etc. *Ibid.*, p. 160.

p. 118. l. 30.   'A Balkan Marseilles.' Alan Palmer, *The Gardeners of Salonika*, p. 14.

p. 120. l. 8.   'If I had commanded it' etc. Villari, p. 58.

p. 120. l. 18.   'The men out here' etc. Jane Dare, *Letters from a Forgotten Army*, p. 16.

p. 121. l. 10.   'Excellent picture of British order of battle.' Villari, pp. 77–8.

p. 121. l. 18.   For a good summary of the arguments of Easteners v. Westerners see the Introduction to Haig's Private Papers, *op. cit.* pp. 31–2. See also, as regards the Balkans, H. Collinson Owen, *Salonika and after*, pp. 205–7.

p. 123. l. 10.   'Sent to Limoges.' Paul Azan, *Franchet d' Espèrey*, pp. 176–8.

p. 125. l. 6.   'Head Westwards for Vienna.' Larcher, *La Grande Guerre dans les Balkans*, gives extracts from d'Espèrey's 1914 memorandum in Annexe 3, pp. 268–9.

p. 125. l. 22.   'A stranger to depression.' Quoted in Barbara Tuchman, *August 1914*, p. 369.

p. 125. l. 24.   'He moved quickly, almost fiercely ...' Brigadier-General Spears, quoted in Palmer, p. 183.

p. 126. l. 1.   'Qualites of the highest rank.' Villari, pp. 201–2.

p. 126. l. 31.   Two thousand prisoners taken. Lloyd George, p. 3208.

p. 127. l. 10.   'Eyes to see with.' Preface by Marshal Franchet d'Espèrey to the Memoirs of Louis Cordier, *Ceux du Premier Armistice*.

p. 127. l. 12.   'Series of forbidding shapes' etc. Cordier, pp. 17 *et seq.*

p. 128. l. 1.   'Ferocious energy.' Quoted in Palmer, p. 184.

p. 129. l. 20.   This forces breakdown from Villari *op. cit.*, pp. 215–16. Azan *op. cit.*, pp. 179–180 has a somewhat different count which gives the Orient Army a slight numerical superiority.

p. 130. l. 5.   'Some old Serbian soldiers.' Cordier, p. 27.

p. 131. l. 8.   'He combines the brains and vices' etc. Mr Valentine Chirol, in a letter to *The Times* of 30 September urging his government to have no truck with the Bulgarian ruler.

p. 131. l. 34.   'True brotherhood of arms.' *Berliner Tagblatt* of 5 August 1918.

p. 132. l. 1.   Peace feelers to Bulgaria. V. H. Rothwell *British War Aims and Diplomacy, 1914–1918*, pp. 215–17.

p. 132. l. 15.   Balfour's 'extravagant suggestions'. *Ibid.*, p. 218.

p. 132. l. 32.   Bulgaria's losses. Stephen Constant, *Foxy Ferdinand, Tsar of Bulgaria* p. 309.

p. 133. l. 15.   'French and Serbian infantry went in.' The most detailed contemporary account of the battle is Villari, Chapter XV; the best modern summary Palmer, Chapter XII. Azan is surprisingly skimpy.

p. 134. l. 21.   Cost of five thousand casualties. V. J. Seligman, *The Salonika Side-Show*, pp. 121–2.

p. 134. l. 30.   British battle losses on 18 September. H. Collinson Owen, pp. 256–7.

p. 136. l. 31.   'The German had won the argument.' Palmer, pp. 211–13.

p. 137. l. 15.   'Fighter planes, like monstrous birds.' Cordier, p. 68.

p. 137. l. 26.   'The defile was choked' etc. Jones H. A., *Over the Balkans and South Russia*, pp. 123–4.

p. 138. l. 6.   British air bombing havoc. Jones H. A., *The War in the Air*, Vol. 6, p. 312.

p. 139. l. 31.   General Lukov's pro-Entente sympathies. Azan, p. 197.

p. 140. l. 5.   Royal train bombarded. Cordier, p. 117 (footnote).

p. 140. l. 25.   'We are coming to help.' Ludendorff, p. 578.

p. 141. l. 10.   'To arrange conditions for an armistice.' Franchet d'Espèrey's telegram to Paris of 26 September 1918, given as Appendix C Villari, p. 273.

p. 141. l. 12.   'Weighty histories.' Larcher, *op. cit.*, p. 235; Gentizon, *Le Drame Bulgare*; and *Schlachten des Weltkrieges*, Vol. 9–11, p. 142.

p. 141. l. 25.   'All suitable courtesy'. D'Espèrey telegram of 26 September 1918.

p. 142. l. 2.   'Only one camera snapped the scene.' Article in *Mosquito* (journal of the Salonika army veterans), Issue no. 139, September 1962, p. 72.

p. 142. l. 17.   'Two illustrious figures.' Azan, pp. 196–7

p. 142. l. 25.   'Huge German staff car.' Villari, p. 246.

p. 142. l. 34.   'You marched against us' etc. Azan, p. 197.

p. 143. l. 10.   Terms given in Villari, pp. 274–5.

p. 144. l. 8. 'It's all finished with Bulgaria.' Cordier, pp. 140–1.

p. 144. l. 26. Germans learn of surrender. *Schlachten des Weltkirieges*, p. 140.

p. 144. l. 32. Rear-guard fight in Skopje. Cordier, p. 141 (footnote).

p. 145. l. 4. Germans defend Sofia. *Schlachten des Weltkrieges*, pp. 142–3.

p. 146. l. 2. '... the end had come.' Churchill, p. 537.

p. 146. l. 4. 'First of props had fallen.' Hankey, p. 840.

p. 146. l. 6. President Wilson hears news. Colonel House, quoted in *Ursachen*, Vol. 5, p. 88.

p. 146. l. 17. 'If one fell away ...' From *The Oxfordshire Hussars in the Great War*, p. 316.

p. 146. l. 24. 'Back door caved in.' Gordon Brook-Shepherd, *The Last Habsburg*, pp. 168–70, for the political aftermath in Vienna of the Bulgarian defection.

p. 146. l. 32. 'The Emperor was not really surprised.' The Empress Zita, in conversation with the author, 9 October, 1978.

p. 148. l. 3. Protocol of Vienna Crown Council Meeting in *Haus, Hof and Staatsarchiv*, Vienna, XXXX, 315 PA Interna, 1918.

p. 148. l. 29. 'How could he break faith?' Niemann, pp. 85-6

p. 150. l. 1. 'Probable it would all be over.' Ludendorff, pp. 579–80.

Chapter 7. *'Jerusalem by Christmas'*

p. 152. l. 18. 'Finally dragged into the war.' For an accurate and readable account of Turkey's manoeuvres see Tuchman, pp. 139 *et seq.*

p. 154. l. 31. 'Exceptionally heavy casualties.' Details of Gaza operation, Cyril Falls, *Armageddon 1918*, pp. 24–6.

p. 155. l. 5. 'A humiliating defeat.' Lloyd George, p. 3219.

p. 155. l. 35. 'Fulfilled, but not cheaply.' Falls, p. 29.

p. 156. l. 10. Transfer of divisions to France. Lloyd George, p. 3221; also H. S. Gullett, *Official History of Australia in the War*, pp. 653–7.

p. 156. l. 24. '... but gaunt ghosts.' Gullett, p. 678.

p. 157. l. 7. 'In the intervals of sight-seeing.' L. S. Amery, *My Political Life*, Vol. 2, p. 143.

p. 157. l. 36. 'A fast-running noose.' Falls, p. 51.

p. 158. l. 6. Details of the British deception plan in Gullett, pp. 685-7.

p. 160. l. 21. All German order of battle details from General Liman von Sanders, *Fünf Jahre in der Türkei*, pp. 271–3.

p. 161. l. 9. For British strengths see Gullett, p. 678.

p. 162. l. 3.   RAF strengths from Falls, p. 32.

p. 162. l. 28.   'The aeroplane, of which these things are foals.' T. E. Lawrence, *The Seven Pillars of Wisdom*, p. 64.

p. 163. l. 5.   'Low morale of his troops.' Von Sanders, p. 273.

p. 163. l. 14.   'Force did least and brain did most.' Lawrence, p. 604.

p. 163. l. 16.   'One of most brilliant cavalry operations.' Falls, p. 11.

p. 163. l. 29.   'From the seaward flank.' These and other details of the battle are taken, except where indicated otherwise, from Falls, pp. 65–86 and Gullett, pp. 692–8.

p. 164 l. 10.   'Offensive had been launched.' Von Sanders, p. 227.

p. 165. l. 24.   'Arab battalions of the coast-guard.' *Ibid.*, p. 281.

p. 166. l. 16.   'Not a single machine took off that day.' Lowell Thomas, *With Allenby in the Holy Land*, pp. 181–5, and H. V. Jones, *The War in the Air*, Vol. 6, pp. 214–16.

p. 166. l. 26.   'Draw out the indignation.' Lawrence, p. 620.

p. 167. l. 4.   'Or destroyed by projectiles.' Von Sanders, p. 275 and p. 281.

p. 167. l. 11.   'It was decisive nonetheless.' Details of the Megiddo engagement, and the capture of Damascus from Falls, pp. 87–100; Gullett, pp. 695–7; and von Sanders, pp. 282–5.

p. 170. l. 2.   'The last of the personnel.' Von Sanders, pp. 284–5.

p. 170. l. 18.   'Its second telling blow.' Details of air attack, except where otherwise stated, from Jones, pp. 224–5.

p. 171. l. 21.   'It was ghastly!' Lowell Thomas, p. 193.

p. 171. l. 27.   'Such a good war.' *My Warrior Sons* (Borton family Diary, ed. by Guy Slater), pp. 198–9.

p. 172. l. 16.   'A sack race ... in Constantinople.' Von Sanders, p. 290.

p. 173. l. 8.   'Four times as many prisoners.' Falls, p. 108, and von Sanders, p. 296.

p. 173. l. 22.   'They were glorious.' Lawrence, p. 655.

p. 174. l. 14.   'The blood of our comrades.' Diary of Lt. Jarolmek, pp. 34–5. Heeresarchiv, Vienna.

p. 174. l. 34.   'We took no prisoners.' Lawrence, p. 653.

p. 175. l. 23.   'Captured and generally sacked.' Falls, p. 143. For the fall of Damascus see especially Gullett, pp. 751–75.

p. 176. l. 6.   'Machine-gunners found such a target.' Gullett, p. 754.

p. 177. l. 6.   'Scrambled eggs in the darkness.' Falls, p. 143.

p. 177. l. 22.   'Triumphal procession about the streets.' Gullett, p. 761.

p. 178. l. 14.   'Only for me ... was ... the phase meaningless.' Lawrence, p. 674.

p. 179. l. 4.   'A more rapid journey home.' Falls, p. 156.

p. 179. l. 12.   Casualty figures in Falls, p. 172.

Chapter 8: *A Beleaguered Fortress*

p. 180. l. 18.   'Which is more doubtful.' War Correspondent of *The Times*, 1 October 1918.

p. 181. l. 23.   'Every orchard felled.' For the construction of the Hindenburg Line see, in particular, Maurice, pp. 131–143.

p. 181. l. 30.   'Neither a line nor a single system.' Frank H. Simonds, *History of the World War*, pp. 246–7.

p. 185. l. 12.   Siegfried cartoon in *Jugend*, 9 September 1918. Peter Liddle Archives.

p. 185. l. 24.   'A co-ordinated attack.' Some of the best contemporary accounts of the Hindenburg Line offensive are in Maurice, pp. 146 *et seq.*; Foch, pp. 205 *et seq.*; Pershing, pp. 607 *et seq.*, and on the German side, Ludendorff, pp. 597–602 and Crown Prince Rupprecht, pp. 356–61. See also, among many other reconstructions, Churchill, pp. 533 *et. seq.* and Lloyd George, pp. 3142 *et seq.*; and for an excellent modern account, John Terraine, *To Win a War*, pp. 139 *et seq.*

p. 185. l. 30.   'At Haig's disposal.' Churchill, p. 533, reading from Haig's own battle maps.

p. 186. l. 2.   'French lost 100,000 more.' Foch, pp. 230–1.

p. 188. l. 35.   'Sister democracy on the opposite shore.' *Australian Official History*, quoted by Terraine, p. 164.

p. 189 l. 21.   'Cutting the Hindenburg Line into little bits.' Lt. P. J. Campbell Diary, p. 117.

p. 191. l. 2.   'Not a distinguished division.' Terraine, p. 165.

p. 192. l. 13.   'Only the white scars ... and lines of wire.' Campbell Diary, p. 119.

p. 193. l. 2.   'Down for the count now.' *Ibid.*, pp. 126–8.

p. 193. l. 13.   'Evidence of the resistance.' Lloyd George, p. 3149.

p. 193. l. 27.   'At last!' Crown Prince Rupprecht, p. 358.

p. 194. l. 4.   'No ground must be yielded too soon.' *Ibid.*, pp. 358–9.

p. 195. l. 11.   'A heavy price to pay.' For general accounts of the Meuse-Argonne battle see Pershing pp. 596–659; Maurice, pp. 146–56 and 189–92; Liddell Hart, pp. 577–85; Forrest Pogue, pp. 194–202; and General R. L. Bullard, *American Soldiers also fought*, pp. 99–112.

Source Notes

p. 195. l. 32.   'The rest walked.' Forrest Pogue, p. 194.

p. 196. l. 2.   'A million express trains.' Bullard, p. 93.

p. 196. l. 23.   'Eight to one.' Liddell Hart, p. 579.

p. 197. l. 12.   'Achieved little at large cost.' Liddell Hart, p. 583.

p. 198. l. 2.   'One huge sea of death.' Wrentmore, p. 165.

p. 198. l. 12.   'Insistence of the French.' Bullard, *op. cit.*, p. 96.

p. 198. l. 21.   'Not such a good showing as expected.' Harvey Cushing, *From a Surgeon's Journal*, Diary entry for 1 October 1918.

p. 198. l. 35.   'Even by some Germans.' Pershing, p. 619.

p. 200. l. 3.   'I shall be wholly delighed.' Foch, pp. 247–50.

p. 200. l. 32.   'No longer be resolved by force of arms.' Ludendorff, p. 580.

p. 201. l. 7.   'No complete official record.' *Deutschland im Ersten Weltkrieg*, pp. 425–426, quotes the papers of Heye and von Quirnheim.

p. 202. l. 7.   'Move the government to decisive action.' Ludendorff, pp. 579–80.

p. 202. l. 22.   'The war was now lost.' *Ursachen*, Annexe 11, pp. 361–68, Ludendorff Memorandum of 31 October 1918.

p. 202. l. 27.   'About to voice them himself.' *Ibid.*, p. 365.

p. 203. l. 6.   'Little respect for common ground.' Even that distinguished 'Westerner' among modern military historians, John Terraine, is at fault here for suggesting, in his *To Win a War* (p. 161) that Ludendorff's *initial* impulse to sue for peace in September sprang from setbacks on the Western Front, an interpretation explicitly contradicted by Ludendorff himself.

p. 204. l. 29.   'The securing of peace.' *Deutschland im Ersten Weltkrieg*, p. 427.

p. 205. l. 8.   Hertling's poor speech. *Ursachen* II, p. 248.

p. 205. l. 24.   Growing opposition to Hertling. *Ibid.*, p. 251.

p. 205. l. 34.   'Re-organization now necessary.' Karl Hertling, *Ein Jahr in der Reichskanzlei*, p. 176.

p. 206. l. 12.   'The situation could only get worse.' Ludendorff, p. 582.

p. 206. l. 30.   'Save whatever can be saved!' *Ursachen II*, p. 262.

p. 207. l. 3.   'Grave-side lamentations.' *Ibid.*, p. 261.

p. 207. l. 11.   Decision to sue for peace. Niemann, p. 88.

p. 207. l. 17.   'With controlled emotions.' *Ibid.*, p. 265.

p. 208. l. 7.   'Until our system has been changed.' *Ibid.*, p. 411.

p. 209. l. 3.   'A very definite attempt to seek peace.' Quoted in *New York Times*, 4 October 1918.

p. 209. l. 7.   'A man of some personal charm.' *The Times*, 4 October 1918.

p. 209. l. 30.   'I cannot understand why it has to be Max.' Prince Max of Baden, *Erinnerungen und Dokumente*, p. 327.

p. 210. l. 5.   'Bad negotiating tactics.' *Ibid.*, p. 326.

p. 210. l. 28.   'No time should be lost.' *Amtliche Urkunden*, quoted in full in Rudin, *Armistice 1918*, pp. 67–70.

p. 211. l. 1.   'Panic now leapt across to the people.' Prince Max, pp. 342–3.

p. 211. l. 7.   'If ... Prince Max is forming a Ministry.' Ludendorff, Urkunden, p. 529.

p. 211. l. 17.   Hindenburg goes to Berlin. Paul von Hindenburg, *Out of my Life*, p. 430.

p. 211. l. 29.   'You have not been brought here ...' Prince Max, p. 346.

p. 211. l. 34.   'Only general replies.' *Ibid.*, pp. 348–9.

p. 212. l. 4.   English text reproduced in Rudin, p. 74.

p. 212. l. 30.   'Like a man condemned to death.' Prince Max, p. 353.

Chapter 9: Home Fires

p. 213. l. 9.   'Important their hopes should not be raised.' *The War Memoirs of William Graves Sharp* (American Ambassador to France 1914–1919), p. 321.

p. 213. l. 14.   War damage to France. *Ibid.*, pp. 296–7; also John Williams, *The Home Fronts*, p. 73.

p. 213. l. 28.   Coal in Paris jeweller's window. *The Times*, 30 September 1918.

p. 214. l. 24.   'White as bread ever was.' *Ibid.*, 5 August 1918.

p. 214. l. 28.   'Restaurants flourished.' Williams, p. 263–4.

p. 214. l. 34.   'Treat both classes of customer equally well.' *The Times*, 9 September 1918.

p. 215. l. 20.   'Stations ... almost as busy with arrivals.' *Ibid.*

p. 215. l. 25.   War-time 'haute couture'. *The Times*, 2 September 1918.

p. 216. l. 14.   'If Clemenceau says ...' Quoted in Williams, p. 261.

p. 216. l. 24.   Britain's breakfast assured. *Daily Telegraph*, 29 July 1918.

p. 217. l. 20.   'Beer ... a necessity for workers.' Caroline Playne, *Britain holds on*, p. 256.

p. 217. l. 30.   Fuel-saving tips. *The Times*, 13 September, 1918.

p. 217. l. 35.   Lights in billiard saloons. *Ibid.*

p. 218. l. 12.   'Temporary oblivion.' Williams, p. 64.

p. 218. l. 21.   'Stick it men!' *Daily Telegraph*, 9 October 1918.

p. 218. l. 30.   Hay restrictions rescinded. *The Times*, 21 September 1918.

p. 218. l. 34.   Britain's bookmakers curbed. *Ibid.*, 7 September 1918.

p. 219. l. 8.   Grouse bags to hospitals. *Ibid.*, 7 August 1918.

p. 219. l. 15.   'Partridge shooting an institution.' *Ibid.*, 2 September 1918.

p. 219. l. 32.   'Put that aside for my pal.' Playne, p. 329.

p. 219. l. 35.   Women eligible as MPS. *The Times*, 19 October 1918.

p. 220. l. 6.   Wave of strikes in Britain. Williams, p. 256.

p. 220. l. 14.   London policemen on strike. Playne, p. 345.

p. 220. l. 28.   'Our country is being disgraced.' Diary of Miss K. Alexander. Peter Liddle Archives.

p. 221. l. 2.   'Our solid British temperament.' *The Nation*, 28 September 1918.

p. 221. l. 20.   'Heated exchange' over sex for GI's. See, for example, *The Times* of 25 and 26 September 1918.

p. 222. l. 5.   'Intern them all!' Williams, p. 254.

p. 222. l. 28.   'Bench determined to stop' fraternization. *The Times*, 2 October 1918.

p. 223. l. 8.   Malnutrition in Germany. All statistics from *Ursachen*, Volume 6, pp. 391–405.

p. 224. l. 18.   Confiscation of civilian clothes. Rudin, p. 13 and p. 35.

p. 224. l. 29.   Overcoats of 'heavy paper'. Williams, pp. 275–6.

p. 225. l. 6.   German train regulations. *Berliner Tageblatt*, 5 August 1918.

p. 226. l. 8.   Richard Strauss in Vienna. *NFP*, 14 October 1918.

p. 226. l. 35.   Account given by the Empress Zita to the author in March 1978.

Chapter 10: The Peace Broker

p. 228. l. 20.   'Cold to the point of rudeness.' Sir A. Willert, *The Road to Safety*, p. 62.

p. 229. l. 36.   '... British world economic domination.' V. H. Rothwell, *British War Aims and Diplomacy, 1914–1918*, p. 279.

p. 230. l. 6.   'League of Nations ... the official instrument of discimination.' W. B. Fowler, *British-American Relations 1917–1918*, p. 210.

p. 230. l. 34.   'Germany should "repay every dollar".' *Congressional Record*, 7 October 1918, p. 11162.

p. 231. l. 7.   'Fourteen Points "only confused the issue".' *The Times*, 15 October 1918.

p. 231. l. 28.   Anti-German war posters. As displayed at the Imperial War Museum in London during the summer of 1978.

p. 232. l. 13. 'I would suggest making no direct reply.' Charles Seymour, *The Intimate Papers of Colonel House*, Vol. IV, pp. 75–6 (henceforth cited as *House Papers*).

p. 232. l. 34. 'A query, not a reply.' R. S. Baker, *Wilson*, Vol. 8, p. 462.

p. 233. l. 5. Rudin, p. 104, reproduces the full American text.

p. 233. l. 18. 'Unless there was a change in Berlin.' Inga Floto, *Colonel House in Paris*, p. 36.

p. 234. l. 6. German note intercepted *'en route'*. Rudin, p. 89.

p. 234. l. 22. French military terms. Foch, pp. 527–8.

p. 235. l. 22. 'A dangerous visionary at that.' Calwell, pp. 136–7.

p. 235. l. 26. 'Wilson is an autocrat.' Christopher Addison, 'Four and a Half Years', p. 575.

p. 236. l. 16. 'Lloyd George irritated with Wilson.' Lord Hankey, *The Supreme Command*, 1914–18, Vol. 2, p. 854.

p. 237. l. 22. Resumption of submarine warfare 'must be assured'. *Amtliche Urkunden*, Document 35A.

p. 237. l. 28. 'Justify the optimists.' Prince Max, p. 370.

p. 238. l. 20. 'We need a breathing space.' *Ibid.*, pp. 371–2.

p. 238. l. 35. 'I thank your Grand-Duchal Highness.' *Ibid.*, p. 389.

p. 239. l. 4. 'A dangerous legend.' *Frankfurter Zeitung*, 11 October 1918.

p. 239. l. 8. German reply of 12 October 1918. *Amtliche Urkunden*, Document 47.

p. 240. l. 1. 'I never saw him more disturbed.' *House Papers*, Vol. IV, pp. 82–83.

p. 240. l. 20. Allied messages to Washington. Quoted in Floto, pp. 36–7.

p. 241. l. 16. English text of Wilson's second note. *Amtliche Urkunden*, Document 48.

p. 242. l. 22. 'Can we accept all Wilson's conditions?' This and the following extracts from intercepted German field post letters dated between 15 and 26 October 1918, reproduced in *Ursachen*, Vol. V, pp. 324–34.

p. 243. l. 28. 'The Kaiser asked me that last Sunday.' Prince Max, p. 332.

p. 244. l. 10. 'The people would choose peace.' *Ibid.*, p. 358.

p. 244. l. 18. 'This upstart on the other side of the ocean.' Niemann, pp. 100–101.

p. 244. l. 10. 'Only summoned at five minutes after twelve.' Prince Max, p. 386.

p. 245. l. 14. 'One of the most dramatic events.' Rudin, p. 141.

p. 245. l. 16. Official protocol of Berlin conference of 17 October. Given textually in Prince Max, pp. 398–421, from which any direct quotations which follow have been translated.

p. 245. l. 34. Ludendorff's account of same. Ludendorff, pp. 604–10, and, much closer to the time than his memoirs, in a long memorandum, *Das Waffenstillstandsangebot*, dated 31 October 1918 and reproduced as Annexe II of *Ursachen*.

p. 245. l. 6. 'How long can the war be conducted?' *Amtliche Urkunden*, Document 56.

p. 248. l. 26. 'I returned in high spirits.' *Das Waffenstillstandsangebot*, p. 367 of Annexe II.

p. 249. l. 4. 'Part of war is luck.' Ludendorff, p. 605.

p. 249. l. 8. 'I lost faith in Ludendorff.' Prince Max, p. 422.

p. 250. l. 8. 'then comes the revolution.' *Ibid.*, p. 428.

p. 250. l. 20. Order to German U-boats. German text in Document 64 of *Amtliche Urkunden*.

p. 250. l. 34. For British Cabinet discussions see, *inter alia*, Calwell, pp. 138–40.

p. 252. l. 14. Account of Wilson's Cabinet meeting in E. N. Hurley, *The Bridge to France*, pp. 332–24.

p. 254. l. 20. This and other details of the Senlis Conference from Foch, pp. 536–40.

p. 255. l. 16. 'We must go on fighting.' Ludendorff, p. 611.

p. 256. l. 3. 'The defeated War Lord should resign!' Prince Max, p. 469.

p. 256. l. 10. 'The decisive factor was the lost trust.' *Ibid.*, p. 47.

p. 256. l. 16. Spa proclamation to troops. Text in Ludendorff, p. 614–15.

p. 256 l. 24. Ludendorff's explanation. *Ibid.*, pp. 615–16.

p. 257. l. 23. 'Ludendorff has been dismissed!' Prince Max, p. 475.

p. 258. l. 1. 'It was as though we could all breathe again.' Letter intercepted by censorship, reproduced in *Ursachen* V, p. 329.

Chapter 11: Landslides

p. 260. l. 8. Withdrawal to the Meuse. Ludendorff, pp. 611–12.

p. 260. l. 16. British re-enter Lille. Gibbs, p. 393.

p. 260. l. 24. Douai a pillaged ghost town. 'The Eighth Division in the War', quoted in Terraine, p. 205.

p. 262. l. 10. 'I don't like those bombs coming in.' Gibbs, p. 395.

p. 262. l. 28. '120,000 battle casualties.' Lloyd George, p. 3149.

p. 264. l. 9.   'We'll take it or report "No Brigade".' Anecdote told in Bullard, p. 110.

p. 264. l. 37.   'Sometimes it's a rifle, sometimes a helmet.' Log book of Captaine Tournaire in *Histoire de la Guerre par les Combattants*, Vol IV, p. 390.

p. 265. l. 8.   '*Hier ruht Smith.*' Bartlett, p. 66.

p. 265. l. 16.   'Three French girls, all dressed up.' Sir William Orpen, *An Onlooker in France*, p. 93.

p. 265 l. 26.   'Captured while sleeping.' Gibbs, p. 389.

p. 265. l. 35.   'War weariness had increased.' Ludendorff, p. 602.

p. 266. l. 6.   'All peace talk must cease.' Rudyard Kipling, *The Irish Guards in the Great War*, pp. 214–15.

p. 266. l. 10.   'The reckless ones became cautious.' Diary of Guardsman W. J. Drury (entry for 1 November 1918). Peter Liddle Archives.

p. 266. l. 20.   'I will never forget my surprise.' Diary of Second-Lt. J. D. Hardman RFC (later Sir Donald Hardman). Peter Liddle Archives.

p. 266. l. 32.   'The sky is covered with our squadrons.' Général H. Colin, *Guerre de Mouvement 1918*, p. 183.

p. 267. l. 9.   'Plenty of fight left.' Hardman Diary, entry for 30 October 1918.

p. 267. l. 20.   'It would still present a challenge.' Hankey, p. 849.

p. 268. l. 17.   'With 200,000 men ...' Azan, p. 211

p. 269. l. 1.   He became 'absolutely furious'. Hankey, p. 842, on whose diary this part of the inter-allied squabble is based.

p. 269. l. 22.   Planning strategy 'on a small hand-atlas map'. Calwell, p. 132.

p. 269. l. 27.   'The Entente possessed no military direction.' Larcher, *La Grande Guerre dans les Balkans*, p. 243.

p. 270. l. 27.   'All this fuss was made.' Lloyd George, p. 3314.

p. 272. l. 5.   E. A. Armstrong in the *Mosquito* (Salonika Army veterans' journal) in October 1963.

p. 272. l. 25.   For a well-documented account of the Mudros armistice negotiations, see V. H. Rothwell pp. 240–44; also Azan, pp. 217–20.

p. 272. l. 32.   'As though for a Spithead review.' H. Owen, *Salonika and After*, p. 272.

p. 273. l. 31.   'He received orders from Clemenceau.' For the relevant exchange between Clemenceau and d'Espèrey, see Azan, pp. 213–16.

p. 275. l. 2.   'They had far outrun their supplies.' Villari, p. 256.

p. 276. l. 30.   Internal re-construction of Austria. For this, and the political events which followed in Vienna and Budapest, see Brook-Shepherd, *The Last Habsburg*, pp. 170–90.

p. 277. l. 29.   'The only solution is a truly federal one ...' The Empress Zita's written record of the event, as given to the author in May 1967.

p. 278. l. 28.   Coronation in Budapest. The Empress Zita to the author in a later conversation on 9 February 1980. She, of course, was crowned Queen of Hungary at her husband's side.

p. 281. l. 12.   For details of the Italian battle plan and dispositions see Villari, *The War on the Italian Front*, pp. 248–52; also Valori, *La Guerra Italo-Austriaca*, pp. 489 *et seq.*

p. 282. l. 18.   'There's a bonus for collecting stinging nettles.' Diary of Hauptmann Radine Kohout, pp. 181–3. Heeresarchiv Vienna.

p. 283. l. 12.   Count Dubsky and his water ration. Unpublished memoirs of Count Gerolf Coudenhove-Kalergi, p. 45.

p. 283. l. 30.   'Was there any point in further fighting?' Major-General Berndt, *Letzter Kampf und Ende der 29 Division*, p. 37.

p. 284. l. 17.   'No fewer than 30,000 deserters.' *Ibid.*, p. 34.

p. 284. l. 28.   'Two rebellious units.' Major-General Ernst Horsetsky, *Die Vier Letzen Kriegswochen*, p. 16.

p. 284. l. 32.   Yugoslav declaration in Vienna. Speech reported in *The Times*, 15 October 1918.

p. 286. l. 6.   'No one can guarantee that the Hungarian troops will ... fight on.' Horsetsky, p. 17.

p. 286. l. 12.   Appeal to Hungarian soldiers. *Ibid.*

p. 287. l. 8.   Unpublished diary of Lt. Colonel Richard (later Lt. General Sir Richard) O'Connor. See also E. C. Crosse, *The Defeat of Austria as seen by the 7th Division*, pp. 21 *et seq.*, which was largely based at the time on O'Connor's account.

p. 289. l. 30.   Heavy Italian mountain casualties. Villari, p. 256.

p. 290. l. 12.   'Scrape together whatever was possible.' Unpublished diary of Colonel Karl Scheller, p. 1284. Heeresarchiv Vienna.

p. 290. l. 24.   'The means were simply not available.' Berndt, p. 65.

p. 290. l. 27.   'Eleven had mutinied almost in their entirety.' Villari, p. 257.

p. 291. l. 12.   'A catastrophe of unpredictable results.' Generaloberst von Arz, *Zur Geschichte des Grossen Krieges*, p. 334.

Chapter 12: 'Finis Austriae'

p. 293. l. 21. 'One overriding aim.' *House Papers*, p. 155.

p. 294. l. 32. 'America had the advantage.' *Ibid.*, pp. 164–5.

p. 295. l. 6. Lloyd George's stand on blockade rights. Hankey, p. 860.

p. 295. l. 24. 'That would never be allowed.' *The Times*, 1 November 1918.

p. 295. l. 35. 'Nations, like animals ...' Hankey, p. 860.

p. 296. l. 7. 'That would amount to a separate peace.' *House Papers*, p. 170.

p. 296. l. 20. 'We will fight on.' Hankey, p. 860.

p. 296. l. 34. Lloyd George's freedom of seas formula. *Ibid.*, p. 862.

p. 297. l. 28. 'I propose terms be submitted straightaway to Austria.' *House Papers*, p. 106.

p. 298. l. 24. Opening of negotiations. Villari, pp. 284-5. Except where otherwise noted, the account of the armistice is based, from the Italian side, on Villari, pp. 281–3; and, from the Austrian side, on Arz, pp. 346–7 and pp. 361–72. These general accounts by no means give the full picture, however, as is shown by some of the hitherto unpublished material quoted below.

p. 299. l. 9. General Weber's unpromising start. Karl Scheller Diary (Annexe), p. 2.

p. 300. l. 1. 'Leave at once ... for the Italian lines.' *Ibid.*, p. 4.

p. 300. l. 22. Another squeal from Vienna. Calwell, p. 146.

p. 301. l. 23. 'The Emperor's trousers.' Hankey, p. 864.

p. 302. l. 24. Károlyi did 'not want a Republic'. Memoirs of Michael Károlyi, p. 108.

p. 303. l. 6. Attempts to steady Hungarian troops. Arz, p. 363.

p. 304. l. 3. Full text resolution in the *NFP* of 22 October 1918.

p. 304. l. 32. Austrian Supreme Command calls for special loyalty reports. Berndt, p. 75.

p. 306. l. 8. Terms telephoned from Paris. Villari, p. 287.

p. 307. l. 14. German fears over armistice. See *Amtliche Urkunden* 86a (Hindenburg's requests).

p. 307. l. 30. 'The most energetic protest.' Arz, p. 366.

p. 308. l. 22. 'I can do no more than ring up Schönbrunn!' Colonel Scheller Diary (Annexe), p. 11.

p. 308. l. 36. 'Certainly lead to a catastrophe.' Arz, p. 368.

p. 309. l. 33.   Austrian telegram of protest over cease-fire. *Ibid.*, p. 371.

p. 310. l. 13.   Badoglio-Weber exchanges. Colonel Scheller Diary (Annexe), p. 15.

p. 311. l. 30.   Confusion at the Tagliamento. Crosse, p. 97.

p. 312. l. 26.   'There is clearly great confusion.' Berndt, p. 99.

p. 313. l. 1.   Show-down at Udine. Berndt, p. 102.

p. 313. l. 24.   'Every soldier found south of this line ...' Arz, p. 378.

p. 313. l. 30.   'Largest march column in military history.' Horsetsky, p. 38.

p. 314. l. 15.   'Trains like moving swarms of bees.' *Ibid.*, p. 39.

p. 314. l. 30.   'So I rang at the door of the Toggenburg Palace.' Coudenhove-Kalergi family diary, p. 60.

p. 315. l. 14.   Prisoner counts. *The Times* of 4 November 1918, quoting official communiqués.

p. 316. l. 1.   Hand-over of Austro-Hungarian fleet. Memoirs of Admiral Horthy, p. 92.

p. 316. l. 26.   Italian take-over of ships. A. E. Sokol, *Seemacht Österreich*, pp. 192–5.

p. 317. l. 30.   Károlyi reaction to armistice. *Károlyi Memoirs*, p. 130.

p. 318. l. 14.   D'Espèrey's dreams of Danubian conquest. Larcher, pp. 253–4.

p. 318. l. 26.   Clemenceau's order to d'Espèrey. Azan, 'L'Armistice avec la Hongrie' in *Illustration* (Paris), 5 November 1921.

p. 319. l. 7.   'We were the "burghers of Calais".' Károlyi, p. 131.

p. 319. l. 16.   'The small and chilly sitting room ...' Károlyi, p. 132.

p. 320. l. 6.   Károlyi-d'Espèrey exchanges. Azan, pp. 229–30; see also Gusztav Grav, *A Forradalmak Kora* (*The Age of Revolutions*), Vol. 11 of the Magyar Szemle Review.

p. 320. l. 28.   'Not today, now I am in Belgrade.' Károlyi, p. 135.

p. 321. l. 14.   French concessions. *Ibid.*, p. 135.

p. 321. l. 20.   Károlyi's telegram to Clemenceau. Azan, p. 232.

Chapter 13: November Nightmares

p. 324. l. 22.   'A private communication.' Prince Max, p. 497.

p. 324. l. 29.   'Under the Chancellor's influence.' *Ibid.*

p. 325. l. 5.   German Socialists turn against monarchy. See, for example, Scheidemann, *Memoiren*, Vol. 11, p. 262.

p. 325. l. 18.   Bavaria warns Berlin. Prince Max, p. 473.

p. 326. l. 22.   'That is why I am leaving this evening.' *Ibid.*, p. 500.

p. 358. l. 13. Kaiser's threat to 'restore order'. *Ibid.*, p. 590.

p. 358. l. 29. 'It is my sacred duty to build a dam ...' Niemann, pp. 133–4.

p. 359. l. 9. Groener ordered to draw up plans. Groener, p. 454.

p. 359. l. 30. Controlling 'a handful of revolutionaries'. Prince Max, pp. 591–2.

p. 360. l. 22. No breakfast for the front-line officers. Groener, p. 458.

p. 361. l. 4. Hindenburg describes the Kaiser's rescue plan. Kronprinz Wilhelm, *Erinnerungen*, pp. 295–8. (The Crown Prince had arrived at Spa at 8.30 a.m. on the morning of the 9th, just as the front-line officers were gathering, and he and the three members of his Army Group staff accompanying him talked to the commanders before and after the meeting.)

p. 361. l. 31. Lengthy period of rest needed. Groener, p. 458–9.

p. 361. l. 34. Raemakers Cartoon. Reproduced in the *Daily Telegraph* of 3 October 1918.

p. 362. l. 25. 'What I have to tell Your Majesty ...' Groener, p. 459.

p. 363. l. 1. Action against 'the rebel cities of the Rhine'. Niemann, p. 135.

p. 363. l. 13. Army 'no longer stands behind Your Majesty.' Groener, p. 460.

p. 363. l. 16. Kaiser's theatrical reactions. Niemann, p. 135.

p. 364. l. 1. 'The Emperor stood there ...' etc. Crown Prince William, pp. 280–1.

p. 364. l. 21. Kaiser to stay King of Prussia. *Ibid.*, p. 283–4.

p. 364. l. 31. 'Those are just words.' *Ibid.*, p. 284.

p. 365. l. 5. Telephone problems with Spa. Prince Max, p. 599.

p. 365. l. 17. 'The die is cast.' *Ibid.*, p. 596.

p. 365. l. 19. Scheidemann resigns. Scheidemann, *Memoiren*, Vol. 2, p. 297.

p. 365. l. 23. 'Now a matter of minutes.' Prince Max, p. 597.

p. 366. l. 4. Abdication announcement by Prince Max. *Ibid.*, p. 599.

p. 366. l. 17. Kaiser tries to retain Prussian crown. *Ibid.*, p. 606.

p. 367. l. 19. 'Breathing heavily, his teeth chattering ...' Niemann, p. 140.

p. 368. l. 4. Discussion of asylum country for Kaiser. *Ibid.*, p. 141, and Groener, pp. 462–3.

p. 368. l. 16. 'As I am no longer Emperor ...' Groener, p. 463.

p. 368. l. 24. Kaiser considers fighting it out. Crown Prince, p. 305.

p. 368. l. 34. 'I must go with you to a neutral state.' *Memoirs of Princess Viktoria Luise*, p. 138.

p. 369. l. 6. Kaiser's farewell letter to his son. Crown Prince, p. 303.

p. 369. l. 22. Kaiser changes his travel plans again. *Ibid.*, p. 306.

p. 370. l. 36. Regency question 'too late, too late'. Prince Max, 600–2.

p. 371. l. 18.	'Pleasant journey' inscription on statue. Incident described in *The Times*, 1 November 1918.
p. 371. l. 28.	Princess Blücher's Berlin diary. Quoted at length in Mordacq, pp. 88–94.
p. 372. l. 9.	'I myself am one of those officers . . .' *Ursachen*, Vol. 6, p. 135.
p. 372. l. 13.	One Berlin army officer resists rebels. *Ibid.*, p. 139.
p. 372. l. 30.	The lone civilian monarchist in Berlin. *Ursachen*, Vol. 5, p. 56.
p. 373. l. 11.	'They are cads about the Kaiser.' War Diary of Miss K. Alexander. Peter Liddle Archives.
p. 373. l. 22.	'Even in this, he was typical!' Empress Zita, in conversation with the author, 9 October 1978.
p. 373. l. 28.	Ebert's strange position. Prince Max, p. 607.
p. 374. l. 6.	Ebert establishes himself. For these political events in Berlin, see Eduard Bernstein, *Die Deutsche Revolution*, pp. 40–50; Hermann Mueller, *Die November Revolution*, pp. 62–70.

Chapter 15: 11 November 1918

p. 375. l. 6.	Mark of authenticity. Foch, p. 303.
p. 375. l. 8.	Puzzled French interpreter. Erzberger, p. 384.
p. 376. l. 5.	For the full text of the armistice discussions arranged in four comparative columns (original terms of Foch; counter-proposals of Germans; Foch's reply to the counter-proposals and final clauses) see *Der Waffenstillstand 1918*, Vol. 1, pp. 23–57.
p. 376. l. 21.	'All submarines.' Wemyss, p. 394.
p. 377. l. 3.	'They only had to come out!' *Ibid.*, p. 393–4.
p. 377. l. 8.	'You sank our ships indiscriminately!' Erzberger, p. 385.
p. 377. l. 24.	German troops in East Africa. *Waffenstillstand*, pp. 40–1.
p. 378. l. 21.	'A nation of 50 millions . . . does not perish.' *Ibid.*, pp. 72–3 gives original German text.
p. 379. l. 1.	Allied cease-fire order. Foch, pp. 319–20.
p. 379. l. 21.	Even a few hisses etc. Eye-witness account from Maarn, given in *Daily Telegraph* of 13 November 1918.
p. 380. l. 1.	'My dog's existence is over.' *Memoirs of Princess Viktoria Luise*, p. 139.
p. 381. l. 10.	Creation of Austrian Republic. Unless otherwise stated, the account which follows of events in Vienna from 9 to 11

November is based on Brook-Shepherd, *The Last Habsburg*, pp. 207–17.

p. 383. l. 15.   Reserve battalion melts away. Unpublished diary of Colonel Carl Wolff, pp. 2–3. Heeresarchiv, Vienna.

p. 383. l. 26.   No rations for Vienna palace guard. *Ibid.*, p. 4.

p. 384. l. 2.   Boroević rescue offer. Friedrich Funder, *Vom Gestern ins Heute*, pp. 549–50.

p. 384. l. 16.   Offer blocked by General Dankl. Brook-Shepherd, p. 206.

p. 385. l. 4.   Coudenhove-Kalergi Diary, entry for 11 November 1918.

p. 385. l. 22.   Clemenceau receives armistice news. Mordacq, p. 43.

p. 385. l. 33.   Colonel House hears the news. *House Papers*, p. 145.

p. 386. l. 3.   'Our Lusitania dead are avenged!' Mordacq, p. 45.

p. 386. l. 14.   Clemenceau's victory speech. *Ibid.*, pp. 118–19.

p. 386. l. 31.   Lloyd George victory speech. *The Times*, 12 November 1918.

p. 387. l. 4.   London street scene, 11 November. Churchill, p. 542.

p. 387. l. 24.   'The whole air filled with … thankfulness.' Unpublished diary of Patricia Hanbury (later Lady Cunninghame Grahame). Peter Liddle Archives.

p. 387. l. 33.   'It's peace all right!' Unpublished diary of Molly Macleod. Peter Liddle Archives.

p. 388. l. 3.   Kent village on 11 November. *My Warrior Sons* (Borton Family Diary), p. 207.

p. 388. l. 15.   Field Marshal Wilson and sobbing woman. Caldwell, p. 149.

p. 388. l. 29.   Wilson address to Congress. Congressional Record, 11 November 1918, pp. 11538–9.

p. 389. l. 10.   'Autocracy is dead!' *House Papers*, p. 145.

p. 389. l. 28.   Allied losses in last phase. Lloyd George, p. 3149.

p. 390. l. 12.   'Those who would not return …' Dorothy Cheney, *Memoirs*. Diary entry for 11 November 1918.

p. 390. l. 22.   '… it ends where it all began.' Alice Lord O'Brian, *Letters from France 1917–1919*. Diary entry for 11 November 1918.

p. 390. l. 30.   'Idleness and cowardice flourish with security.' Baroness Ernest de la Grange, *Open House in Flanders*. Diary entry for 11 November 1918.

p. 391. l. 2.   'An immense and majestic crowd of poilus.' Jacques Bouis, *Notes d'un Agent de Liaison*, p. 211.

p. 391. l. 8.   Gunners kissing their horses. Diary of Gunner Bruce Ross of 13th Field Artillery Brigade. Entry for 11 November 1918. Peter Liddle Archives.

p. 391. l. 16.   'It is indeed God who ... has saved them.' Maréchal Fayolle, *Cahiers Secrets*, p. 312.

p. 391. l. 22.   'Everything went on as usual.' Major-General O'Ryan, *The Story of the 27th Division*, p. 397.

p. 391. l. 31.   '... probably the last German killed.' Adrian Keith-Falconer, *The Oxfordshire Hussars in the Great War*, p. 339.

p. 392. l. 2.   British battery goes on firing. From the BBC's Radio Four programme broadcast at 10.15 a.m. on 11 November 1978.

p. 392. l. 7.   German machine gunners ceremonial farewell. *The History of the 62nd (W.R.) Division*, p. 150.

p. 392. l. 16.   'No cheering and little outward excitement.' *Ibid.* (footnote).

p. 392. l. 32.   'Impossible to forget those ... who had not come through.' *The Gloucestershires in the First World War*, p. 349.

p. 393. l. 10.   'Oh God, what a war ... What a peace!' P. J. Campbell Diary, p. 172.

p. 393. l. 18.   'And what happens now?' C. H. Dudley Ward, *History of the Welsh Guards*, p. 289.

p. 393. l. 22.   '... on this day ... I found something wrong ...' Orpen, p. 98.

Selected Bibliography
of Works Consulted

(Excluding Official War Histories,
unpublished diaries and periodicals,
as identified separately in the Source Notes)

1 English

Addison, Rt. Hon. Christopher, *Four and a Half Years* (Vol. 2) London 1934

Amery, L. S., *My Political Life* (Vol. 2) London 1953–5

Balfour, Michael, *The Kaiser and his Times* London 1964

Banks, Arthur, *A Military Atlas of the First World War* London 1975

Barker, A. J., *The Neglected War* London 1967

Baring, Maurice, *R.F.C., G.H.Q.* London 1920

Buchan, John, *Episodes of the Great War* London 1936

Bartlett, S. Ashmead, *From the Somme to the Rhine* London 1921

Bentinck, Lady Nora, *The Ex-Kaiser in Exile* London 1921

Blaxland, William, *Amiens 1918* London 1968

Boraston, J. H., *Sir Douglas Haig's Despatches* London 1919

Brook-Shepherd, Gordon, *The Last Habsburg* London 1968

Calwell, Major-General Sir C. E., *Field Marshal Sir Henry Wilson* London 1927

Churchill, Winston S., *The World War 1916–1918* London 1927

Constant, Stephen, *Foxy Ferdinand* London 1979

Coombs, Rose E. B., *Before Endeavours Fade* London 1976

Cornwall, James Marshall, *Foch* London 1972

Crosse, Rev. E. C., *The Defeat of Austria as seen by the 7th Division* London 1919

Dare, Jane, *Letters from a Forgotten Army* London 1920

Dewar, G. A. B., *Sir Douglas Haig's Command* (Vol. 2) London 1922

Duff Cooper, *Haig* (2 Volumes) London 1935

Falls, Cyril, *Armageddon 1918* London 1964

Fischer, Fritz, *Germany's Claims in the First World War* London 1967

Gibbs, Sir Philip, *The War Despatches*, London 1964

Hankey, Lord, *The Supreme Command* (Vol. 2) London 1961

Haig, Field Marshal Sir Douglas, *Private Papers* London 1932

Hart, Captain Liddell B. H., *History of First World War* London 1930

Hart, Captain Liddell B. H., *Foch, The Man of Orleans* London 1933

Hart, Captain Liddell B. H., *The Other Side of the Hill* London 1951

Headlam, C., *The Guards Division in the Great War* (Vol. 2) London 1924

Jones, H. A., *The War in the Air* (Vol. 6) London 1931–7

Jones, H. A., *Over the Balkans and South Russia* London 1923

Keith-Falconer, Adrian, *The Oxfordshire Hussars in the Great War* London 1927

Kipling, Rudyard, *The Irish Guards in the Great War* London 1923

Lawrence, T. E., *Seven Pillars of Wisdom* London 1928

Lawrence, T. E., *Revolt in the Desert* London 1928

Liddle, Peter, *Testimony of War* Wilton (Salisbury) 1979

Lloyd George, David, *War Memoirs* (Vol. 6) London 1936

Macartney, C. A., *Hungary, a Short History* Edinburgh 1963

Macartney, C. A., *The House of Austria and the Later Phase* Edinburgh 1978

Massey, W. T., *Allenby's Final Triumph* London 1920

Maurice, Major-General Sir F., *The Last Four Months* London 1919

Middlebrook, Martin, *The Kaiser's Battle* London 1978

Montgomery, Sir A., *The Story of the Fourth Army* London 1920

Morrison, L. G., *The 8th of August 1918* London

Murray, Arthur, *At Close Quarters* London 1946

Orpen, Sir William, *An Onlooker in France* London 1921

Owen, H. Cullison, *Salonika and After* London 1919

Palmer, Alan, *The Gardeners of Salonika* London 1965

Playne, Caroline, *Britain holds on* London 1933

Repington, Lieutenant Colonel C., *The First World War* (Vol. 2) London 1920.

Rothwell, V. H., *British War Aims and Diplomacy* Oxford 1971

Ryder, A. T., *The German Revolution of 1918* London 1967

Ryder, A. T., *Twentieth Century Germany* London 1972

Seligman, V. J., *The Salonika Sideshow* London 1919

Slater, Guy (ed), *My Warrior Sons* London 1973

Terraine, John, *To Win a War* London 1978

Selected Bibliography

Terraine, John, *Douglas Haig* London 1963
Thomas, Lowell, *With Allenby in the Holy Land* London 1938
Ward, C. Dudley, *History of Welsh Guards* London 1920
Wavell, Lieut. General A. P., *The Palestine Campaign* London 1928
Wemyss, Lady, *The Life and Letters of Lord Wemyss*
Willert, Arthur, *The Road to Safety, a study in Anglo-American relations*
    London 1952
Williams, John, *The Home Fronts* London 1972
Wyrall, Everard, *History of the 62nd West Riding Division* London 1925
Zeman, Z. A. B., *The Break-up of the Habsburg Empire* Oxford 1961

2   French

Azan, Paul, *Franchet d'Espèrey* Paris 1949
Benoist-Mechin, J., *Ce que demeure* Paris 1942
Bouis, Jacques, *Notes d'un Agent de Liaison* Paris 1922
Boillot, F., *Un officer d' infanterie à la Guerre* Paris 1927
Bugnet, Charles, *En écoutant le Maréchal Foch* Paris 1929
Buxtorf, A., *En Italie avec la 24ième Division* Nancy
Charles-Roux, F., *La Paix des Empires Centraux* Paris 1947
Clemenceau, Georges, *Grandeurs et Misères d'une Victoire* Paris 1930
Colin, General H., *Guerre de Mouvement 1918* Paris 1935
Cordier, Louis, *Ceux du Premier Armistice* Clermont-Ferrand 1936
Daille, M., *La Bataille de Montdidier* Paris 1924
Debergh et Gaillard, *Chemins de l'Armistice* Paris 1968
Ducasse, Andre, *Balkans, 14–18* Paris 1964
Fayolle, Marechal, *Cahiers Secrets de la Grande Guerre* Paris 1964
Foch, Marechal Ferdinand, *Mémoires* Paris 1931
Grange, Baronesse Erneste de la, *Open House in Flanders* London 1929
Isorni, Jacques, *Philippe Petoeni* (2 Volumes) Paris 1973
Larcher, M., *La Grande Guerre dans les Balkans* Paris 1929
L'Hopital, Rene, *Foch, l'Armistice et la Paix* Paris 1938
Modelin, Louis, *Foch* Paris 1929
Mangin, General, *Comment Finit la Guerre* Paris 1920
Maricourt, Baron André, *Foch* Nancy 1920
Mordacq, General, *La Verité sur l'Armistice* Paris 1929
Pedroncini, G., *Pétain, Général en Chef 1917–1918* Paris 1974
Recouly, Raymond, *Le Mémorial de Foch* Paris 1929

November 1918

Renouvin, P., *L'Armistice de Rethondes* Paris 1968
Sarrail, General, *Mon Commandement en Orient* Paris 1920
Serringy, General, *Trente Ans avec Pétain* Paris 1959
Weygand, General, *Le 11 Novembre* Paris 1947
Weygand, General, *Foch* Paris 1947

3   American

Aldrich, Mildred, *The Peak of the Load* London 1919
Alexander, R., *Memories of the World War 1917–18* New York 1931
Allen, Hervey, *Towards the Flame* London 1934
Baker, Roy Stannard, *Woodrow Wilson, Life and Letters* New York 1927–9
Bullard, General R. L., *American Soldiers also Fought* New York 1936
Cheney, D., *Memories, November 1917–March 1919* Hartford 1930
Cushing, Henry, *From a Surgeon's Journal* London 1936
Fowler, W. B., *British-American Relations 1917–1918, The role of Sir William Wiseman* Princeton 1969
Frothingham, Thomas G., *The American Reinforcement in the World War* New York 1927
Harbord, Major-General J. G., *The American Army in France 1917–1919* Boston 1936
Judy, Will, *A Soldier's Diary* Chicago 1931
Kennan, George F., *American Policy 1900–1950* Chicago 1951
Lansing, Robert, *The Big Four* Boston 1921
Leland, Captain C. G., *From Shell-Hole to Chateau with No. 1 Company* New York 1950
Mamatey, Victor S., *The United States and East Central Europe 1914–1918* Princeton 1957
Mayer, A. J., *Political Origins of the New Diplomacy 1917–1918* Yale, New Haven 1959
O'Brian, Alice Lord, *No Glory* (*Letters from France 1917–1919*) Buffalo 1936
Palmer, Frederick, *Bliss, Peacemaker* New York 1934
Pershing, John J., *My Experiences in the World War* London 1931
Pogue, Forrest C., *George C. Marshall, Education of a General* New York 1963
Rickenbacher, E. V., *Fighting the Flying Circus* New York 1919

Selected Bibliography

Seymour, Charles, *Woodrow Wilson and the World War* Yale, New Haven 1921

Seymour, Charles, *The Intimate Papers of Colonel House* (Vol. IV) London 1928

Sharp, William Graves, *War Memories 1914–1919* London 1931

Tuchman, Barbara W., *August 1914* London 1962

Wheeler, Curtis, *Letters from an American Soldier to his father* Indianapolis 1918

Wrentmore, E. L. *In Spite of Hell* New York 1958

4   German

Baden, Prince Max von, *Erinnerungen und Dokumente* Stuttgart 1968

Bernstein, Eduard, *Die deutsche Revolution* Berlin 1921

Binding, Rudolf, *Aus dem Kriege* (Transl.: London 1925)

Bose, Major Thilo von, *Die Katastrophe des 8 August 1918* Berlin 1930

Bülow, Prince von, *Denkwürdegkeiten* (Vols 2 and 3) Berlin 1930

Cramon, General A. von, (translation) *Quatre Ans au GHQ Austro-Hongrois* Paris 1922

Dieterich, General D., *Weltkriegsende an der Mazedonischen Front* Oldenburg 1925

Erzberger, Matthias, *Erlebnisse im Weltkrieg* Stuttgart 1920

Foerster, Wolfgang, *Der Feldherr Ludendorff im Unglück* Wiesbaden 1952

Groener, General Wilhelm, *Lebenserinnerungen* Göttingen 1957

Hertling, Graf von, *Ein Jahr in der Reichskanzlei* Freiburg 1919

Hindenburg, Gert von, *Hindenburg, Soldat und Staatsmann* Berlin 1932

Hindenburg, Paul von, *Aus meinem Leben* Leipzig 1920

Kabisch, Ernst, *Der schwarze Tag* Berlin 1934

Kürenberg, Joachim von, *War alles falsch?* (*Das Leben Wilhelm II*) Bonn 1951

Kutscher, Hans, *Admiralsrebellion oder Matrosenrevolte?* Stuttgart 1933

Ludendorff, General Erich, *Meine Kriegserinnerungen* Berlin 1919

Ludendorff, General Erich, *Urkunden der obersten Heeresleitung 1916–1918* Berlin 1922

Michaelis (edited), *Die Ursachen des deutschen Zusammenbruchs* (especially Nos. 2 and 6 of the 16 volumes) Berlin 1929

Muller, Hermann, *Die November Revolution* Berlin 1928

November 1918

Niemann, Alfred, *Kaiser und Revolution* Berlin 1922
Niemann, Alfred, *Kaiser und Heer* Berlin 1929
Noske, Gustav, *Von Kiel bis Kapp* Berlin 1920
Nowak, Karl Friedrich, *Der Sturz der Mittelmächte* Munich 1921
Payer, Friedrich, *Von Betthman-Hollweg bis Ebert* Frankfurt 1923
Petzold, Joachim (ed.) *Deutschland im ersten Weltkrieg* Berlin 1969
Rupprecht, Kronprinz von, *Mein Kriegstagebuch* Munich 1929
Sanders, General Liman von *Fünf Jahre Türkei* Berlin 1920
Scheer, Admiral, *Deutschland's Hochseeflotte im Weltkrieg* Berlin 1920
Scheidemann, Phillip, *Der Zusammenbruch* Berlin 1921
Sendtner, Kurt, *Rupprecht von, Wittelsbach* Munich 1954.
Stegemann, Hermann, *Geschichte des Krieges* Stuttgart 1921
Stutzenberger, Adolf, *Die Abdankung Kaiser Wilhelms* Berlin 1937
Tirpitz, Admiral Hans von, (translation) *Memoiren* London 1928
Tschuppik, Karl, *Ludendorff, Die Tragödie des Fachmanns* Vienna 1930
Viktoria Luise, Princess, (translation) *The Kaiser's Daughter* London 1977
William II, Kaiser (translation) *My Memoirs* London 1922
William, Kronprinz, *Erinnerungen* Stuttgart 1922
Zedlitz-Trützschler, Graf Robert, *Zwölf Jahre am deutschen Kaiserhof* Berlin 1924

5 Austro-Hungarian

Arz, Generaloberst, *Zur Geschichte des Grossen Krieges* Munich 1924
Benedikt, Heinrich, *Geschichte der Republik Oesterreich* Vienna 1954
Berndt, General, *Letzter Kampf und Ende der 29 Division* Reichenberg 1928
Csokor, Franz Theodor, *3 November 1918* Vienna 1936
Eisenmenger, Anna, (translation) *Blockade Diary 1914–1924* London 1932
Funder, Friedrich, *Vom Gestern ins Heute* Vienna 1952
Horsetsky, Major-General Ernst, *Die vier letzten Kriegswochen*
Horthy, Admiral, (translation) *Memoirs* London 1956
Karolyi, Catherine, *A life together* London 1966
Karolyi, Michael, *Memoirs* London 1956
Kleinwächter, Friedrich, *Von Schönbrunn bis St. Germain* Graz 1964
Lichem, Heinz von, *Die Geschichte der Kaiserschützen* Graz 1977

Selected Bibliography

Lorenz, Reinhold, *Kaiser Karl* Graz 1959
Sokol, A. E., *Seemacht Öesterreich* Vienna 1972
Werkmann, Karl, *Deutschland als Verbündete* Berlin 1931
Werkmann, Karl, *Der Tote auf Madeira* Munich 1923

6 Italian

Cadorna, General Luigi, *La Guerra alla Fronte Italiano* Milan 1921
Diario della Guerra, *Italia* Series, Vol. 4 Milan 1919
Giacomelli, Antonietta, *Vigilie, 1914–1918* Florence 1919
Orlando, Vittorio Emanuele, *Memorie* Milan 1960
Salandra, Antonio, *L'Intervento* Milan 1930
Valori, *La Guerra Italo-Austriaca* Bologna 1925
Villari, Luigi, *La Campagna di Macedonia* Bologna 1922

APPENDIX A

President Wilson's Peace Programme

A. *The Fourteen Points, 8 January 1918*

1. Open covenants of peace, openly arrived at, after which there shall be no private international understandings of any kind but diplomacy shall proceed always frankly and in the public view.

2. Absolute freedom of navigation upon the seas, outside territorial waters, alike in peace and in war, except as the seas may be closed in whole or in part by international action for the enforcement of international covenants

3. The removal, so far as possible, of all economic barriers and the establishment of an equality of trade conditions among all the nations consenting to the peace and associating themselves for its maintenance.

4. Adequate guarantees given and taken that national armaments will be reduced to the lowest point consistent with domestic safety.

5. A free, open-minded, and absolutely impartial adjustment of all colonial claims, based upon a strict observance of the principle that in determining all such questions of sovereignty the interests of the populations concerned must have equal weight with the equitable claims of the government whose title is to be determined.

6. The evacuation of all Russian territory and such a settlement of all questions affecting Russia as will secure the best and freest co-operation of the other nations of the world in obtaining for her an unhampered and unembarrassed opportunity for the independent determination of her own political development and national policy and assure her of a sincere welcome into the society of free nations under institutions of her own choosing; and, more than a welcome, assistance also of every kind that she may need and may herself desire. The treatment accorded Russia by her sister nations in the months to come will be the acid test of their good will, of their comprehension of her needs as distinguished from their own interests, and of their intelligent and unselfish sympathy.

7. Belgium, the whole world will agree, must be evacuated and restored, without any attempt to limit the sovereignty which she enjoys in common

431

with all other free nations. No other single act will serve as this will serve to restore confidence among the nations in the laws which they have themselves set and determined for the government of their relations with one another. Without this healing act the whole structure and validity of international law is forever impaired.

8. All French territory should be freed and the invaded portions restored, and the wrong done to France by Prussia in 1871 in the matter of Alsace-Lorraine, which has unsettled the peace of the world for nearly fifty years, should be righted, in order that peace may once more be made secure in the interests of all.

9. A readjustment of the frontiers of Italy should be effected along clearly recognizable lines of nationality.

10. The peoples of Austria-Hungary, whose place among the nations we wish to see safeguarded and assured, should be accorded the freest opportunity of autonomous development.

11. Rumania, Serbia, and Montenegro should be evacuated; occupied territories restored; Serbia accorded free and secure access to the sea; and the relations of the several Balkan states to one another determined by friendly counsel along historically established lines of allegiance and nationality; and international guarantees of the political and economic independence and territorial integrity of the several Balkan states should be entered into.

12. The Turkish portions of the present Ottoman Empire should be assured a secure sovereignty, but the other nationalities which are now under Turkish rule should be assured an undoubted security of life and an absolutely unmolested opportunity of autonomous development, and the Dardanelles should be permanently opened as a free passage to the ships and commerce of all nations under international guarantees.

13. An independent Polish state should be erected which should include the territories inhabited by indisputably Polish populations, which should be assured a free and secure access to the sea, and whose political and economic independence and territorial integrity should be guaranteed by international covenant.

14. A general association of nations must be formed under specific covenants for the purpose of affording mutual guarantees of political independence and territorial integrity to great and small states alike.

Appendix A

B. *The Four Principles of 11 February 1918*

1. That each part of the final settlement must be based upon the essential justice of that particular case and upon such adjustments as are most likely to bring a peace that will be permanent.

2. That peoples and provinces are not to be bartered about from sovereignty to sovereignty as if they were mere chattels and pawns in a game, even the great game, now forever discredited, of the balance of power, but that,

3. Every territorial settlement involved in this war must be made in the interest and for the benefit of the populations concerned, and not as a part of any mere adjustment or compromise of claims amongst rival states; and

4. That all well-defined national aspirations shall be accorded the utmost satisfaction that can be accorded them without introducing new or perpetuating old elements of discord and antagonism that would be likely in time to break the peace of Europe and consequently of the world.

C. *The Four Points of 4 July 1918*

1. The destruction of every arbitrary power anywhere that can separately, secretly, and of its single choice disturb the peace of the world; or, if it cannot be presently destroyed, at the least its reduction to virtual impotence.

2. The settlement of every question, whether of territory, of sovereignty, of economic arrangement, or of political relationship upon the basis of the free acceptance of that settlement by the people immediately concerned, and not upon the basis of the material interest or advantage of any other nation or people which may desire a different settlement for the sake of its own exterior influence or mastery.

3. The consent of all nations to be governed in their conduct toward each other by the same principles of honor and of respect for the common law of civilized society that govern the individual citizens of all modern States in their relations with one another; to the end that all promises and covenants may be sacredly observed, no private plots or conspiracies hatched, no selfish injuries wrought with impunity, and a mutual trust established upon the handsome foundation of a mutual respect for right.

4. The establishment of an organization of peace which shall make it

certain that the combined power of free nations will check every invasion of right and serve to make peace and justice the more secure by affording a definite tribunal of opinion to which all must submit and by which every international readjustment that cannot be amicably agreed upon by the peoples directly concerned shall be sanctioned. These great objects can be put into a single sentence. What we seek is the reign of law, based upon the consent of the governed and sustained by the organized opinion of mankind.

D. The five particulars of 27 September 1918

1. The impartial justice meted out must involve no discrimination between those to whom we wish to be just and those to whom we do not wish to be just. It must be a justice that plays no favourites, and knows no standards but the equal rights of the several peoples concerned.

2. No special or separate interest of any single nation or group of nations can be made the basis of any part of the settlement which is not consistent with the common interest of all.

3. There can be no leagues or alliances or special covenants and understandings within the general and common family of the League of Nations.

4. And more specifically, there can be no special, selfish, economic combinations within the League, and no employment of any form of economic boycott or exclusion except as the power of economic penalty by exclusion from the markets of the world may be vested in the League of Nations itself as a means of discipline and control.

5. All international agreements and treaties of every kind must be made known in their entirety to the rest of the world.

APPENDIX B

The Armistice Convention With Bulgaria

Signed 29 September 1918

I. Immediate evacuation, in conformity with an arrangement to be concluded, of the territories still occupied in Greece and Serbia. There shall be removed from these territories neither cattle, grain, nor stores of any kind. No damage shall be done on departure. The Bulgarian Administration shall continue to exercise its functions in the parts of Bulgaria at present occupied by the Allies.

II. Immediate demobilization of all Bulgarian armies, save for the maintenance on a war footing of a group of all arms, comprising three divisions of sixteen battalions each and four regiments of cavalry, which shall be thus disposed: two divisions for the defence of the Eastern frontier of Bulgaria and of the Dobrudja, and the 148th Division for the protection of the railways.

III. Deposit, at points to be indicated by the High Command of the Armies of the East, of the arms, ammunition, and military vehicles belonging to the demobilized units which shall thereafter be stored by the Bulgarian authorities, under the control of the Allies. The horses likewise will be handed over to the Allies.

IV. Restoration to Greece of the material of the IVth Greek Army Corps, which was taken from the Greek army at the time of the occupation of Eastern Macedonia, in so far as it has not been sent to Germany.

V. The units of the Bulgarian troops at the present time west of the meridian of Uskub, and belonging to the XIth German Army, shall lay down their arms and shall be considered until further notice to be prisoners of war. The officers shall retain their arms.

VI. Employment by the Allied Armies of Bulgarian prisoners of war in the East until the conclusion of peace, without reciprocity as regards Allied prisoners of war. These latter shall be handed over without delay to the Allied authorities, and deported civilians shall be entirely free to return to their homes.

VII. Germany and Austria-Hungary shall have a period of four weeks to withdraw their troops and military organizations. Within the same period the diplomatic and consular representatives of the Central Powers, as also their nationals, must leave the territory of the Kingdom. Orders for the cessation of hostilities shall be given by the signatories of the present convention.

[Signed] General Franchet D'Espèrey
André Liapchef
E. T. Loukof

General Headquarters,
29 September 1918, 10.50

APPENDIX C

The Armistice with Austria-Hungary

I. Military Clauses

1. The immediate cessation of hostilities by land, sea and air.

2. Total demobilization of the Austro-Hungarian forces operating on the front from the North Sea to Switzerland.

Within Austro-Hungarian territory, limited as in clause 3 below, there shall only be maintained as an organized military force a [maximum of 20 divisions], reduced to pre-war [peace] effectives.

Half the divisional, corps and army artillery and equipment shall be collected at points to be indicated by the Allies and United States of America for delivery to them, beginning with all such material as exists in the territories to be evacuated by the Austro-Hungarian forces.

3. Evacuation of all territories invaded by Austria-Hungary since the beginning of war. Withdrawal within such periods as shall be determined by the commander in chief of the Allied forces on each front of the Austro-Hungarian armies behind a line fixed as follows: From Piz Umbrail to the north of the Stelvio it will follow the crest of the Rhetian Alps up to the sources of the Adige and the Eisach, passing thence by Mounts Reschen and Brenner and the Heights of Ötz and Ziller. The line thence turns south crossing Mount Toblach and meeting the present frontier [of the] Carnic Alps. It follows this frontier up to Mount Tarvis and after Mount Tarvis the watershed of the Julian Alps by the Col of Predil, Mount Mangart, the Tricorno (Terglou) and the watershed of the Cols di Podberdo, Podlanischam and Idria. From this point the line turns south-east towards the Schneeberg, excluding the whole basin of the Save and its tributaries; from the Schneeberg it goes down towards the coast in such a way as to include Castua, Mattuglie and Volosca in the evacuated territories.

It will also follow the administrative limits of the present province of Dalmatia, including to the north Lisarica and Trivania and, to the south, territory limited by a line from the [shore] of Cape Planca to the summits of the watershed eastwards so as to include in the evacuated area all the valleys and water courses flowing towards Sebenico, such as the

Cikola, Kerka, Butišníca and their tributaries. It will also include all the islands in the north and west of Dalmatia from Premuda, Selve, Ulbo, Scherda, Maon, Pago and Puntadura in the north up to Melida in the south, embracing Sant'Andrea, Busi, Lissa, Lesina, Torcola, Curzola, Cazza and Lagosta, as well as the neighboring rocks and islets and [Pelagosa], only excepting the islands of Great and Small Zirona, Bua, Solta and Brazza.

All territory thus evacuated [will be occupied by the troops] of the Allies and of the United States of America.

All military and railway equipment of all kinds, including coal, belonging to or within those territories, to be left *in situ* and surrendered to the Allies according to special orders given by the commanders in chief of the forces of the Associated Powers on the different fronts. No new destruction, pillage or requisition to be done by enemy troops in the territories to be evacuated by them and occupied by the forces of the Associated Powers.

4. The Allies shall have the right of free movement over all road and rail and waterways in Austro-Hungarian territory and of the use of the necessary Austrian and Hungarian means of transportation.

The armies of the Associated Powers shall occupy such strategic points in Austria-Hungary at such times as they may deem necessary to enable them to conduct military operations or to maintain order.

They shall have the right of requisition on payment for the troops of the Associated Powers wherever they may be.

5. Complete evacuation of all German troops within 15 days, not only from the Italian and Balkan fronts, but from all Austro-Hungarian territory.

Internment of all German troops which have not left Austria-Hungary within that date.

6. The administration of the evacuated territories of Austria-Hungary will be entrusted to the local authorities under the control of the Allied and Associated armies of occupation.

7. The immediate repatriation without reciprocity of all Allied prisoners of war and interned subjects and of civil populations evacuated from their homes on conditions to be laid down by the commanders in chief of the forces of the Associated Powers on the various fronts.

8. Sick and wounded who cannot be removed from evacuated territory will be cared for by Austro-Hungarian personnel who will be left on the spot with the medical material required.

Appendix C

II.   *Naval Conditions*

1. Immediate cessation of all hostilities at sea, and definite information to be given as to the location and movements of all Austro-Hungarian ships.

Notification to be made to neutrals that freedom of navigation in all territorial waters is given to the naval and mercantile marines of the Allied and Associated Powers, all questions of neutrality being waived.

2. Surrender to the Allies and the United States of America of 15 Austro-Hungarian submarines, completed between the years 1910 and 1918, and of all German submarines which are in or may hereafter enter Austro-Hungarian territorial waters. All other Austro-Hungarian submarines to be paid off and completely disarmed, and to remain under the supervision of the Allies and United States of America.

3. Surrender to the Allies and United States of America with their complete armament and equipment of 3 battleships, 3 light cruisers, 9 destroyers, 12 torpedo boats, 1 mine layer, 6 Danube monitors, to be designated by the Allies and United States of America. All other surface warships, including river craft, are to be concentrated in Austro-Hungarian naval bases to be designated by the Allies and United States of America and are to be paid off and completely disarmed and placed under the supervision of the Allies and United States of America.

4 Freedom of navigation to all warships and merchant ships of the Allied and Associated Powers to be given in the Adriatic and up the River Danube and its tributaries in the territorial waters and territory of Austria-Hungary.

The Allies and Associated Powers shall have the right to sweep up all mine fields and obstructions and the positions of these are to be indicated.

In order to insure the freedom of navigation on the Danube, the Allies and the United States of America shall be empowered to occupy or to dismantle all fortifications or defense works.

5. The existing blockade conditions set up by the Allied and Associated Powers are to remain unchanged and all Austro-Hungarian merchant ships found at sea are to remain liable to capture, save exceptions which may be made by a commission nominated by the Allies and United States of America.

6. All naval aircraft are to be concentrated and immobilized in Austro-

Hungarian bases to be designated by the Allies and United States of America.

7. Evacuation of all the Italian coasts and of all ports occupied by Austria-Hungary outside their national territory, and the abandonment of all floating craft, naval materials, equipment and materials for inland navigation of all kinds.

8. Occupation by the Allies and the United States of America of the land and sea fortifications and the islands which form the defenses and of the dockyards and arsenal at Pola.

9. All merchant vessels held by Austria-Hungary belonging to the Allied and Associated Powers to be returned.

10. No destruction of ships or of materials to be permitted before evacuation, surrender or restoration.

11. All naval and mercantile marine prisoners of war of the Allied and Associated Powers in Austro-Hungarian hands to be returned without reciprocity.

APPENDIX D

Conditions of an Armistice with Germany

A.   On the western front.

I. Cessation of hostilities on land and in the air six hours after the signature of the Armistice.

II. Immediate evacuation of the invaded countries: Belgium, France, Luxembourg, as well as Alsace-Lorraine, so ordered as to be completed within fifteen days from the signature of the Armistice. German troops which have not evacuated the above-mentioned territories within the period fixed will be made prisoners of war. Joint occupation by the Allied and United States forces shall keep pace with evacuation in these areas. All movements of evacuation or occupation shall be regulated in accordance with a note (annex No. 1), drawn up at the time of signature of the Armistice.

III. Repatriation, beginning at once, to be completed within fifteen days, of all inhabitants of the countries above enumerated (including hostages, persons under trial, or convicted).

IV. Surrender in good condition by the German Armies of the following war material:

> 5,000 guns (2,500 heavy, 2,500 field).
> 25,000 machine guns.
> 3,000 trench mortars.
> 1,700 Fighting and bombing aeroplanes – in the first place, all D7's and all night-bombing aeroplanes.

The above to be delivered *in situ* to the Allied and United States troops in accordance with the detailed conditions laid down in the note (annex No. 1) determined at the time of the signing of the Armistice.

V. Evacuation by the German Armies of the districts on the left bank of the Rhine. These districts on the left bank of the Rhine shall be administered by the local authorities under the control of the Allied and United States Armies of Occupation.

The occupation of these territories by Allied and United States troops shall be assured by garrisons holding the principal crossings of the Rhine (Mainz, Coblenz, Cologne), together with bridgeheads at these points of a 30-kilometer radius on the right bank, and by garrisons similarly holding the strategic points of the area.

A neutral zone shall be reserved on the right bank of the Rhine, between the river and a line drawn parallel to the bridgeheads and to the river and 10 kilometers distant from them, between the Dutch frontier and the Swiss frontier.

The evacuation by the enemy of the Rhine districts (right and left banks) shall be so ordered as to be completed within a further period of 16 days, in all 31 days after the signing of the Armistice.

All movements of evacuation and occupation shall be regulated according to the note (annex No. 1) determined at the time of the signing of the Armistice.

VI. In all territories evacuated by the enemy, evacuation of the inhabitants shall be forbidden; no damage or harm shall be done to the persons or property of the inhabitants.

No person shall be prosecuted for having taken part in any military measures previous to the signing of the Armistice.

No destruction of any kind to be committed.

Military establishments of all kinds shall be delivered intact, as well as military stores, food, munitions and equipment, which shall not have been removed during the periods fixed for evacuation.

Stores of food of all kinds for the civil population, cattle etc., shall be left *in situ*.

No measure of a general character shall be taken, and no official order shall be given which would have as a consequence the depreciation of industrial establishments or a reduction of their personnel.

VII. Roads and means of communications of every kind, railroads, waterways, roads, bridges, telegraphs, telephones, shall be in no manner impaired.

All civil and military personnel at present employed on them shall remain.

5,000 locomotives and 150,000 wagons, in good working order, with all necessary spare parts and fittings, shall be delivered to the Associated Powers within the period fixed in annex 2, not exceeding 31 days in all.

5,000 motor lorries are also to be delivered in good condition within 36 days.

The railways of Alsace-Lorraine shall be handed over within 31 days, together with all personnel and material belonging to the organization of this system.

Further, the necessary working material in the territories on the left bank of the Rhine shall be left *in situ*.

All stores of coal and material for the upkeep of permanent way, signals and repair shops shall be left *in situ* and kept in an efficient state by Germany, so far as the working of the means of communication on the left bank of the Rhine is concerned.

All lighters taken from the Allies shall be restored to them.

The note (annex 2) defines the details of these measures.

VIII. The German Command shall be responsible for revealing within 48 hours after the signing of the Armistice, all mines or delay-action fuses disposed on territories evacuated by the German troops, and shall assist in their discovery and destruction.

The German Command shall also reveal all destructive measures that may have been taken (such as poisoning or pollution of wells, springs, etc.).

Breaches of these clauses will involve reprisals.

IX. The right of requisition shall be exercised by the Allied and United States armies in all occupied territories save for settlement of accounts with authorized persons.

The upkeep of the troops of occupation in the Rhine districts (excluding Alsace-Lorraine) shall be charged to the German Government.

X. The immediate repatriation, without reciprocity, according to detailed conditions which shall be fixed, of all Allied and United States prisoners of war, including those under trial and condemned. The Allied Powers and the United States of America shall be able to dispose of these prisoners as they think fit. This condition annuls all other conventions regarding prisoners of war, including that of July 1918, now being ratified. However, the return of German prisoners of war interned in Holland and Switzerland shall continue as heretofore. The return of German prisoners of war shall be settled at the conclusion of the peace preliminaries.

XI. Sick and wounded who cannot be removed from territory evacuated by the German forces shall be cared for by German personnel, who shall be left on the spot with the material required.

B. *Dispositions relating to the eastern frontiers of Germany.*

XII. All German troops at present in any territory which before the war formed part of Austria-Hungary, Roumania, or Turkey, shall withdraw within the frontiers of Germany as they existed on August 1, 1914, and all German troops at present in territories which before the war formed part of Russia, must likewise return to within the frontiers of Germany as above defined, as soon as the Allies shall think the moment suitable, having regard to the internal situation of these territories.

XIII. Evacuation of German troops to begin at once, and all German instructors, prisoners and agents, civilian as well as military, now on the territory of Russia (as defined on August 1, 1914) to be recalled.

XIV. German troops to cease at once all requisitions and seizures and any other coercive measures with a view to obtaining supplies intended for Germany in Roumania and Russia (as defined on August 1, 1914).

XV. Annulment of the treaties of Bucharest and Brest-Litovsk and of the supplementary treaties.

XVI. The Allies shall have free access to the territories evacuated by the Germans on their eastern frontier, either through Danzig or by the Vistula, in order to convey supplies to the populations of these territories or for the purpose of maintaining order.

C. *Clause relating to East Africa.*

XVII. Evacuation of all German forces operating in East Africa within a period specified by the Allies.

D. *General clauses.*

XVIII. Repatriation without reciprocity, within a maximum period of one month, in accordance with detailed conditions hereafter to be fixed, of all interned civilians, including hostages and persons under trial and condemned, who may be subjects of Allied or Associated States other than those mentioned in Clause III.

Appendix D

Financial clauses.

XIX. With the reservation that any subsequent concessions and claims by the Allies and United States remain unaffected, the following financial conditions are imposed:

Reparation for damage done.

While the Armistice lasts, no public securities shall be removed by the enemy which can serve as a pledge to the Allies to cover reparation for war losses.

Immediate restitution of the cash deposit in the National Bank of Belgium and, in general, immediate return of all documents, specie, stocks, shares, paper money, together with plant for the issue thereof affecting public or private interests in the invaded countries.

Restitution of the Russian and Roumanian gold yielded to Germany or taken by that Power.

This gold to be delivered in trust to the Allies until peace is concluded.

E.   Naval clauses

XX. Immediate cessation of all hostilites at sea, and definite information to be given as to the position and movements of all German ships.

Notification to be given to neutrals that freedom of navigation in all territorial waters is given to the navies and mercantile marines of the Allied and Associated Powers, all questions of neutrality being waived.

XXI. All naval and mercantile marine prisoners of war of the Allied and Associated Powers in German hands to be returned without reciprocity.

XXII. To surrender at the ports specified by the Allies and the United States all submarines at present in existence (including all submarine cruisers and minelayers), with armament and equipment complete. Those that cannot put to sea shall be deprived of armament and equipment, and shall remain under the supervision of the Allies and the United States. Submarines ready to put to sea shall be prepared to leave German ports immediately on receipt of a wireless order to sail to the port of surrender, the remainder to follow as early as possible. The conditions of this article shall be completed within 14 days of the signing of the Armistice.

XXIII. The following German surface warships which shall be

445

designated by the Allies and the United States of America, shall forthwith be disarmed and thereafter interned in neutral ports, or, failing
them, Allied ports, to be designated by the Allies and the United States
of America, and placed under the surveillance of the Allies and the
United States of America, only caretakers being left on board, namely:

> 6 battle cruisers.
> 10 battleships.
> 8 light cruisers (including two minelayers).
> 50 destroyers of the most modern type.

All other surface warships (including river craft) are to be concentrated in German naval bases to be designated by the Allies and the
United States of America, completely disarmed and placed under the
supervision of the Allies and the United States of America. All vessels of
the auxiliary fleet are to be disarmed. All vessels specified for internment
shall be ready to leave German ports seven days after the signing of the
Armistice. Directions for the voyage shall be given by wireless.

XXIV. The Allies and the United States of America shall have the right
to sweep up all minefields and destroy all obstructions laid by Germany
outside German territorial waters, and the positions of these are to be
indicated.

XXV. Freedom of access to and from the Baltic to be given to the navies
and mercantile marines of the Allied and Associated Powers. This to be
secured by the occupation of all German forts, fortifications, batteries
and defence works of all kinds in all the routes from the Cattegat into
the Baltic, and by the sweeping up and destruction of all mines and
obstructions within and without German territorial waters without any
questions of neutrality being raised by Germany, and the positions of
all such mines and obstructions to be indicated, and the plans relating
thereto are to be supplied.

XXVI. The existing blockade conditions set up by the Allied and
Associated Powers are to remain unchanged, and all German merchant
ships found at sea are to remain liable to capture. The Allies and United
States contemplate the provisioning of Germany during the Armistice as
shall be found necessary.

XXVII. All aerial forces are to be concentrated and immobilized in
German bases to be specified by the Allies and the United States of
America.

XXVIII. In evacuating the Belgian coasts and ports, Germany shall abandon, *in situ* and intact, the port material and material for inland waterways, also all merchant ships, tugs and lighters, all naval aircraft and air materials and stores, all arms and armaments and all stores and apparatus of all kinds.

XXIX. All Black Sea ports are to be evacuated by Germany; all Russian warships of all descriptions seized by Germany in the Black Sea are to be handed over to the Allies and the United States of America; all neutral merchant ships seized in the Black Sea are to be released; all warlike and other materials of all kinds seized in those ports are to be returned, and German materials as specified in Clause XXVIII are to be abandoned.

XXX. All merchant ships at present in German hands belonging to the Allied and Associated Powers are to be restored to ports specified by the Allies and the United States of America without reciprocity.

XXXI. No destruction of ships or of materials to be permitted before evacuation, surrender or restoration.

XXXII. The German Government shall formally notify all the neutral Governments, and particularly the Governments of Norway, Sweden, Denmark and Holland, that all restrictions placed on the trading of their vessels with the Allied and Associated countries, whether by the German Government or by private German interests, and whether in return for specific concessions, such as the export of shipbuilding materials, or not, are immediately cancelled.

XXXIII. No transfers of German merchant shipping of any description to any neutral flag are to take place after signature of the Armistice.

F. Duration of the Armistice.

XXXIV. The duration of the Armistice is to be 36 days, with option to extend. During this period, on failure of execution of any of the above clauses, the Armistice may be repudiated by one of the contracting parties on 48 hours' previous notice. It is understood that failure to execute Articles III and XVIII completely in the periods specified is not to give reason for a repudiation of the Armistice, save where such failure is due to malice aforethought.

To assure the execution of the present convention under the most favorable conditions, the principle of a permanent International Armistice Commission is recognized. This Commission shall act under

447

the supreme authority of the High Command, military and naval, of the Allied Armies.

The present Armistice was signed on the 11th day of November 1918, at 5 o'clock A.M. (French time).

F. Foch	Erzberger
R. E. Wemyss	A. Oberndorff
	v. Winterfeldt
	Vanselow

Index

THE WESTERN FRONT, 1918

Scale of Miles

| 0 | 50 | 100 | 150 | 200 |

———————— Limit of German Advance, 1918

— — — — — Armistice Line, 11th November, 1918

————— Railways

N O R

NOR
SEA

ENGLAND

THE HAGUE

LONDON

Thames

OSTEND

BRUGES

GHENT

ANTW

FLANDERS

CALAIS

Passchendaele

COURTRAI

BRUSS

Ypres

BELGI

BOULOGNE

St Omer
Hazebrouck

Lys

TOURNAI

LILLE

Bellecourt

NAN

Schelde

MONTREUIL

DOUAI

Mons

Sambre

ENGLISH CHANNEL

ARRAS

CAMBRAI

Abbeville

AVESNES

Somme

Bapaume

La Capelle

P

Péronne

Homblières

AMIENS
Boves

ST QUENTIN

Caix

Vendhuile
Tergnier

R

Mezières

Oise

Laon

D

Y

COMPIÈGNE

SOISSONS

Aisne

Grandpr

Crépy

Villers Cotterêts

RHEIMS

SENLIS

Château Thierry

Marne

PARIS

GHQ
Château
Bombon

Seine

F   R   A   N   C   E